MOBILE INTERACTION DESIGN

MOBILE INTERACTION DESIGN

MATT JONES
University of Wales Swansea

and

GARY MARSDEN
University of Cape Town

John Wiley & Sons, Ltd

Telephone (+44) 1243 779777

Email (for orders and customer service enquiries): cs-books@wiley.co.uk
Visit our Home Page on www.wiley.com

Other Wiley Editorial Offices

John Wiley & Sons Inc., 111 River Street, Hoboken, NJ 07030, USA

Jossey-Bass, 989 Market Street, San Francisco, CA 94103-1741, USA

Wiley-VCH Verlag GmbH, Boschstr. 12, D-69469 Weinheim, Germany

John Wiley & Sons Australia Ltd, 42 McDougall Street, Milton, Queensland 4064, Australia

John Wiley & Sons (Asia) Pte Ltd, 2 Clementi Loop #02-01, Jin Xing Distripark, Singapore 129809

John Wiley & Sons Canada Ltd, 22 Worcester Road, Etobicoke, Ontario, Canada M9W 1L1

Wiley also publishes its books in a variety of electronic formats. Some content that appears
in print may not be available in electronic books.

Library of Congress Cataloging-in-Publication Data

Jones, Matt, 1968-
Mobile interaction design / Matt Jones and Gary Marsden.
p. cm.
Includes bibliographical references and index.
ISBN-13: 978-0-470-09089-3 (pbk.)
ISBN-10: 0-470-09089-8 (pbk.)
1. Mobile communication systems – Design and construction.
2. Human-computer interaction. I. Marsden, Gary. II. Title.
TK6570.M6J66 2005
621.384 – dc22

2005025158

British Library Cataloguing in Publication Data

A catalogue record for this book is available from the British Library

ISBN-13: 978-0-470-09089-3 (PB)
ISBN-10: 0-470-09089-8 (PB)

Typeset in 10/11 Bembo by Laserwords Private Limited, Chennai, India
Printed and bound in Great Britain by Bell & Bain, Glasgow
This book is printed on acid-free paper responsibly manufactured from sustainable forestry
in which at least two trees are planted for each one used for paper production.

To:

Clare, Sam, Ben and Rosie (Matt)
&
Gil, Holly and Jake (Gary)

CONTENTS

Preface xv
Acknowledgements xix

PART I: INTRODUCTION 1
Chapter 1: Possibilities 3
Key points 3
1.1 Introduction 4
1.2 What are mobile devices? 6
1.2.1 Communication or information device? 9
1.2.2 Appliance or Swiss army knife? 11
1.2.3 Cherished device or commodity tool? 13
1.3 Impoverished or extraordinary interfaces? 14
1.3.1 The Fastap keypad 15
1.3.2 Peephole displays 16
1.3.3 Accommodating human capabilities and limitations 17
1.4 Impoverishing interactions? 28
1.4.1 Reasons for poor design 28
1.4.2 Impacts of poor design 29
1.5 Outline of the rest of this book 35
Summary 36
Workshop questions 36
Designer tips 36

Chapter 2: Products for people 39
Key points 39
2.1 Introduction 40
2.2 Useful 41
2.2.1 Function before form 41
2.2.2 Evolving uses 42
2.3 Usable 43
2.3.1 Usable in itself 44
2.3.2 Usable in life 51

2.4 User experience 54
 2.4.1 Strong identity 55
 2.4.2 Interaction as package 58
2.5 Technology acceptance 63
Summary 64
Workshop questions 66
Designer tips 66

Chapter 3: Innovating 67
Key points 67
3.1 Introduction 68
3.2 Technology-centered approaches 69
3.3 Transferring from the desktop 74
 3.3.1 Applications 75
 3.3.2 Interface styles 78
3.4 Building on past mobile success 81
3.5 Drama 83
3.6 Frameworks for human-centered thinking 85
Summary 89
Workshop questions 89
Designer tips 90

PART II: DEVELOPING EFFECTIVE MOBILE APPLICATIONS 91
Chapter 4: Interaction design 93
Key points 93
4.1 Introduction 94
4.2 Designing what? Designing how? 94
4.3 Understanding users 96
 4.3.1 From biology to psychology 96
 4.3.2 Field studies 97
 4.3.3 Direct questioning 99
 4.3.4 Distilling the findings 100
4.4 Developing prototype designs 100
 4.4.1 Shaping and managing the design space 100
 4.4.2 Prototyping 105
4.5 Evaluation 106
 4.5.1 Testing with users 107
 4.5.2 Testing in the absence of users 109
4.6 Iterative development 112
4.7 Multiple viewpoints 113

4.7.1 Many techniques and tools 113
4.7.2 Many disciplines 113
4.7.3 Participation and collaboration 116
4.8 From interaction design to deployment 117
Summary 118
Workshop questions 118
Designer tips 119

Chapter 5: Watching, asking, probing 121
Key points 121
5.1 Introduction 122
5.2 Focusing the study 124
5.2.1 How focused should the study be? 124
5.2.2 Finding people to study 125
5.3 Top techniques for understanding people 129
5.3.1 Observing 130
5.3.2 Enquiring 138
5.3.3 Diary studies 141
5.3.4 Discount methods 145
5.3.5 Focus groups 149
5.3.6 Creatively engaging methods 151
5.4 Making sense of observations 155
5.4.1 Activities 155
5.4.2 Analysis perspectives 156
5.5 Personas and scenarios 160
5.5.1 Personas 160
5.5.2 Scenarios 163
Summary 167
Workshop questions 167
Designer tips 168

Chapter 6: Prototypes 169
Key points 169
6.1 Introduction 170
6.2 What is a prototype? 170
6.3 Different prototypes for different purposes 170
6.4 Low-fidelity 171

6.4.1 Self-checking 171
6.4.2 Communicating with others 173
6.4.3 Interaction prototyping 174
6.4.4 Empowering users 176
6.5 Higher-fidelity 178
6.5.1 Deciding what to prototype 178
6.5.2 Hardware and software integration 178
6.6 Finishing the process 186
6.6.1 Evolutionary 186
6.6.2 Revolutionary 186
6.6.3 Process 187
6.7 Issues in prototyping 189
6.7.1 Some considerations 190
6.8 A final note on development 191
Summary 192
Workshop questions 192
Designer tips 192

Chapter 7: Evaluation 195
Key points 195
7.1 Introduction 196
7.2 Classifying evaluation 196
7.3 'Quick And Dirty' 197
7.4 Conceptual model extraction 197
7.5 Direct observation 199
7.5.1 Finding out what users are thinking 199
7.5.2 How to record observations 200
7.5.3 How to not bias the experiment 203
7.5.4 Happy users 203
7.6 Interviews 204
7.7 Questionnaires 205
7.8 Non-user methods 207
7.8.1 Heuristic evaluation 207
7.8.2 No people whatsoever 209
7.9 Experimental evaluation 209
7.9.1 Hypothesis 210
7.9.2 The users 211

7.9.3 Tasks 212
7.9.4 Experiment design 212
7.9.5 Conducting experiments 213
7.9.6 Experimental results 214
7.10 Considering context – evaluating mobile systems 214
7.10.1 Physical context 214
7.10.2 Technological context 216
7.10.3 Social context 216
7.10.4 Other contexts 217
7.11 Complementary evaluation 218
7.12 Conclusion 219
Summary 219
Workshop questions 219
Designer tips 220

PART III: DESIGN GALLERY – DIRECTIONS AND GUIDELINES 221
Chapter 8: Controlling Complex Functions 223
Key points 223
8.1 Introduction 224
8.2 Menus and memory 225
8.3 Hierarchical menus 225
8.3.1 Learning structure 225
8.3.2 Improving classification 226
8.3.3 Context information 227
8.4 Icons 227
8.5 Manuals 233
8.5.1 Online manuals 233
8.5.2 Website manuals 234
8.6 No menus? 234
8.6.1 Data structures 235
8.6.2 Alternatives 235
8.6.3 Design ideas – data structures 238
8.6.4 Evaluation via experiment 238
8.7 More complex menus 242
8.8 Some concluding thoughts 244
Summary 245
Workshop questions 245
Designer tips 245

Chapter 9: Information access 247
Key points 247
9.1 Introduction 248
9.2 Small-screen impacts 250
9.2.1 Lessons from the past 251
9.2.2 Impact on browsing complex content 255
9.2.3 Impact on searching 256
9.3 Designs for browsing 258
9.3.1 Guidelines 259
9.3.2 Schemes 261
9.3.3 Packaging content 271
9.4 Improving search 272
9.4.1 Assessing sets of results 272
9.4.2 Judging the value of individual results 274
9.5 Mobile information ecologies 280
9.5.1 Fitting in 280
9.5.2 Case study: the laid-back search tool 283
9.5.3 Peer-to-peer schemes 286
Summary 287
Workshop questions 287
Designer tips 288

Chapter 10: Beyond text – using images on mobile devices 289
Key points 289
10.1 Introduction 290
10.2 Ethnography 290
10.2.1 Where have all the photographs gone? 291
10.2.2 Digital ethnography 292
10.3 Finding photos 292
10.3.1 Meta-data 293
10.3.2 Meta-data management 294
10.4 Browsing photos 294
10.4.1 Timeline 295
10.4.2 Treemaps 295
10.4.3 RSVP 296
10.4.4 Speed Dependent Automatic Zooming 298
10.5 Downscaling case study 300
10.5.1 Arranging photos 300

10.5.2 Screen size 300
10.5.3 Write once, run anywhere 301
10.5.4 Meanwhile, back with the users 301
10.5.5 User testing 304
10.5.6 Platform 306
10.6 Advanced technology 306
10.7 What are photos for? 307
10.7.1 What are we sharing? 309
10.7.2 Using audio with photographs 311
10.7.3 Video 311
10.8 Looking to the future 312
Summary 312
Workshop questions 313
Designer tips 313

Chapter 11: Impacting the community; impacting the world 315
Key points 315
11.1 Introduction 316
11.2 The digital divide 316
11.3 Mobiles work 316
11.3.1 The rise and rise of mobile technology 317
11.4 Planning a project 318
11.5 That culture thing 320
11.6 Case studies 325
11.6.1 Empowering people – Cybertracker 325
11.6.2 Education 327
11.6.3 Communitization 328
11.7 Call to arms 333
Summary 333
Workshop questions 333
Designer tips 334

Resources 335
References 339
Credits 365
Index 367

PREFACE

Computers anytime, anyplace. This long-term research goal is daily becoming more and more of a focused reality. The mobiles are amongst us. And devices we carry around in our pockets are more powerful than those on board the rockets that took the first people to the moon. But where are we going, today? How should these handhelds, smartphones, PDAs, embedded systems and even implants change our lives?

Mobile marketing tells us they will transport us, not to a new planet, but to a whole new world of exciting, life-enhancing possibilities. We will communicate and relate in better ways; become more creative, better informed, better educated; and live in enhanced communities and societies as smart mobs swarm into action – all the while becoming more efficient and effective in our working lives.

And yet, back home, unset digital clocks on microwaves, VCRs and DVDs blink a stark warning: '00-00'. The dazzling possibilities on offer as we buy a new mobile, or are given one by our work IT department, seem all too often to crumble in our hands. Resigned disappointment follows. It shouldn't be this way.

We tell our students that computing is awe-inspiring, and humbling because it is about changing the world, for good. It's the new architecture – about building the places (that have been called 'interspaces') in which people will work and play. We expect much of our buildings: they need to have firm foundations, solid structures, pleasing esthetics. We should expect the same of emerging mobile systems. All too often, though, they are more akin to summer sandcastles, decorated with alluring shells, overwhelmed by the ocean of real-life contexts and needs.

There are, of course, great examples of mobile design, and we celebrate some of these in the book: our aim is not to berate designers, but to look for ways of dealing with the challenging issues they face every day.

We focus on providing advice and examples that will help overcome the human factor and usability problems seen in many mobile products and services, so that their potential can be fully met. Anytime, anywhere? No, what's needed is mobiles that work at the right time, and that know their place – that fit in.

There's still time to make things better, and now is a good time to start. Mobile application development is where the web was in the early 1990s – taking its first steps, on the edge of a flowering of services and technologies. So, where are you going to take us?

WHAT'S COVERED

Computer science, psychology, sociology, marketing, and usability engineering – they're all in the mix here. Ingredients to point the way to better products and design processes.

There are lots of human–computer interaction, usability, and human factors texts available. This book, though, presents key concepts, principles, guidelines and practices of user-centered approaches in a way that differs in three respects.

Most obviously, it's all about mobiles – these systems are becoming so important there's a need for a book that speaks directly about them. Mobiles also present new human-factor challenges, and we draw these out, with specific recommendations for both how design projects should be carried out and how the interfaces and interactions should be structured. Finally, we've tried to make the text as accessible and fun to read as possible – after all, designing the future should be something you should enjoy and be passionate about!

There are three parts to the book: *Introduction, Developing effective mobile applications*, and *Design gallery – directions and guidelines*. The first part aims to challenge your thinking about what mobiles could or should be, as well as examining the innovation and development approaches you could take – and the implications of these – as you seek to develop effective products and services.

Part II presents a range of techniques and tools you can use as you go about investigating user needs and developing potential interactive solutions. Although there's a strong emphasis on the process, a process that is applicable to more than mobile development, it is full of example mobile concepts and systems to help illustrate the points and stimulate your own designs.

The final part, the *Design gallery*, applies what we've been talking about in the earlier parts of the book to important aspects like mobile information access and the handling of rich media such as photographic images. This part of the book brings together the research we've done along with that of many others over the last 10 years, to give practical pointers to the sorts of interaction design users will find effective and pleasing.

In each chapter, you'll find three elements to help you understand and make use of the material:

- **Exercises**: design questions and challenges; usability puzzles that can be solved by applying the approaches we cover.
- **Workshop questions**: suggestions for deeper discussions and activities, particularly useful in a group setting.
- **Designer tips**: practical, challenging suggestions to help improve design products and process. We've been involved with mobile interaction design for around a decade now; these tips come from the hard lessons we've learnt during our successes and failures.

At the end of the book you will also find the *Resources* section provides additional pointers to useful sources of inspiration and information; from blogs to conferences to attend. We will be updating this content on the book's website.

WHO SHOULD READ THIS BOOK?

This book is for anyone who wants to extend their understanding of effective human-centered design, learning about and applying it in the increasingly significant context of mobile systems.

- **If you are a student or an educator** ... this can be the textbook of a first course on human–computer interaction, having the advantage of dealing with technologies and use-contexts that are highly engaging. If you've already done an introductory course, the material here can be the basis for a more challenging, extended exploration of design practices; we've taught such courses to graduate students ourselves. An example syllabus is given on the accompanying website (see **`http://www.wileyeurope.com/go/mobile`**).

- **If you are a mobile system interaction designer or software engineer (or want to be one!)** ... the book will give fresh perspectives on the goals of and approaches to mobile interaction design. It also highlights, in an integrated way, state-of-the-art approaches to service and product provision. You can use it to check your own ideas and provoke new ones.
- **If you are an industrial or academic mobile researcher** ... from our own experience, we know how difficult it is to step back and understand this fast-evolving field whilst engaged in research projects. Drawing on a great deal of research published in the main international conferences and journals, we try to do just this. Those working on the topics of information access, image access and mobile communities will be given insights into the current and evolving thinking surrounding these application areas.
- **If you are a mobile business/marketing analyst or strategist or a student in these areas** ... the book provides an analysis to help explain previous hits and flops as well as pointing the way for successful future innovation.

A WORD OF WARNING

This book is mostly academic in tone, but you will notice a lot of personal opinion in here. This is intentional and there are lots of reasons why we wanted to write this way. Firstly, we are passionate about what we do and it is hard to convey passion in a traditional academic writing style. Secondly, we wanted to add some value to the book beyond going to Google and typing in "Mobile Interaction Design". We have been working in this area now for 10 years as researchers, consultants and lecturers, so hope that our opinions are helpful.

ABOUT THE AUTHORS

MATT JONES

Matt has recently moved from New Zealand to Wales (UK) where he is helping to set up the *Future Interaction Technology Lab* at Swansea University. He has worked on mobile interaction issues for the past 10 years and has published a large number of articles in this area.

He has had many collaborations and interactions with handset and service developers, including Orange, Reuters, BT Cellnet, Nokia and Adaptive Info, and has one mobile patent pending.

He is an editor of the *International Journal of Personal and Ubiquitous Computing* and on the steering committee for the Mobile Human–Computer Interaction conference series.

Matt is married with three mobile, small children; when he's not working he enjoys moving quickly on a bike whilst listening to music and the occasional podcast.

More information at www.undofuture.com.

GARY MARSDEN

Gary is currently employed as an Associate Professor in the Department of Computer Science at the University of Cape Town in South Africa where he has worked since 1999. He moved there primarily because his office in London had no windows. Whilst in London, he worked at the Interaction Design Centre at Middlesex University. It was here that he met Matt, and where they both started working in the field of Mobile Interaction Design. Prior to that, he had been lecturing and completing his PhD in the Computer Science Department at Stirling University in Scotland.

Although his background is in computer science, moving to South Africa has forced him to reconsider his views about technology in general, and HCI in particular. This has resulted in him becoming increasingly convinced of the importance of an ethnographic and action-research based approach to interaction design – most abstract and clean theories of technology and HCI seem to fall flat in the developing world. It's unlikely he will ever figure out a foolproof method for running successful interaction design projects in the developing world, but he will have a lot of fun trying.

More information at www.hciguy.net.

ACKNOWLEDGMENTS

Many people have helped us shape the content of this book. We are very grateful for all the conversations, email exchanges, encouragement and, of course, research papers provided by colleagues in the HCI community around the world. Anonymous reviewers at various stages in the manuscript preparation also gave us useful guidance. We are grateful to Gaynor Redvers-Mutton for commissioning the book and to our editor, Jonathan Shipley, and project editor David Barnard, for all their helpful advice.

During the writing, we had the chance to talk through issues with inspiring individuals. Their contributions have been used directly (as, for example, interview material) or indirectly here. Thanks, then, to Ben Bederson, Jason Brotherton, Ann Blandford, David Cairns, Paul Cairns, Fabio Crestani, Matthew Chalmers, Susan Dray, Elise Levanto, Stefano Mizzaro, Carl Gutwin, Scott Jenson, Ben Shneiderman, Phil Stenton, Jenny Tillotson, Don Norman, Teresa Peters, Jenny Preece, Yin Leng Theng, Marion Walton and Kevin Warwick.

The following also gave us their time but in addition helped Matt in arranging meetings and visits at their organizations during a sabbatical, fact-finding trip in 2004: Steve Brewster (University of Glasgow), Mark Dunlop (Strathclyde University), Panu Korhonen (Nokia), Cliff Randell (Bristol University) and Harold Thimbleby (then of UCL Interaction Centre; now at Swansea University).

'Our' research work was done in collaboration with others, all of whom made significant contributions. We are especially grateful for the enjoyable and stimulating work times we have had we these collaborators and friends over the years: David Bainbridge, Edwin Blake, Kevin Boone, Andy Cockburn, Sally Jo Cunningham, Shaleen Deo, George Buchanan, Norliza Mohd-Nasir, Pritti Jane, Steve Jones, Dynal Patel, Harold Thimbleby and Nigel Warren.

Waikato University, New Zealand, provided funding for Matt's sabbatical trip in 2004 and Gary's sabbatical trip to New Zealand in 2003. At Waikato, the HCI and New Zealand Digital Library research groups provided a great environment in which to nurture ideas. Thanks especially to Mark Apperley (for helping in the laid-back thinking), Dana MacKay (who offered up interesting thoughts on social interaction), Dave Nichols (for many good pointers to useful material), Bill Rogers (for early morning encouragement and discussions), Kirsten Thomson (for helping organize usability studies) and Ian Witten (for sage advice on the joys of book writing). Additional thanks to the many students at Waikato who have helped make the work fun, including Gareth Bradley, Tim Barnett, Jason Catchpole, Anette Olsson and Rachel Hunt.

Gary's colleagues at UCT have been very understanding about giving him time to complete this book; his head of department, Prof. Ken MacGregor, has been particularly forbearing. Besides the academic staff, one of the great joys of working at UCT is being surrounded by enthusiastic post-graduate students. Many of these have provided valuable feedback on early drafts of the book, Richard Schroder, David Nunez and Dynal Patel in particular. These students and the other members of the Collaborative Visualisation Group are undertaking work which really will change the world. Also, many honors students have contributed to the content of this book by implementing some of the systems discussed. Specifically, the classroom system was implemented by Dominic Gruijters, Brendan Fry and Steve Reid. The Greenstone communitization software was implemented by Rob Cherry, Alan Haefele, Dynal Patel and Nessen Ramsammy. Finally, we would like to thank bridges.org for letting us quote the Real Access criteria.

Various funding bodies have supported the work mentioned here. We are thankful to the Engineering and Physical Sciences Research Council (UK), the Foundation for Research in Science and Technology (NZ), ACM/SIGCHI (USA), the National Research Federation (SA), the Telkom/Siemens Centre of Excellence (SA), Microsoft Research (UK), Microsoft South Africa (SA), the University of Waikato (NZ), and the University of Cape Town (SA). We would also like to thank HP and bridges.org for donating over 80 PDAs to support our research.

Our wives and children have put up with, supported and constructively distracted us during the long process. Thanks beyond expression to Clare, Sam, Ben and Rosie (Matt), and Gil, Holly and Jake (Gary).

PART I
INTRODUCTION

CHAPTER 1	**POSSIBILITIES**	3
CHAPTER 2	**PRODUCTS FOR PEOPLE**	39
CHAPTER 3	**INNOVATING**	67

CHAPTER 1
POSSIBILITIES

OVERVIEW

1.1. Introduction
1.2. What are mobile devices?
1.3. Impoverished or extraordinary interfaces?
1.4. Impoverishing interactions?
1.5. Outline of the rest of this book

KEY POINTS

- 'Mobile' means more than 'mobile phone': handhelds, wearables, badges, RFID tags and even implants will play an important part in the future.
- The emerging technologies offer interesting interaction possibilities involving audio, touch and gestures.
- There are competing visions of what mobiles should do and be – are they for communication or information? Fashion or utility?
- While some feel that these small devices have 'impoverished interfaces' the bigger problem is the impoverished designs being developed.
- Interaction design is about finding the right ways to deploy the dazzling new technological capabilities to meet real user needs.
- Without effective interaction design, there will be negative emotional, economic and ethical impacts.

1.1 INTRODUCTION

For two billion people, the mobile phone (or 'cellphone') is an essential part of everyday life. It's a business tool to clinch important deals; a 'remote control' for the real world, helping us cope with daily travel delay frustrations; a 'relationship appliance' to say goodnight to loved ones when away from home; a community device to organize political demonstrations.

This most pervasive of devices has been used in times of great tragedy and personal loss – who can forget reports of poignant emergency last calls and texts; in joy and excitement; and, more banally, in many simple moments of commuter boredom. It's a device that is truly a *personal* technology, helping people to feel safer, less lonely, more human.

The statistics associated with the uptake and use of mobile phones are staggering. Many European countries have a penetration rate approaching 100% and, in places like Italy and Finland, it's not uncommon to find people who have several handsets. Mobile ownership certainly outstrips personal computer ownership dramatically, despite the technology being relatively new. While in 1993 there were fewer than 10 million subscribers worldwide, by mid-2003 there were 10 times this number in China alone. In the same year, on average, Singaporean users sent and received over 200 text messages a month, contributing to the worldwide traffic of many billions of text messages monthly.

BOX 1.1 HOW TIMES HAVE CHANGED

While today, anybody and everybody, at least in the Western world, can be a mobile user, things were very different half a century ago, as Jon Agar notes (Agar, 2004):

In 1954, the Marquis of Donegal heard that the Duke of Edinburgh possessed a mobile radio set with which he phoned through to Buckingham Palace – and anyone else on the network – while driving in London. The Marquis was more than a little jealous, and enquired of the Postmaster General whether he, too, could have such a telephone. The polite but firm reply was 'no'. In the mid-1950s, if you were the husband of the Queen you could have a mobile telephone connection to the public network. But if you were a mere marquis, you could go whistle. ■

Despite this satisfying success story, there have been some disappointments in the way other aspects of the mobile market have developed over recent years. While the first quarter of 2005 saw a further 180 million-plus telephone handset sales, *just* – the 'just' emphasizing how spectacular telephone sales were – three million people bought a handheld computer. On top of this, the mobile telephone industry's pleasure in money made from basic services is tempered by unenthusiastic consumer responses to some advanced devices and services. Even with a great deal of marketing, early attempts to convert users to technologies such as WAP, video calling, and a whole host of mobile payment schemes, flopped.

Why are basic mobile devices (phones) and services (voice and messaging) so successful, while the uptake of the more advanced gadgets and applications is frustratingly sluggish? Answer: the former meet basic human desires in simple, direct ways.

So, what's the trick to spotting and developing successful future mobile user experiences – ones that really connect with what people want, and operate in straightforward, satisfying ways? Answer: interaction design, the focus of this book.

As a practice, interaction design owes much to the long-established discipline of Human–Computer Interaction (HCI) and the associated usability industry. Through the efforts of researchers and practitioners, over the past several decades, methods, tools and techniques have evolved to help designers identify the needs of their users and to develop systems that support their goals in effective and efficient ways.

Interaction design, though, extends the mainstream practices. It goes further, being concerned more about crafting a poetic 'customer experience' rather than prosaically delivering 'ease-of-use' (Thomas and Macredie, 2002). As an interaction designer you have to have passion and heart: whereas usability is often seen as a privative – something you notice only when it is not there – interaction design is about making a statement.

Terry Winograd, a pioneer of HCI, compares interaction designers to architects. The job is about building spaces – or, as he dubs them, *interspaces* – for people to coexist and communicate (Winograd, 1997). Now, think about some of the great buildings around the world – wonderful cathedrals like St Paul's in London or Gaudi's Sagrada Familia Church in Barcelona, and dazzling modern-day constructions like the Guggenheim Museum in Bilbao. Or consider more private places – your favorite holiday retreat and home itself. The architects of these buildings clearly thought about how to make sure they are workable and functional, helping inhabitants carry out their worship, visits, jobs, holidays or domestic lives. But what makes these sorts of places truly successful is not just their basic 'usability'. These places inspire, excite, lift the spirits or provide comfort.

BOX 1.2 MOBILE LIFE

Over the past few years there have been many news media stories highlighting impacts of emerging mobile-phone based technologies on societies and individuals. Here are just a few examples:

'Photo lead in credit card fraud – A photograph taken by a quick-thinking passer-by on his mobile phone could help trace a gang of credit card fraudsters.' (*BBC News Online*, 19 September 2003)

'Don't smoke, light up a mobile phone, it's safer – The next time you feel the urge to indulge your craving for nicotine try lighting your mobile, not literally though. British psychologists say those desperate to kick their weed could soon resort to a small program on their cell phones or PDA which would display a series of dots on the screen. Looking at the flickering images, or conjuring up different mental pictures, can help stop ➤

cigarette cravings, claim scientists at the British Association's science festival in Salford, Greater Manchester.' (*The Economic Times*, India, 13 September 2003)

'Mobiles "betray" cheating Italians – A new survey published by Italy's largest private investigation company says that in nearly 90% of cases, it is the mobile phone which reveals or betrays extramarital activities.' (*BBC News Online*, 15 September 2003)

'U r sakd – Accident Group's 2,500 staff received a series of text messages on their mobile phones, telling them to call a number. There, a recorded message from the company's insolvency administrators at PricewaterhouseCoopers informed them that "All staff who are being retained will be contacted today. If you have not been spoken to you are therefore being made redundant".' (*Economist Magazine*, 5 June 2003) ■

This book is about shifting the mobile design perspective away from 'smart' phones, to people who are smart, creative, busy, or plain bored. Our aim is to help you to overcome the frustrations of the previous disappointing handheld 'revolution' by providing the billions of potential mobile users with future products and services that can change their (or even the) world.

In the rest of this chapter, we set the scene by first considering different perspectives on what mobile devices are, or should be. Then, we look at the evolving diversity of mobile interaction technologies. If you are a designer used to working with conventional interactive systems (say a website developer), you might feel the mobile environment is rather impoverished in comparison; we aim to alter your perspective.

While some might feel the technology itself reduces the range of user experiences, we believe the bigger problem is poor design choices; so, to end, we highlight some of the reasons for and implications of bad mobile design, hopefully motivating you to read the rest of the book.

1.2 WHAT ARE MOBILE DEVICES?

There's no doubt, then, that we are in the era of the mobile and will see an increasingly dazzling and sometimes bewildering diversity of devices and services. Indeed, if you ask the question 'what is a mobile?', even today, the answer isn't straightforward.

We could describe them in terms of the types of function they provide: some allow you to organize your appointments and to-do lists; with others you can create Multimedia Messages (MMS), a picture with a soundclip, perhaps, to send to a friend; many provide desktop-type applications – like word-processing – viewed through a small screen. Full-color games are possible with a range of handsets, and there's a potential market of medical devices that could monitor your vital life signs day by day. Of course, devices that allow many or all of such functions are possible, too.

EXERCISE 1.1 MY MOBILE IS . . . ?

Get a group of friends or colleagues to complete this sentence: "*My mobile is . . .* ".

What sorts of answer did you get? Classify them in terms of function (keeping in touch, checking the news, etc.), context of use (home, work, leisure, etc.), and emotional issues (attachment to the device, frustrations it causes, and so on). ■

Another way of distinguishing the different types of device is by form factor and the physical elements users can interact with. They range in size from handheld devices to jewel-sized sensors and badge-shaped displays. Most have physical buttons you can press and many have touch-sensitive displays. Then there's usually a stylus, cursor control pad or wheel for pointing to and selecting from the information displayed. Less conventionally, some devices are beginning to have position, movement and tilt sensors; even squeezing is being considered as an interaction method.

Some users are more attached to their mobiles than others. Most see their mobiles as an accessory they carry around – another portable object like a wallet or paperback book; in contrast, others, like the well-known 'Cyborg', Kevin Warwick, see the future of mobiles as lying *beneath* the skin, through the use of surgically implanted devices (Warwick, 2002).

BOX 1.3 IMPLANTING YOUR MOBILE?

An interview with Kevin Warwick

Kevin Warwick, professor of cybernetics at Reading University, UK, shocked the scientific establishment in the late 1990s by implanting microprocessor circuitry in his arm. Since that time, he has continued to experiment on 'upgrading the human' through implants.

MJ: Your use of implants, to many, seems at best hyper-futuristic, at worst quite strange. Will the types of approach you use ever become mainstream?

KW: I used to work for British Telecom [the major telecoms provider in the UK] and in the 1970s we were looking at mobile telephony, but the mainstream management view was that the technology would never be used pervasively. Now, 30 years on, everyone has a mobile.

MJ: So where are we with implants in development terms? ➤

KW: Well, implants are already used to help people overcome some disabilities – cochlear implants to help those with impaired hearing are good examples. For the more radical work – such as that we've pioneered to explore the possibility of people communicating directly using their nervous systems – we are many decades or more years off before it becomes widely viable.

MJ: ... and when implanting technology does become easy, what will be the 'killer apps'? What will be the SMS of implants?

KW: Enhancing communication and relationships. My wife and I took part in an experiment where her nervous system and mine were directly connected with implants in each of us transmitting and receiving nerve pulses from each other. We'd just finished the 'official', independently observed test, when I felt a little pulse of electricity in my arm. I knew my wife was sending me a signal – it was a 'wow' moment. Imagine if we could move on from simple dots-and-dashes and send thoughts and feelings.

MJ: Some of the things you're proposing could be done without implants – think about a phone you squeeze, and someone else holding their device feels your touch. Why, then, are you so interested in embedding these devices into the body itself?

KW: Because I want to see how the nervous system accommodates, adapts (or rejects) the new possibilities. We know the brain is very good at adapting to new configurations – people who have suffered strokes, for example, can recover some of their abilities by the brain effectively rewiring itself. How, then, will the brain cope if we wire in extra sensors, providing it with new inputs – say, infrared – for instance?

MJ: This book is about mobile interaction design – for your special type of mobile device, what's the process you use?

KW: I'm a cybernetics professor – for me it is about fusing technology and humanity. So, unlike traditional human–computer interaction design, we are not 'user-centered': it is *not* all about the human. Rather, we think about how the technology and human can work together. We start, then, often by thinking about the technology and how to apply it to enhance the human experience. I think there's a big danger of focusing too much on what people think they want or need – sometimes, only when they experience a new technology can they articulate its value to them and help shape its development. Of course, we also work with a wide range of people who bring other perspectives, from bio-ethicists to anthropologists and neurosurgeons.

MJ: You see a positive future for implants, but is there a darker side to the technology?

KW: Of course you could construe all manners of frightening future scenarios: people with implants might get viruses – not biological but digital ones; hackers could tap into your nervous system, and so on. The constructive thing to do, though – and this applies to more conventional development – is to start thinking through the human and social implications from the start, designing in an attempt to ensure positive outcomes. ■

Wearable computing researchers are also beginning to see their devices as *part of* them, rather than *apart from* them. Take Thad Starner and his co-researchers at Georgia Tech. His team are developing wearable systems with tiny head-mounted displays embedded in a prescription set of glasses, a simplified keyboard and a backpack containing a fully featured computer (Starner, 2003). Less extreme wearables include wristwatch-come-web browsers and badges that are mini public information displays (Falk and Björk, 1999). (See Color Plate 1.)

For other devices, their mobility comes not from the people carrying them but by virtue of being embedded in a vehicle – car navigation systems are increasingly popular, and luxury models can offer small-screen, passenger Internet access systems.

In this book, there is an emphasis on handheld, small-screen devices like PDAs and mobile phones. However, many of the issues and ideas we discuss are just as relevant to the larger devices, like tablet-sized PCs, and the more diminutive ones, like tiny button-sized gadgets.

But let's not get carried away and overwhelmed by the range of devices, functions and application areas (dozens of new ones are being envisaged every day, after all). Let's step back and consider what users might want out of a mobile – the role they should play.

1.2.1 COMMUNICATION OR INFORMATION DEVICE?

Until the end of the 1990s, there were two types of handheld device that supported quite different sets of user needs. There were the mobile phones, for keeping in touch, and PDAs or handhelds, for information management.

Communication-oriented mobile devices have been around somewhat longer than the information-focused ones. Predecessors of modern mobile phones first emerged when Bell Labs launched its radio telephone service in 1946. Then, the devices were vehicle-bound, used by dispatch drivers, doctors and other emergency service personnel. Thirty years later, in 1975, Martin Cooper of Motorola was granted a patent for the cellular handset technology that has enabled mass use of wireless communications.

John Sculley first applied the term Personal Digital Assistant (PDA) in 1992 when talking about the Apple Newton, a hand-sized information organizer. However, small computer-like devices were widely available eight years earlier in 1984 when Psion launched the successful handheld Organizer. Over the 20 succeeding years, many other manufacturers, like Palm with its PalmPilot range and Microsoft with a 'pocket' version of its operating system, have entered the market, providing devices that have offered a range of information processing facilities from simple diary and contact management through to spreadsheet applications. Medical professionals, traveling salespeople, and others who have to spend a large part of their time away from a conventional office have been enthusiastic early adopters of these developments; indeed, there are even books – such as *Handheld Computers for Doctors* (Al-Ubaydli, 2003) – aimed at helping these users get the most out of their devices.

The barriers between the two mobile species began to break down from around 1997 onwards. Mobile phones started to offer access to web-like information using a variety of innovations, the best known being the Wireless Application Protocol – used in Europe and North America – and i-mode which dominated Japan. In addition, like all computing devices, their processors became faster and faster and their onboard storage capacities ever faster. To make use of such resources, manufacturers competed to provide additional features like diaries, games and even text editors. Some phones – the Communicator series from Nokia and the advanced Sony Ericsson devices are good examples – support many of the functions found in PDAs.

Meanwhile, as phones became more like PDAs, handhelds sprouted stubby aerials and gained wireless communication card slots, so users could communicate with each other, placing calls and sending text messages as well as connecting wirelessly with information services.

The trend, then, is clear: increasingly, people will be able to carry mobile devices that are both communication and sophisticated information devices. Indeed, many of the mobile devices people buy will have such abilities built in as standard. But will their owners actually use them both to communicate – by voice, messaging and other emerging services – and to manage and access information?

Lots of commentators certainly see a future full of satisfied handheld users, talking, messaging, playing games, and accessing the net. In a book about Nokia's approach to designing usable phones, Turkka Keinonen sees it this way:

Mobile phones used to be functionally direct replacements of their wired forebears. Now they have suddenly become platforms for entertainment and commerce and tools for information management and media consumption. (Lindholm *et al.*, 2003, p. 6)

Others, though, feel the research community and mobile industry are focusing too heavily on developing services that provide mobile users with 'content'. Richard Harper, an influential communications researcher, puts it this way (Harper, 2003):

. . . mobile devices will be first and foremost about offering users the ability to keep in touch with friends, family and colleagues, and that this will take precedence over technologies and applications that will offer information access and use.

He argues that the communication potential of devices has hardly begun to be tapped:

If one thinks about human communication in the [sic] general, one will note that exchanges between people are not all the same, as if a hello were the same as a summons, as if a whisper from a lover is the same as a bellow from the boss. Yet if one looks at current communications applications and protocols one will see there are few alternatives made available to the user, and people cannot vary the way they call their friends, partners or colleagues, except perhaps through the use of text.

EXERCISE 1.2 ENHANCING EXPRESSIVENESS

What features might a future mobile device have to help users express themselves more fully when communicating with another person in another location? Discuss the pros and cons of each proposal. ■

Harper worries that as people, in his view, will carry mobiles mainly for communication, the drive to provide information-centered products might have a damaging impact on the overall usefulness and acceptance:

Many information delivering services and products, for example, require larger screens than most current GSM devices do, and this may lead to expanding the form factor to a level that makes constant carrying difficult or at least irritating and burdensome.

Unlike others, then, Harper sees the brightest future of mobiles lying in a device that is specialized in providing users with ways to communicate, with revenues from such services vastly outselling the information-based ones.

1.2.2 APPLIANCE OR SWISS ARMY KNIFE?

Perhaps, though, the real issue is not whether mobile devices should focus mainly on communication or information processing. There is a broader concern – should one device try to do everything for a user or should there be specialized tools, each carefully crafted to support a particular type of activity?

This is the debate over the value of an 'appliance attitude' in mobile design. Should we focus on simple, activity-centered devices – ones that might well combine task-specific communication and information facilities – or look to providing a 'Swiss Army Knife' that has every communication and information management feature a manufacturer can pack into it?

Kitchen toasters have a simple purpose – to quickly tan pieces of bread, transforming them into something appetizing for breakfast. They are focused-function, easy-to-use appliances. Often, they are put to work with other appliances – a bread-making machine to provide a fresh, warm loaf in the morning; an electric carving knife for slicing pieces into just the right thickness.

In contrast, the Swiss Army Knife – a pocket-sized device with a set of retractable tools, from blades to tweezers – is not an appliance; it is trying hard to be a do-it-all, multi-purpose gadget. Don Norman sees it this way:

Sure, it is fun to look at, sure it is handy if you are off in the wilderness and it is the only tool you have, but of all the umpteen things it does, none of them are done particularly well. (Norman, 1999, p. 71)

Some techno-prophets, like Norman, foresee a future where the computer becomes less like a Swiss Army Knife and more like a toaster – a future where it evolves into an appliance; an information appliance, that is.

In Norman's vision, we will surround ourselves with many such devices, just as we currently fill our homes and offices with books, lights, notepads and picture frames. Each appliance will help users do a specific activity – like writing, their hobby, or communicating – and they will support these in simple, direct ways. The tools will also be able to effortlessly communicate with the others:

. . . use an appliance for one activity, then point it at a target appliance and push the 'send' button: whoosh, the information is transmitted to the other. (Norman, 1999, p. 52)

At first glance, the simplifying appliance attitude seems particularly well suited to small, mobile devices. Multitudes of features frustrate users even when they use a PC with a high-resolution display, full keyboard and mouse; in the mobile context, each additional function might be a further ingredient for disappointing user experiences. Then, there's the design liberation offered by the vision of devices working together. No need to worry that the handheld has a small display – just find a nearby large screen for a more comfortable read.

However, an important objection to this sleek simplicity is the possibility that users will be overwhelmed by the number of appliances they will need to support their everyday tasks. For mobiles, the problem seems even more pressing – just how many gadgets will people be able to carry around with them on a daily basis? Norman suggests that when traveling, there will be a preference for a Swiss Army Knife, all-in-one, computing device, such as a portable PC, trading off its convenience against lower usability.

It is probably too early to dismiss the notion of mobile appliances, though, and to assume people will only ever want to carry around one device. Look inside the bag you carry to work – it might well contain a book or magazine (a reading appliance), a phone (a communication appliance), pictures of your favorite people (a photo appliance) and a notepad (a writing appliance). Technological developments – making mobiles lighter, foldable and flexible – could make the appliance approach tenable.

Returning to the present, however, we see that most mobile devices are certainly not appliances; they are do-everything, solve-it-all, shrunk-down personal computers. Industry bodies, manufacturers and service providers don't appear to see this as a problem; indeed, all seem to be proud of the complex miniatures they are producing, convinced that users want to carry around one device to fit all the different tasks they face each day. Take this statement from the International Telecommunications Union, quoted in an *Economist Magazine* article, which discusses advanced, third-generation (3G) products:

The 3G device will function as a phone, a computer, a television, a pager, a video-conferencing centre, a newspaper, a diary and even a credit card ... it will support not only voice communications but also real-time video and full-scale multimedia ... It will also function as a portable address book and agenda, containing all the information about meetings and contacts ... It will automatically search the Internet for relevant news and information on pre-selected subjects, book your next holiday for you online and download a bedtime story for your child, complete with moving pictures. It will even be able to pay for goods when you shop via wireless electronic funds transfer. In short, the new mobile handset will become the single, indispensable 'life tool', carried everywhere by everyone, just like a wallet or purse is today. (Economist, 2004b)

The market has, though, shown some signs of appliance-flavored thinking with devices which are optimized for particular types of activity. The BlackBerry, for instance, is focused on keeping professionals in touch with their email and important data. Meanwhile, several phone manufacturers are producing entertainment-style appliances, optimized for image capture, games and music enjoyment. The notion of using mobile devices together with other pieces of technology is also being put into practice – for example, there are set-top boxes to receive data from mobile phones and display it on the television screen.

Of the two early and classic handheld computer types – Palm's PalmPilot and Microsoft's Windows CE/PocketPC devices – the former had a greater appliance feel to it, supporting frequent short bursts of activity, such as looking up a telephone number or jotting down a note. The instantaneous, unobtrusive qualities that characterize information appliances were pursued throughout the product's development (Bergman and Haitani, 2000). Meanwhile, the Microsoft approach has tended towards replicating the flavor of their desktop products in shrunk-down form; as one of the designers puts it:

Windows is installed on a great number of PCs, both in the office and home environments. It makes sense to leverage familiar design in new emerging platforms. (Zuberec, 2000, p. 128)

While there is limited evidence of appliance thinking in the commercial world, research labs are testing a range of possibilities. Consider, for example, Cameo, designed for professionals who take care of elderly people living independently in the community (Andersson, 2002). The device supports six functions, including handling of alarm alerts sent from the carer's clients, taking photos of the client's environment to inform the wider care team, and a memo recorder.

1.2.3 CHERISHED DEVICE OR COMMODITY TOOL?

Most users have very little emotional attachment to their toaster or dishwasher – they are, after all, just appliances: tools to get a job done. Lots of mobile users, though, really care about the devices they carry around with them, their choice of device reflecting something about who they are, or want to be.

Designers have recognized this, particularly in the styling of the physical features of the devices they build. As an extreme example, take Vertu, which markets itself as a luxury mobile communications company. It handcrafts handsets using precious metals, jewels and distinct design. Such attention to detail comes at a price – in 2005, their range retailed at between $9000 and $30 000 (Vertu). The company's products appeal to those concerned with making an *haute-couture* statement that they feel reflects their high status. In contrast to the short life most mobiles have, the company expects people to hold on to their expensive model for many years, valuing them as they would a precision-made watch. The phone is engineered so that new developments in technology can be accommodated without having to dispose of the handheld entirely.

It seems that the biggest challenge watchmakers at the higher end of the business face today is to sustain the emotional attachment people have for their watches. There are hints that many people could (or already have) become just as emotionally attached to their sleek new GPS-enabled, tune-playing, video-showing, time-managing camera-phones as they once were to their wristwatches. (Cukier, 2005)

Right at the other end of the market are the disposable phones. Just buy it, use up the pre-paid credit and throw it away. These phones are simple and functional, with the only user interface being a touchpad for dialing calls.

Between Vertu and the throwaways, there are many mainstream devices designed with an eye to image, style and fashion. One of Nokia's early imaging phones (the 7600) was marketed on its website in this way:

Introducing a bold icon for the age of mobility. The distinctly new-paradigm Nokia 7600 imaging phone is a synchronous blend of torqued curves and the latest technology. It's compact, futuristic, and conveniently contoured to fit your palm. (Nokia, a)

BOX 1.4 JUST ANOTHER TOOL? PICK-UP-AND-USE MOBILES

Not all mobiles are well-loved, personal devices with one long-term user who wants to personalize and adapt it to suit their specific needs and image. Some are mobile equivalents of familiar walk-up-and-use technologies like cash-dispensing machines and public transport ticket vending devices. ➤

FIGURE 1.1

MyGROCER showing small screen display attached to shopping cart

An obvious place for these pick-up-and-use technologies is supermarkets. The MyGROCER system (Kourouthanasis and Roussos, 2003), for example, illustrated in Figure 1.1, uses a PDA-type device built into a shopping cart, helping the user navigate to grocery promotions and to keep track of their purchases. Less sophisticated versions of this approach are now in common use in supermarkets around the world. Researchers have also taken mobile systems into museums and art galleries, with visitors being handed devices to use for the duration of their visit. ■

1.3 IMPOVERISHED OR EXTRAORDINARY INTERFACES?

It is all too easy to despair at the seemingly limited interaction abilities a mobile device has. The tiny, fiddly keypad; the low-resolution, small screen – surely, such input and output technologies will always mean these devices will be the impoverished relations of the richly expressive desktops? If you are a designer who has worked with conventional technologies – perhaps used to producing slick websites for large-screen viewing – you might well feel handhelds offer you little room to develop creative interactions your users will find fulfilling.

This sort of thinking needs to be challenged. The much-reduced physical size of the devices does seem to be a big limitation on the possibilities for rich interaction, but there are technology developments that will allow designers to effectively address the mobile context.

While we emphasize the importance of understanding users throughout the book – their needs, capabilities and limitations – paradoxically, a look here at input and output technologies nicely highlights the importance of this human-centered style. We will see how insights into aspects of human nature, from basic physiology through to social protocols, can lead to more effective technologies for the device and user to communicate.

By facing the challenge to build extraordinary interfaces that go beyond the normal and expected, highly usable input and output approaches will emerge. Already, some interesting new ways of increasing the bandwidth between user and device have been demonstrated in research labs.

But let's begin by considering the two much-derided interaction 'failings' of small devices – their tiny keypads and Post-it note-sized screens. How can a small handheld device allow the user to interact in ways they are familiar with on their PC, that is, by pressing discrete keys to input characters and having a large display area? Two interesting technologies, the first a commercial design, the second coming out of a HCI research lab, illustrate imaginative ways of making up for the physical lack of space for a keypad and a display.

1.3.1 THE FASTAP KEYPAD

Standard mobile phones use the ISO keypad layout – 12 keys, 10 for the numbers 0–9, the other two for the characters * and #. Eight of the numeral keys also each have three alphabetic characters associated with them (e.g., '2' has 'abc' and '6' has 'mno').

Entering more than a few words with such a condensed keypad can be very laborious. The basic entry technique is called multi-tap. For each character, the user has to potentially press a key several times to select the actual input they want. For instance, entering 'CAN' would involve pressing key '2' three times for 'C', pressing it once again for 'A', and finally hitting '6' twice for 'N'. Clearly, such an approach slows a user down – one study, for example, showed that compared with a conventional keyboard, where people can achieve 60 or more words per minute (wpm), multi-tap reduces this sprinting pace to an ambling 21 wpm for experts (Silfverberg *et al.*, 2000).

Basic multi-tapping was enhanced significantly with the introduction of the dictionary-based, predictive text method patented by Tegic, known as T9. Users press keys just once and the system, using a dictionary lookup, presents the most likely word(s) as the input progresses. Silfverberg's comparison with multi-tap showed that it has the potential to allow a user to double their text entry speed to 40 wpm.

Instead of relying on user effort as in the multi-tap case, or the sort of clever software processing that T9 uses, the Fastap keypad manages to squeeze a full alphanumeric keyboard with 50 independent keys in a third of the space of a business card (Levy, 2002). That's 3.3 keys per square centimeter while other similar-sized keypads provide around 1.2.

The approach actually involves two keypads, one raised above the other (see Figure 1.2). The upper provides mainly for alphabetic input, while the lower provides for digits. The keys are positioned so each has a similar amount of space to a conventional, full-size keyboard, leading, it's claimed, to increased comfort. While users are typing, they do not have to worry about pressing a key exactly. If they hit several keys in one go, a technique called 'passive chording' allows the system to unambiguously work out what entry a user intended. In passing, note that *active* chording has been used for entering text while mobile, too. Here the user has to press *groups* of keys – a chord – simultaneously to enter text. The Twiddler (see Figure 1.3) uses 12 keys in its chording system, for instance.

Cockburn and Siresena (2003) wanted to find out how this new keypad compared with the text entry performance of multi-tap and T9 systems. They did this by carrying out a controlled, scientific experiment (we will explore this type of evaluation method and alternatives in Chapter 7).

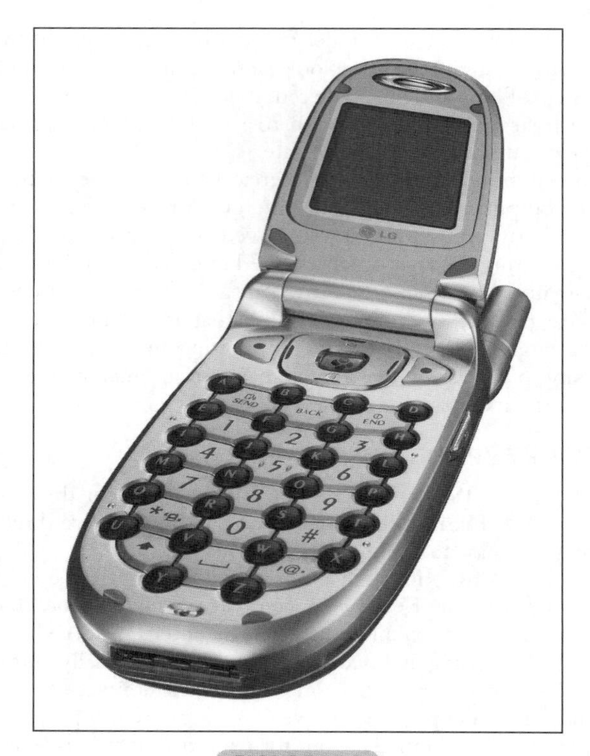

FIGURE 1.2

Fastap keypad

The first time users tried the different methods, Fastap was the most successful. With Fastap, they could enter a text message at an average rate of 6.3 wpm; in contrast, not all could complete the task using multi-tap or T9 and the input rates dropped to 3.6 and 3.9 wpm, respectively. The technique had the advantage of requiring no training, and when users were asked about the schemes they were more satisfied with the novel approach. They also liked the 'modeless' style of data entry: that is, they didn't have to work in different ways depending on whether they were entering numbers or words. Modes in interactive systems are known to cause people difficulties. We will look at the issues of mobiles and modes in more detail in Chapter 8.

1.3.2 PEEPHOLE DISPLAYS

While the Fastap keypad makes the physical keypad seem much larger than it really is, the Peephole display does the same for a handheld's screen area. Instead of trying to clutter the small screen with information, with this approach the display acts as a small window – the peephole – onto a much larger display area (Yee, 2003).

The handheld is given positional sensors that tell the system where the device is, relative to the user. The user moves the device around, left and right, up and down, and as the position of the handheld changes, the display is updated to show another portion of the bigger picture. This virtual,

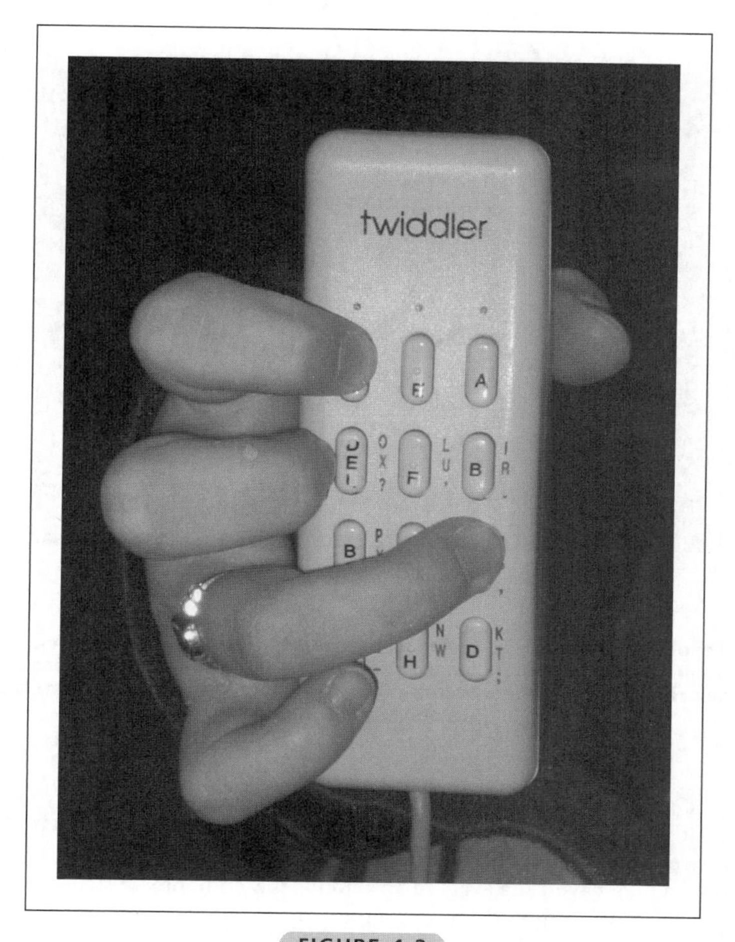

FIGURE 1.3
The Twiddler – active chording for text entry (Lyons *et al.*, 2004)

large-scale display might be showing a map, a list of names in an address book, or a figure the user wants to draw.

Figure 1.4 shows one of the prototypes in use, providing what is dubbed a personal information space. The user can move the device to view different parts of a sort of virtual desktop, with different applications and information being placed around the user.

1.3.3 ACCOMMODATING HUMAN CAPABILITIES AND LIMITATIONS

Sit in a café and watch how people interact with each other and the world around them. The PC's interface abilities, envied by handheld developers who see it as highly expressive, looks completely unsophisticated and simple in comparison. Yes, people do write things down for others to read – a waiter writing a bill, for example – and they show each other documents: "would you like to see

FIGURE 1.4

Peepholes in action – accessing a large personal information space via a small window. Image shows user operating a PDA. Moving the device to their right allows them to access a Doodle Pad application; to their left is a calendar application

the wine menu, ma'm?". But much more nuanced interplays are occurring, too. "Touch that bottle of red wine – is it the right temperature?" "What did my partner's sigh mean?" "Such a dramatic hand movement over on Table 5, what's going on?".

Some HCI researchers have long wanted to endow the computer systems they envision with similarly 'natural' ways of communicating. Despite the ability of people to sense and express themselves in many ways, there's been a great deal of frustration with machines that can only respond to discrete inputs – on the whole, that means key pushes – and present information predominantly in a visual form, with a few beeps or, at most, a sequence of notes.

Handhelds are proving to be both an outlet and an additional motivation for novel interaction research – for these gadgets, advanced approaches are seen not as luxury added extras, but as necessities. Extending the repertoire of input and output forms – or modalities, as they are called – is seen as a way of allowing the user and device to communicate more completely and in ways that better fit with mobile demands. When someone is walking around a new town, hurriedly trying to locate a meeting place, they will probably want to pay attention to street signs, traffic and landmarks and not have to exert all their mental abilities on interacting with their handheld.

As we will see below, there is a wide range of developments in mobile interaction techniques that are trying to better exploit users' capabilities. Some address human auditory (hearing) abilities, others haptic (touch and movement sensing) abilities. Then there's increasing interest in exploiting people's gestural skills, such as the expressive movements users can make with their hands or head; and the ways in which users can deploy multiple means to express their needs are also being accommodated.

Auditory Interfaces

If you listen to a piece of music, your brain has the ability to accurately distinguish between subtle variations in the intensity, pitch, duration and quality (or timbre) of the notes you hear. For some time, researchers have explored using such cues to enhance the user experience, particularly in terms of the feedback an interactive system gives about the effect of something a user has done.

Auditory icons, such as familiar, natural sounds, were proposed by Bill Gaver to supplement visual cues (Gaver, 1989). A file dropped into the trashcan, then, would not only disappear but cause a metallic, crashing sound to be played. Moving a document over your desktop becomes more realistic as you hear a shuffling sound and see the icon shift position.

Earcons are also non-speech sounds but are synthetic, systematic sequences designed to convey structural information about an interface, such as what part of a menu hierarchy a user is currently perusing (Blattner *et al.*, 1989).

In the new, mobile context, the sophisticated hi-fi abilities of some phones are already important: many users enjoy downloading ringtone melodies and there are 'Top 10′ style ringtone charts that track the most popular. (In June 2005, a quirky mobile ringtone 'sung' by a frog topped the pop music charts, displacing Coldplay! The mobile's influence on everyday life continues to surprise.) But, from an interaction design perspective, auditory input–output is also very attractive.

Stephen Brewster and his team at Glasgow University, for example, are looking at additional interactive uses of the sound channel. In one experiment, he added earcons to the buttons in a PalmPilot calculator; when touched, each button made a distinct sound. This auditory feedback helped users enter data more effectively and they preferred the approach over the calculator that had mute buttons (Brewster, 2002).

The most expressive sounds that we humans make are, of course, those that convey language. So there's been a lot of interest in investigating effective ways to enable users to talk to their devices, using speech recognition techniques, and to listen to spoken output via speech synthesizers. While both recognition and synthesis systems can now produce reasonably high-quality results and can operate fairly robustly at the desktop, it is worth noting that the places people want to use their mobile devices and the sorts of input they want to make often present difficult challenges to the technology (see Box 1.5).

BOX 1.5 THE TROUBLE WITH SPEECH

Speech recognition and synthesis look natural choices for mobile interaction, but there are problems:

- **Noise.** Background noises of say a train or a busy street can still lead to severe degradations in accuracy and cause generated utterances to be misheard or missed altogether.
- **Spontaneity.** At the desktop, people might well want to express full sentences carefully, in dictation-style mode, but when on the move they are likely to utter ➤

spontaneous commands, requests and clarifications which could be full of difficult-to-handle content. This speech-in-action will contain lots of false starts and stumbles – "umm ... when's my next ... no ... tomorrow's appointment", for example – which people can handle easily but can cause recognizers to falter quickly.

- **Out-of-vocabulary words.** Recognizers rely on dictionaries, but words that people want to use in the street, including names of people and places – "meet Jaydon at Te Papa", for instance – might well not be in the lexicon. Similarly, accurate synthesis of such phrases is also difficult.
- **Cognitive burden.** Attending to speech consumes much of a user's cognitive processing abilities. Think carefully, then, about the situations where speech output is essential and limit the amount of information delivered. ■

One system that has tried to leverage the benefits of speech for mobiles and to address some of the problems is MIT Media Lab's Nomadic Radio (Sawhney and Schmandt, 2000). The system is really a sort of mobile messaging appliance, providing access to email, personal notes, calendar entries, news broadcasts and the like. Users don't have to grapple with interaction devices like screens or a keyboard; instead all of these services are accessed mainly through audio input and output. Voicemail and other audio-based information, like news summaries, are simply played to the user, but text-based information, like email, is first converted to speech using a synthesizer. There are also auditory cues to indicate events like message arrival and system breakdowns. A technique called spatialized audio gives the user the impression that different sound sources are coming from distinct locations around their head – news to the left, voicemail to the right, and so on. Meanwhile, speaking to the system – "Go to my messages", "I am confused, what can I say?" – is the way the user accesses information and controls the system's operation.

Haptic Interfaces

As you flick through this book's pages, your fingers will sense the movement of the pages, even the slight air movements the action generates. Using these inputs, you'll be able to approximate how near you are to the section you really want to read. Carry a stack of books from a library and your sense of touch will be supplemented by your abilities to perceive movements, such as beginnings of a topple, as the top books begin to slide out of your hands. Haptics, then, involve feedback from touch and movement sensors in the skin, muscles, the inner ear and some other organs. Mobile researchers have become increasingly interested in putting such capabilities to use.

Mobile phones have long had very simple haptic interfaces; instead of ringing and disturbing an important meeting, they can be set to 'vibrate mode' to provide discreet notification. This approach, though, can only communicate one 'bit' of information: the vibrations are either on or off, indicating that there is a call/message or not. In contrast, the TouchEngine vastly expands on this limited vibra-vocabulary (Poupyrev *et al.*, 2002). Sony researchers who developed the system were motivated by physiological experiments showing how sensitive and discriminating our sense of touch can be. We can notice two stimuli just 5 ms apart – or twice as fast as a blink – and can sense displacements on our palm as low as 0.2 microns in length, much smaller than a single pixel on a mobile phone display.

The TouchEngine uses a haptic actuator, set inside the handheld, to convert electrical signals into motion. With its added abilities, the mobile can give the user touch-based feedback by moving part of the PDA screen, or the entire screen. But what useful extra information can this device communicate?

Its inventors experimented with a range of possibilities, from notification of incoming calls to attempts to convey more complex information. Instead of simply telling the user there's an incoming call, the user can be given information about who the caller is, or the urgency of the call, by varying the rhythm, intensity and gradient of the vibration.

Another application that was tried was a tactile progress bar. While a visual progress bar – such as the one you see when waiting for information to download from the Internet – is useful when there is spare screen space and the user can give their attention to monitoring it, as on the desktop, its merits in the mobile case are less clear. As an alternative, then, the TouchEngine can present a tactile-based progress bar. The handheld emits short pulses, decreasing the period between each such 'click' the nearer the task is to completion.

A further prototype implemented a touch-based version of the paper-shuffling auditory icon mentioned earlier. The user tilts the handheld to view a map. As the map slides, instead of playing a sound conveying paper movement, the device generates a scratching tactile pattern that becomes a simple pulse when the edge of the map is reached.

Vibrations and force feedback will quickly become common, but there are examples of interfaces that go beyond providing feedback via touch and involve the user in touching, grasping and otherwise manipulating the device (Harrison *et al.*, 1998). The Gummi interface illustrates how very 'hands-on' interaction with computing devices could become in the longer-term (Schwesig *et al.*, 2003). The proposal is for devices that you can actually twist and bend to express your needs. Imagine a display you can grasp with both hands, one on either side of the screen, flexing it upwards and downwards to control the amount of zoom on a map or other document. To try the concept, the researchers combined a non-flexible TFT screen – the sort of display found on handhelds today – with touchpads on either side. The user squeezes the pads, simulating the sorts of bending movements that researchers envisage with future display technologies (see Figure 1.5).

Gestural interfaces

You can powerfully and quickly communicate by moving your hands, nodding your head, pointing a finger. Research into gestures, from simple movements of a device to complex head nods, promises to provide useful ways to enter information and control future commercial mobiles.

EXERCISE 1.3 GESTURES AND LARGE SCREEN INTERACTION

Imagine a large screen display that the presenter can interact with by using gestures. Instead of having to click a button or move a mouse, they control the information being shown using body movements; but what should those movements be? Design prototype gestures for the following types of control:

- Next slide
- Previous slide ➤

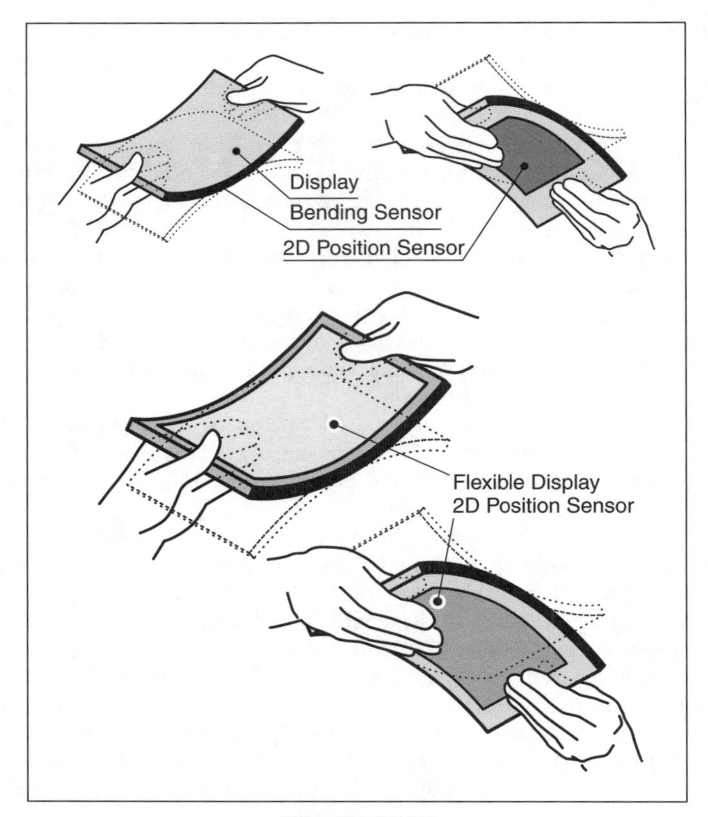

FIGURE 1.5

The Gummi interface – bend the display to interact

- Zoom in to magnify the display
- Zoom out to reduce the view
- Remove some information
- Remove the complete document from the display.

Think about the mapping between the gestures and the actions – do they seem natural? How does the system know when the presenter is giving it an instruction as opposed to simply gesturing to the audience?

Perhaps the most successful and best known gesture-like interfaces are those for text input and editing on handheld computers. The unistroke method (Goldberg and Richardson, 1993) and the

Graffiti handwriting technique used in the early PalmPilots are examples of approaches that use simple, distinct gestures, expressed using a pen stylus, for both alphanumeric characters and editing commands, such as deleting text or changing from lower case to upper case.

Stylus or finger-based movements can also control an application as well as being used to enter text. Examples of such approaches are seen in the SmartPad (Rekimoto *et al.*, 2003) and TouchPlayer (Pirhonen *et al.*, 2002).

SmartPad is for mobiles, with the basic push-button keypad being supplemented with a sensing grid that can detect the user's light touch, a bit like the touchpad mice used on some laptop computers. Pick up a mobile and sweep your finger across the keypad, to the left or right, or try a circular movement. These are easy to do, even one-handed, and if your phone is equipped with a SmartPad, those movements could be interpreted as a wish to view an alternative page of content – forward or back – or as a virtual jog-wheel control for scrolling through information.

The TouchPlayer, prototyped on a PocketPC-type device, gives the user eyes-free control of a music application by combining simple gestures and auditory feedback through the earcons mentioned earlier. If you want to skip forward to the next track, you move your finger to the right; to increase the player's volume you make a circular sweeping movement, like turning a knob.

In both prototypes, the use of gestures allows the designer to achieve two important things:

- Overcome the lack of physical space for input. The gestures avoid the need to add additional physical buttons or other controls to the device or clutter the limited screen space with buttons and other widgets.
- Accommodate the use-conditions likely with the devices. Mobile users are unlikely to want or be able to give their full attention to interacting with their devices. For example, many music players are used while people are jogging vigorously on a treadmill in the gym; their exercise experience will be affected if they have to try to concentrate on a small screen, locate a button or menu, and activate a function.

Moving up from these micro-gestures, the next type of gesture being researched involves the device itself. Here, tilt-based systems are important and have been used for both text, cursor and application control:

- **Text and cursor control**. In one tilt-to-write system, found to be almost 25% faster than multi-tap, different characters are selected depending on the positioning of the device (Wigdor and Balakrishnan, 2003). In another prototype, cursor movement is controlled by tilting. Incidentally, this system also embodies two increasingly important elements of mobile interaction design – fun and pleasure. The user experience is similar to moving a knob of butter around a frying pan: the steeper the tilt, the faster the cursor runs down the screen (Weberg *et al.*, 2001).
- **Application control**. Two of the systems we've already mentioned – the Peephole and the TouchEngine – allow users to interact by moving the handheld up and down and left-to-right for information viewing, such as scrolling through a list. In another experimental effort, Ken Hinckley and a team from Microsoft Research looked at an alternative application of movement. They were interested in finding a way to switch on a handheld's memo-recording function (Hinckley *et al.*, 2000). Many PDAs have a button, often on the device's side, that if pushed activates the recorder. Hinckley and his team thought about a way of saving the user the trouble of explicitly pressing 'record'. To do this they built a prototype that can recognize when the user intends to store a voice message. Using a number of sensors, such as one to measure the

handheld's proximity to other objects and others that indicate how the device is being held, the prototype is able to detect when the user brings the handheld up to their head, holding it like a mobile phone, and then starts recording. It's easy to imagine extensions to this sort of idea: move your music player to the center of your body, near your heart, and access your favorite playlist; or touch it on your leg and listen to the music you like to jog to.

All of the gestures discussed so far are small-scale ones – you would hardly notice someone performing them. If some research prototypes make it out of the lab and into the street, though, you might come across people who seem to be behaving rather strangely. These systems involve users in more extravagant, obvious movements to express their needs. Take, for example, one mobile system that uses nod-recognition to control selections from a menu presented through audio (Brewster *et al.*, 2003). Like Nomadic Radio, via spatialized audio, the user perceives different sound sources coming from different positions relative to their head. To select a source, the user nods in its direction.

An evaluation of this system's usefulness showed that people were able to walk around and control the system effectively by nodding. The effort they put into interacting with the system, though, did slow them down – their pace slowed by nearly a third. This is a good reminder that interacting on the move will disrupt something else the user wants to do – you need to minimize the effort required to use your system.

While such schemes sound odd, with the potential to make users feel self-conscious as they walk down the street, you have to remember that little more than a decade ago, even talking into a phone in public would have marked you out as an eccentric. Now with hands-free headsets, self-talkers and gesturers are a common sight in all major cities.

BOX 1.6 AROMATIC OUTPUT?

An interview with Jenny Tillotson

Input and output based on vision, audio and even touch will be common and conventional in mobile devices. Our ability to perceive and respond to smell, though, has been relatively underexploited.

This paucity of investigation is being addressed by groups of researchers interested in aromatic output. Aromas have advantages, it's argued, of being highly evocative while also being unobtrusive – a form of interaction that fits well with the goals of ambient and ubiquitous computing. Aromatic output could enhance websites or games or, more banally, be added to calendar applications:

...pick up the children at 3.30... the aroma of baby powder wafts across the room at 3.00 p.m. as a gentle reminder of the upcoming appointment. (Kaye, 2004)

Jenny Tillotson, a researcher at Central St Martin's College of Art, London, has been investigating the use of aromas in a mobile context since 1997. A fashion designer, ➤

she explores the integration of scent-output technologies with fabrics, leading to radical, wearable computers.

MJ: What motivated you to consider the use of smell?

JT: My main focus is wellness: how can technologies enhance physical and emotional well-being? Aromas are known to have calming and healing properties and I want to see if and how aromatic output can be triggered and generated using the clothes people wear.

MJ: Many researchers with a technology background are building 'wearable computers'. How does your approach differ?

JT: First off, I'm an artist so the places I seek my inspiration for concepts are probably quite different from those of the technologist. For example, I often look to nature and biology to see how animal and plant life interact or are structured. When I was working on a honey-type aroma output, I modeled the output device – the fabric – closely to honeycomb structures. Secondly, my wearables are less utilitarian than many other visions: so, I envisage the fabric generating a localized 'scent bubble', providing aroma molecules for the right moment for the right effect, triggering new emotions and enhancing the intimate contact with other living things. I hope we will develop a new hypersensitivity, learn new and stimulating pleasures and recreate lost memories all through the aromas delivered by the technology.

MJ: Picking up on the utility of this approach, are you exploring the use of this for more mundane applications?

JT: Well, there's the 'scent clock', an aroma-based way of telling the time. In aromatherapy there are a range of distinct smells, or 'notes'. We're looking at associating these with specific minutes and hours. But the aim is to go beyond the simple function of informing the wearer of the time and to provide aromas which will be useful in terms of evoking and shaping emotions. You could imagine too a mobile phone that not only has a ring tone but a scent tone; as you bring the phone to your head you are given a slight aroma based on who the call is from, or perhaps the purpose of the call.

MJ: There's also a lot of interest in conventional mobile design in community aspects of the technology to allow people to relate, share experiences and collaborate. You talk about 'enhancing the intimate contact with other living things' – can you give an example?

JT: Perfume obviously impacts on more than just the wearer and is used to signal subtly from one person to another. The aromatic clock output, then, would affect not just the wearer but those standing close by too. Inter-person interaction has been a ➤

very important motivation for my work, but again, my take on it is quite different from the 'hard' technological approaches you commonly see. So, there have been quite a few mobile dating-type research prototypes – when your device notifies you that someone you might be interested in is in the vicinity. In our concept, sensors in your garments could be programmed to detect someone whose pheromone profile is of interest to you and to send them a sample of your own pheromones. Love is literally in the air. ■

Multi-modality

Think back to the café scene – when you see someone pointing to the menu, they are probably speaking too, saying perhaps "What's that dish like?". If the person is only speaking or pointing, we could describe them as operating in a unimodal way; they are using just one method to communicate. By combining two or more ways to express themselves, they are being multimodal in their interactions. In our café example, employing two modalities can help in two ways. First, it reduces the amount of communication effort between customer and waiter; the customer doesn't have to refer verbosely to the dish, saying perhaps "What's the *Spaghetti al forna Italiano* like?". Instead, they can abbreviate the full description to just 'that dish'. Second, imagine the noise from an excited party at a nearby table drowning out part of the customer's request; in this case, the waiter can use the other input, the pointing, to help understand what's being asked.

As we have seen, as technology develops we're likely to see mobiles that can support several modalities – sound cues, speech input and output, touch and gestures, for example. These communication forms can be combined, just as they are in human-to-human interactions, to make for less cumbersome dialogs and to help resolve ambiguous input. The advantages of a multimodal approach could be particularly welcome in the mobile case. Hurried users will appreciate the shortcuts multimodality provides, saving them from having to spell out their needs laboriously as they might have to if just one input technique were available. Users are also likely to make more input errors with their mobiles: a mis-selected option when using a stylus while walking; a strangely pronounced spoken command uttered while stressed. The redundancy provided by using more than one input will help the device to be more accommodating.

The QuickSet multimodal system, described by Sharon Oviatt, demonstrates some of the potential advantages of using multiple inputs for mobiles (Oviatt, 1999). QuickSet is a tablet-sized computer, equipped with speech input and pen-driven gesture interaction. In one trial, users were asked to operate the system in a fire and flood control simulation – they had to imagine they were in charge of coordinating rescue services in a disaster, an increasingly important use of handhelds. They could talk to the system and gesture at the same time, issuing commands like "Show me the hospital" while pointing to a location on the map, or circling a part of the display and saying "Zoom in" to see an enlarged view. Multimodality improves the accuracy of the system in recognizing what the user wants to do. Speech recognition systems often cope badly where there is a lot of background noise, but with QuickSet, using extra gestural inputs, error rates are reduced by up to 35%.

Designing for some, Benefits all

In the 1980s, few in mainstream HCI research were interested in users who had special needs – visual, hearing or cognitive impairments, for instance – although there were some notable exceptions (see Edwards and Long (1995) for a review). Fortunately, this lack of activity has been vigorously redressed and now there's the flourishing research area of universal accessibility. As well as benefiting minority user groups, these efforts have improved the lives of many users.

A good example from mobiles of how design for special needs leads to a much wider win is the predictive text system, T9, known to most users through its use in mobile phone text messaging. Originally, its developers were looking at ways to help impaired users enter text on a conventional PC. Their target users could control only their eye movements, so the question was how such limited interaction could be used for input into the computer. The answer involved designing a pair of glasses capable of spotting where the wearer was gazing. As the eye can focus accurately on only eight regions, the developers grouped letters together and placed them on distinct parts of the screen. Then, as the user looked at different letter clusters, a dictionary process gave the users potential word matches as input progressed.

Just as the eye-gaze users were limited with their eight input regions for text entry, so are standard mobile phone users, with only a small set of buttons on the keypad. Tegic, the company that licenses T9, saw that the specialized input technology, designed for challenging users, could be effective in accommodating device limitations as well. As the company's website puts it:

Soon, [the developers] realized that this technology could benefit a much broader audience who was struggling with the same small form factor issues. (Tegic)

So, as a mobile developer, it's worth your while to keep track of the work going on in the universal usability field (see *Resources* at the end of the book). There will be other innovations, like T9, driven by users who themselves have 'limited bandwidth' for interaction, and these may well transfer to mobile devices that have restricted input–output capabilities.

Just as design for limited ability users has led to benefits for all, mobile design will help enhance conventional, fully featured computers. Non-mobile developers, then, should certainly pay attention to all the novel input and output schemes being explored for mobile devices. The mobile space has some key advantages as a breeding ground for effective interaction design. There's the obvious need to innovate to overcome the form-factor problems and impacts of the context these devices are used in. But there's also less clutter, less distractions as a clean, simple design is sought. On a conventional PC, in contrast, with its huge screen space there's a real temptation to add more and more to the interactive possibilities; just look at the over-featured software we're all familiar with.

Novel Technology Problems

Technological developments, then, allowing interactions ranging from tilting to touching, from speaking to nodding, will add to the designer's repertoire. You need to be aware, however, of some side-effect design problems these new techniques will pose. Key presses and mouse movements, though inappropriate in some mobile situations, do have the advantage of being unambiguous and discrete. Getting robust recognition of inputs like speech and gesturing in real-world contexts remains an unsolved problem.

Even when the techniques are highly reliable, you will still have to make difficult design choices as to which to use. Just as conventional software developers tend to add new features to their applications continually, there will be real pressures to give devices all the latest, most dazzling interaction technologies. Although you might find it hard to persuade your colleagues, particularly those in marketing, to resist bloating the devices in this way, you should certainly put up a good fight, insisting on selecting those that will give the user simple, direct, unnoticeable ways of communicating their needs.

1.4 IMPOVERISHING INTERACTIONS?

The mobile's small screen, limited keypad or other interaction limitations should not be used as an excuse for bad interaction design. If a customer complains how hard it is to access a mobile's functions, a defensive response might be "What do you expect on such a small screen?". While device characteristics – things you might have no control over – could lead to some user problems, your interaction design choices will have the bigger impact on the quality of interaction.

Every day we encounter many examples of poorly thought-out interactions, and not just in computer systems. How many times have you tried to pull on a door handle, only to find, silly you, that you should have pushed? Or struggled to work out how to operate the shower-come-bath unit in your hotel room? Yearning for a refreshingly warm post-journey soak, you find yourself doused by a blast of cold water from the shower. Did the designers consider how much frustration, wasted time and disappointment they were sowing when they made their choices?

If there are problems with simple things like doors and showers, is there any hope for the far greater complexity in interactive computer systems? Any PC user will be familiar with the meaningless error messages, inappropriate interruptions and teeth-clenching frustrating events like sending email after email without the attachments being attached.

Sadly, as new technologies come along, old mistakes are repeated, and mobiles are certainly not immune. Over the years, mobile users have found themselves lost as they attempt to navigate the increasingly complex set of functions their devices provide (we'll explore this further in Chapter 8). They've been perplexed by the techno-vocabulary littering the interfaces – from 'data bearers' to 'gateways' – failing to cope with the degree of technical expertise required to set up 'fun' applications like multimedia messaging. And many have been angered when half-way through composing a special text message when the phone rings, the mobile switches into 'call' mode and their efforts are lost.

1.4.1 REASONS FOR POOR DESIGN

Why do developers repeatedly inflict poor experiences on their users? Three key reasons are:

- perceived financial cost of better design;
- an overwhelming emphasis on technology over purpose; and
- a lack of user-based 'debugging'.

Financial Short-Termism

A product's price is a highly visible factor used by customers to help them choose between one option and another. Very much less visible, at first glance, is the quality of the interaction design. In store, a device that will provide many happy years of pleasant, effective use could look much like another which will frustrate, confuse and annoy. As quality interaction increases production costs, a manufacturer might feel less motivated to invest in careful design: what's the point if you can sell lots of devices anyway, through slick marketing and competitive pricing? As we will see later, this is a rather short-sighted view.

Techno-Fixation

Technological wizardry is exciting to developers and users. As we have seen already, there will be lots of novel, interesting – and some even effective – ways for users to interact with their mobile devices. For the developer, it is easy to be tempted to always try to add the most impressive features.

The user, in turn, may feel like a second-class citizen if their device does not offer the latest, fastest, fully featured innovations.

Walk into any consumer electronics store and you'll find 'demonstration' modes on many gadgets – one press turns the passive device into a sophisticated seducer, lights flickering, displays animated as you're given a tour of the seemingly unlimited potential the device has to change your world. It's very hard not to get caught up in the drama of these shows, but when you get home, after the purchase, the user experience might be a lot less palatable (Thimbleby, 1996a).

Some developers might also argue they have enough to cope with, just to get the complex technology to work. Sure, trying to get a device to switch robustly between the local WiFi connection in a coffee bar to a cellular network channel, all without the user noticing, *is* technically very challenging and the achievement laudable. But these issues should not mean that users' complex, diverse needs are overlooked. What's the point of technical mastery if the user's experience is dull and desperate? It's like a master chef baking the finest Belgian chocolate cake, full of clever layers of flavor, only to expect diners to consume it through a straw.

Overlooking the real bugs

Designers can also easily gain a false sense of satisfaction with the products they develop. If you spend many months working on a system, spotting its technical failings – bugs that cause the device to malfunction or stop working altogether – is relatively easy, but gaining a sense for the interaction glitches is much harder to do.

Part of the problem is to do with the designer psyche. When you use something you've designed yourself, you will approach the interaction with a very different perspective from your target user. You are the device's creator with a detailed insider's knowledge of the system's design. What seems almost mystically bizarre to the user will be straightforward and systematic to you. Furthermore, having exerted a great deal of intellectual effort and time in developing a design, you will also find it hard to criticize the outcomes. In fact, spotting flaws at a late stage will cause unpleasant emotional tension, something psychologists term 'cognitive dissonance'; to overcome this feeling, you're likely to rationalize away the problems, saying things like "it's not that big a problem" or "it's the user's fault, they need to read the manual".

User-bug blindness also comes from external sources. Marketer-borne feedback might also encourage design over self-confidence. Marketing needs to sell a company's products and the first group to buy into a new technology, the so-called early adopters, might well share your positive views on the product's design or be more tolerant or more able to cope with its failings (Norman, 1999, pp. 34–46).

The answer, then, is to expose ordinary users to early designs to which you're less committed, and see what they really think. Failing to do this will mean that fatal interaction flaws will be found too late; then the shock in glimpsing the difference between your perception and that of others can be quite profound, like listening to a tape-recording of your speech and wondering, "Do I really sound like this?".

1.4.2 IMPACTS OF POOR DESIGN

But why should you care whether or not your designs are well received? What should motivate you to invest additional resources into producing better interactions? Three things to consider are the emotional, economic and ethical impacts of your work.

Emotional Impact

Coming to the realization that your designs are poor when it is too late is an emotion worth avoiding. The thought of your design causing millions of despairing sighs is a great motivator to improve the approach and outcomes of your work. Most designers design in order to produce something of value that others – not just other designers – will enjoy and gain satisfaction from. The dream of hundreds of thousands or even millions of people having a better day because of your designs is a highly appealing one.

As a designer, it is really important to understand that the choices you make will have a significant impact on your users' emotions, stress levels and mental energy. Sadly, most people's experience is that technology affects them negatively more than it does positively. The media have made great play of 'computer rage', with a well-known piece of TV news footage showing an employee aggressively destroying his workstation, symbolic of the bad emotions technology is seen as fostering. To bring a degree of scientific objectivity to the apparently widespread poor experiences, a group of researchers set out to assess the frustration levels computer technology brings into people's lives (Ceaparu *et al.*, 2004). The results are disturbing, particularly for mobile developers.

People rated themselves as often being very frustrated with their computers. Situations causing most frustration were error messages, non-robust data connections, system freezes, excessively long downloads, and missing or hard-to-find system features. With mobiles, all of these factors can be exacerbated and we might expect even higher levels of frustration. For example, small displays could lead a designer to produce shorter, even more cryptic error messages, and feature lists that are difficult to navigate, and connection reliability and data transfer speeds can also be lower.

The research also found that you are more likely to have a higher immediate level of frustration if some technology problem occurs during an important task. Interruptions when you are involved in something less critical cause lower levels of emotion. Mobile users will often be relying on their devices to help them just-in-time, under pressure – "I need those sales figures, right now". So again, raised negative emotional responses seem probable.

While the study asked users to subjectively assess their feelings, frustration does have very real physiological impacts: poor design strains the body. Richard Hazlett of the Psychiatric Department at Johns Hopkins medical school, illustrates this, demonstrating the link between facial muscle activity and frustration levels (Hazlett, 2003). He showed that badly designed interfaces – such as websites that are difficult to use – generated distinct patterns of electrical activity, reflecting the degree of muscle tension.

Some researchers are interested in measuring such physiological responses in order to produce systems that can relate to people on an emotional basis – indeed, there's a whole research area known as 'affective computing' (Picard, 1997). Imagine, then, a handheld that can monitor your stress levels from the sweatiness of your hand as you grip it, and adapt the way it interacts with you. While such efforts are interesting, for most of us involved in design the aim should be to reduce the level of frustration and stress our users suffer in the first place.

Economic Impact

People waste one-third to one-half of the time they spend in front of the computer (Ceaparu *et al.*, 2004). Some of this unproductive time is spent trying to fix problems; the rest is time taken up in repeating work that was lost because of the problem, such as restoring a mistakenly deleted file. Coping with fixing the problems wastes most effort: users spend between a quarter and a third of their computer time just trying to get back to a productive state after interruption.

For many years now, usability evangelists have used economic arguments to urge companies to take interaction design issues seriously, some even suggesting that global productivity is being affected through difficult-to-use systems (Landauer, 1996). Jacob Nielsen, one of the most successful and vocal of the ease-of-use gurus, puts it this way: "...usable design saves money and saves jobs" (Nielsen, 2003).

Lots of the marketing associated with mobiles speaks loudly of the economic gains in having the ability to communicate and access information whenever and wherever needed. Given such claims, and the lack of spare time mobile users tend to have, they will be especially displeased if they suffer the degree of wasted time common in other computer systems.

There is an additional economic incentive for mobile developers to produce devices and services that users take up and use extensively. Globally, and particularly in Europe, network operators have spent many billions of dollars on acquiring licenses to operate advanced services. In addition to these vast sums, a great deal of expenditure has gone into rolling out the infrastructure needed to provide coverage for all the hoped-for sophisticated mobile interactions. Shareholders will want these investments to pay off as soon as possible, but every device and service that is difficult to configure, hard to operate or frustrating to use will further lengthen the already long period before their patience is rewarded.

Ethical Impacts

Stressed users, lower productivity and reduced revenues are one thing; lost lives, a damaged environment and unhealthy consumer attitudes are rather more serious.

Mobiles in safety-critical situations

'Killer App' is an IT industry cliché, but the drive to find an essential application all users need is strong one, more so for mobiles. Although it may be hard to discover that 'killer' to supplement the surprise success of text messaging, unwittingly many current devices and services are potential killers themselves.

In the UK there are over 40 million mobile phone users. If each of these wastes 60 seconds a day trying to operate their device, every day a lifetime of human effort dies, wasted. While such a statistic might be a fun way to motivate your colleagues to take interaction design seriously, there are application areas where real deaths might be caused through impoverished interactions. For certain interaction design products, reducing user fatalities would seem, therefore, to be the 'killer app' – a key justification for the methods we discuss in this book. Simply put, basic design improvements might save lives.

First, take transport. There have been several cases of aircraft crashes or near-catastrophes arising from difficult-to-use systems, poor error messages and the like. Even pilots, who are highly trained individuals and experts at coping with complexity, have at times struggled with the technology. Mass-produced mobile technology is promising to bring complexity down to earth, with feature-laden devices available to every car driver:

> ... *one of the processors embedded in your car could signal your PDA that it's time for an oil change. The request for an appointment is simultaneously received by your cell phone, which interacts transparently with the PDA to schedule both the appointment and the oil change.* (Di Pietro and Mancini, 2003)

A car radio analysis showed how a range of interaction design problems might lead to a driver being seriously distracted (Marsden *et al.*, 1999). Examples include:

- Routine tasks when operating the radio taking a long time, requiring the driver's full attention
- Drivers having to move their head closer to the device, reducing their road vision, to read a display

- 'Time-outs' that undo a sequence of user settings if the driver fails to complete the process in time, encouraging them to persist in interacting with the radio when they should return their full attention to the driving conditions.

Radios are relatively simple compared to the navigation and route guidance systems, traffic congestion monitors and other services becoming available to drivers. Poor interaction designs will distract drivers from what they should be doing – driving – and serious accidents will happen.

Medicine is another domain where safety is key and poorly designed systems have the potential to cause tragic outcomes. Hospitals are full of high technology, employed to help practitioners to diagnose, treat and monitor patients' conditions. As these systems are introduced, there's a growing awareness of errors that might be caused by poor interaction design. Chris Johnson, who has studied many air traffic incidents, sees similar problems for medicine. Just as 'fly-by-wire' aircraft require pilots to become computer operators, clinicians' dependence on complex medical systems is increasing. One case he relates clearly illustrates how failings in interface design could seriously affect patients. A drug infusion device, used to deliver medication in a controlled way, displayed drug unit information in an inconsistent way, switching from micrograms (MCG) to milligrams (MG):

When using the dose calculator function for a nitroglycerin drip, the program changes from MCG on one screen to MG on the next screen. A provider trying to start an IV infusion quickly may not notice the change and continue on programming the infusion. At the end the decimal point is not easy to read and the dosing error may not be noticed. The error described allows for only 10% of the desired dose to be delivered. (Johnson, 2003)

Handhelds and other mobiles are joining the ensemble of devices found in clinics. Doctors and nurses refer to their PalmPilots to look up drug information or to jot down some observations for later use. There are also plans to extend the use of wireless devices within many hospitals.

Patients themselves are also getting their hands on healthcare mobiles. Some of these monitor vital signs. Patients might wear a number of sensors – to track the heart rate, pulse and breathing rate – with the readings sent to a walkman-sized mobile device worn on the belt (McGarry *et al.*, 2000); Exercise 1.4 illustrates an interface design for this sort of application.

Going on the previous evidence of errors caused through badly designed interfaces, more and more medical mobiles, used by both trained professionals and ordinary people, can only mean there is plenty of room for future serious interaction failings.

EXERCISE 1.4 INTERFACE DESIGN FOR A MOBILE VITAL SIGNS MONITOR

Figure 1.6 shows one of the proposed interface designs for a wireless vital signs monitor. The top indicators show the battery level and whether one or more of the patient's vital signs are approaching a problematic level. The lower section gives readouts of the patient's heart rate, with the panel displaying 'HEART' also capable of displaying scrolling pager-like messages. The middle portion of the interface gives the current ➤

time. Function display options allow the user to view other vital signs information such as breathing rate.

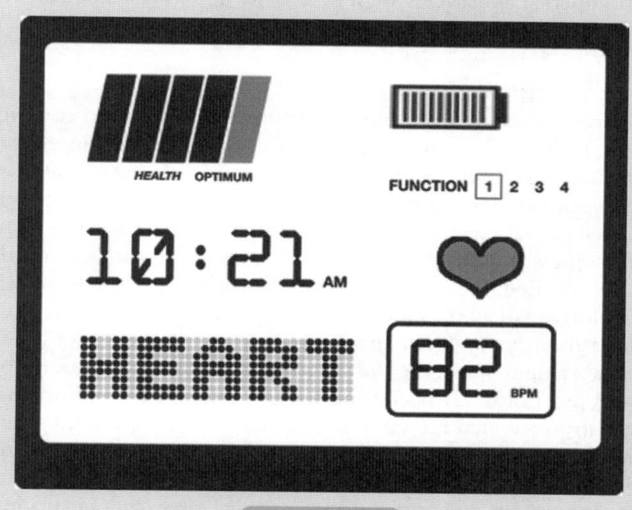

FIGURE 1.6

Vital signs wearable monitor prototype (adapted from McGarry *et al.*, 2000)

Think about possible problems that might arise through this interaction design. Sketch out alternatives. Improvements could include:

- Replacing function numbers with icons (heart, lung shape, etc.)
- Replacing scroll buttons with direct access – one button for each function
- Making bar chart easier to interpret by, e.g., renaming '*HEALTH* OPTIMUM' legend and redesigning layout
- Placing battery indicator in alternative location – closeness to health bar chart could lead to confusion. ■

Mobiles and environmental problems

In the words of Jonathan Ive, vice-president of industrial design at Apple and designer of iMac and iPod:

Maybe it's too pragmatic, too modest but I guess we can design products that people will actually want to keep, even when they are technologically obsolete. (Ive, 2004)

In the United Kingdom, millions of tonnes of electronic equipment are thrown away every year (Thimbleby and Jones, 2002). The mobile mass market heightens this serious threat to the environment. The disposable phones, mentioned earlier, are obvious potential landfill contributors, but even expensive devices, ones you might expect purchasers to hold on to for some time, are being discarded and dumped at a relatively high rate. Why does this happen and how can interaction designers make a difference?

Developing unhealthy attitudes

Studies of how technologies mature, from innovative novelty through to commodity, provide some answers. When a new technology comes along, it might not be advanced or robust enough to satisfy user needs. During this development phase, you might expect people to buy a device – say an early handheld without wireless connectivity – and to upgrade when another emerges that is better able to meet their needs, such as connecting to remote information sources. However, at some point, the technology should mature so that users' technological needs for performance, reliability and so on are satisfied. At this point, Don Norman argues, interaction designers become particularly valuable (Norman, 1999). When anyone can supply the required technology, one way to differentiate products in order to compete is by providing excellent user experiences.

Now, while undeniably there are some unmet technological needs with mobiles, fueling current upgrade behaviors, the technology is becoming mature enough to support many user goals. The mobile industry needs strong-willed interaction designers able to spot and articulate these cases, as well as companies that are courageous enough to invest in products that provide effective, fulfilling user experiences – products that users have no reason to discard too quickly.

Even if the technology exists to satisfy a user's needs, they can be made to feel dissatisfied, perceiving there to be a better solution they should buy into, and persuading them to dispose of their current device. One way this happens is through what's called 'feature creep' – the adding of extra, not necessarily widely used, facilities in successive product upgrades.

Here's the scenario. An interaction designer studies users, identifies a clear need, and sees that the technology exists to supply this amply. The designer then produces a design for a system that simply supports the user as they carry out their goals. Time passes, and the company decides to release another version of this device with 10 extra features. Despite the fact that none of these might be used, or even useful, to most of its customers, users will be tempted to upgrade – after all, who wants to feel left behind? Even if they don't want to purchase the new version, they may be forced to so that their device remains compatible with those of colleagues and friends who have upgraded: if all your friends are sending multimedia messages but your phone cannot receive them, what will you do? This upgrade cycle – and the associated refuse – can continue indefinitely. Another battle you may have to face as an interaction designer, then, is persuading engineering and marketing colleagues to resist the apparently easy money to be made through feature expansion.

Persuading companies to change their strategy might sound like an impossibly ambitious task for any one interaction designer. Individual designers can, though, easily begin to make a difference in smaller ways. A poor interface to a technology that is adequate in all other senses – fast enough, robust enough, etc. – will breed dissatisfaction in the user who might feel they have to buy an alternative device that appears easier to use. Designers who write meaningless error messages, fail to give feedback to let a user know the results of their actions, or make it difficult to find important features, might be motivated to better practices if they remembered that each poor design choice could lead to another green field being turned into a rubbish site.

BOX 1.7 FLOWERS FROM DEAD MOBILES

Working with Motorola, researchers at Warwick University in the UK have developed mobile phone covers which, when planted, naturally degrade and grow into a flower. Work was motivated by the environmental impact of increasing mountains of disposed mobile phones. See Figure 1.7 and Color Plate 3.

FIGURE 1.7
Graceful degradation

1.5 OUTLINE OF THE REST OF THIS BOOK

We've already seen what mobiles *could* be; the rest of the book is about what they *should* be and how to go about attaining these ideals.

In the next two chapters of this introductory part, we'll consider what design qualities people will value in mobiles they buy, and the approaches you could use to ensure these are crafted into your products.

After this scene setting, we go into the detail of how to design mobile interactions. Part II – *Developing effective mobile applications* – explores the techniques you can use to gain insights into user needs as well as examining the process of turning these into reality, and seeing how the prototypes fare, through evaluation.

Throughout the book, we'll be presenting useful pointers, provocations and guidelines to help you design. These are drawn from the work of many others as well as ourselves. The third part – *Design gallery* – is dedicated to raising the issues and presenting advice on important elements in many mobile interactive systems: things like navigation, information presentation, sophisticated visualizations and collaboration.

SUMMARY

It's easy to have a limited vision of the mobile future – mobiles as just supercharged phones, carried in the pocket. But mobiles have the potential to be key building blocks in the new, digitally augmented world. If designers and developers simply view them as consumer gadgets, sophisticated trinkets, a great opportunity will have been lost. The technology is personal and pervasive, and poor interaction design will have serious impacts – for users and the industry. Careful, inspired innovations can change the world, bringing pleasure, helping businesses and even saving lives.

WORKSHOP QUESTIONS

- The MediaCup shown in Color Plate 1 has a processor and memory embedded in its base. It can communicate with other devices (including other cups) placed nearby. What uses might such a device have?
- Human–computer interaction educators tend to stress the importance of maintaining 'implementation-free' thinking and prototyping for as long as possible in the design process. To what extent do you think this is possible or desirable in the mobile context?
- Predictive text systems use dictionaries to find the best single word matches for a string of text. How could you potentially improve the quality of the word suggestions a system makes and what data structures would you need to furnish your design?

DESIGNER TIPS

- *Develop an 'appliance attitude' to the applications and devices you are working with. Identify a small, coherent set of functions users really want and deliver them in a simple, direct way. If you want to – or have to – provide many other features, hide them away.*

- *Start to think now how you might employ the more advanced input–output technologies being developed – how your current designs might change if your users could squeeze or tilt, for example. But also begin to develop resistance to using every innovation in all your applications.*
- *Keep track of the work being done on universal usability – research into how disabled users might be better served by technology. These people have 'impoverished' interfaces and the work might inform your challenged devices.*
- *If you've been working in HCI for some years on non-mobile projects, relax as you move to this new area. Mobiles require more than utility/task-focused thinking; try to consider enjoyment, pleasure and fun in your designs.*

CHAPTER 2
PRODUCTS FOR PEOPLE

OVERVIEW

2.1. Introduction
2.2. Useful
2.3. Usable
2.4. User experience
2.5. Technology acceptance

KEY POINTS

- Successful mobile products are ones that are useful and usable, and provide a coherent, comprehensive user experience.
- If a mobile does not provide highly valued functionality, it will not be used, no matter how well designed the interface is.
- A mobile's usability is affected by two factors: its intrinsic ease of use – the way it presents its functionality, the feedback given to users and more; and how well it fits in with other resources at the user's disposal.
- A user's perception of a mobile's usability is affected by far more than just the device's quality. The customer support provided, its interaction with network services and even the explanation of pricing plans matter too.
- Research from business schools and information science departments on technology acceptance has provided useful tools to assess the reasons for success and failure of mobile products.

2.1 INTRODUCTION

How do you see the lives of your users? Some technologists seem to have a dangerously distorting image in their minds as they develop products: the user as patient, requiring a sort of healing by technology.

With this world view, users are seen as being in dire need of the latest gadgets and services in order to help them untangle work or social complexities. They are inefficient in carrying out their activities, or worse still, incompetent to complete their tasks without the support digital products can provide. Their lives are empty and meaningless, having to be filled by new electronic experiences; and they have to be distracted from the unexciting realities of everyday living. This negative attitude perhaps fueled the Millennium Bug panic of the last years of the 1990s. How would the world cope if computer systems stopped working?

Instead of seeing people as hapless, helpless and hopeless, a far more constructive thing to do is to focus on their abilities to be creative, to self-determine and to cope – to understand that if all the lights had gone out on 1 January 2000, communities would have adapted, survived and probably held parties.

Ben Shneiderman, in his book *Leonardo's Laptop (Human Needs and the New Computing Technologies)*, presents a far healthier attitude to users and their lives, setting out a manifesto for applying technologies in ways that build on and enhance people's abilities; as he puts it:

The old computing was about what computers could do; the new computing is about what users can do. (Shneiderman, 2002, p. 2)

Most people lead full, busy, interesting and interested lives. They will not take up a technology unless there is a very good reason to do so. A new mobile product will click with people if it allows them to achieve something significant while fitting in with the other things that fill their lives. On top of these two critical success factors, products should be pleasing, charming, delightful and enjoyable, rather than annoying, bland, frustrating and dull.

The things we design, then, need to be useful and usable, and provide an overall enlightening user experience.

BOX 2.1 'USERS'?

Throughout this book – and any book about interactive systems development – you'll often come across the word 'user'. Although it's a convenient, accepted shorthand way of describing the people who make use of computer-based systems, it may not help foster good attitudes towards them, as Aaron Marcus, a usability consultant, notes (Marcus, 2003).

First, it could create a gulf – 'them and us' – between the designer and the person who will use the products: *we* designers design and develop the product, then after all the effort is complete, *they* use it. Interaction design involves people ➤

participating throughout the design process. Secondly, the term has negative connotations of dependence: it conjures up an image of people who need a technological fix to survive.

Marcus reviews the alternatives to 'user', including: *participant, addict* (some marketers of interactive products really do want you to become hooked), *consumer, guest* or *visitor* (particularly suitable for e-commerce sites), *players* (for gaming applications) and *readers* (for content-based services).

As a designer, you will find it helpful not thinking about an abstract, distanced 'user'. Alternative general terms, like those Marcus suggests, can help, but better still you should keep in mind some specific, real characters, visualizing the surroundings they live in and the things they do. In Chapter 4, we will look at the useful tools of personas and scenarios that can help you do this. ■

2.2 USEFUL

2.2.1 FUNCTION BEFORE FORM

As mobile interaction researchers and designers, a real motivation should be discovering things that people really want to do – things they can't do without. Right from the start of any design project, seek to produce services that people will want to use over and over again, happy to spend their time and money on.

In the words of Scott Jenson, Head of Jenson Design and former director of product design at Symbian, "People would walk over glass to send a text message" (Scott Jenson, personal communication). Text messaging, even with the sorts of improvements discussed earlier such as predictive text and more effective keypads, seems a difficult activity, yet people do it and enjoy it. It's a good example to demonstrate that a seemingly poor user interface will not terminally undermine a much-wanted service. Conversely, an excellent interface will not lead people to use a service if its value to them is low.

This primacy of function over form is amusingly discussed by Nigel Derrett in his analysis of a musical mobile, the bassoon (Derrett, 2004). This wind instrument is very difficult to learn: it can take hundreds of hours to become even competent; thousands to become a professional. It has a complex, not at all 'user-friendly' interface: the five finger holes, 24 keys and a 'whisper key lock' make it difficult to handle, requiring fiddly finger placements and dexterous gymnastics to produce the right notes. Derrett's experiences with the instrument led him to propose a law of interface design, named after the company that was responsible for the bassoon's key and hole system:

Heckel's Law: The quality of the user interface of an appliance is relatively unimportant in determining its adoption by users if the perceived value of the appliance is high.

Heckel's Inverse Law: The importance of the user interface design in the adoption of an appliance is inversely proportional to the perceived value of the appliance. (Derrett, 2004)

To stress his point, he argues that if the only thing stopping an interactive system being successful appears to be its interface design, it's probably not a device really worth having.

Now one take on 'Heckel's laws' is that interaction design is something that adds little value to the product's overall worth. Indeed, for many years there were difficulties in persuading companies to seriously invest in the sorts of user-centered design methods discussed in this book. Instead, products were made 'user-friendly' right at the end of the development cycle. The process was like sprinkling chocolate on top of a cappuccino, quick and far less important than activities involved in creating what lies beneath.

Look again, though. The laws talk about *interface*, but interface is not *interaction*, and interface design is not interaction design. While interface design is focused on the detailed look-and-feel of a product, interaction design is a far more wide-reaching endeavor: it is about understanding the goals people want to achieve with the technology. So a key purpose of the process is to identify the role – the functions – mobiles will have.

2.2.2 EVOLVING USES

In the early days of mobile devices, the roles they would play in people's lives seemed obvious. The mobile world was about powerfully equipping traveling workers, the so-called 'road-warriors', to become clinically efficient and effective, making quicker, bigger deals and staying leaps ahead of competitors.

In a Nokia study of i-mode, the services most highly regard by users – email and mobile data communication – were indeed business-oriented (Lauridsen and Prasad, 2002). Corporate users of these services, however, are not just the stereotypical, testosterone-driven, sales-force members of old; all sorts of people are now using mobiles to take their work out of the office.

An interesting nascent trend, then, sees information workers eschewing desktop-type PCs in preference to laptops: they use their portable computer in the office, while they are commuting, and then back at home. Mobile network operators are capitalizing on these user leanings by marketing high-bandwidth wireless slot-in cards.

At the start of the first mobile revolution, the talk was all of services on a mobile phone or small handset; now the operators are realizing that one of major ways they can generate revenue is by simply being effective mobile Internet service providers.

As the business mobile market broadens with the user base becoming more diverse, the industry will have to further accommodate the change in its customers and design around their needs; whereas the 'road-warriors' might be pleased to be early adopters of techno-centered gadgets and services, such designs will not be universally attractive.

The Nokia survey also showed the significance of non-business uses of mobiles. Popular leisure i-mode services included ringtone downloads, entertainment services, games and animations. These sorts of offerings have grown in popularity in Europe over recent years.

For interaction designers, the exciting but problematic nature of mobiles is that they don't conform to the work-centered notion of computing. While business-type goals and tasks are relatively easy to analyze and represent, the mobile reaches out into many other areas of people's lives and allows a blurring of the boundaries between work and leisure.

The rise of the sorts of lifestyle applications seen in i-mode also reminds us that not all useful things are fast, efficient and result driven. Life is more than speedy decisions and quick transactions. People often involve themselves in activities over long periods of time, being creative and reflective.

'Blogs' are important evidence of these sorts of needs: since 1999, 'blogging' – the writing of an online public diary – has become highly popular. Mobile developers, keen to tap into the trend, created mobile blogging software to allow people to post entries from their mobile phones.

When you develop mobile services, don't just think about fast-paced, always-on, always-connected interaction. How could you help users slow down with more relaxed styles? Here's an example by a group that's been developing 'slow technology' (Hallnäs and Redström, 2001). Most doorbells simply play the same, short jingle each time they are pressed. In the slow-technology doorbell, every time you press the button you hear only a short piece of the full tune. Only over time, after several visits, can the whole melody be appreciated.

How could you apply this design in the mobile context? Well, perhaps each time someone calls your mobile, you might get to hear a short piece of a caller-selected ringtone; over time you get to piece together the bigger melody, the process acting as an extra, little bit of shared experience that builds your relationship.

EXERCISE 2.1 CALLER TUNES AND PERSONALIZATION

Some network providers allow a subscriber to specify an audio track – say a piece of music – to be played when a caller rings them, replacing the standard 'connecting' tones. What is the rationale behind this, what problems may occur, and how could things be improved?

Comments: the service aims to appeal to the desire by many owners to personalize their technology. Other forms of customization, such as downloading of screen savers or ringtones, have been very popular. However, in these cases, the user's choices are exposed in a limited way, to themselves and people in close physical proximity. These constraints explain the attraction of personalization – the user has some control over who is given insight into their personality and can gage other people's reactions directly. With basic caller tunes, the user cannot be sure whether it is appropriate or desirable for a caller to hear their choice. An improvement would involve playing a tune only to a caller explicitly placed on a list by the user. ■

2.3 USABLE

Perhaps you can relate to the experience of excitedly buying a new gadget or subscribing to a new mobile service only to lose interest or hope in it soon afterwards. Over the past decade, there have been many handheld devices that supported functions that looked useful – from helping to schedule appointments, to accessing emails remotely, to manipulating photo albums. However, after the first few months of proud use, again and again users have abandoned these devices, leaving them to linger in their desktop cradles, or to gather dust in a bag.

Poor usability comes in two forms. First, there's the question of whether the device or service is usable in itself. From this intrinsic, low-level, ease-of-use perspective, devices are often just plain difficult to operate. Take the task of jotting down a note: pen and paper have a satisfying, simple usability; meanwhile, on a handheld, the sluggish interaction – selecting the note application from a menu, choosing an input mode and the like – can clip the wings of any inspired thought.

Usability is also about whether the device works in harmony with the things around it. Poor usability can come when there's a lack of thought into how the mobile might integrate with a user's other resources and the way they wish to carry out their work and broader lives.

2.3.1 USABLE IN ITSELF

In *The Psychology of Everyday Things*, Don Norman gives classic and enduring advice on how to design products that make sense to their users. People have to be able to work out how to easily turn their goal – such as silencing their device during a meeting – into system actions by, say, pressing a mute button. Besides this, in all the interactions they have with the device, they need to be able to see what their actions have achieved – how the system has changed.

To help designers, Norman sets down four principles of good practice that promote these ease-of-use essentials (Norman, 1988):

- Ensure a high degree of **visibility** – allow the user to work out the current state of the system and the range of actions possible.
- Provide **feedback** – given continuous, clear information about the results of actions.
- Present a **good conceptual model** – allow the user to build up a true picture of the way the system holds together, the relationships between its different parts and how to move from one state to the next.
- Offer **good mappings** – aim for clear, natural relationships between actions the user performs and the results they achieve.

BOX 2.2 GOLDEN RULES OF DESIGN

As well as Don Norman, many other people have proposed guidelines for effective usability. One set which is widely cited is Ben Shneiderman's *Eight Golden Rules of Interface Design* (Shneiderman, 1998).

Strive for consistency	Make sure the application is internally consistent, for example by using the same terms for the same things. Be consistent with other applications users might come across – don't be tempted to do things differently unless there is a good reason. Be consistent with users' wider life knowledge and experience. ➤

Enable frequent users to use shortcuts	Phone designers have long used numeric shortcuts to cut down on menu navigation. Another example is the mapping between a mobile phone keypad and the visual icon grid seen on some smart phones – on holding down a key, the function that is spatially related to the key is activated. Allow users to define 'favorites' or most-used features; consider tracking usage and providing access to most-used functions directly (beware of trying to be too clever – automatically adapted menus, etc., have been shown to be problematic).
Offer informative feedback	Provide feedback as quickly as possible. Indicate any delay to the user with a realistic presentation of progress. Avoid jargon – relate error and other messages to the user's task.
Design dialogs to yield closure	Give users a sense of beginning, middle and end in their interactions. Text messaging task flow in many devices is a good example of a well-structured, simple dialog.
Strive to prevent errors, and help users to recover quickly from them	With limited controls closely placed (both physical buttons and on screen), watch for mistaken input. On screen, avoid making controls too small or placing them too closely together. Give helpful feedback on invalid input, highlighting it and requiring that only the erroneous input is fixed.
Allow 'undo'	Make it easy for the user to reverse mistaken input or actions.
Make users feel they are in control of a responsive system	With the move to provide more sophisticated media types and interactions on mobiles (photos, video, music, etc.), even with the increased processing/memory power available there is the danger of sluggish, clunky systems – consider the delays currently seen in many phone photo applications while images are stored and retrieved. Careful, resource-efficient approaches are needed.
Reduce short-term memory load	Avoid burdening the user with complicated numbers, codes, sequences, etc., as far as possible. ■

EXERCISE 2.2 APPROPRIATE FEEDBACK?

On a popular mobile phone, when the battery level is low, the device alerts the user by playing a polyphonic jingle and by displaying a colorful, full-screen warning message. This activity further reduces the power available; furthermore, the owner may not even benefit from this performance if their phone is out of earshot. How could the user be better warned of the impending battery failure while preserving the remaining power as long as possible?

Comments: the warning should be given in a less power-hungry way and at a time when the user will actually notice it. For example, when they go to make a call and the power is low, before connecting, the device could play a short spoken message, ''Battery level is low'', while the user is holding the device to their ear. ■

Living up to these ideals when designing mobiles can be a challenge. How do you make a system's functions visible and give good feedback when the device has such a small display and when users can't always give it their full attention?

Or, what about communicating the conceptual model effectively? Users see new services through the lens of their previous experiences with other systems. As the developers of the early pocket versions of Windows found, the slightest interface hint of the desktop PC experience could usher in possibly unhelpful user expectations.

BOX 2.3 "IT DOESN'T LOOK LIKE A CAMERA"

Getting the affordances right

The perceived affordances of an object – be it a telephone handset or a web form – are the ways the user believes they can interact with it. If you design a mobile with a turnable, flippable screen and the user can't see how to turn or flip it, the affordances are being badly communicated.

Many single-purpose mobile devices, like a simple cellphone, digital camera or music player, have well-designed affordances. As you pick up a camera, you quickly discover which way to hold it to your face and where to press to capture the image. When listening to music on the move, your fingers can feel their way to the controls that increase the volume or pause the music without your having to look at the device.

Many mobiles are now multi-purpose: they are a camera, a telephone and a music player all in one. A team from the Ericsson Usability Lab studied whether such ➤

a multi-function device can give the sorts of clear affordances seen in simpler appliances (Goldstein *et al.*, 2003). They asked a group of users to carry out a range of tasks on a prototype with similar characteristics to many early sophisticated phone–PDA combinations: a cover that could be flipped open to reveal a stylus-operated, touch-sensitive screen, with a camera lens on the phone back. Trial activities included picture taking, placing of phone calls and music playing.

FIGURE 2.1

It's a camera; now it's a PDA; now it's a phone – communicating affordances through careful design ➤

While users completed their assignments quite effectively, there were problems in terms of efficiency and satisfaction. In the photo tasks, although the phone had a 'shutter' button on the back, instead of using it, users tended to opt for navigating through the camera options using the stylus and on-screen menus to access the image capture tool. Those who did find the button tried to press it downwards and not inwards, as the designer expected.

What users were doing was transferring their understanding from previous experiences to the new device. To them, the design suggested a computer application and this led them to interact with the menu software rather than just pressing a button, and since on many cameras the shutter button is mounted on the top of the device and operated by pressing downwards, they tried to use the phone's shutter button in the same way. On top of this, the design promoted one-handed operation which, while great for messaging and phone calling on the move, led to poor, shaky images.

The study points to the need for designers to look at earlier mobiles – cameras, music devices, watches, etc. – and see these as useful reference or source models of how form and function can be communicated. Some developers are showing a strong understanding of the advantages of effective affordance presentation. Take the Sony Ericsson S710a (Figure 2.1). It has been consciously styled to look like a camera that the user can hold in two hands. Turn it around, though, and it neatly presents its communication functions: "In horizontal mode, you have the perfect camera. Vertically held, it has the look, feel and satisfaction of a mini organizer, phone, gaming and messaging device." (Sony)

Some TV remote controls offer different views of the device's functionality: a simple set of features as a top layer, but by sliding down a cover, more extensive abilities are given to the user. Mobile phone manufacturers do this too by providing certain features when the phone is in one form and then if flipped or twisted open, other functions become available.

With developments in physical technologies, it is possible to imagine a much more dramatic reconfiguring of the form factor: physical buttons, sliders or touchpads might emerge from the skin of the device, providing the advantages of appliance-style thinking to a multi-purpose product. ■

Designing-in these desirable qualities is not, though, an impossible task. In fact, the principles can be a useful spur to generate innovative approaches to interaction:

- Visibility and feedback
  - Visibility and feedback are not dependent on visual display. Don't rely simply on the small display provided by most mobiles. Additional technologies such as haptic or auditory ones (discussed in Chapter 1) provide new possibilities.

  - Content should not be the only concern. It's tempting to focus on trying to use the entire small screen to display information content, but you must also ensure that device controls are made clear to the user (see Box 2.4).
  - Visibility is not about being all-seeing. You do not have to present everything to the user at once. The Peephole system described in Chapter 1, for example, cleverly allows the user to see different tools and information depending on the position of the device.

- Conceptual frameworks
  - Look at other things people use when mobile and see whether their attributes can help inform design. Box 2.3 discusses this further.
  - Employ terminology that makes sense to the user. For example, some mobile services still suffer from appearing to be designed for network engineers.

- Mappings
  - Make direct manipulation more direct. Graphical User Interfaces (GUIs) revolutionized conventional computers. Before them, interaction involved command-line entry: black screens with a blinking cursor, with users entering complex, almost mysterious, commands and receiving little feedback. In the GUI environment, not only can the user see what functions are available and how their actions have affected the system state, but they can directly manipulate the system: dragging and dropping, pointing and clicking (Hutchins *et al.*, 1985). Mobiles offer the opportunity for extending the notion of direct manipulation – the things a user wants to do and the way they do them can be more closely coupled. Prototypes like the bendable Gummi interface seen in Chapter 1 are harbingers of the possibilities.

BOX 2.4 VISIBILITY AND MAPPINGS

Semi-Transparent Widgets

How do you efficiently use a small screen space to communicate both the information users want and the controls – button and scrollbar widgets and so on – they need to operate the service? Tomonari Kamba and team tackled this problem and proposed the use of semi-transparent text and widgets for PDA devices (Kamba *et al.*, 1996).

In their prototype, text is displayed at 80% translucency, and control objects (like the buttons at the bottom of the screen in Figure 2.2) at 20%. The text is placed 'on top' of the widgets. So, in our example screenshot, if the user quickly taps the stylus on the link 'Greenpeace', the system responds by jumping to the relevant section of information, but if they hold down the stylus, the user 'passes through' the text and the widget below becomes active. ➤

FIGURE 2.2

Semi-transparent text and widgets as a way of overcoming small screen space while not compromising the principle of visibility (Kamba *et al.*, 1996)

Lift to zoom out: a good mapping?

In the Peephole system (see Chapter 1) the user lifts up the handheld toward them to see less detail (zoom out) and moves the device away from them to zoom in, getting more detail. In a map application, then, raising the handheld toward your face would show you more of an area overview; lowering would allow you to see more of the street-level information.

But is this mapping a good one? In the informal, small evaluation presented by the technique's inventor, it was preferred over the seemingly more obvious alternative – zooming in by raising the device, zooming out by lowering it (Yee, 2003).

At first glance, this seems strange. Think about reading a newspaper or magazine: if you raise it toward your face, you see more detail, not less; and if you want to scan the whole page, you might lower it to see an overview. But remember that in the Peephole system the conceptual model being employed is of the handheld as a window onto an information source rather than as an information carrier itself. Pulling this window toward you is pulling it away from the information source, hence you see less detail; lowering it is like placing it nearer to the source, giving a closer view. ➤

Good-Looking Design, Poor Mapping

Figure 2.3 shows a prototype screen design for a mobile phone-based games portal. Users push the device's joystick-type control to select from the Games, Chat, Comics or Puzzles channels. Which way would you push the joystick to open the Chat channel?

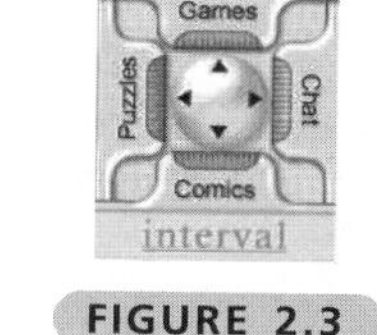

FIGURE 2.3
Mobile games portal

The obvious answer seems to be 'to the right', but the designers have a different view. The concept employed is one of drawers which you pull to open and push to close. So, to open Chat, you move the joystick to the left; to open Games you move it downward, and so on. Early evaluation led to a refined design that made the mapping between action and effect clearer. ■

2.3.2 USABLE IN LIFE

Even when a device is easy to operate and plainly communicates the effect of interacting with it, the test comes when it is deployed in the complex, messy world of real situations. When a user calls on its services in everyday use, it might still disappoint dramatically.

This sort of real use is markedly different from the rehearsals and play-acting that come when a device is examined in isolation, as a thing on its own. A system can appear impressive, reasonable and effective to a customer watching an in-store demonstration, or while working carefully through a manual soon after a purchase, or when playing with the device to discover features; but when it has to be used in the wild, as it were, in tandem with the world around it, the usability can break down quickly.

Whenever someone is trying to achieve something – to satisfy their goals – they will draw on a wide range of resources. Take the task of getting from A to B, finding your way to a new location. Sure, a mobile interactive service could be really helpful but you're also likely to glance at bits of paper (perhaps a reminder of the exact address), look at street signs, keep an eye out for landmarks, or ask people in the street.

As another example, consider the goal of finding a good restaurant in an unfamiliar city. You could use a mobile restaurant guide service, but in addition you might also check out the recommendation with good local knowledge – asking a kiosk holder, for example – and even decide to walk to the place itself and see what it is really like, taking in the route, enjoying the character of the area.

Or, what about all the technological scenarios for Radio Frequency Identification (RFID) chips? These are mobiles of a sort – postage stamp-sized chips that contain data to identify the object they are attached to and that can be interrogated wirelessly.

Supermarkets are very keen on this technology as a replacement for barcodes. One use they have in mind is automated checkout: as you walk up to the counter, a scanner probes the trolley, picking up the radio signals from all tags, and within seconds you're presented with your bill. The advantages seem obvious, but if this sort of scheme is to work from a human point of view, thought needs to go into providing some of the features of today's person-operated checkouts.

Watch people at the checkout – they make last-minute decisions as they place items on the conveyor belt, deciding for example to reject an earlier selected item; they keep an eye on the till display to verify the prices; and they sort their goods into bags, one for frozen goods, another for vegetables and so on. It's not impossible to couple benefits of the new technology with the advantages of the old, for example by providing shopping trolleys with separate compartments for the different types of foodstuff. The problem is that when a new system is conceived, there's the danger of focusing only on the disadvantages of the old approach, jettisoning all positives in the process.

As designers, we shouldn't resent the fact that our technological offerings aren't complete solutions that do everything for the user. Think back to the restaurant guide scenario: it could be tempting to enable a mobile to provide pictures, even a live video feed from the restaurant to give a sense of ambience, and complete details of the menu, all with the aim of giving the user such a perfect set of information that they don't need to visit the restaurant unless they really want to eat there. But to do so misses the point of people enjoying the exploration. Instead, as designers, we should look to how mobile services might work together with the other available resources out there already.

To get across this notion of people making use of interdependent resources and activities as they work to achieve their goals, Bonnie Nardi and Vicki O'Day coined the phrase 'information ecologies' (Nardi and O'Day, 1999). Their definition of these ecologies is really helpful in getting the role of mobiles into perspective:

We define an information ecology to be a system of people, practices, values and technologies in a particular local environment. In information ecologies, the spotlight is not on technology, but on human activities that are served by technologies. (Nardi and O'Day, 1999, p. 49)

If we don't understand these ecologies, we can introduce mobiles that inhibit or devour the other species – the other resources – with disastrous effect. Just as in a natural ecology, the sustainability and quality of our lives with mobiles depends on ensuring that all the resources we need work well together. Ecological thinking prompts designers to think up new roles for mobiles that naturally grow out of the current situation and, as the development progresses, to be sensitive to the 'fit' of the new with the old.

Much new technology is presented as an opportunity for new, exciting opportunities, filled with shining-faced people in perfect worlds. But we are *ecological*, not *technological* – we humans mess up the clean, clear visions produced by developers and tech-marketers. We have lives, not opportunities; old as well as new; depression as well as excitement. Designers need to understand and work with this reality, rather than ignoring or, worse still, trying to demolish it.

BOX 2.5 MOBILES AND THE MYTH OF THE PAPERLESS OFFICE

In the early 1970s the notion of the 'paperless office' began to emerge in visions produced by technology researchers and was hyped by journalists in search of a strong story. You only have to look around your own workplace to see that this has yet to become a reality.

Richard Harper and Abigail Sellen have examined actual paper use over the last few decades, and find that in contrast to the paper-free dreams, the reality is of ➤

workplaces filled with ever-increasing numbers of printed documents (Harper and Sellen, 2001). In 1987, 60 million tonnes of paper were used; that rose to 150 million ten years later. Technology, like email which has increased paper use by 40%, is fueling demand for output rather than dampening it. From a case study of the International Monetary Fund, Harper and Sellen found that only 14% of work involved just digital documents; in 86% of cases, paper documents, usually in conjunction with online resources, were consulted.

One type of paper species you'd probably find in anyone's information ecology are the sticky notes, called Post-its in many parts of the world. These small pieces of paper are used to convey chunks of information, greetings or reminders. They are what have been called 'micronotes' (Lin *et al.*, 2004). You'll see them stuck to folders, on doors, atop of piles of paper, providing a colorful messiness to offices and homes.

How could the sort of useful clutter provided by these notes work in a mobile technology context? One approach would be to allow people to attach digital messages to locations, ready for others to receive later. Imagine enjoying a restaurant and leaving a message 'outside' it, rating it highly; as your friend walks by, their mobile is triggered with a message and they can take a closer look.

The Stick-E Note system was an early demonstration of the idea, with one application scenario being a tour of Disney World (Pascoe, 1997). Visitors who carried a mobile enabled with location-aware software were able to pick up place-specific information as they wandered around the theme park. The GeoNotes service takes things further with the aim of allowing anyone to post messages (Espinoza *et al.*, 2001).

However, such virtual notes don't have the tangibility and visibility of paper: it's so easy to spot those brightly colored small squares of paper around your office, but what about hidden digital messages? How would you make people aware of these lurking location-based digital messages? There are lots of possibilities – for example, augmented reality techniques could be used. The user might wave their handheld around in front of them viewing an image of the location on the device's screen; overlaid on the real world image could be icons indicating messages from colleagues and friends.

An alternative future could see mobile technology used in a way that combines the advantages of the digital world with those of the physical one. Mark Weiser who, ironically, worked at Xerox Parc, where the paperless office myth seems to have originated, explored such a future through the 1990s, developing 'ubiquitous computing' devices (Weiser, 1993).

One such type of device was called Tabs (Color Plate 4), inch-sized mobile devices with small screens, that could wirelessly communicate. Think of hundreds of these littered around your office space, acting much in the way Post-it notes do. Piles of paper would be supplemented with piles of these Tabs, for storing ideas or passing onto someone else.

While the Tabs were, through technological necessity, rather cumbersome, ongoing developments such as e-paper could see Weiser's dream fulfilled in a more elegant way. ■

2.4 USER EXPERIENCE

In the nineteenth century, mobile writing desks were very popular – the laptops of an earlier era (see Figure 2.4). Opening one up provides a sloped flat surface for placing a sheet of paper, and receptacles to hold ink, nibs and pens. Lifting the writing area uncovers further storage for paper and other materials.

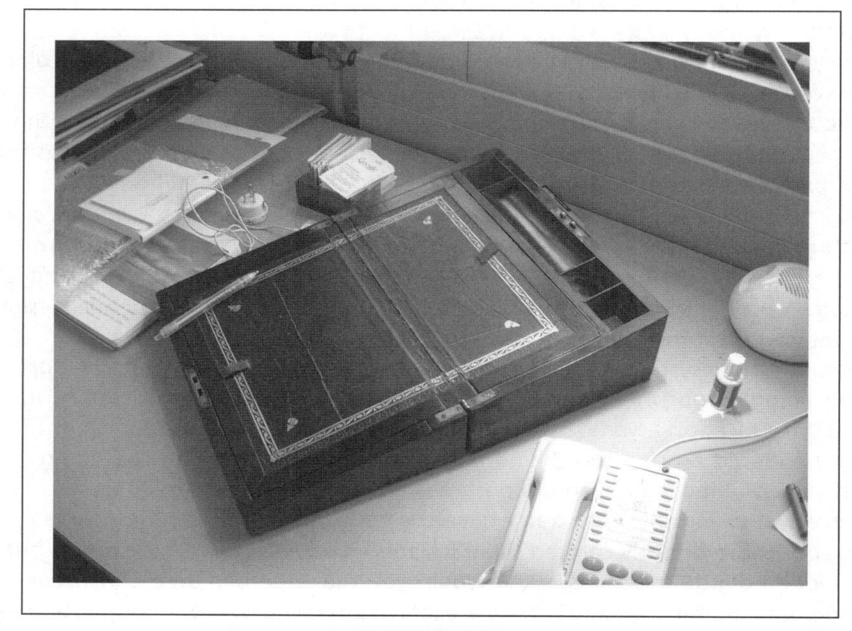

FIGURE 2.4
Portable writing desk – the nineteenth-century laptop

These devices were undoubtedly useful – people needed to send off correspondence while traveling. They were also a good fit with the wider context of use, being reasonably easily portable, storable and robust.

More than this, though, they provided a highly crafted, pleasant experience. For the British civil servants posted far from home, running the Empire in unfamiliar, sometimes difficult circumstances, these boxes could provide a little home comfort through the quality of craftsmanship. Using one, you get a firm feel from the writing surface, helping your words flow as you press down with the ink pen; the look of the smooth, small storage places and the way the lid lifts and the drawers slide are all delectable too. The graft of writing the draft of this chapter was made more palatable by using one.

How do modern mobiles compare? The ubiquitous computing, or Ubicomp, movement – the notion of computing technology being everywhere and anywhere – has fertilized much of the research and development in mobile computing. One of its goals is to make technology disappear, or as Mark Weiser, the founder of the field, eloquently expressed it: 'to make computing get out of the way' (Weiser, 1993).

With many mobiles, though, computing technology is still very much in the way, degrading the experience of using the tools. People's lives are already full and complex, and rather than delectable designs we see distasteful ones that add to the load, forcing users to grapple with getting their mobile to work.

Let's now consider two useful ways of improving the overall user experience. The first concerns the identity of a product – the message the design sends to the user; the way it makes them feel and act. Then there's the need to extend the influence of interaction design beyond the technology itself to the whole package presented to the user: the marketing, customer care, charging plans, etc. In both cases, the aim is to present the user with an experience that is solid, distinct, understandable, trustworthy and satisfying. Just like the writing desk.

2.4.1 STRONG IDENTITY

Making computing disappear, as Weiser encouraged, is about tidying away the technology so the user's own needs can remain in the foreground. It doesn't mean that products and services should not have clear, discernible, likeable identities. When people use a mobile, they should know they are using it and enjoy the experience, much like the nineteenth-century correspondents and their writing boxes.

Think about some highly successful interaction designs – the web services provided by sites like Amazon and eBay. When people shop at these places, they feel like they are *going* to a *place*, to spend some time and money, rather than experiencing 'interactions' ethereally in cyberspace.

However distinct such web experiences are, though, you can't actually touch or hold a website in the palm of your hand. Mobiles have the potential to communicate even more powerfully at this level to the user. They have the advantage over other interactive systems of being physical, graspable, touchable objects.

Now, in some development projects, the designer gets the opportunity to influence the form of the physical elements and how these relate to the software functions they encase. In the previous chapter, we saw some examples of how they might marry up physical device features and operations to provide effective experiences. A landmark model of the way the physical elements can be used to give a product a strong identity, and high usability, is seen in Apple's iPod (see Box 2.6).

BOX 2.6 INTERACTION AS BRAND

Apple has long had a reputation for producing technology with high design values and excellent usability. It was one of the first computer companies to see the value of making ease and pleasure of use a key part of its brand.

The iPod (Figure 2.5) is Apple's portable music player, a hard drive capable of storing many thousands of tracks. It's a much-desired device, by 2004 gaining almost iconic and cult status (witness the way owners would subtly acknowledge each other by spotting the white earbud headphones they sported). ➤

FIGURE 2.5

Mantelpiece collectable – the Apple iPod

Its casing is sleek and smooth but so is the interaction design. Indeed, the product's strong, attractive identity owes much to the simple yet powerful controls presented to the user: just six easy to understand buttons, operating all music selection and playing functions as well as its other features such as the alarm clock and calendar.

All interactive products should have controls with such powerful simplicity; for mobiles it is particularly important. Littering the small form-factors with multiple ➤

hard-to-operate controls not only impacts the quality of the esthetics but will distract the user from what they really want to do, causing them to pause and struggle to remember the sequence of operations. With the iPod, it's quite possible to carry on jogging, say, while increasing the music's volume; or to find quickly just the right piece of music to match the mood, before the moment passes.

The iPod's wheel and central action button contribute greatly to the design effectiveness. They work well for two reasons:

- **Excellent mappings.** The movement used to scroll – rotating the finger clockwise or anticlockwise – gives a good sensation as your skin glides over the white solid-state wheel. The gesture also has what psychologists would describe as a direct and clear mapping. That is, the action and its results are obviously linked: moving your finger clockwise means 'more', anticlockwise 'less'. A tap on the action button, like a click of a mouse, confirms a choice or makes a selection.
- **Consistency.** While the wheel is used to control a large number of features, the uncomplicated mapping always holds; there is a high degree of consistency in the way it works. If you're scrolling through a list of music, 'more' means scroll forward, 'less' backward; when you are listening to a track, 'more' increases the volume, 'less' decreases it; and so on.

Watch people listening to their car radio while driving. You might well see them tapping out the tune on the steering wheel as they wait in traffic. Or notice how fellow train travelers sometimes twitch their fingers to the beat of the music they are listening to on their portable players. People are moved by their music and the iPod's design allows them to operate it in an almost rhythmic, flowing fashion. The device's design is in tune with its purpose.

Apple also understands that usability depends on more than just how a mobile works in isolation. They realized that it had to work well with other interactive services. Both their PC-based music library software and their web-based music store, which sells single tracks, integrate effectively with the iPod.

Nokia is another mobile company that has invested heavily in ensuring their brand is known for its innovative interaction design. One of their trademark controls, seen on a highly successful range of phones, was the NaviKey – with this key, most of the phone's functions can be accessed using a single physical key whose meaning is displayed as a 'soft-key' in the display located above the button. The importance of the design to the marketing is described in this way by Nokia insiders:

With ... the Navi-Key UI, we raised the visibility of the UI even further by naming and trade marking the NaviKey. An easy-to-remember name given to a tangible UI element, let us transform the abstract concept of usability from something hard ➤

to understand into a concrete product attribute. The message to consumers was as follows: anybody can master this phone since it is operated with only one key. (Lindholm *et al.*, 2003)

In appraising its success, the designers pick out some of the same qualities embodied in the iPod:

- Reduction in the number of buttons
- Learnability of the concept
- The way the design can accommodate a wide range of interactions. ■

Even if you have no control over the physical form of the device, such as in all those cases where you are developing a new service for handsets produced by a third-party manufacturer, you can still think carefully about which of the available physical buttons, wheels, sliders and display elements you should use and in what ways they are best deployed.

Identity, however, comes from more than just the device's physical aspects. Just as the impression we form of a person is a complicated function of their physical attributes, how they present themselves and their character traits, the identity of a mobile will be influenced by everything the user interacts with. The controls selected, fonts employed, prompts displayed and features available are just some of the elements you need to consider.

And, in considering these things, you need to bring to bear your own, well-articulated design attitude. If you have what's been called a clear 'editorial voice' that you apply consistently, you will be more effective in developing products with character.

As an analogy think about the debate over personalized information and editor-produced content. When the web was young, there were many predictions that tailored content would become preferable to the sorts of edited content provided by traditional newspapers and magazine. A decade or so later, on the web, edited newspaper and magazine content still make up some of the most popular online offerings. Editors use their creative abilities to provide a coherent, comprehensive publication, something with an opinion; in contrast, automatically selected or agent-filtered information can be bland and lifeless. Clement Mok, former creative director of Apple, when asked about some of the failings of the information architecture profession, put it this way:

People still like to be led through information and resources that have a very distinct point of view. That piece of the equation is often missing. (Mok, in Anderson, 2000a).

Learning to be an interaction designer, therefore, involves finding and using your editorial voice.

2.4.2 INTERACTION AS PACKAGE

What's important is the entire experience, from when I first hear about the product to purchasing it, to opening the box, to getting it running, to getting service, to maintaining it, to upgrading it. (Don Norman, in Anderson, 2000b).

Interaction design should be seen as having a wide sphere of concern. A case study that shows that there is (or should be) much more to the process than screen design was provided by Leysia Palen and Maryam Salzman (Palen and Salzman, 2001). After tracking some 19 new mobile phone owners for the first six weeks after their purchase, they saw that the perception of usability went far beyond the handset design. As well as a device's hardware and software, they identified two other elements of the system that affected users' experience: what they called *netware* and *bizware*.

Netware

Netware comprises all of the added services a network operator provides – voicemail, call identification, etc. They critically impact on the perception of the service experience. Poor netware interaction design can drastically impact the overall quality of service a user feels they are getting. If the design team overlooks the control of the network services and the way they are integrated with the handset, the good design of the device's own interactivity will lose much of its luster.

In the case study, users had to be adept not just at operating their handset but at using other systems – such as a website – to configure the network services. This led to all sorts of user frustrations. One problem, for example, involved a service to divert calls made to a customer's home phone to the mobile phone. Once activated, turning off this service was not a trivial matter. The subscriber had to call an automated line and go through a series of steps. The process was so complicated that customers found they were unable to turn the service off. Then, in order to be able to receive calls at home, the only solution was to switch off their mobile. This clearly frustrated people, as a comment from one customer who was finding the 'service' a great inconvenience, shows:

It's really a drag, because I have to have my phone turned off, if [my wife] is at home and wants to get phone calls, which is really kind of – what's the word? – cancels the point of having a cell phone.

The need for effective netware design is increasing as more and more services are added. Already there are additional offerings that have had usability problems. So when many networks first started to provide features such as picture and multimedia messaging, and the backup of device-based information over the network, users had to struggle to set the services up, often having to enter control parameters, addresses and so on manually.

For more sophisticated network services, like those that allow a user to disclose their availability (selecting settings such as "I'm busy" or "I'm bored") or to indicate their location, netware usability is going to a deciding factor in the appeal.

Wherever possible, configuring, initializing and updating of netware should be invisible to the user – set up either at the point of purchase or over the network. However, where it is important that the user has some manual control over network services, such as adjusting call forwarding options, Palen's and Salzman's investigation demonstrates that as much of this as possible should be carried out directly from the handset with a few steps. Users should be able to easily get an overview of the options they've set and turn them on and off quickly, all from the device.

Bizware

'Bizware' – the customer service center, call plan choices, even the telephone bill format – can also seriously affect the formation of the customer's relationship with the service they are subscribing to. Poor pricing of a data service, or a bad explanation of the costs, for example, can reduce the uptake more dramatically than a badly designed way to access the service. Again the way many mobile network operators handled the initial introduction of advanced services in these terms seems to have affected the rate of uptake.

Orange, a mobile network provider, has from its launch focused on attempting to make the customer's experience a highly enjoyable one. As Apple did with personal computing, Orange worked hard from the start at marketing their services as usable and user-centered rather than technology-driven. For example, as they moved to offer more complex services in 2003, they developed initiatives to help users experiment and learn about the new possibilities, such as offering in-shop 'training'.

BOX 2.7 NOKIA AND USER EXPERIENCE

An interview with Panu Korhonen, senior manager, interaction design, Nokia

MJ: What contributes to the 'user experience' associated with a product?

PK: Anything and everything to do with the product – the product itself, the services, what the out-of-the-box process is like, the documentation and so forth.

MJ: And what makes the experience a good one?

PK: The way I see things relates well to Don Norman's framework in his book, *Emotional Design* (Norman, 2004). Experiences with our products come at the three levels. So, in the first tenth of a second, how does the product look and feel (that's the visceral response)? Then, does the product allow the user to build a sort of relationship with it: straightforward at first to pick up the basics and then perhaps some ways to extend their skills with the right amount of challenge at the right time? This is the 'behavioral' response – overall we want products that are not 'clunky' but provide a smooth, enjoyable sense. Finally, there's the reflective and social side of the experience – how does the product help people to view themselves? The social value of the products comes from a whole range of factors, from coolness and branding through to functionality.

MJ: To achieve this degree of excellence, what sorts of skills do you look for in your group members?

PK: We've got many people with psychology and sociology backgrounds but also designers and programmers to produce concepts and prototypes. As we do a lot of usability testing, skills in designing and running experiments are very useful. Another important skill is common sense – knowing about everyday life and the other (non-technology things) that fill people's time and interests. ➤

MJ: In thinking about the user experiences, what drives your group?

PK: Well, obviously, an understanding about the users themselves but also a number of other factors. The technology that's available or will be available has to be considered; we have roadmaps of the sorts of device and services that will come on stream over the next years. Then there are the sorts of business model that might be offered – what users will be happy to pay for – and network operators' views are also important to us. ■

BOX 2.8 WHY IS SMS (TEXTING) SO SUCCESSFUL?

If you had proposed SMS ten years ago as a potential 'killer app', what sort of reaction do you think you'd have received? Most probably, the response would be disbelief: how could a medium that conveys only 160 characters, entered via an awkward typing method, be effective?

Putting aside these seemingly fatal failings, texting scores well in terms of our three important characteristics of successful services: usefulness, usability and user experience.

First, it is highly useful for a range of purposes: families, friends and colleagues can use it to keep in touch, and it can be a channel for information services such as those that deliver news and sports headlines. Then, its lightweight and low-profile nature means it fits in well with the other aspects of people's lives: that is, it has everyday usability. Finally in terms of user experience, the service has a number of advantages: it has good netware usability; it can be configured and activated without the user's involvement (though this wasn't always the case); users perceive it to be instantaneous and a way of being very directly in contact with others; and it even allows people to be reflective, fostering a creative crafting of messages and the contemplation of previously received texts.

Scott Jenson, Head of Jenson Design and former director of product design at Symbian, has pondered the SMS success story, in an effort to see if and how multimedia messaging (MMS) could be another winner. The SMS success factors he considers include the following (Jenson, 2004):

- **Costs.** Some people feel that a significant part of the SMS phenomenon can be accounted for by the low cost of texting relative to voice calls, a factor particularly important to teenagers. However, research has shown that this not the biggest driver of the uptake, and that people can spend a substantial amount of money on sending messages – sent messages generate more messages as the to-and-fro of text conversations develop. Messages can also lead to voice calls as, for example, when someone calls to clarify or gossip about a text. A similar 'virtuous circle' has ➤

been seen with i-Mode where online information – like the name and other details of a restaurant – leads to a later voice call.

- **Low intrusion.** People can read and respond to a message whenever they like. Furthermore, they can decide on the pace of this response. Some people, for example, react immediately to every message, using SMS as a form of instant messaging; others may look only when they are coming to or leaving their workplace.
- **Expressiveness and meaning.** Marketers of multimedia messaging have used the slogan 'a picture's worth a thousand words' to highlight the benefits of MMS over SMS. But carefully crafted texts, perhaps with the correspondent's own adapted vocabulary, can be highly expressive and convey significant meaning to the recipient, treasured for some time.
- **Turn-taking.** The technology is a social one. It allows people to participate in a controlled, equal way. I send a message to you; I wait; you respond; then it's my turn again.
- **Privacy.** Overhead conversations present obvious difficulties, but texts allow a degree of private communication in public spaces. Although it might be distracting, during a meeting it's possible to say ''I love you'' to someone in another city while communicating with a colleague at the other end of the room as you attempt to clinch a deal.

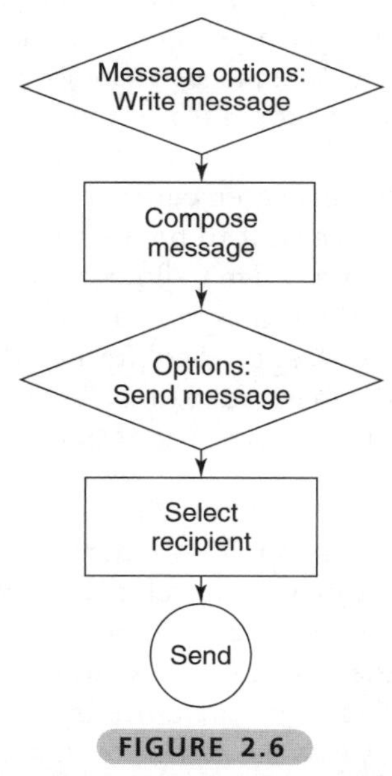

FIGURE 2.6

SMS task flow: simple and direct (adapted from Jenson, 2004) ➤

> But what about the basic usability of the service which, as we said, seems poor with its limited message length and text entry method? While these are problems, the interaction design is effective: Jenson illustrates this by pointing out the simple, linear directness of creating and sending a message (see Figure 2.6). As he notes, "... it is hard for the consumer to make a mistake in that there are very few wrong turns to take". ■

2.5 TECHNOLOGY ACCEPTANCE

Our discussion on what makes a people-centered product, one they will want to buy, use and keep, reflects the thinking of the HCI research and practice community over the past several decades. This community is made up of predominately those working in computer science and the 'ologies' (psychology, sociology, anthropology).

Another group of researchers, those in business schools and Information Science departments, have also been keenly investigating the factors that make a technology a sensational success or a disappointing flop. This work – studying technology acceptance and adoption – has led to a range of models that predict the likely uptake of an innovation (see Figure 2.7 for an example).

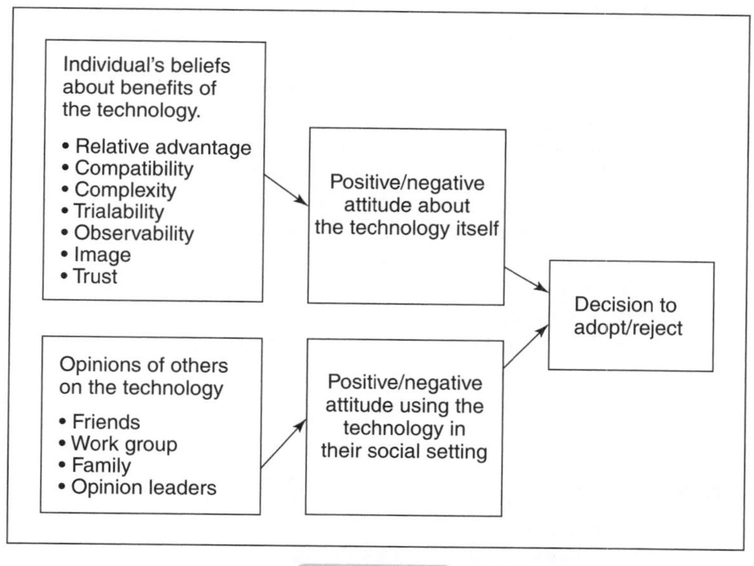

FIGURE 2.7

Technology acceptance model – whether a person adopts a technology depends on their individual beliefs and the influence of those around them (adapted from Barnes and Huff, 2003)

TABLE 2.1

Technology acceptance and interaction design

Interaction design terminology	Technology acceptance model terminology
Usefulness	Relative advantage
Intrinsic usability of service	Complexity; compatibility (with previous services/technology); observability
Ecological usability	Compatibility (with life/culture); observability; image; trust; opinion of friends, family and other groups
User experience	Trialability; observability; image; trust; reaction of friends, family and other groups

Interestingly, the sorts of qualities identified in this research have striking similarities to the notions that HCI practice has developed and that we've highlighted in terms of usefulness, usability and user experience (see Table 2.1).

Interaction designers commonly collaborate with colleagues from marketing and other business units; these people may be more familiar with the language of technology acceptance, so it could be worth couching discussions in these sorts of terms.

Technology acceptance models can be useful at assessing novel concepts and prototypes. They can also be employed in trying to understand why a previous service was successful, so that future ones can emulate their adoption. Stuart Barnes and Sid Huff did just this for i-Mode, the phenomenally successful mobile Internet service developed by the Japanese Telecom provider, NTT DoCoMo. In 2004 this service boasted 41 million Japanese subscribers – that's 32% of the population – and 3 million elsewhere in the world (Barnes and Huff, 2003).

The perspective provides some useful pointers into why the uptake of the system was so great. As Table 2.2 illustrates, some of i-Mode's staggering success can be explained by Japan-specific aspects: the culture is very conformist, so people eagerly adopt a technology that looks like it is going mainstream; and the alternatives were poor – unlike in the UK or USA, for example, few Japanese had access to the Internet at home. However, other success factors are more transferable, such as the focus on a small select set of services, vetted by the trusted NTT, and the low costs of trying a new feature. Some of these winning formulas have been replicated by other operators; Orange, for example, ran a 'Try' campaign in 2004 when it allowed free use to novel services for a limited period of time.

SUMMARY

Many of today's mobile products and services fail to deliver on the range of key qualities we've discussed here. Sure, there are good examples everywhere of devices that are attractive in terms of their industrial design, their esthetic appeal; but, apart from a handful of cases, the success is only skin-deep. Now, while products certainly can be sold purely on the

way they look and the array of sophisticated technology they contain, without addressing real user needs and the spectrum of usability issues developers are missing opportunities to build a loyal customer base – customers who are able and willing to actually use the product, generating further service revenues, over an extended period.

TABLE 2.2

i-Mode and the technology acceptance model (based on Barnes and Huff, 2003)

Factor affecting uptake	i-Mode
Relative advantage – To what extent does this innovation add value to the user?	Prior to availability, access to the Internet for Japanese users was low
Compatibility – How consistent with previous experience? How does it fit with lifestyle and attitudes of the user?	Carefully designed to fit telephone handset – network provider had a high degree of control over handset design. Service played on Japanese enthusiasm for hi-tech, especially in young people (hence games, etc.)
Complexity – How easy does it appear to be to use?	Handset design included a command navigation button with simple menus, special browser to reduce complexity, and control of content. Users able to personalize
Trialability – Is it cheap and easy for user to play with innovation before committing to adopting (or rejecting) it?	Pay-as-you-go encouraged experimentation (*cf.* long contracts); low cost of use promoted sharing of handsets for others to trial services
Observability – Are the results of using the service obvious, by the users and others?	Quick responsiveness of network allowed users to see immediate effect of actions, and handsets often used in public, so effectiveness of services observable by others
Trust – How good a relationship does the user expect with the provider?	NTT already trusted brand and initially carefully controlled the sorts of site available; clear pricing policies helped
Image – How does the innovation enhance the user's own self-esteem and the image they project to others?	Perceived as increasing social status

WORKSHOP QUESTIONS

- Usability guidelines such as those we've seen in this chapter can be used both to help generate designs and to check proposals. Generally in both cases, the design activity is done by a human. How might a computer system be used to automatically generate or check an interface design?
- When you buy a new gadget (mobile, DVD or computer), what information and activities are your top priorities as you begin to open the packaging?
- For a mobile device you own, create a set of resources that would give the user a good 'out-of-the-box' experience. Imagine your user opening the package containing the device – what instructions, manuals or other things might they find and in what order?
- Use the technology acceptance model discussed in Section 2.5 to explain why ringtone downloads to mobile phones have been so successful, while the late 1990s 'Internet on the phone' (WAP) services failed to appeal in Europe.

DESIGNER TIPS

- *If your design proposal doesn't contain at least two functions that will compel your user to carry their device with them, think again.*
- *Ignore notions like 'user-friendly' and others that might lead you to 'dumb down' your designs. 'User-accommodating', 'user-appealing' and 'user-appreciated' should be your goal.*
- *Check each design proposal you generate against the well-known usability guidelines. Can your user work out what to do? Are they given immediate and meaningful feedback as they push buttons, select options and so on? Does your proposal provide a satisfying way to step through and complete a task?*
- *Don't overestimate the importance of your designs – be ecological, think about the other resources available to users.*
- *Learn the language of your colleagues – business strategists and marketers. Couch your proposals and critiques in terms of technology acceptance models and the like.*

CHAPTER 3
INNOVATING

OVERVIEW

3.1. Introduction
3.2. Technology-centered approaches
3.3. Transferring from the desktop
3.4. Building on past mobile success
3.5. Drama
3.6. Frameworks for human-centered thinking

KEY POINTS

- Interaction design is not solely about giving users more of what they already have; it can also turn the accepted order on its head, redefining what successful applications are.
- Some approaches to innovation distance the user, with their lives and contexts being perceived only dimly or merely imagined. This can lead to products that fail to fit into the real world. Designers need to consider issues of complexity, integration and scale.
- Technology can inspire designs right from the start of the development process. Interesting, intriguing working prototypes can prompt users to articulate their future needs.
- Just because an application or interface style is successful on the desktop does not mean it will enjoy similar appeal when mobile.
- At the opposite end of the spectrum to the user-peripheral innovation approaches, there are tools that help designers generate new people-focused ideas for mobile services. These draw on an understanding of human values and motivations.

3.1 INTRODUCTION

There are billions of users waiting for innovative mobile services that are useful and usable, and offer a distinctly satisfying user experience. Handset developers, network operators and third-party mobile software developers are all eagerly attempting to discover the products that will really take off.

The opportunities are great, but as we saw in Chapter 1, there have already been disappointments and the potential for failure is high. How, then, can you innovate services in such a way that increases the chances of success and reduces the risk of costly flops?

In this chapter, we take a look at a spectrum of innovation strategies. They differ in terms of what drives the process. In some cases, the development is shaped by a desire to produce products that have the latest, most sophisticated technology; in others, previous market success is used to highlight possible future 'winners'; meanwhile, the imagination and creativity of the designer is clearly an important factor in many cases.

As we work through some alternatives, you'll notice that the strategies become more and more 'user-centered'. The 'user' becomes less abstract and more involved, their real lives and concerns being used both to select the sorts of services developed and to shape the form these new products take.

None of the approaches here, though, is the complete answer; by looking at them, we will see their advantages and drawbacks, setting the scene for the interaction design methods and guidelines that we focus on in the rest of the book.

BOX 3.1 INNOVATION

Without innovation, organizations and economies are doomed to stagnate, or worse, wither. Governments understand this, putting effort into developing innovation policies, providing funding for innovation parks and centers, and linking businesses with other partners such as universities. Commercial concerns recognize it by reinvesting substantial proportions of their revenues back into research and development. Nokia, for instance, invested 13% of their net sales into research in 2003 (Nokia, b).

'Innovation' conjures up breakthrough, paradigm shifts, major change. Certainly there are innovations that do that – the mobile phone itself is one – but in *The Innovator's Dilemma*, Clayton Christensen presents a more useful taxonomy of innovative technology, making the distinction between inventions that are sustaining and those that are disruptive (Christensen, 2003).

Sustaining innovations are those that give customers more of what they already have and want. So when camera phones first appeared, the image quality was low, but consumers soon demanded higher-resolution devices to match conventional digital camera quality. Initially, services associated with these phones were simple messaging ones, but as image quality improved there were innovations to exploit the more advanced capabilities; now you can walk up to a public booth in a shopping mall, wirelessly connect to it from your camera phone and produce high-quality ➤

prints. Multimedia messaging innovates in this way too – the thinking behind it was that as texting was so successful, customers would be even more enthusiastic about messaging facilities that also allowed images and audios to be sent.

Some sustaining innovations are incremental in nature. A manufacturer that develops technology for a one-gigabyte, postage-stamp sized hard drive for a mobile phone will work to further extend the engineering to produce a five-gigabyte version. But sustaining innovations can also involve radical enhancements, introducing distinct types of technology or approach.

As an example, consider how mobile phone attributes such as display font size, brightness and speaker volume can be adjusted. Most devices allow the user to manually control these or to set up profiles for different contexts such as 'outdoors' and 'meetings'. Mäntyjärvi and Seppanen (2002), though, describe a prototype that employs sensors to monitor the user's context (such as environmental noise, the user's walking speed, etc.). This information is used to automatically adapt the settings. If, for instance, the user is walking quickly to the bus stop in the evening while checking the timetable on the phone, the font size and the backlight illumination might be increased to help them read the information.

Disruptive technologies, in contrast, disrupt the status quo; they turn the accepted order on its head. Where sustaining innovations build in a managed, predictable way, with the aim of making products more and more successful, disruptive ones redefine what success is. Because these innovations are so different from the present working order, they can easily be rejected or sidelined: as Christensen notes, at first these technologies appear to be a bad business proposition, since they appear to give customers not more of what they want (the sustaining model) but less. SMS was such a disruptive technology, its eventual mass appeal at first being overlooked. Who would want to use such a poor means of communicating when they could talk to someone anytime, wherever they wanted?

Christensen's insights came from his analysis of the hard-disk drive industry. There he found that the established companies were very good at innovating in sustaining ways but poor in seeking out and developing disruptive technologies. The message to big mobile companies like Nokia and Motorola is to be wary of the new entrants to the market. ■

3.2 TECHNOLOGY-CENTERED APPROACHES

In 1965 Gordon Moore, of Intel Research, predicted that the number of transistors squeezed onto an integrated circuit board would be doubled every two years or so. And, while the number went up, the cost of manufacture would stay the same.

This law, dubbed Moore's law, has held true, and is expected to do so until at least the end of 2010: back in 1970 there were 1000 transistors per chip; by 2000 there were 42 000 000. What this means, in short, is that if you wait two years, you can do as much as you do today, in processing terms, at half the cost. The next time you bump into a computer science researcher, tease them by telling them to take a two-year vacation – when they return they might find the problems they are addressing have been solved by the improvements in the underlying technology!

Moore's law means that current mobile devices have more power than fully fledged PCs of the early 1990s. As well as processing speeds, there have also been great advances in display technology, storage capacities and battery life. A lot of these technical innovations allow users to do more of what they are doing already – to display higher-quality images, store more data locally on the mobile, and so on. As we saw in Chapter 1, there are also developments leading to intriguing new ways for the user to provide input and get output from the device.

Mobile technology companies, handset developers like Nokia and Samsung, and software providers like Microsoft, all keep a very close eye on the emerging hardware. Indeed, if you are an interaction designer in a company like these, you will be made very aware of the technology 'road-maps' that play an important role in product strategies. These plot out the types of hardware that will be commercially available usually over a five- to ten-year period: location-tracking hardware in every phone by 2007; tilt-based sensors commonplace by 2008, etc.

Faced with this inevitable technological progress, it is very hard not to let these innovations drive the development of mobile products and services. After all, your customers will all want the newest, most exciting features, won't they? In a technologically centered development environment, device manufacturers will attempt to fill the products with as many of the novelties as possible, and service providers will seek out applications that can make use of them.

But heed the warnings of such a techno-fixation from the recent mobile past. In the late 1990s, European network operators paid tens of billions of dollars in licensing fees for broadband wireless capabilities. Their eagerness, now somewhat regretted, betrayed an "if we build it, they will use it" mentality and the assumption that large numbers of subscribers would highly desire – and be willing to pay for – fast access to video and other data-intensive services.

For the communications industry, video telephony has been a particularly potent technological obsession. Barry Brown, a tech-anthropologist – one of a growing breed who study not lost tribes in far-flung lands, but the communities of concrete-jungle-inhabiting, sophisticated users – charts this fixation, from early attempts by AT&T (in 1971) through to recent mobile service providers' attempts at encouraging face-to-face calls on the move (Brown, 2002). This enthusiasm on the part of operators persists in the face of 30-plus years of evidence that people just do not like the idea of seeing who they are calling.

However, we are not arguing that you should ignore technological developments. Many of the innovations have the potential to greatly enhance users' experience: context-aware technology, touchable interfaces, robust speech recognition, etc., will undoubtedly provide designers with better ways to meet users' needs. As Jakob Nielsen points out (see Box 3.2), one of the factors contributing to early WAP service failure was the small monochrome screens most mobiles had when the services first emerged; now larger displays in full color are possible.

EXERCISE 3.1 RINGTONES FOR NON-MUSICIANS

Putting aside implementation issues, how could you allow users to customize their ringtones without having to become trained musicians? (See Figure 3.1.) ➤

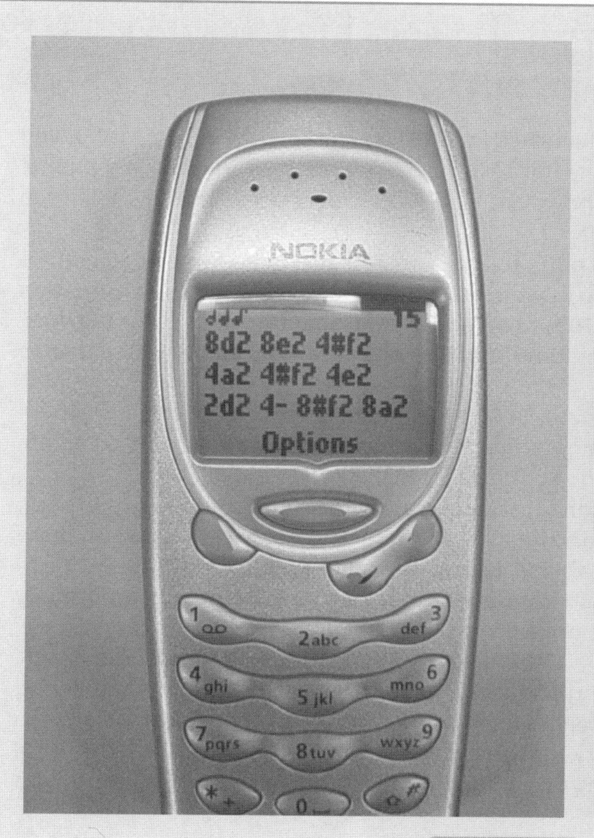

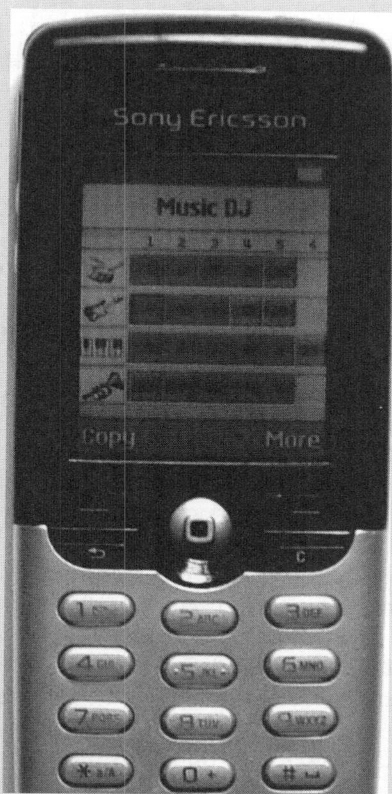

FIGURE 3.1

Command line vs graphical user interface: technological developments and improved user experience

Left: ringtone composition application on a low-resolution, monochrome display. Right: a tune being composed on a device with a more sophisticated screen. Clearly, the display technology improvements enhance the presentation of melody and reduce the complexity of composing a tune. The example shows too the progression in mobile interfaces following that of the desktop computer – from command line to graphical

Comments: users could be allowed to adjust musical attributes of existing ringtones, such as the pitch and tempo. Alternatively, they could use a tool to join small snippets of pre-recorded melody together to form interesting compositions. A more sophisticated service could see users humming their tune and having this automatically rendered as a musical tune. ■

BOX 3.2 THE FALL AND RISE (PERHAPS) OF WAP

Early commercial WAP services were launched in 1999 and marketed widely the following year with slogans like 'surf the mobile net'. Much was promised – the web on a phone, in fact. By the middle of that year, however, WAP was widely perceived as a failure, a real disappointment; a backlash began.

Jakob Nielsen, renowned usability guru, found that users struggled for several minutes to complete simple tasks like checking news headlines or finding TV program information (Nielsen, 2000b). When questioned, 70% of his participants said they would not use WAP in the future, one noting that it would be cheaper, and faster, to buy a newspaper to find the information.

The usability arm of service consultants SERCO found similar failings: in one test where users had to find an address in a business directory, only two of 12 users could complete the task, taking over 20 minutes to do so (Heylar, 2002).

These and other studies have highlighted several factors, in addition to the poor, misguiding marketing that led to the failure of these early services. Some of these factors – the so-called 'back-end usability' issues – are being addressed through technological developments; others (the 'front-end' ones) need designers to purposefully design services that support users' mobile needs.

With careful user-centered design, effective services should be possible with WAP. By 2003, the industry stopped talking about the technology and focused on marketing the usefulness and benefits of the services they were offering over the protocol. Usage figures released by the WAP industry that year suggest this shift may rescue WAP, with users accessing hundreds of millions of pages, mainly for downloading ringtones and games.

- Back-end usability issues
  - Cost of services: early services were charged by time connected; given the difficulty of using the WAP sites, this could mean, as Nielsen notes, that it would be cheaper to make a phone call to find the information.
  - Low bandwidth.
  - Small screens, often showing only 5 to 8 lines of text in monochrome.
- Front-end usability issues
  - Technology-oriented terminology confuses users: 'cache', 'certificate', and so on, need to be expressed in more meaningful ways.
  - Poorly repurposed web content: many services took website content and re-presented it for the mobile device with minimal redesign. Not only was ➤

much of the content itself of little value for mobile users; the way it was communicated was also inappropriate. (Chapter 9 looks at ways of improving this situation.)

- Clumsy, tedious interactions: services often required multiple steps to log on, find information, etc. Connecting to an email service, for example, could take several minutes – all charged – simply to enter the username and password.
- Confusing navigations: many services required users to make choices from a series of menus. As well as the time needed to locate information, in the SERCO study, users were confused by the way the WAP 'back' button worked. They expected the WAP 'back' to operate in the same way as in the in-built phone menus – taking them up a level menu hierarchy rather than back to a previously viewed page (which might not be the next level back in the menu structure). (Chapter 8 deals in detail with the problems of menus and navigation on mobiles.)
- 'Walled gardens': service providers attempted to restrict users to accessing a limited set of controlled content. ■

Conventional human-centered development approaches shy away from thinking about technology – 'the implementation' – until after all user needs are really thought through and understood. The advantage of such a strategy is that the design process is not distracted or stifled early on by detailed design considerations. For mobile-style innovations, though, there do seem to be benefits in allowing technology to be a more active ingredient in the innovation cauldron.

One illustration of what's possible is described by Yvonne Rogers and her team (Rogers *et al.*, 2002). Their aim was to innovate in a 'technology-inspired' way; that is, they gave users interesting, strange technology to play with. They were not interested in defining specific services, but rather wanted to explore the possibilities new technologies offered with respect to leisure and learning. The aims of the study were threefold:

first . . . to design the experience so success/failure is not an issue. A second [aim] is that the technology should not be the focus of the experience. A third is that what we provide should be genuinely entertaining and, in some ways, challenging.

This, then, is not technology 'push' where the goal can be to try really hard to make the technology succeed and be at the center of what the user does; nor is it a purely user-centered 'pull', with technology being deployed and then critically evaluated to see whether it meets some previously well-defined needs. Instead, technology is being used as a thought-provoking tool, prodding the user to give a response, in a way

. . . not dissimilar in its aims to a familiar technique for innovation in modern art, where there is a history of experimenting with new combinations and juxtapositions.

This approach is a type of 'probe' – tools we will learn more about in Chapter 5. At this point, though, it is worth noting that these techniques are good at disruptive-type innovation (see Box 3.1 for a definition); they can help users to see their world in entirely new ways.

BOX 3.3 SMS SERENDIPITY

SMS – text messaging – was an unexpected, but very welcome, chance success story for the mobile industry. It was not developed through a careful study of users, there were no pilot user tests, and the interface was not designed to allow efficient communication.

You could take this case to heart and decide not to spend time and money on deeply involved user-centered design processes – instead, why not spend the interaction design budget on generating as many services as possible, in the hope that some will be the real winners? This approach, however, is like arguing against regular employment over spending money on buying lottery tickets. SMS is a 'winner', yes, but we are less likely to hear about the many failures that cost far more than an investment in focused design activities.

The SMS case does provide several positive pointers for designers, however. First, some SMS qualities, like simplicity, directness and flexibility of use, could be built into other services. Second, services could be designed in ways that allow users to find uses rather than being too constrained; that is, to cater for the adaptive and subversive user. Finally, SMS is a strong reminder of the need to keep a careful watch on how people are actually using existing technologies, to discover the unexpected, informing later versions of a device or service. ■

3.3 TRANSFERRING FROM THE DESKTOP

One obvious innovation strategy is to take approaches successful on the PC and to bring them to the mobile. This can be done either at an application level or in terms of the look and feel of the interface presented to the user.

At an application level, the benefits seem clear. The reasoning goes like this – if something is highly desired already on the PC then why not allow users to have it on the mobile too? Apart from the comfort of seemingly certain success in developing a cross-over, there are two other attractions to the approach. Such applications may allow users to carry on activities started on the desktop when they are mobile: if a user has been working on a document, why not let them view and even edit it as they work away from home? What's more, the degree of re-learning they will need in order to use the system effectively will be minimal.

At a user interface level, giving the mobile a familiar look and feel might also help to cut down on the learning needed to use the device. On top of this, it could be useful in marketing – "buy our products, the ones with the reassuring look and feel" – the interface, then, acting as a key brand element.

As we will see, however, just because a type of application or style of interface works well on one platform does not necessarily mean it will be so effective on another.

3.3.1 APPLICATIONS

In the search for highly attractive mobile services, there have been many attempts to bring widely used PC applications to the small screen. A good example that highlights the thinking and the pitfalls is Instant Messaging (IM).

This PC application is highly popular, especially among teenagers. Being able to see which friends or colleagues – often known as 'buddies' in IM speak – are online at the same time, and to send them a message, helps enhance people's sense of being part of a community; IM acts, as it were, as a 'social glue'.

Given the apparent similarities with SMS, in terms of both purpose (fast, one-to-one communication) and appeal to younger people, wireless providers have looked at offering IM-type services on mobile devices. Meanwhile, research into how and why people use IM on PCs hints at some problems: simply providing similar features on a mobile will not necessarily be the runaway success these providers may hope for.

Rebecca Grinter and her colleagues uncovered several salient aspects of teenager IM use on the large screen, each raising challenges for mobile versions of IM (Grinter and Palen, 2002):

- Teenagers used IM in parallel with other computer-based activities like web surfing, doing schoolwork or emailing. They were, then, multitasking. On a small screen, how do you allow a user to monitor messages and carry out other activities?
- Often they had more than one IM window open, being involved in concurrent conversations with different groups of people. How can more than one chat thread be supported when the screen space is limited?
- IM was seen as a 'quiet' technology that could be coordinated with other activities without great disruption. When you are at a PC, your other activities are information based, so switching from typing a document to greeting a friend is not highly disruptive. When you are mobile, many of your other activities are physically based – walking, looking for landmarks, dealing with a customer – requiring a different frame of mind.
- IM was seen as a free activity – there were no worries about the length of time spent communicating with friends. However, on mobiles these chats could become very costly: one New Zealand operator, for instance, charged 20 cents (about US 10 cents) per message in 2004.

The market problems might be resolved relatively simply, such as by charging a flat rate for all IM use in a month, but the interaction design challenges are more complex.

Hubbub, an experimental messaging service developed by AT&T (Figure 3.2), sheds some further light on the appeal or otherwise of mobile Instant Messaging and interaction details that need to be tackled (Isaacs *et al.*, 2002). Hubbub can be used from a PC, like conventional IM, and via wireless devices like a PDA.

In a study of its use, while people rated the service highly, only three of 25 participants elected to use mobile devices. Even for this small group, their handheld IM conversations accounted for just 8–20% of their total use of the service. The researchers suggest mobile uptake might improve when handheld costs, wireless service and network reliability improve. A more fundamental problem could be that while users find it effective to chat while doing other computer tasks, when genuinely mobile they have little desire or opportunity to do so.

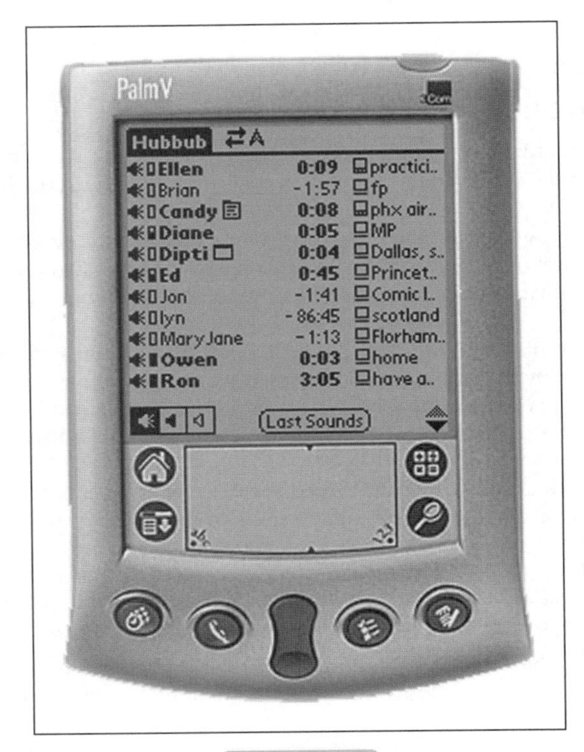

FIGURE 3.2

Hubbub, a mobile Instant Messaging application. View shows contact names and current location and status

IM can be a really important tool to keep in touch when away from family, friends and colleagues when traveling (Nardi, 2000). While mobile IM might not be attractive as an 'always there', pervasive device activity, as it is on the PC, it might be seen as a very helpful way for people to communicate at prearranged times, or when they have some unproductive periods with little else to do. So, a traveling business person, back in her hotel room after a day's work, might switch on her handheld, access IM and chat with her children; or a bored passenger, during yet another long wait in the airport lounge, could flip open his device to see whether any colleagues back at base were available for a catch-up chat. Alternatively, during such free periods, the traveler could allow the device to notify them when someone they could talk with was available. To satisfy such needs, however, a mobile IM service has to integrate with conventional PC services. Currently, some mobile network operators only allow users to communicate with others who are using the same service via a mobile device.

Even where a desktop application seems a good candidate for transplanting to the mobile platform, some interaction redesign is likely to be needed. The Hubbub study illustrates the sort of additional thinking you might have to put in when moving from the desktop to the street.

Hubbub's mobile interface does not insist on precise input; there are no obtrusive word predictors or spell checkers. A user can also send short audio messages, sequences of notes – a form of the auditory earcons mentioned in Section 1.3.3 – to convey messages like 'hi', 'talk?' and 'OK'. Such design choices help mobile users to participate efficiently without having their contributions stilted by the technology.

While customizing an interface to fit the mobile can lead to long-term benefits, in the short term users may have some difficulties with the new version: that is, differences in the way something operates compared to an earlier learnt system, even if it supports previously met functions, can disrupt the user's experience, as an early piece of research on desktop word processors illustrated (Karat *et al.*, 1986). In that experiment, experienced users were asked to carry out tasks on the system they knew well. Then they did similar things on a new word processor. For half of the people involved in the trial, this new system was very close to the older one, offering the same functions via menus that were organized in familiar ways. The system the other half of the subjects used, while providing functionality consistent with the old application, used a different menu organization. This group performed less well, completing tasks more slowly.

EXERCISE 3.2 ICONS AND COMMUNICATING A MOBILE USER'S CONTEXT

In conventional desktop Instant Messaging, each chat participant (often called 'buddies' or 'contacts') is represented by an icon. These give cues about the user's availability – minimally, they can show whether the user is online or not. Make a list of the sorts of information a user might wish to communicate about their mobile context. For each item, say how this status information might be set, and design a small graphical icon to depict it. Show your icons to someone else and ask them to say what they think they mean.

Comments: when thinking about the ways status information can be set, there are two main options: either manual or automatic. In the manual case, where the user explicitly changes their profile, you need to think about quick ways to toggle through the alternative settings with perhaps short-cuts (e.g. single button-pushes) for the most important (e.g. to switch between 'available' and 'unavailable'). There is also the issue of how to ensure the user is aware they are still in one mode (e.g. 'unavailable') when they wish to be in another (a simple, but sometimes frustrating, solution is to employ time-outs where settings revert to the standard after a specified period). In the automatic case, think about which contextual factors might be sensed to update the settings (e.g. fast movements mean the user is in a rush and unable to interact leisurely with the device or other people). Be warned: effectively second-guessing users has long been a goal of interactive system researchers – think of Microsoft 'Clippy' – and is really hard to do. ■

BOX 3.4 PUSH-TO-TALK

While text-based instant messaging might not be such a big hit on mobiles, voice versions could be more popular, as a study by Allison Woodruff and Paul Aoki of the Palo Alto Research Center (PARC) suggests (Woodruff and Aoki, 2003).

Push-to-talk is a feature being provided by a number of mobile telephone networks around the world. It allows walkie-talkie type communication – users press a button to send a voice message directly to one or more other subscribers.

In the PARC study, a group of young people were observed using the technology. What the researchers found was that the service enabled a range of communications, including:

- Chit-chat: gossip-type conversation over the day
- Extended presence: keeping in touch with loved ones
- Micro-coordination: sending messages in order to organize activities and rendezvous
- Play, e.g. sending each other funny sounds or comments.

Many of these sorts of interaction are of course seen in SMS; however, the participants showed they particularly appreciated the very low interactional costs of using the voice approach and the lack of the 'persistence' of messages (the audio messages were not stored, unlike text messages), allowing them to engage without the risk of being held to account later for what they said.

All the participants enjoyed the service and were moderately enthusiastic about using it in the longer term. ■

3.3.2 INTERFACE STYLES

Designing a new system to accommodate a user's previous knowledge and experience at the interface and interaction level seems sensible in attempting to promote the product's adoption and in reducing the amount of relearning. Such motivations are noted by some researchers to justify their attempts to provide a full QWERTY keyboard for mobile devices (Roeber *et al.*, 2003).

In early versions of the Microsoft operating system for PocketPCs, the aim was to replicate the desktop interface experience extensively – the goal was Windows on a small screen. But the effect was a less than usable experience, as one of the developers recounts:

From a usability standpoint, interface consistency was not enough to ensure success in the first iterations of the Palm-sized PC . . . If quick data entry lookup was a key requirement for the product, then it wasn't being satisfied with the multiple screen taps necessary to acquire information. So, while familiarity and functionality were satisfied, usability was not. (Zuberec, 2000)

Microsoft's competition, in the form of Palm, approached the problem quite differently. The PalmPilot developers rejected the idea of emulating the PC experience. Noticing big differences between the ways people used PCs and PDAs, their whole approach was to make things simple, direct and fast to complete. With a PC, people work for extended periods on a word processor or spreadsheet; handhelds, in contrast, are used in short bursts, many times during the day. As Rob Haitani, one of the early designers, says:

You have to ask yourself if the usage pattern is diametrically opposite, does it make sense to copy the design paradigm, and our response was no. (Bergman and Haitani, 2000)

The PocketPC Windows developers learned from their experiences and later versions were more mobile-adapted.

BOX 3.5 SHRINKING TO FIT

One approach to design is to take existing applications on one platform and refit them for the smaller screen. This is Microsoft's advice for adapting applications for their Smartphone from the PC or PocketPC (Microsoft, a). Note that the 'Common Dialogs' referred to here are the dialog boxes used to select a file, and a 'Spinner' control is an interface element that allows users to toggle through a list of options using arrow buttons on the phone.

Microsoft's general guidelines

To design an effective user interface (UI), here is a procedure you should follow to optimize your results.

Step 1: Review your current UI for the desktop version of your application or PocketPC.

- Locate all unnecessary interface elements and remove them.
- Locate all elements that are not supported and remove them or replace them with Smartphone elements.
- Try to avoid dialogs that pop up dialogs that pop up dialogs, . . ., and so on.

Step 2: Put all interface elements under each other instead of having them side-by-side.

- Use descriptive labels on top of elements instead of to the right or left (see Figures 3.3 and 3.4).
- You can have longer dialogs since they scroll automatically. ➤

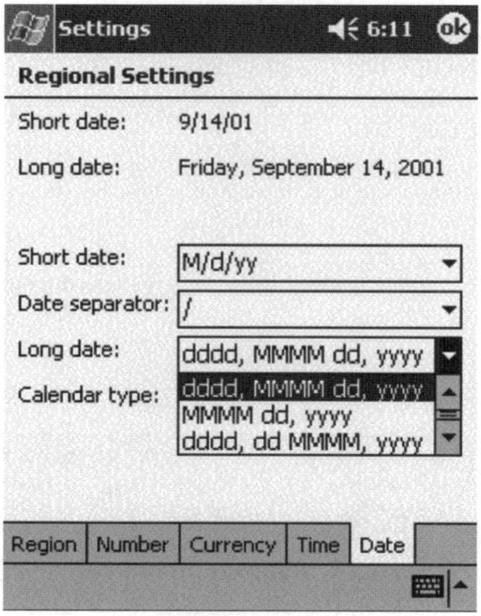

FIGURE 3.3

PocketPC user interface

FIGURE 3.4

Smartphone user interface ➤

Step 3: Locate all Common Dialogs and remove them. If your application requires the user to select a file, do the following:

- Store such files in '/My Documents'.
- Load the list of all those files into a Spinner control.
- Show the Spinner control instead of the Common Dialog.

Step 4: Reduce the number of menus to one and menu items to 4–8.

Step 5: Define your SoftKeys. If you have a menu, use SoftKey 2. Otherwise follow this guideline: use SoftKey 1 for 'OK' or any other positive selection (i.e. 'Yes', 'Done' or 'New') and SoftKey 2 for 'Cancel', negative selection (i.e. 'No') or any further actions.

Step 6: Test your application user interface with one hand.

Force yourself to operate even the emulator with just one hand to ensure it will work to the satisfaction of the user. ■

3.4 BUILDING ON PAST MOBILE SUCCESS

Instead of trying to take well-known PC services and shrinking them, another possibility is to look at what has worked on mobiles and see how to build on these successful services. On mobile phones the obvious winners are voice and messaging, and many providers are looking at how to extend the ways people can use these methods of giving and receiving information (see Box 3.6).

BOX 3.6 EXTENDING THE SUCCESS?

Voice and text messaging enjoy a success that service providers would like to extend. There are a range of possibilities, some commercially available; but which ones will really fit with users' needs?

- Push-to-talk: simply press a button on the phone to talk directly, walkie-talkie fashion, to another user (see also Box 3.4).
- TAP: send a message containing just the sender's name and time, a simple, fast way to tell someone they are on the sender's mind (Jenson, 2004). ➤

- Voice SMS: send short voice messages directly to another phone (Jenson, 2004).
- Picture/multimedia messaging: enrich text messages with photos, music or video.
- SMS to voice: type a text message and send it to a non-text-capable phone, the system converting text to speech.
- Fixed phone SMSing: have a fixed phone that can display and send text messages.
- SMS archiving: access all the text messages you've sent or received via a website when you are at a PC at home or work. ■

As the mobile IM case shows, just assuming that variations of an effective form of service will also be highly desirable is naive. Be wary of complicating a simple but effective service, like SMS, and weakening its power by doing so.

Multimedia Messaging (MMS) is an attempt to provide SMS users with richer ways of getting their message across. However, as Scott Jenson explains, in its initial form it failed to add substantial value to users:

MMS assumes its value is based upon the value of SMS . . . [but] Current user research implies the true value of SMS is based on a complex series of social and interactive attributes which don't seem to be greatly enhanced by digital photos. There indeed may be great value to sending photos, but it will be a new, currently unknown value. (Jenson, 2004)

MMS also breaks the simple interaction model seen in SMS. Figure 3.5 illustrates a typical task flow with users having to complete a complex series of steps, potentially involving repeated activities such as selecting and attaching sounds or image. Compare this with the simple, linear sequence that characterizes SMS (see Figure 2.7 in Chapter 2).

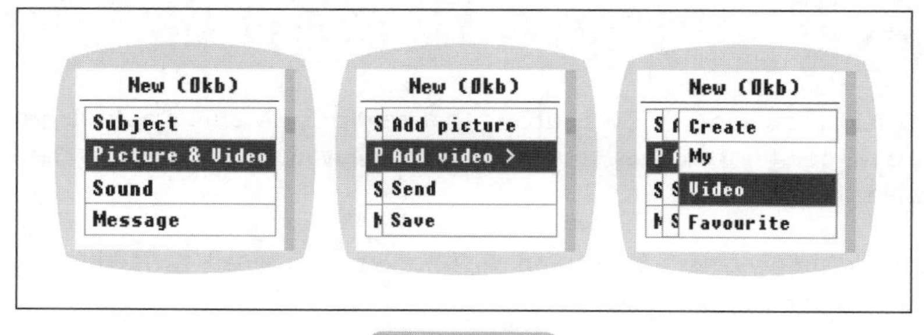

FIGURE 3.5

MMS task flow: creating an MMS can be complicated (inspired by Jenson, 2004)

3.5 DRAMA

Playwrights create both worlds and characters to act in them. They know everything about the creatures they conjure up, limiting their interactions with the world they inhabit. The focus in on defining the lives of a handful of individuals, with a story that carefully weaves their actions into the meaningful whole.

As a mobile designer, you might see yourself as a bit of a playwright, developing 'scripts' for how people will use the technology, imagining how it will be employed in a world you invent. But what seems useful and viable in interaction terms, when imagined, may be hopelessly ineffective in the real world. When conjuring up users and their worlds, the scale and complexity of the actual world is easily overlooked.

Take some of the proposals for location-based, targeted mobile marketing: 'money-off' coupons and the like. The possibilities opened up by the technology seem very useful and potentially lucrative, and a whole range of applications have been suggested. Some examples, from an IBM researcher, give a flavor of the exciting drama we might all be involved in:

Notify a consumer as they enter a shopping center that an office supply store's back-to-school sale is over in two hours; ... Send tourists brief multimedia descriptions in the Washington, D.C. Mall as they enter each monument's surrounding area; ... Inform lottery players that they are close to the 'pot of gold at the end of the rainbow' and they should look for someone dressed as a leprechaun ... (Munson and Gupta, 2002)

Sounds convincing? Who would turn down the opportunity to receive such timely information, helping save (or win) money and to make the most of a visit? But how would you cope with the deluge of messages when every store, public authority and lottery-running organization can send you 'useful' information? Email spam will seem harmless by comparison, if there aren't easy-to-operate mechanisms for users to control the type, number and occurrence of such mobile interruptions. Such mechanisms will be a major usability challenge for the industry.

It is easy, too, to overlook the social, group effect of these notifications if you are simply imagining one user feeling pleased to have received a useful message. Take the blinkers off and visualize hundreds of people in a busy shopping mall all hearing about the last moments of a shop sale; a highly unpleasant, unfulfilling shopping experience is guaranteed for all as shoppers rush and converge on the store – not so much a case of a 'smartmob', more a smarting one.

On top of this problem of managing scale, add the issues of integrating these types of service into the other things a user is doing and wants to achieve. Imaginary users have nothing else to do except play a part in the system being envisioned – they are waiting for the designer's cues. So, in the mobile notification case, the assumption seems to be that users are keenly waiting for their next stage direction: "turn left now for a bargain!", "look up and see Abraham Lincoln", "There's the leprechaun!".

Real people might well have other things on their mind, like rushing through a shopping mall to pick up their children, or they might simply want peace to reflect on a visitor attraction. Next time you visit an art gallery, watch how some people stand for long periods in front of a painting, in awe and silence, then imagine a flurry of mobile 'educational' messages interrupting this peace.

The gap between fantasy and reality was also seen in a major magazine advertising campaign for a hi-spec phone during 2004. The glossy advert tells the story of how a father, away on a business trip, can still read stories to his children using the device. He sits in his hotel room, looks into his video phone, and his little ones at home watch him on another mobile while tucked up in bed on the other side of the planet.

Anyone with young children will immediately spot the limitations of such a vision. Putting aside the wisdom of entrusting a small child with an expensive handset – one of ours recently dunked a handset in a cup of milk – the technology does not supply what the child (and adult) really enjoys: close, physical contact. Cuddling, not content, is king.

You cannot imagine what your users will want to do – you have to keep a careful watch.

BOX 3.7 PICTURE PHONES AND PARENTS

Sam, a four-year-old, loves spending hours making complex constructions out of wooden blocks or Lego. When it was time to tidy up at the end of the day, there were always tears; he just could not bear to see his creations so quickly dismantled and put away. When his father bought a mobile phone with a built-in camera, things changed. One day, Sam said "Daddy, give me your phone, want to take a picture". Slightly bemused, Dad handed the phone over, set it to picture mode and watched as Sam carefully photographed his tower. "Look, Daddy, a picture", Sam happily said, "now we can take it down". No request was made to print or store the photo. Ever since, Sam has used the mobile to momentarily document his work.

A simple real-world example that illustrates how a designer's plotline falls apart is played out millions of times a day at major international airports around the world. With global roaming, when a passenger arrives in a new country, as soon as they turn on their phone they'll receive several messages welcoming them to the region and offering them networks to choose from. This 'service' can be extremely annoying when all you want to do is send a text message or place a quick call to tell friends you've arrived. After coping with the initial interruptions, heralded by a series of message arrival beeps, you may then need to spend a minute or so deleting messages now cluttering your device's message memory.

3.6 FRAMEWORKS FOR HUMAN-CENTERED THINKING

Psychologists have long been interested in what motivates people, identifying the activities that drive them. Similarly, any visit to a bookstore will confirm the ongoing popularity of books that discuss methods, habits and techniques for successful living.

Ben Shneiderman has drawn on these traditions to produce a framework to spot the sorts of future devices, applications and services people will want (Shneiderman, 2002). He strongly argues we all want to be creative, to be involved in transforming ourselves and others. His recommendation to technology innovators is to support these needs. He breaks this creative process down into four activities:

- Collecting (gathering information)
- Relating (communicating with others)
- Creating (innovating)
- Donating (disseminating the results of the creativity).

All of this creativity involves relating to others. Some of these relationships are close and personal (relating to oneself, family and friends), others are organizational (colleagues and neighbors), and there are large, societal interconnections too (citizens and markets).

Putting the activities and relationships together forms the ART, the Activities Relationship Table, a tool for generating human-focused technology ideas (see Table 3.1). You can use this table to generate ideas for candidate mobile products. For any square in the table, ask the familiar brainstorming questions of what, how, where, when and why. What might a person want to communicate to their friends and family? (Their mood, current activities, perhaps?) Why might someone want to remain in touch with a large group of people while mobile? (To check or make bids on an auction site, in the way a mobile service offered by eBay does, or to keep track of important developing new stories, for instance).

EXERCISE 3.3 USING ART TO GENERATE POTENTIAL MOBILE SERVICES

Using Shneiderman's ART framework:

- What information might you want to gather from the strangers you repeatedly see on your commutes to and from work, in the coffee-shop where you buy your ➤

TABLE 3.1

Mobile applications activities and relationships (adapted from Shneiderman, 2002)

Relationships	Activities			
	Collect information	Relate communication	Create innovation	Donate dissemination
Self	Reminders (capture things you want to follow up later – a book in a store, advert in the street)			
Family and friends		Find a friend (locate contacts in a city you are visiting)	Mobile blog (write notes, send photos to your personal diary)	
Colleagues and neighbors	Network effectively (pick up the contact details of groups of people you meet, quickly)	Info-doors (send messages to a digital display on your office door)		
Citizens and markets		Click-n-pay (m-commerce); on-the-go bidding (in online auctions when away from the desktop)		Tourist tips and recommendations (if that sought-after attraction is closed, let others know)

morning takeaway, or in the doctor's waiting room when you take your baby for its regular check-ups? How could this information be collected via mobile devices and what use might it be?

- Nokia launched a service in mid-2005 to allow users to create a sort of web page on their phone that other users in close proximity can view. Where would this application fit in Table 3.1? ■

Another framework for thinking through user needs is provided by usability consultants Aaron Marcus and Eugene Chen (Marcus and Chen, 2002). They suggest exploring different 'spaces' in which mobiles will have a role:

- Information (services ranging from weather reports to diary assistants)
- Self-enhancement (the mobile as a memory aid, health monitor, etc.)
- Relationships (with the device extending existing social interactions)
- Entertainment (services include games and music with an emphasis on short bursts of content)
- m-commerce (the e-coupons we mentioned earlier would fall into this category).

While taxonomies like ART help you think through design proposals from a human perspective, they are only a start to a process and certainly do not provide the guaranteed successful choices. Innovations need to be tested with real users, so use these thought-tools to begin the ideas-bubbling process and then build prototypes, evaluate and refine them (see Box 3.8).

BOX 3.8 MESSAGING TO YOUR OFFICE DOOR

One idea for linking mobiles to other information devices is the InfoDoor (Shneiderman, 2002). Place PDA-sized networked displays on office doors and allow the office owner and others to post messages remotely. These digital noticeboards might function either banally as electronic nameplates or in a more sophisticated way, for instance in displaying a message sent to tell visitors you're stuck in traffic.

While the idea is appealing, building and testing such proposals with actual users is vital if you want to uncover problems and understand nuances of use, as Keith Cheverst and his team discovered when they built the Hermes system at Lancaster University in the UK (Cheverst *et al.*, 2003). Every office door was given a message pad with messages sent via text message, email or a web interface. Visitors can also use the system to leave a message to the absent occupant; when this happens a text message is sent to the room owner's mobile phone prompting them to pick up the note via the web.

When the system was deployed in the trial, one problem was the users' perception of its reliability. On a number of occasions, room owners would send a text message only to discover later that it had not been delivered to their door. To strengthen trust in the system, the prototype is being modified to send a confirmation SMS back to the sender when their message has been successfully displayed on the door.

Skeptics might feel all this technology is overkill – why not just phone the departmental secretary and ask them to pin up a message? Cheverst's user test showed, however, that the system encouraged message sending that would not occur otherwise. Messages such as "in big q at post office ... will be a bit late" were seen as too unimportant to bother a secretary with, but could be quickly and easily sent from the mobile. ➤

The Hermes system also usefully illustrates the notion of viewing mobiles as just one of an ensemble of devices – a collection of things that work together to provide useful services. In contrast, some mobile manufacturers and network operators are jealously guarding their networks and devices. ■

BOX 3.9 TECHNOLOGY VERSUS USER-CENTERED DESIGN

Jesper Kjeldskov and Steve Howard have reported on an interesting attempt to compare technology and user-centered design approaches (Kjeldskov and Howard, 2004). They put together two teams each made up of interaction design researchers and industrial practitioners, engineers and students. The brief was for the teams to develop prototypes for a context-aware mobile system to promote and support the use of public transport in Melbourne, Australia.

One group used the classic user-centered approaches, immersing themselves in users' lives through interviews, field studies and the like; the other team took a strongly technology-driven approach, taking hardware features such as location sensing capabilities, and producing prototypes that made use of these.

The user-centered team produced a range of ideas, such as an MP3 player complemented with speech output to guide users to their destinations, and a foldable mobile office to be used while traveling by the city's trams. They then further developed one of the prototypes, called TramMate. This system gave users travel information linked to the appointments logged on their mobile. It could alert them when they had to depart to catch the tram, tell them how to get to tram stations based on their current location, and give other useful information such as travel times and route changes. The TramMate prototype was not a functional one; rather it was presented as a series of sketches.

The technology-driven group focused on exploiting the potential of GPS (for navigation) and GPRS (for data transmission). The working prototype they ended up with had some similarities with TramMate from a functional perspective, providing textual route descriptions and annotated maps based on the user's current location. However, the interface was very different: users had to look up tram timetable information manually as there was no link to their appointments diary, and updates to the information to reflect the user's change of location happened only when the user actively requested them.

In comparing the two outcomes, the user-centered approach was seen as very useful in producing prototypes that accommodated current practice and perceived needs as well as in envisioning some more radical concepts. However, the real-world usability and feasibility could not be easily tested. In contrast, the technology-centered ➤

strategy identified some of the technical constraints that would have to be addressed as well as providing a functional prototype that users could try out in realistic contexts. In doing this, usability and broader use issues were identified.

The study suggests that designers should combine technology with user-centered design methods in their attempts to envision future mobile services. ■

SUMMARY

Inspiration for new services can be spurred in several ways. Tracking technology evolutions, asking questions like "What novel experiences will this make possible?" and "How might the technology change the established ways of looking at communication, information access, social interactions, etc.?", is one way. Then there's history to draw on – looking at successful non-mobile applications, to consider which might transfer to the small screen, and analyzing existing mobile winners in an attempt to divine effective extensions. Design is not a mechanistic, clinical activity, and the role of the designer's imaginative flair should not be downplayed. But design should also not be purely an art, and there's the science of disciplines like psychology and sociology which can be applied in a generative way. However, each of the methods considered here has pitfalls.

Technology-centered approaches can lead to follies, with vast sums spent on providing a highly sophisticated service that no one wants. Failing to notice the differing requirements of a mobile context when looking to past applications is easy to do too. When we dream or imagine, we can quickly suspend the constraints and messy nuances of reality; what appears a great innovation might fail to scale, crumbling in the bright lights of our complex world. Finally, just as self-help books can only generalize about the human condition, providing starting points for readers to address their own problems, human-centered frameworks such as ART are springboards: their advice needs to be tested and refined by engaging with actual users.

WORKSHOP QUESTIONS

- Look in business and technology magazines (such as *The Economist* and *Wired Magazine*) and find examples of the ways new devices and services are marketed. Critique the storylines and characters being presented – does the innovation really fit? How would it scale? How could you improve on it?
- Shneiderman was inspired by Stephen Covey's *Seven Habits of Highly Effective People* (Covey, 1990) and Maslow's hierarchy of human needs. Visit a bookstore and select another of the

top-selling self-help books. What values and needs does it address? How might a mobile service be designed to accommodate these?

- Design a set of auditory tones (they could be auditory icons or earcons – flick back to Section 1.3.3 to remind yourself about the difference) that could communicate another user's mobile status. The application context is push-to-talk type services; the user presses a button to contact a friend or colleague and the system responds to give their status if not they are not available.

DESIGNER TIPS

- *Before transferring a successful service – like instant messaging – from desktop to the mobile, ask yourself how much of the service's appeal is dependent on its non-mobile context.*
- *When integrating a mobile with a desktop service, adopt the maxim 'everything, underwhelmingly'. That is, provide access to as much of the user's data as possible (and remember many mobiles will soon have vast on-board storage) but at the same time provide a small set of mobile-adapted tools to manipulate and view it. For a word-processing application, for example, users will want to annotate draft documents created on the desktop – the device might allow them to highlight text using a joystick and select from a set of predefined notes like 'follow-up' or 'unsure', or it could employ voice-notes. In terms of information access, automatically extracted summaries of previously viewed or available content will be important.*
- *When looking at previous mobile success stories, step back from the details of the service and look for the general qualities they embody. SMS is a winner because of the simple interaction model it uses, the satisfying sense of closure it gives (with a clear beginning, middle and end to the interaction), and the range of uses it can be put to.*
- *Brainstorming is clearly an important part of innovation. Let your imagination run free, and strive to change the world – people who communicate and relate better; improved understanding within and across organizations and cultures; greater access to the democratic process . . . Look to sociological insights into what drives people, what they hold dear. After each ideas-generating session, nominate one team member to be an enthusiast and another a skeptic: the enthusiast should talk up the proposal, thinking of extensions; the skeptic should focus on flaws, puncturing any unrealistic, over-positive groupthink.*

PART II
DEVELOPING EFFECTIVE MOBILE APPLICATIONS

CHAPTER 4	**INTERACTION DESIGN**	**93**
CHAPTER 5	**WATCHING, ASKING, PROBING**	**121**
CHAPTER 6	**PROTOTYPES**	**169**
CHAPTER 7	**EVALUATION**	**195**

CHAPTER 4
INTERACTION DESIGN

OVERVIEW

4.1. Introduction
4.2. Designing what? Designing how?
4.3. Understanding users
4.4. Developing prototype designs
4.5. Evaluation
4.6. Iterative development
4.7. Multiple viewpoints
4.8. From interaction design to deployment

KEY POINTS

- Interaction design creates a plan specifying the user needs in terms of required functionality, how this functionality is to be accessed and controlled, the presentation of content, system state, help and feedback information, and the way the system is to integrate with other resources in the user's context.
- This plan is used by software engineers as they code the application. It should influence broadly – from data structure design to screen layout planning.
- The process involves watching people in order to understand user needs, developing prototypes using design skills, guidelines and case studies, and being humble as these are evaluated and seen to fall short, and to need refining. Each of these activities will be carried out repeatedly.
- Users should be involved at all stages of the process. Identifying representative users of the services can be more difficult than in desktop system development.
- The interaction design team ideally should draw on a range of skill sets – computer science, marketing, graphic design, sociology and psychology are all important.

4.1 INTRODUCTION

Most of the approaches we've reviewed up to now are really focused on making things. A helpful view of the interaction design process is that it's about *making sense of things* (Dykstra-Erickson *et al.*, 2001). As we have seen, products 'make sense' to users when they do something useful, do it in harmony with the rest of the things in the user's life and have a well-articulated, strong identity.

The purpose of this chapter is to give an overview of the processes involved in interaction design, drawing out the common types of approach and technique. If you are already an interaction designer, some of what we say will be familiar, but do read on as there are additional considerations and strategies in the mobile context that we highlight. If you are new to the field, what follows is a nutshell description of the entire interaction design discipline, showing you how things fit together and relate to the wider development process. In the three chapters that follow, we will look in much more detail at how you might successfully deploy an interaction design process in mobile development; look out for pointers in this chapter to further details in the book.

4.2 DESIGNING WHAT? DESIGNING HOW?

What is this 'interaction' that's being designed? Well, it's not purely something the technology 'does' – the interactive facilities the device or service provides. Nor is interaction just a property of the people who use it – the ways they react to or perceive the system. Rather, it's about the relationship between the technology and users in the wide context that they are placed within.

In working towards an effective interaction design, you will be involved in three main types of activity:

- **Understanding users –** having a sense of people's capabilities and limitations; gaining a rich picture of what makes up the detail of their lives, the things they do and use.
- **Developing prototype designs –** representing a proposed interaction design in such a way that it can be demonstrated, altered and discussed.
- **Evaluation –** each prototype is a stepping stone to the next, better, refined design. Evaluation techniques identify the strengths and weaknesses of a design but can also lead the team to propose a completely different approach, discarding the current line of design thinking for a radical approach.

Clearly, there are many variations on these general phases (see, for example, Preece *et al.*, 2002). In the later chapters that look at the activities in detail, we will concentrate on the issues, approaches and case study examples that are most illuminating to the mobile context.

Each of these activities may well draw on some of the techniques touched on in the previous chapter. So in understanding users, you might consider using an emerging technology to provoke responses about future needs, and a starting point for new concept prototypes could be previously successful services.

Interaction design, though, is distinguished in two ways from other development methods. Firstly, in terms of the breadth of its vision: as we've said, it's not just about the technology or people, but about building infrastructure that will improve the way life is experienced and lived. Secondly, coming back down to earth, in order to live up to this ideal it's also about being completely grounded and guided by an understanding of the impact of design choices on people who will end up using the systems.

Unlike some of the other strategies, interaction design is also intensively participative and collaborative. That is, you will work with many different stakeholders – engineers, industrial designers and, crucially, representatives of the user community – all throughout the project.

It's also an evolutionary process – ideas will come, fail and fade, and be replaced by better and better proposals. You will learn that one design is never enough, and failing is a constructive rather than a destructive experience.

BOX 4.1 INTERACTION DESIGN DEFINED

At first glance, 'interaction design' might appear to be a modern, web-age replacement term for more familiar, decades-old terms such as 'usability engineering' and 'human–computer interaction'. In fact, though, it has been in use for quite some time – IDEO designers used it in a 1995 article, describing activities that had been going on for 10 years (Spreenberg *et al.*, 1995) – and it has a distinct set of concerns.

Giving a short, pithy definition of interaction design, though, is not easy. It's been used to describe activities involved in creating things from e-commerce websites to GPS navigators, and by people who come from a range of backgrounds including the arts, industrial design and marketing.

Jenny Preece, Yvonne Rodgers and Helen Sharp, in a textbook on the subject, define it this way:

... designing interactive products to support people in their everyday and working lives. (Preece *et al.*, 2002, p. 6)

Two key words in their definition are '*products*' and '*everyday*'. 'Products' reminds us that in many cases, the goal is to get consumers to buy the results – interaction designers do not just work on in-house, corporate core systems where the end-users have little choice but to take what they are given. 'Everyday' further emphasizes the broad remit – the products that designers envision will assist people to do all sorts of things that are important to them, like shop, care for their health, further educate themselves and pass leisure hours in pursuing a hobby.

For outsiders, and people starting to learn about interaction design, the danger is to see the activity as one concerned only with providing a 'skin' to the product – an activity performed only after the more important work of coding which constructs the skeleton and guts of a system. But, while apologizing for repeating ourselves, we stress that interaction design does not equal interface design. Interface design is about the 'statics' – screen layout, how you communicate content and system control information – like the scenery in a play. Do interaction designers need to address these things? ➤

Absolutely, but they come later. What's important upfront are the dynamics – first understanding the key needs of the user and then constructing the way the system cooperates with the user.

Continuing the play metaphor, interaction design is about the acting on the stage, how one scene moves to the next, the relationships between the central characters and the themes the playwright is trying to communicate. Shakespeare, in *As You Like It*, wrote: "All the world's a stage, And all the men and women merely players." It's not too fanciful to suggest that the job of an interaction designer is to create places for people to play out their lives (remembering to ensure these places and lives reflect reality and not fantasy); or, as Terry Winograd eloquently puts it, interaction design is about the construction of "the 'interspace' in which people live, rather than an 'interface' with which they interact" (Winograd, 1997). ■

4.3 UNDERSTANDING USERS

Anything you can learn about your users will help you produce better designs. Some of the knowledge you need is already out there – biologists, psychologists, sociologists and anthropologists have carried out many experiments and field studies, providing useful insights into what humans can do and cope with. We'll be bringing together some of the most important findings specifically for mobiles in several of the chapters that follow. You'll also need to go and carry out your own first-hand investigations, doing field studies, running focus groups, and performing interviews. (Chapter 5 explores the range of approaches in detail.)

4.3.1 FROM BIOLOGY TO PSYCHOLOGY

A few years ago, a UK private healthcare organization ran a TV advert detailing some of the incredible complexities and abilities of a human body: the number of times the heart beats in a lifetime, the number of neuron connections in the brain, the reaction times in danger. The advert ended with the slogan 'you are amazing'.

Developing a design attitude that considers users as 'amazing' is much healthier than some of the ideas that have tended to dominate interactive technology developments in the past: users have been seen at best as simple folk who need things to be made 'friendly' or 'easy'; at worst as characters full of 'weaknesses', like vagueness, illogicality and emotion (Norman, 1994).

If you know what makes people 'amazing', even at the basic biological level, your mobile design choices can be better informed. Developers of the tactile interfaces we encountered in Chapter 1, for example, are exploiting the human skin's ability to perceive very rapid stimulations.

You also need to get beneath the skin, understanding what goes on inside your user's head when they interact. This sort of knowledge comes from cognitive psychology, a science focused on mapping out how humans process and respond to the world. Cognitive psychologists have developed theories addressing lots of aspects relevant to system design, like visual processing, human memory and learning.

Let's consider, as an example, knowledge of human short-term or working memory. This memory is the mental piece of scrap paper we use as we complete our goals. Experiments have shown that this memory is small – it can store something of the order of five to seven chunks of information – and it rapidly decays.

While such facts are interesting in themselves, how are they relevant to an interaction designer? Such insights can be particularly helpful when making specific design choices at a detailed level. So, if you didn't appreciate the limitations of short-term memory, you might produce a design that overloads the user; when this happens, people make mistakes. Take menu-based voice interfaces for telephone systems, in which a remote system speaks a series of options and the user responds with key presses. If you give users too much to think about, in terms of either the number of options or the process of selection ("press 1 to forward, 9 to delete, 3 to play, ..."), they will forget choices and make incorrect selections.

EXERCISE 4.1 DESIGN FOR THE ELDERLY

In many of the main markets for mobiles, populations are aging with life expectancy increasing. While the current generation of older people might not be attracted by advanced mobile services, future older users (including you!) who have grown up with the technology might be an important segment of the market. However, little work has yet been done on design for this group.

- What distinct attributes should be accommodated when designing for this group?
- Take a mobile interface you are familiar with (e.g. the main options menu on your phone) and critique its design with respect to the needs of older users. Then, show the interface to an elderly person and ask them to comment on it. Compare their remarks with your critique.

Comments: you should consider both physical and cognitive attributes. For example, vision might be impaired, dexterity reduced, and memory less able. There are also issues relating to leisure time (this group has more), disposable income (usually less, though in some cases considerably more), and key concerns (family, status quo, health and security, for instance). ■

4.3.2 FIELD STUDIES

Understanding general human characteristics is important, but getting to know your particular group of users is vital. To do this, you can use a set of techniques to observe and probe the people and situations of interest.

In human-watching terms, no-one gets closer to the action than an anthropologist. Being an anthropologist is about being completely immersed in a community, often spending a large amount of time with the group being studied. The aim is to document the detail of the way the group is organized, relates and develops.

For interaction design, a branch of anthropology called ethnography has been gaining prominence for some time; initially the techniques were used to study complex work practices like air traffic control, but they are highly applicable to mobile design.

The anthropologist has become a must-have employee of many companies:

... corporate anthropology is now mainstream, particularly among technology firms. Indeed, when he was informed that IBM Research had hired Ms Blomberg as its first anthropologist in December 2002, Paul Saffo of the Institute for the Future exclaimed "Just now? How embarrassing." (*Economist*, 2004a)

Ethnographic methods focus on producing an account of what is going on in real situations by observing the moment-by-moment behavior of people interacting with others and their environment over extended periods of time. The ethnographer collects first-hand, eyewitness evidence of how people do their work or leisure in the actual setting, rather than in artificial environments such as a laboratory or focus-group interview room.

Just how immersed and intense studies can get is highlighted by Allison Woodruff and Paul Aoki's report on their study into the use of push-to-talk mobile phones (Woodruff and Aoki, 2003). Woodruff lived with four of the participants and joined them in many of their social and work activities for a week. She eavesdropped on conversations (audible through the phones' loudspeakers), recorded over 50 hours of conversations and ended up with a corpus of over 70 000 words of dialog between the participants.

Such intense effort is immensely rewarding. After a period of observation, you come back full of anecdotes and an overview of the field setting. You'll have many 'a-ha' moments when things suddenly make sense. You can also give some authentic reactions to design proposals the team generates; you know what it's like to be the user (Button and Dourish, 1996).

One way to understand the ethnographic process, and the way it links into the bigger design process, is to think of front-line war reporters and studio news anchor people. The ethnographer is the war reporter; the design team members, back at home, are the news anchors.

Reporters have to respond to spontaneous 'live' questioning by news anchors, but they also need to be able to step back and provide a considered overview of the situation for viewers. So, the ethnographer's job is to portray the action in a vividly colorful way both in responding to design team questions and by providing an account resulting from careful reflection.

As Button and Dourish note, the activity is less one of data collection and more of a writing-up, presenting descriptions and explanations of what was observed. As an interaction designer you will be well aware of the need to involve the user, but relying only on their subjective rationalizations of their behavior probably won't give a full account of the situation. The explanations they offer might well be influenced by what they think you want to hear, or what they would like to believe about themselves. Your job, then, is to provide objectivity out of subjectivity. You will be fully involved with people, watching them, talking to them, looking at the documents and other artifacts they use, meanwhile stepping back and asking "what does all this action mean?".

While ethnography is a core, field-study activity, as we will see in the next chapter there are other in-situ methods you can use.

BOX 4.2 REPORTING AND ACCOUNTING: MOBILES AND GENDER

Finding out how people view mobile technology is an important part of innovating new, successful designs. But as well as being immersed in the users' world, as an investigator you need to be able to go beyond what users tell you. As an example of the mix of reporting, analyzing and accounting that goes on in ethnographic-type investigations, take some comments from Sadie Plant on mobile use and gender (Plant, 2001). The first paragraph is straight reporting; in the other two, she steps back and offers some insights on what she's seen, too.

A number of males also confessed to being inhibited when their companions displayed mobiles of higher specification or aesthetic quality than their own. Others said they had been keen to display their mobiles while they were top-of-the-range or state-of-the-art, but had stopped doing so when their models fell behind.

It was also observed that 60% of lone women had a mobile on show. ... Many women saw this reflecting their own experience of the mobile as a valuable means of keeping unwanted attentions at bay. A mobile projects an image of self-containment, and can even legitimize solitude: I'm not alone, I'm with my mobile phone.

While the public display of a mobile phone is often a matter of fashion, style, covert social messages and hidden agendas, it should also be remembered that it is a functional device whose display is nothing more than a practical need to keep it at hand. ... Many western men tend to carry their mobiles in their pocket or hand. ... Arab women prefer robust models which can survive life in voluminous handbags. ■

4.3.3 DIRECT QUESTIONING

During the field studies, it's likely you will gently prod your users, using techniques like the unstructured interview, where you ask broad, open-ended questions, but it is important not to disrupt and influence too much what you are observing.

There will be times, though, when you will want to be a little more intrusive. You might want to call in some users and interview them, or get them together in focus-group style discussions. These sessions can then be used in three ways:

- To validate your impressions and interpretations from the field
- To help piece together the disparate field observations
- To gain additional information on situations and time periods when you just could not be present in the field.

For mobile interaction design, the out-of-field techniques are particularly important. Ethnography in fixed locations is easier than in situations where mobile technology is used. The ethnographer can make a camp in the workplace, for instance, and get comprehensive access to many of the things they need to study; all the action is out in the open.

When everything really is in the open and out-and-about, things become harder. People will be using mobiles, or doing things that could benefit from a mobile service, when they are in the street, or traveling away from their own workplace, or having lunch on a park bench. Although desirable, it is impossible to be with these mobile users all the time, in every place they go. Furthermore, if you are studying a fixed situation, like a workplace or home, there's a background that stays relatively stable, and you can focus on dynamics; with mobiles, all the changes of scene can camouflage the key activities you need to understand.

4.3.4 DISTILLING THE FINDINGS

For all of the effort in the field studies and other user explorations to pay off, the results need to be made palatable for the next stages of design. Accounts, then, must be written up using language that the rest of the design team can understand, rather than being more appropriate for a scholarly, sociological seminar or journal.

One way that findings can be made to come alive is to give them skin and bones, creating believable characters (called personas) and writing stories (called scenarios) about what these characters do, and where and how they do it. Unlike the completely fictitious, imagined users and storylines discussed in the previous chapter, these are documentary-type characters, grounded in reality.

There are also more engineering-flavored tools for representing users' key activities. These include methods, like hierarchical task analysis, that attempt to identify a user's goals and then present the activities needed to achieve these in a structured way, from the top (main activities) downwards (sub-activities, sub-sub-activities and so on).

4.4 DEVELOPING PROTOTYPE DESIGNS

Armed with ethnographic accounts, personas, scenarios and other characterizations of the users and their needs, constructive design can begin.

4.4.1 SHAPING AND MANAGING THE DESIGN SPACE

At every step of the design process, from coming up with an innovative mobile concept through to the detailed specification of how, say, service availability information is presented to the user, the number of possible design options can be vast. Many of the potential solutions will be poor, many others just sufficient; but there will be a small number of potentially excellent ones, the proposals you need to unearth and polish.

So the challenge is to prune this enormous design space so you can focus on the best. A good way of doing this is to assess every proposal against the real-world insider knowledge gained from the sorts of approaches outlined above. Scenarios, personas and task analysis representations can all act as a form of designer consciousness. They can speak the uncomfortable words of criticism, prompting you to confront aspects of the design that jar with what's known about the context you are designing for. *Would your characters really want that feature? When would they use that service?*

BOX 4.3 DESIGN STARTING POINTS

Some guidelines are about shaping your attitude toward or your perspective on design; others are more to do with helping you decide the shape of controls or widgets. To illustrate the range of advice available, consider the following design pointers.

- **Design for truly direct manipulation.** Direct manipulation revolutionized the desktop experience. The blinking command line cursor was replaced by a graphical interface where the user could point and click, drag and drop. These are successful not only because they make the functionality of the system visible, reducing load on short-term memory, but also because their mode of operation fits well with people's desire to interact and manipulate the world in direct, tangible ways.
  - The user experience of GUIs on a desktop, though, does not really come close to the sorts of direct manipulation we carry out daily in the world. We touch, pick up, examine, place and even throw objects. Mobiles of the future could offer a far richer experience; as Hiroshi Ishii puts it, we could ''turn the world itself into an interface'' (Ishii and Ullmer, 1997).
  - *Direct combination*, for example, has been proposed as a means for hyper-direct manipulation (Holland *et al*., 2002). Point at an object – say a document – with your mobile to select it; point to another object – say yourself – and the document is automatically emailed to you.
  - Alternatively, simply allow the user to see their body as part of the interface (this has been termed 'embodied interaction'). Already there are simple consumer products demonstrating this approach – take Sony's Playstation EyeToy, for example, with gamers using hand gestures and other body movements to interact with the software.
- **Design for ecological use.** Recognize that the user will have other resources to hand as well as their mobile – from documents to signposts, from landmarks to desktop computers. Consider ways of using these resources – for example, how could mobiles be used to capture information relating to the physical world around them and then use this to access information resources?
- **Design for maximum impact through minimum user effort.** Many usability guides encourage designers to keep things simple. However, it is easy to turn this advice into tedious, limited and banal designs. As we will see in Chapters 8 and 10, though, it is possible to have engaging, flexible interaction frameworks which are still simple for the user to understand and use. ➤

- **Design for personalization.** Mobiles are personal technologies – users develop a greater sense of attachment to them than to other computing devices they encounter. Devices and services should allow users to adapt and personalize them both in terms of their look (note the popularity of altering ringtones and screensavers on phones) and functionally, setting up menu options, etc.
- **Design for play and fun.** Users will appreciate the opportunity to have fun with their mobile. Fun involves a sense of enjoyment, pleasure, looseness and lighthearted-ness. To enhance the fun in your design, consider, for example, alluring metaphors, compelling content, attractive graphics, appealing animations and satisfying sound (Shneiderman, 2004).
- **Design for one-handed use.** Often, preferred use will be one-handed (even for devices that offer two-handed use). Even when there are other options available (e.g. stylus) it is worth designing as if only one-handed use is possible, as this can force you to focus on direct, simple designs (Nikkanen, 2003). ■

Another way to reduce the seemingly overwhelming set of design possibilities is to draw on the past experience of others. Large numbers of guidelines already exist to point toward effective design choices: most focus on non-mobile systems (but are still often applicable); some deal more directly with mobile issues.

One sort of guideline provides high-level advice; these are design ideals or principles that will help you question the fundamental roles of mobile services and the way these services should be delivered. We saw some of these thought-provoking questions in Chapter 1 when we explored what mobiles could or should be. Other designer aids are much more directed – for example, many mobile platform developers have written interface-style guides (see Box 4.4 for two example excerpts). The International Standards Organization has also been actively involved; adhering to their advice can not only improve the user's experience but also enhance the credibility of your designs as well as the process pursued in developing them (Bevan, 2001).

BOX 4.4 PLATFORM DESIGN GUIDELINES

Many mobile platform and product developers have published user interface guidelines on the web. Below are two extracts; in the *Resources* section at the end of the book we give a list of URLs to others.

Extract from the UIQ (User Interface platform for Symbian devices) guide for menu presentation:

- Make the text for menu commands as short as possible. ➤

- Use an ampersand (**&**) rather than the word **and**.
- Use dividers to group similar menu commands together, and to separate them from commands that are unrelated but appear on the same menu. Don't overuse them. If you're starting from the menu layout below, a useful rule of thumb is that you should add no more than one extra divider.
- Do **not** use ellipses (...) to indicate commands that lead to dialogs. This is another simplification in UIQ. A menu command is a menu command, whether it leads to instant action or a dialog.
- ...
- The **Delete** menu command should always be the final command on the application menu, separated from other commands by a divider. Change the *command type* to reflect the type being displayed, e.g. **Delete contact** or **Delete message**. (Symbian)

Extract from the Microsoft Smartphone menu guide:
On Windows Mobile-based PocketPCs, a pop-up menu displays additional commands for a screen item. The pop-up menu appears when a user taps and holds the stylus on the screen item. If the user taps any other area of the screen, the pop-up menu disappears.
Consider the following when you include pop-up menus in an application:

- Where possible, display the pop-up menu to the right of and below the screen item.
- In general, commands on the pop-up menu should also be available from menus and buttons on the menu bar. For more information, see Menu Bars.
- To minimize stylus movement, list commands from top to bottom in order of expected frequency of use.
- Actions that are difficult to recover from, such as delete, should be placed at the bottom of the pop-up menu. (Microsoft, b) ■

In terms of managing the design space, you have to cope with the dual nature of the interaction design process. First, design can be a very fast-paced, energetic activity. You will often find yourself in participative, collaborative sessions with groups of people coming at the issues from different viewpoints – marketers, software engineers, end-users – with the ideas flowing freely. Whiteboards will be filled with colorful sketches; flipchart papers will be rapidly written on, torn off and placed round the room; and Post-it notes will be doodled on and stuck onto some other design artifact.

In such an environment, it's very easy to overlook a good proposal, or to lose the design history – the steps you took and the reasoning you went through to get to your design. There are a number of techniques, called design rationale methods, that can help capture the designs and the thinking behind them as the design progresses (see Exercise 4.2) (MacLean *et al.*, 1989).

The second face of design is far more introverted – design at times is a very quiet, considered process. The documents you generate during the exciting, creative sessions are used as the basis for reflection. Away from the dynamic environment of collaborative sessions, alone or with others – a user or another design team member – you can review the rationale behind the current designs. *Are they really well founded? Is there enough detail for the next phase? What about that initial design we rejected – perhaps it does have some merits?*

EXERCISE 4.2 DESIGN RATIONALE

QOC is a design rationale method (MacLean *et al.*, 1989). Its three elements are:

- **Questions**: key design challenges
- **Options**: potential answers or solutions to the questions
- **Criteria**: ways of assessing the alternatives.

The analysis is presented graphically with lines drawn between the options and criteria. A solid line indicates a positive connection (option satisfies criterion) while a dotted one signals a negative assessment (option does not satisfy connection). Figure 4.1 shows a partial analysis for a mobile weather service question. Complete it by specifying options and drawing lines between these and the given criteria.

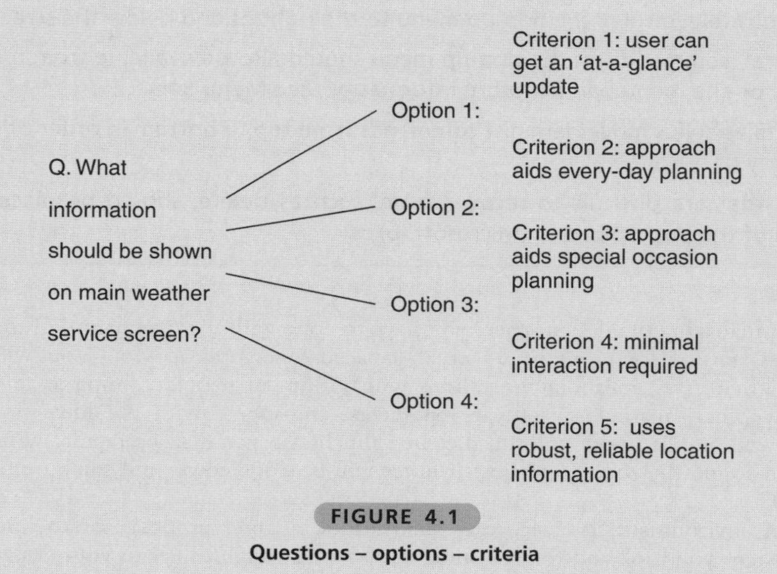

FIGURE 4.1

Questions – options – criteria

Comments: in thinking about options, accommodate both the location(s) and time periods the user may be interested in. Think too about supplementary detail that is not shown on the main screen but accessible from it. ■

4.4.2 PROTOTYPING

It's easy to think you have a good idea, fully formed and clear, while it's still just in your head. When you try to write it down, though, you will often find it hard to express your thoughts in a simple way. Usually, the problem is twofold: there are conceptual weaknesses with the ideas and they need time to mature; and you need to experiment and refine how you articulate your thoughts.

Drafting out a document can help you with your thinking and improve the way your ideas are expressed. Some people don't like showing early drafts of their work to others; they want to perfect it before exposing it – and themselves – to an audience. But early and repeated feedback from others is a sound way of working toward a better final document.

Interactive system prototyping is like document drafting. The purpose of a prototype is to pin down the design team, to make them articulate their proposals in forms that can be used and reviewed by others. Prototypes are the fuel of interaction design – vital in driving the progress, in generating and improving ideas and in involving people. Indeed, Daniel Fallman argues persuasively that prototyping – what he calls sketching – is the archetypal design activity, the core process that allows a designer to understand the problem and frame a solution (Fallman, 2003).

BOX 4.5 WHAT IS DESIGN?

Daniel Fallman reviews alternative perspectives on design, identifying three main standpoints (Fallman, 2003):

- As a scientific process (the 'conservative account')
- As an art form (the 'romantic account')
- As an ad-hoc activity, as he puts it 'a bustle with reality' ('the pragmatic account').

As a designer, you might then see yourself as one or more of the following:

- A scientist or engineer who works progressively from a set problem toward solutions, using guidelines, design knowledge and a scientific, rational approach
- A creative genius, an artist who mysteriously or mystically brings a product to life, using your craft knowledge and imagination, inspired by art, music, poetry and drama
- A '*bricoleur*', a person who tinkers toward a solution, using tools and materials to hand, engaging with the situation (a thoughtful 'hacker', if you will).

Fallman argues that none of these accounts is adequate on its own. He presents a helpful notion of design as an 'unfolding', where the problem and solution are not seen as separate but evolve through a process of 'sketching' (prototyping). ■

Prototyping needs to start early in the design process and continue throughout. There are all sorts of ways that prototypes can be presented – from a paper sketch to functional, computer-based ones which users can interact with (Svanaes and Seland, 2004). Particularly in the early stages of design, it's important to steer clear of focusing on the final system implementation. Thinking about implementation too early can reduce design quality in two ways:

- Good proposals can be stifled by a resistance to any design that might not be fully implementable in the development environment – cries of "it can't be done!" from your software engineer colleagues. In reality, even when there are technical limitations, it is often possible to code up the essence of a great implementation-independent idea.
- Looking to the implementation can also lead to a low-level mindset of making the widget shape the focus, rather than the relationships between a user's action and the system's reaction. This is a bit like a house builder trying to position light switches before the room's beams are fitted together.

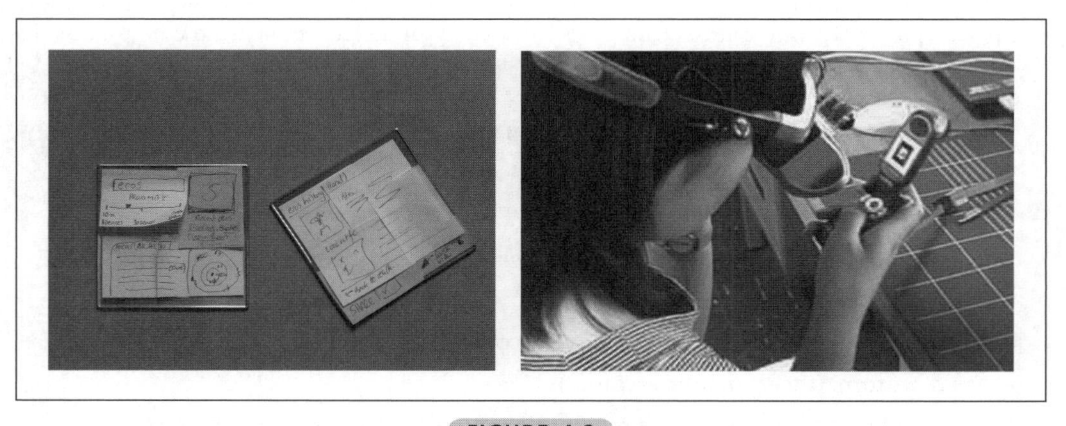

FIGURE 4.2

Examples of mobile prototypes

Left: paper-based prototype for a peer-to-peer local search application. Right: contrasting with this is a physical working prototype where the user interacts with the handset and views results on the device's 'screen' via a head-mounted display (Nam and Lee, 2003)

While you should keep away from implementation considerations as long as possible, that does not mean that every prototype should not be as realistic as possible. The comments you get from your users will be about the specific prototype you show them, the reactions and suggestions being very much driven by its actual form and features. For mobiles, this desire to produce prototypes with realism is driving some innovative new prototyping techniques, as we'll see in Chapter 6.

4.5 EVALUATION

Prototypes, however simple, are there to be judged. As design proposals emerge, they need to be assessed to see whether they achieve what they set out to achieve. A big part of this process involves asking users to evaluate them, but there are other, less costly techniques for gaining rapid feedback on what works and what is likely to cause user problems. Again we give below a flavor of what's involved, and talk more about issues and methods later (see Chapter 7).

4.5.1 TESTING WITH USERS

Standard, conventional testing practice – for the kind of interactive system you have on your desktop – involves bringing representative users to a usability testing facility, presenting them with a prototype and asking them to complete some specific tasks. Their completion times, their accuracy and the sorts of errors they make are all recorded for later analysis.

This quantitative data might be compared with the performance seen in competing designs in order to work out which of the proposals is best. Alternatively the design can be judged against some prior performance levels set by the team (e.g., "the average completion time should be 20 seconds", or "from out-of-the-box to network-connected should take no more than 5 minutes"). Users' subjective responses, the things they say about the system, can also be scrutinized; these qualitative insights can further help shed light on what works and what doesn't.

But are usability labs and conventional testing approaches really appropriate for mobiles? Surely only on-the-move, in-the-wild evaluations are useful? While such streetwise evaluation methods are essential, a conventional usability laboratory can still be very effective. There will be many details of a design that are best explored in isolation from the distractions of the real world where the mobile will eventually be used. Take the case of a project to develop a wearable mobile for service technicians (see Figure 4.3). Lab-based experiments were used to find the smallest usable size for buttons on the touch screen panel; it turned out to be 0.3 square inches (Fallman, 2002).

There will also be cases where it will pay to use a lab to assess the relative advantages of a series of potential designs before embarking on a more costly field-trial. For example, researchers who

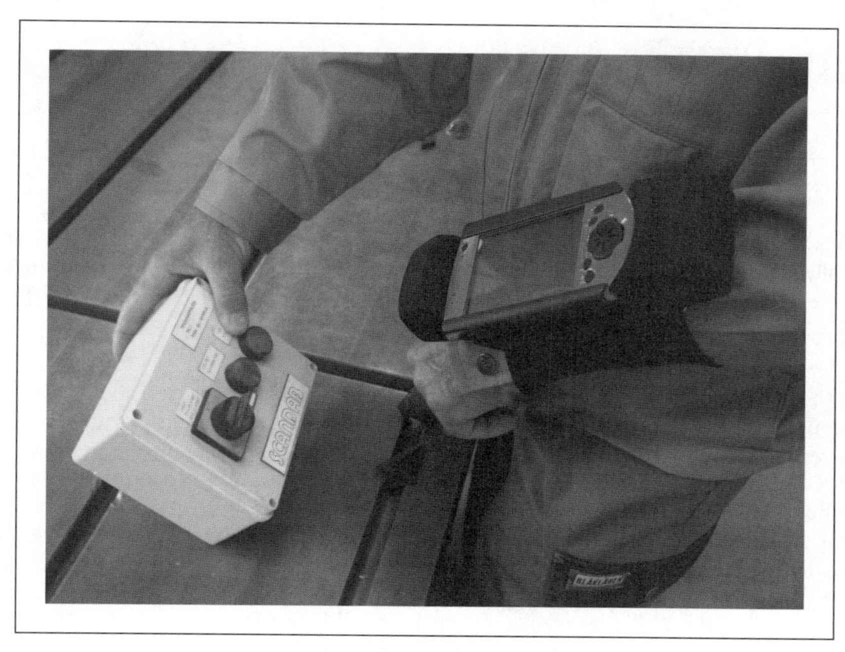

FIGURE 4.3

Mobile wearable for service technicians (Fallman, 2002)

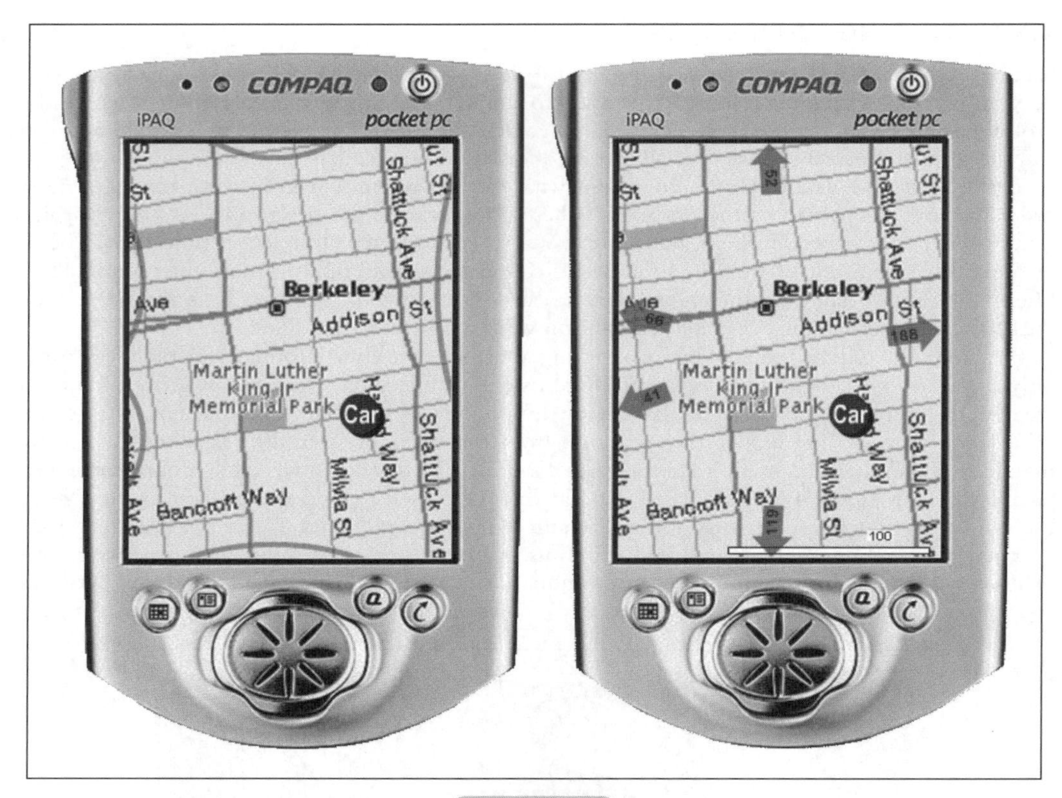

FIGURE 4.4

Haloes for better map navigation (Baudisch and Rosenholtz, 2003)
The Halo technique (left) was compared experimentally to an alternative design (right). Haloes graphically indicate both direction of target and distance, with closer targets being represented by smaller arcs. The alternative approach uses arrows combined with numeric indication of distance. The Halo approach led to time savings of 16–33%

developed the Halo technique – a method for giving mobile users information about the proximity of landmarks on a map (see Figure 4.4) – used conventional, controlled scientific methods. A handheld display was emulated and presented to users on a desktop computer screen; the performance of the design was compared with another prototype that gave less sophisticated landmark hints (Baudisch and Rosenholtz, 2003).

You will, however, almost certainly want to see how users cope with your proposed mobile in realistically demanding situations. Taking this to the extreme, Jason Pascoe and colleagues studied the use of a PDA-based wildlife tracking system for ecologists in Africa: these users interacted with the system, recording their observations while close to wild animals (Pascoe *et al.*, 2000). How your users really cope with the system while in the wild, surrounded – be it by animals or cars – amidst the heat of the day, or the cold of an early city morning, will be rather different from their reactions while sitting comfortably in a softly furnished test suite.

There are other challenges for mobile evaluations (Thomas and Macredie, 2002). While it's easy to measure performance in terms of time, how do you measure attributes like 'unobtrusiveness' or the device's effectiveness at providing 'ambient awareness'? Think too about study duration: typical lab-based studies last between 15 minutes and an hour, but you might be interested in how your users adapt and adopt your services over much longer periods. In one six-week mobile phone study, for instance, people's perceptions of mobile services favorably improved over the period of the study (Palen and Salzman, 2002). To help track such changes, the researchers used a voicemail diary, encouraging participants to phone in and record their thoughts on the service, and rewarding them one US dollar for every comment.

4.5.2 TESTING IN THE ABSENCE OF USERS

Regardless of whether they are brought into the lab, or followed in the field, involving users is costly – it takes up your and their time, and you often have to pay them to participate. Some evaluation techniques do not need a user to be present and can provide rapid insights into the design qualities.

Scott MacKenzie demonstrates, for example, the usefulness of analytical models in determining the efficiency of different text entry methods for mobile devices (MacKenzie, 2002). He shows how to calculate the KSPC (key strokes per character), which is the average number of basic input actions, such as touching a key – like a mobile phone button, for instance – or gesturing with a pen-like stylus, needed to enter a text character. We won't explain here how the calculation is made; the point is that while these sorts of model approaches do not replace user testing, they can cut down wasteful repeated studies. As MacKenzie puts it, "... potential text entry techniques can undergo analysis, comparison and redesign prior to labor-intensive implementations and evaluations."

In passing, if you interested in text-entry efficiency, it is worth looking at the KSPC for a range of common entry mechanisms, as shown in Table 4.1. As MacKenzie notes, it is likely that the methods with the lowest KSPC – the least effort for users – will give the best throughput of characters; from his results, then, the best approach is the unistroke method (gestures with a stylus) used together with word-level prediction.

TABLE 4.1

Keystrokes per character (KSPC) comparison of text entry methods (adapted from MacKenzie, 2002). The smaller the value of KSPC, the more efficient the input technique

Interaction technique	KSPC
Multi-tap	2.0342
T9	1.0072
QWERTY	1
Word prediction (keypad, $n = 10$)*	0.8132
Word prediction (keypad, $n = 2$)	0.7086
Word prediction (stylus, $n = 10$)	0.5000

*n is the number of alternative word options displayed in schemes that use word prediction.

In addition to model-based, performance-predictive schemes, other popular non-user based testing methods include the heuristic review where the design is checked against good design rules-of-thumb, and the expert-based review where someone who has lots of experience in designing mobile interactions uses their knowledge of what works to spot weaknesses in the design (see Box 4.6).

BOX 4.6 EXPERT INSIGHTS

An interview with Scott Jenson, Head of Jenson Design (a product design consultancy) and former director of product design at Symbian

MJ: How did you get into mobile design?

SJ: I was working for Apple and had the chance to be on the Newton concept. Then, when I moved to London, I knew I just had to get into the mobile phone area as that's where all the exciting design was – and is – going on. So, I ended up leading the DesignLab, working on projects such as the QUARTZ, which turned into the interface for devices like the Sony Ericsson P800 and P900.

MJ: What did the DesignLab do?

SJ: There was a lot of usability testing and design refinement. So, we had three full-time people whose job was to create functional prototypes using Macromedia Director; then we'd review, user-test and change these designs. Sometimes this included taking the prototypes to different countries to see how they worked, or not, with a broad range of people. We'd also work on trying to define new concepts for mobile interaction and services and in these cases we'd think more about the design semantics.

MJ: 'Semantics'?

SJ: Yes, design is about semantics and syntax. First, you need to see what people do and what they want – the semantics – and then you have to find a way of making this possible – the syntax. I was involved in thinking about lots of early WAP services; the trouble was that the industry in general focused on and promoted a sort of syntax-focused design; worse still, lots of the offerings had many syntax errors, with users having to carry out many steps just to get a simple piece of information.

MJ: In doing all these activities within a fast-paced, commercial environment, what did you learn about design?

SJ: Well, first, design needs to know its place. It's not the only thing that's needed for a successful product – functionality, price, marketing, fashion, brand: lots of things have ➤

a major impact too. As part of this 'team player' attitude, you have to accept that design is the art of compromise.

MJ: Can you give some examples of this pragmatic approach?

SJ: It comes in all sorts of forms. So, take the Sony Ericsson P800/P900 – we wanted to build a device that was a PDA and phone combined. Now Palm already had a very successful UI concept that really worked, but we couldn't over-copy this as we wanted a distinct but also effective interface. Then, there were the rapid changes and additions to the platforms we were working with – so, we started with one set of devices in mind and then a company came along with another platform with a smaller display and a jog-wheel instead of a stylus. And, of course, when the design goes into production there are lots of times when something just can't be done given the time and technical constraints; as a designer you then need to work with the engineers to try and retain as much of your idea as possible. So, for example, on a phone platform we worked on, for technical reasons, we had to have a 'sync' folder for email synchronized with the desktop client, and an 'inbox' for messages received when mobile. What we actually wanted was a single view of the 'inbox' combining all the user's mail; so, we had to produce a 'hack' with a process that read mail from both sources and put it in a third on the device.

MJ: How did the DesignLab work to be what you've called a 'team player' within the company?

SJ: Design is an inherently social process. From the very start we'd ensure we had buy-in from key groups – our initial brainstorm sessions would, for instance, include software engineers. Then, when we produced the final design, before the development began, we'd draw up a 'design manifesto' spelling out our interaction concept in terms of purpose, functionality, marketing and the like, and get this signed off by a 'champion' from marketing, the technical team and the DesignLab.

MJ: Now that you've moved into independent consulting, what sorts of approach do you get from potential clients?

SJ: A whole range. The classic case is a company that phones you up and says "we've got two weeks to ship, can you look at the icons". At the other end of the extreme, I'll be asked to generate 'blue-skies' concepts for future services.

MJ: When you're shown concepts or designs, how do you assess them?

SJ: First, I'll be asking "what's the value of this?" – that is, will people really want it? Take the iPod music player. It's really easy to articulate what the value is – "it lets me take all my music with me"; compare that with mobile Instant Messaging – "it allows ➤

me to be online and show you my availability if I've set it''. So, a quick test is to try and sum up the value in one sentence. Next, I assess it from my strong belief in simplicity. I was looking at a service recently that had all sorts of functionality with many, many nested menus. I sat down with the design team and tried to figure out the three key things that people wanted to do; then we hid all the rest of the functionality for the power users.

MJ: When you see UI 'bugs' in the systems, how do you help companies work on them?

SJ: First, you need to judge how important the bug is. Some usability people can be too pedantic and perfectionist: if you look at any mobile, you'll find lots and lots of problems, but not all of them will have a noticeable impact on the users' experience. One technique I use is to think in terms of a 'red card' (this bug needs sorting out) and a 'yellow card' (it's a problem, but a lower-priority one). Once you've spotted the problems, it depends how near to shipping the product is – if it's late, then quick hacks, help text and manuals can be a fix until version 2; if it's early on, you then need to persuade the developers why change is needed. ■

4.6 ITERATIVE DEVELOPMENT

One of the first software development models to be developed was called the Waterfall Model (Royce, 1970). As water leaps off a ledge it falls quickly downwards, dragged inexorably to the base; similarly in the waterfall software model, development flows top-downwards, the system design moving from the abstract to the implementation through a series of well-defined phases. As each phase is completed it is 'signed off' and the next is commenced.

With interaction design there are some dependencies between the activities outlined in the previous sections. So it would be unwise to attempt to generate scenarios, the stories of use, before you have been immersed in the users' world, for instance; and evaluation can obviously happen only after there is something to evaluate.

However, design is certainly not a case of following a simple checklist, moving with certainty from problem to solution. The design process does not proceed in a one-way, clear-cut fashion. Rather, many prototypes are built, designs being formed and reformed over and over again. Your skills in understanding users' needs and your ability to shape and manage the design space, as well as your prototyping and evaluation expertise, may all be needed as each new design emerges.

In many of the projects we've worked on, then, the development process has proceeded thus. First, we do some ethnography and other types of in-situ study. Back at the office, we sift through our observations, extracting themes and issues. We call in users to interview, cross-checking with what we found earlier, and we return to the field to do more focused studies, guided by the initial fieldwork. Next come some prototypes that we take back to the field and put in the hands of potential users, both to check our assumptions and to further draw out possible opportunities and needs (the prototypes here thus acting as a fact-finding tool). More prototypes follow which are critiqued by us, other expert designers and users back at the lab. We usually develop a couple of competing proposals and get them to a status that allows them to be evaluated in a controlled test.

After refining the 'winning' system further, we might then deploy it in the field to see how it performs in context over time.

Although this oversimplifies the case a little, engineering and interaction design differ in the way they approach problems and solutions. In engineering, the aim is to take a clearly defined problem – say a bridge that can withstand gale-force winds and heavy vehicles – to produce an effective, robust, stress-tested solution. As an interaction designer, though, you will often find yourself trying to form a view about what the problem actually is as much as producing the solution. As designs develop you might well experience self-doubt, needing to reassess your certainties about what your users value, leading you to go back to further field observations, for example.

4.7 MULTIPLE VIEWPOINTS

Interaction design is a stimulating and demanding job. Part of the interest, and some frustration, results from the need to employ diverse techniques, to accommodate discordant attitudes and viewpoints, and to actively involve people with differing backgrounds and sets of skills.

4.7.1 MANY TECHNIQUES AND TOOLS

The previous sections present a sketch of the design process. In all of the main activities, there is a wide range of design techniques that can be used; Table 4.2, adapted from Dykstra-Erickson *et al.* (2001), gives a feel for the diversity of options available. At least three factors will influence the choice of methods:

- The nature of the project
- The team's skills
- The culture and style of the company you work for.

While you won't need, or be able to use, all the available approaches every time, it is usually helpful to deploy more than one technique for a particular purpose: field studies combined with interviews, expert evaluations with design walkthroughs, and so on.

Design, then, can learn from geographical surveying: to find an object's location, two or more readings are taking from known points. In design, this triangulation process means taking two or more perspectives to understand a situation more accurately (Mackay and Fayard, 1997).

4.7.2 MANY DISCIPLINES

The sorts of skills needed to produce effective interfaces have changed greatly in the past 40 or so years, as Jonathan Grudin notes (Grudin, 1990). While today, interaction design draws on many distinct disciplines, including computer science, marketing, sociology and the arts, things were not always as cosmopolitan.

At first, in the 1950s, computers were like newborn infants, adored by engineers and programmers. Interactions were unsophisticated and simple, and the main skills needed to produce effective interfaces came from electrical engineers.

By the 1960s, programmers were the predominant computer users, interacting with programming development software. These users were like schoolteachers – willing to put the effort into understanding the growing child while educating it to do useful things. Technical developments in

TABLE 4.2

Diversity of techniques useful in interaction design (inspired and adapted from Dykstra-Erickson *et al.*, 2001), showing approaches organized by phase. These techniques have evolved from diverse disciplines – from ethnography to marketing, from arts to computer science

Finding out about use	Analyzing user data	Generating ideas	Designing systems	Evaluating systems
Naturalistic observations	Event coding (classifying and categorizing observations)	Oral brainstorming	Paper prototyping	Longitudinal (longer-term) field deployment
Contextual inquiries (field interviews shaped by user activities)	Task analysis (identifies structures in actions user carries out to reach goals)	Notecard brainstorming	Video prototyping	Usability study (e.g. review by usability experts)
Question-naires	Survey analysis	Video brainstorming	Software / hardware simulation	Lab trial
Focus groups	Persona and scenario analysis (consolidating observations into focused descriptions of typical users and uses)	Focus troupes (acting out potential uses)	Wizard of Oz (simulation where investigator plays role of system, responding to user interactions)	Design walkthrough (using psychology-based assessment tools to measure impact on learning, errors of design, etc.)
Lab studies to assess specific behavioral / cognitive characteristics	Log analysis (data mining techniques to assess interactions with existing devices / services)	Bodystorming (brainstorm-ing carried out in field – i.e. designers take their bodies to the context)	Functional prototype	Focus groups

TABLE 4.3
(continued)

Finding out about use	Analyzing user data	Generating ideas	Designing systems	Evaluating systems
Probes: cultural, mobile, technological (tools and techniques aimed at prompting responses in engaging ways)		State-of-art review (analysis of published example designs and issues relating to area of concern)		Diary study
Diary study (self-report technique where user regularly completes diary entries relating to their activities / experiences)				

computer science, such as operating systems and high-level languages, were the keys to improving the ways programmers and computers communicated.

It took until the 1970s for the term 'user interface' to come into parlance, with end-user terminals and non-technical users. At this stage, as Grudin eloquently puts it, the computer had grown up and began making its first steps into the community, a place full of people with less commitment and time to adapt to it – it had to fit in. From this point, human-factors specialists, cognitive psychologists and the like become important.

In the 1980s and 1990s, computers increasingly moved out of the back office and onto the desks of many employees. Soon the need became apparent to understand how groups of people work together, supported by interactive systems. At this time, sociologists, anthropologists and the like came to the fore.

In recent years, computing technology has reached out even further, from the workplace to every place, into consumer products, becoming a backcloth to ordinary life. To meet the needs of this development stage, interaction design is further drawing on marketing and artistic disciplines. Nokia, then, have thought about phones for different segments of the consumer market: there are 'classic' styles for 'controller'-type consumers, fashion-oriented ones for the 'expressors', and a premium look is targeted at 'impressors' (Lindholm *et al.*, 2003). Meanwhile, the role of art-inspired approaches is concisely argued by the Royal College of Art's Interaction Design Department:

... most hi-tech products and services are still a long way from meeting people's everyday needs and desires. We require fun as well as function, poetry as well as power. (RCA)

4.7.3 PARTICIPATION AND COLLABORATION

For much of the last century, many workers were seen as cogs in a wheel. Their jobs and work practices had to be fine-tuned in order to make the overall process more and more effective. This mechanistic management style was fathered by Frederick Taylor who published *The Principles of Scientific Management* in 1911 (Taylor, 1998). In it, he laid out approaches to carefully specify how jobs should be carried out, the tools to be used, and how the work environment should be controlled. For employees, these approaches saw a dramatic loss of autonomy.

While widely deployed, such methods were challenged in Scandinavian countries. These nations, with a long tradition of social justice, developed participative and cooperative work design techniques. The thinking behind these approaches is that as well as being simply more humane, they increase productivity by nurturing commitment and enthusiasm in everyone involved.

Collaborative work practices have long been seen as important in computer technology development. The developers who build a system and the people who will use it are brought together, to work as equals in the development process. Everybody can contribute and each contribution is as welcome as the next – there is a notion, then, of equal opportunity.

Many variants of such participatory design (PD) methods exist; indeed, by 2001, Michael Muller, who has been involved in shaping key techniques, counted 61 separate approaches with seven different lifecycles (Muller, 2001). Participants come together and use low-tech objects, such as Post-it notes and marker pens, to work on specifying elements of the Graphical User Interface (GUI).

Many of the methods were developed in the era of desktop computers and GUIs. For mobile design, they need to be adapted for several reasons (Bødker and Buur, 2002):

- **Need to express novel interaction elements.** Post-it notes, cards, marker pens and the like are excellent for prototyping GUI widgets – buttons, scroll bars, etc. – and their relationships on screens on forms. But what about the non-visual elements in mobile interactions and how a device and its environment might relate?
- **Need to accommodate mobile use-contexts.** In conventional participatory design, teams meet in a laboratory, or an adapted meeting room. For the sorts of office-type systems the techniques were invented for, this sort of arrangement is more than satisfactory. Participants have a clear shared understanding of the office place environments the system will be used in; they can easily communicate their experiences away from their actual workplace. The complexity and diversity of use-contexts for mobiles make using a conventional meeting place less attractive.
- **Need to involve engaged, true stakeholders.** In pure participatory design, the users involved are the ones who will actually end up using the systems. With many mobile systems, the aim is to produce services which will be used by a mass market – the people you involve in the design effort might be potential users, but they will have less of a commitment than those workers who knew they would be definitely affected by the final design outcome.

The 'collaboratorium' is one approach to overcoming such problems (Bødker and Buur, 2002). Participants use props and work together in locations – both indoors and outdoors – that better accommodate the features of mobile use. An example of the use of the collaboratorium is reviewed in Box 4.7.

BOX 4.7 THE 'COLLABORATORIUM'

The collaboratorium is a forum for participatory design for mobile and ubiquitous computing (Bødker and Buur, 2002).

Adapted participatory design methods were used in a study with Danfoss, an industrial manufacturer of sensors. The aim was to see how new mobile and ubiquitous computing technologies might be used to improve the work at wastewater plants.

The researchers brought together participants who included Danfoss development engineers, marketers, interaction designers and anthropologists. Users were also chosen carefully to be 'exemplary future users of the technology, as the goal of this project was to design instruments for a general market rather than to redesign the equipment of the participants' particular plants'.

In one full-day session, the participants worked together on three activities:

- **Design game.** Team members sat round meeting tables indoors and played a board game. The board represented a plant layout and pieces of differently shaped and colored foam were used to represent components like sensors and displays. The first part of the game was aimed at creating a shared understanding. The second part was aimed at redesign – justifying and leading to new technology ideas.
- **Movie making.** The teams were then taken outdoors to visit a plant. As they walked round the site they related what they were seeing to the board game representation. Each team had to decide on one promising innovation they had identified in the earlier game and then produce and film a script of it in action. For these films they used props (e.g. blocks of foam to represent handhelds).
- **Presenting movies.** All the participants then came back to the meeting room and showed each other the movies. Issues with the proposal along with new insights were then discussed. ■

4.8 FROM INTERACTION DESIGN TO DEPLOYMENT

The process of interaction design ends up by producing a blueprint for the new service. This plan will typically include working prototypes, detailed paper designs and accompanying explanations for the implementation team.

In non-mobile developments, these design outputs are often used by just a team of software engineers; however, for mobile systems, they may well also inform industrial designers and hardware specialists.

Having spent a great deal of effort in carefully understanding user needs and documenting designs which will lead to a useful, usable user experience, the next phases of development can invoke anxiety or even despair. Excellent interaction designs do not guarantee similarly successful end products: implementers can poorly translate the plan or simply override your decisions with what they see as their better approach. To avoid this fate, understand and keep close to the developers (Poltrack and Grudin, 1994).

- **Get commitment and input.** To stop designs being compromised at later stages, involve the implementers in all phases of interaction design.
- **Communicate the design effectively.** One appealing approach is to give the developers a package consisting of a prototype and its manual and then challenge them to deliver an implementation that lives up to your hopes (Norman, 1999). Making the implementation fit the manual is better than the common practice of asking some hapless technical writer to explain the quirks and errors in the final system (Thimbleby, 1996b).
- **Remain involved.** Become part of the implementation team, ask to see each implementation prototype, and prompt the implementers to test versions of the system with users.

SUMMARY

Mobile interaction design is about the stuff of people's lives, focused on understanding and developing blueprints for systems that permeate the broad spectrum of their experiences – at home and work, while shopping and traveling, supporting their everyday and extraordinary needs. It involves being immersed in the richness of the detail, while being able to spot and articulate themes. And, all the while, these users are included and participate in the design activities: they'll certainly be observed and interviewed; they might well assist in building various prototypes; and their reactions to proposals have to be gleaned and channeled into refining the designs.

The mobile context offers some particular challenges to designers, ranging from philosophical difficulties in effectively framing potential future uses of emerging technologies, to practical ones such as the problems of watching users on the move. A palette of methods exist and designers draw on several at each stage, to give themselves different but complementary viewpoints. Some of these are qualitative, aimed at providing nuanced descriptions and interpretations; others are quantitative, giving empirical data such as task completion times and user ratings in a prototype evaluation. At the end of the design process, the baton is passed to the software engineering team; but a wise interaction group will stay closely involved until shipping.

WORKSHOP QUESTIONS

- If you're a computer scientist, software engineer or programmer, this book might be the first time you've come across interaction design notions. Think about how you previously perceived the 'user interface'. When you have developed programs in the past, what have you done to try to make this interface usable?

- Imagine you've just completed the interaction design for a new mobile service for a large broadband mobile network operator. What pressures might the development team face that might lead to the design being compromised? How might you work to reduce the implications of such influences?
- Computer scientists need to understand human issues; that seems obvious. But how can computer science fundamentals – the core algorithms and data structures, for instance – be applied to improve the user interface?

DESIGNER TIPS

- *Build up your own archive of design ideas and methods by creating a 'memorial box' or scrapbook of things you've tried or seen elsewhere. Fill it with photos, sketches, cuttings from magazines and conference papers. Frequently, flip through it leisurely; reflect on what you've learnt. Share this personal resource with colleagues.*
- *During a design project, keep everything you produce. It's easy to forget to document the process, and something like the urgent need to refer to a long-cleaned whiteboard is a harsh reminder. At the end of each day's work, get everyone on the team to scan through this record and to choose one item that they wish to discuss first thing the next day. If each aspect of your designs cannot be rationalized with respect to this history, think carefully about how you are proceeding.*
- *Keep your eyes open to life – read about architecture, art, economics, the latest scientific and sociological findings. Plenty of newsstand magazines are helpful in this respect –* The Economist, NewScientist *and* Wallpaper *are examples. But remember that very few people are renaissance types who can master both art and science – surround yourself with others who have complementary skills.*
- *If your design process does not involve field (e.g. ethnographic observations and longitudinal evaluations* in situ*) and non-field (e.g. post-field data analysis and lab trials) in equal measure, you should look at redressing the balance.*
- *Involve programmers in the design process. Do this not only because you want buy-in but because computer science – which is all about managing and structuring resources and complexity – has a lot to say about how an interface might be constructed (see Chapter 8 for a detailed illustration).*

CHAPTER 5
WATCHING, ASKING, PROBING

OVERVIEW

5.1. Introduction
5.2. Focusing the study
5.3. Top techniques for understanding people
5.4. Making sense of observations
5.5. Personas and scenarios

KEY POINTS

- Investigative methods can inspire and inform design, helping to suggest starting-points for new mobile services as well as nurturing emerging ideas via a rich understanding of current and future user contexts, activities and attitudes.
- Typically, a series of field studies are carried out involving naturalistic observations and in-situ interviews. These are complemented with follow-up interviews and focus groups to reflect on field findings and to fill any gaps arising from difficulties in observing all aspects of mobile situations. Self-reporting tools, such as diary studies, are also often employed.
- For mobile services, there is a role for a newer breed of creatively engaging investigative method: various types of probe (such as cultural and technological) and role-playing are examples.
- Given the pressured product development cycles that characterize the mobile industry, 'discount' investigation methods are often necessary and appropriate: focused, short ethnographic studies and the use of data mining techniques to analyze usage logs are examples.

- **The potential ocean of user data needs to be distilled. A range of analysis techniques exist – some look at the data from a sociological perspective, others more from a system engineering one. In all cases, the aim is to understand and communicate the structure, patterns and trends that characterize the activities important to users and the situations in which these are performed.**

5.1 INTRODUCTION

To be a successful interaction designer, prepare yourself, from the very start of each project, to be surprised, enlightened and delighted as you get to know your users.

- Imagine you've been set the task of extending ringtone download services. The intention is to provide ways for the users to browse and select melodies interactively on the handset itself. The assumed market are the current enthusiastic adopters – teenagers – but on one of your field visits, you discover a mother rocking her crying baby while using her phone to play a lullaby melody (Gaver *et al.*, 2003). You begin to think about this user group's needs and wonder about a service that might meet them – simple access to sets of lullabies and baby-oriented images that can be waved in front of a distressed infant's eyes.
- Put yourself in the place of a designer looking at providing travel directions via a mobile system. Initially, you imagine people will use the service on their own, but during field studies you see people working together as they try to find a location: couples in cars, one driving and the other navigating; and groups of people in the street huddled round a map, trying to orientate themselves. These observations lead you to ponder whether and how the proposed service could support such collaborative activities. Your fieldwork also highlights the wider 'social issues' of navigation. On an in-car navigation system study, one of the drivers had a rental car with an on-board system, but his friends didn't:

  ... locations were planned over breakfast with other members of the group based on tourist leaflets and atlases. On deciding to leave, the other cars were forced to wait many minutes while the navigation system was programmed. There was social pressure just to go. (Curzon *et al.*, 2002)
- You're investigating the use of SMS texting in lectures. You build a prototype that allows students to send questions and suggestions anonymously to a 'whiteboard', visible to everyone in the audience. At first, your idea was to help shy or intimidated students get direct access to the lecturer without having to raise their hand in a large class situation. However, in some early field trials, you see students 'subverting' the original plan by posing and answering questions themselves – one student asks a question, another replies. It starts you thinking about how groups of people situated together – in classrooms, sports domes, restaurants, etc. – might work together as 'immobile', mobile communities (Jones and Marsden, 2004).

- Or, what about mobile messaging in mental healthcare situations? You've been asked to explore ways of helping patients keep in touch with their support team while living semi-independent lives within the community. You propose a direct link between the patient and a specific member of the team: the patient can send a text message that will be delivered to their carer. However, when prototyping, the care team professionals say they'd prefer all messages from patients to be available on an open message display, viewable by the whole team. This scheme would allow them to cover any staff absences and reduces the risk of patients becoming too dependent on a particular member of the team (Cheverst *et al.*, 2003).

Talk to an experienced designer and they will tell you that one of the most fulfilling, stimulating, but also overwhelming and tedious phases of the job is this process of understanding your users' lives and how technology might fit. It's a bit like doing a very large, complex jigsaw puzzle, except that you don't have the lid with a photo of the completed picture to guide you, and you keep finding new pieces; bit by bit, though, you have to begin to see patterns that help you make sense of the situation.

To play this jigsaw game, ideally you'd need to invisibly track the users, all day long, hovering silently, noting what they do and when, along with the sorts of things they use to complete their activities. You would have to be with them at their workplaces, follow them during their commutes, and sit with them when they unwind at home. On top of all this, you need to get inside their heads, to probe the motivations and intentions they have while mobile. Now, while invisibility cloaks or omniscient mirrors are a mainstay of fantasy writing, we have to think of more practical ways of approximating their powers.

In this chapter we consider techniques to give you access to users' important moments, situations, attitudes, needs and desires without having to spend years in long-term relationships with them. We've put together this toolkit by reviewing a large number of reports on mobile development. Our aim is to identify the most frequently used approaches in industry and research labs.

Because mobile product life-cycles are short, we emphasize observation gathering and analysis techniques that can be used to provide rapid results; while all of the tools we discuss can be used in a pragmatic way, there are some, termed 'rapid' or 'discount' methods, which appear particularly useful in mobile development.

Weeks or months of observations are wasted unless you can mold them into forms that succinctly, yet richly, communicate the salient aspects of your users' lives. So we end the chapter by looking at how the data might be analyzed and represented in order to be useful to the design team.

Along the way, we present examples and case studies to illustrate the approaches and give findings that are of interest in themselves.

EXERCISE 5.1 SUPPORTING COLLABORATIVE, MOBILE NAVIGATION

You have been asked to design a mobile service that provides route navigation information; the aim is to lead the user from their starting point to a destination. The intended platform is a pocket-sized PC that includes a high-resolution display and audio output facilities. ➤

Discuss design considerations for the following three contexts. Consider the types of route information and the means of presenting it, along with ways users might interact with the application:

- Pedestrian navigation
- In-car use for driver-only situations
- Collaboration between driver and passenger.

Comments: navigation information may be presented textually, graphically and via audio. Some of these modes, and combinations of them, will be more appropriate in certain situations than others. For the driver alone in the car, spoken instructions would seem the most useful; in the street, directional graphics to point the way may be more effective. A range of levels of information abstraction may be helpful to users: pictures or descriptions of landmarks along the route are examples of low-level, detailed information (shown to be particularly useful for older users), while more abstract map overviews can be vital aids for planning. ■

5.2 FOCUSING THE STUDY

Before you can observe your users, you need to identify what you are interested in and who you should watch to gain insights: the first important job, then, is to be clear about the focus of your study.

5.2.1 HOW FOCUSED SHOULD THE STUDY BE?

At the beginning of a project, you should consider the following four questions:

- Who are we interested in? That is, what is the profile of our users: their age range, socioeconomic background, skills and interests?
- What is the domain we are focusing on – the work world of company managers? Education? Healthcare? Leisure time?
- What broad user-goals are we keen to support? Helping people to work together? Providing them with diversions during commute time?
- Are there any technology constraints? Some clients might want you to particularly consider situations where their products might play a role. For example, an image-processing company commissioned a study on how camera-type devices might be used in the workplace (Brown *et al.*, 2000).

Some studies will be rather unfocused: "go and find some inspiration for a new mobile service", your client may say. Here, the user profile, domain and activities are undefined. Others will be far more constrained: "see how middle-managers might use our new notepad-like mobiles in work", for instance. Between these extremes will be briefs such as "look at ways of supporting visitors to a city". Here, the profiles and user goals are broad, so in our example some visitors will be on business, others there for leisure; there will be young and older people, singles and groups; and they will have goals as varied as coordinating travel plans, locating a friend in the city, and finding local sites of interest.

Some studies will be more about inspiring design, others about informing design. 'Inspiring' is about coming up with well-founded departure points in a strategic way:

The starting point for strategic design is very vague, and typically involves a new technology, an attractive user group, or an interesting social phenomenon. The objective is to design new product concepts that become profitable new businesses within a few years. (Korhonen, 2000)

In contrast, 'informing' is more concerned with giving authoritative direction to a project that has pressing commercial deadlines. The more imprecise your answers are to the four questions, the closer your work will be to an inspiring activity; the more specific you can be, the more the work will be about informing design. In most projects you will be likely to be involved in a process that is part-way between providing inspiration and information.

If you are given a very vague brief, you should ensure your client understands the implications and are happy to be paying for 'blue-skies' investigations. If, though, they present a very specific set of requirements, try to widen the scope, questioning their constraints: so, in terms of profile, many mobile organizations focus on groups of young people and teams of knowledge workers. What about the elderly, or family groups, or (of interest for those developing peer-to-peer mobile services) strangers who find themselves co-located?

5.2.2 FINDING PEOPLE TO STUDY

Sampling

The Scylla of overgeneralizing from a limited number of contacts is accompanied by the Charybdis of bogging down when users disagree. (Grudin, 1991)

Identifying the right types of people to watch is a critical skill. You can futilely spend much time following one group of people, while in contrast a single person may be highly illuminating. See Table 5.1.

The standard advice when selecting people to observe is to choose a *representative sample*. That is, a group that typifies the larger, entire population – so if you are developing a service for young, middle-income adults, the sample you study should include the range of people found in that category.

If you are looking at something that can be quantified – given a value – in a simple way, like voting intention, then the sampling task is reasonably simple: just select a large enough number of people using standard sampling methods. So, asking five colleagues about their voting plans in a national election will give you no useful information; randomly questioning 5000 will.

Scientific sampling methods may be useful in some limited design cases, where a specific, usually numeric answer is being sought. But what about the usual situation where you are really interested in far more nuanced aspects of user need? How many people should you study when you want to understand, say, the ways people manage their relationships? And, who should these people be?

Now, suppose you had enough resources to explore these sorts of issues by questioning a scientifically representative sample – surely, that would best? Certainly, you would amass a vast amount of data, but you would very likely be overwhelmed, unable to make out the interesting, important features – the things that stick out and catch your eye – in the users' behavior patterns. Your discernment would be drowned by a flood of distracting, irrelevant detail.

Rather than becoming debilitated trying to ensure a 'representative' group, take a more practical, iterative and dynamic approach to subject selection; as David Millen puts it:

One of the major goals . . . is to observe and understand interesting patterns or exceptional behavior and then to make practical use of that understanding. The sampling strategy should, therefore, aid the researcher to identify such behaviors in a reasonably efficient manner. (Millen, 2000)

Millen goes on to identify useful characters to recruit when looking to get quick inspirations into life. The aim is to purposefully use judgment to select key informants whom he categorizes as field guides, liminals, corporate informants, and exceptional informants:

- **Field guides**. If you've ever been on a game safari, you'll know you can spend hours or days driving around on your own and only ever seeing antelope. Hire a game-park guide and they can take you to the interesting places. In interaction design, field-guides are people who know the lie of the land: the individuals, groups and their dynamics, the organizational politics, etc. They can point out who, when and where to watch. These people have lots of access to others: think secretaries and managers in a corporate setting, and community workers for the street.
- **Liminals**. Look for the people who are accepted by most people – the ones everyone is happy to share a coffee with – and who move freely between a number of subgroups. They'll also be the ones with insight, able to explain group behaviors and in-jokes. They are, in a way, introvert–extrovert types: full of life in the group, very much part of the action, but also people who muse and reflect on what's going on.
- **Corporate informants**. Your organization may have people – such as marketers and service staff – who already spend much time with your future users; they can provide eye-witness information and help identify users who could be guides and liminals.
- **Exceptional informants**. These are the rare, 'guru' types that deliver highly original, 'disruptive' insights. They are usually very well connected and respected by their peers.

Another form of directed selection is seen in *theoretical sampling*. This is deployed in the *Grounded Theory* approach to user studies (we'll look at this method in a little more detail in Section 5.4.2). Here, the types of people you choose are guided by the 'theory' (the framework you build to understand the users and their behavior) that develops during the study. So, as you study, you refine the user characteristics you are interested in, and then find further participants to investigate. Iterative, evolutionary sampling like this is beneficial regardless of how you initially choose your subjects.

Recruiting, Motivating and Retaining Subjects

When you have an idea about who you are going to target, the hard work of recruiting subjects begins. Good ones are like valuable employees and it pays to consider ways of encouraging their effective participation and long-term involvement.

- **Direct, unsolicited approaches.** Watch market researchers in a busy high street; it's a thankless job. Most people they attempt to stop for a quick survey or interview hurry past, shaking their heads in irritation at the attempted intrusion. To make matters worse, these data collectors cannot approach everyone, as they are usually given a profile of the type of person to look for – targeting, for example, mainly middle-aged affluent-looking people. You could attempt to use such a technique when studying people for a system design. You might stand in a busy thoroughfare where people are mobile – like a shopping center or train station – and approach people in this direct, unsolicited way. But the benefits of the approach do not outweigh the costs. Lurking in places where mobile users congregate – airports, hotels, bars, cafés, clubs, busy streets – can, though, be a good way of identifying interesting people to talk to. People such as hotel concierges, taxi drivers, café owners and community leaders are surrounded by mobiles every day.

- **Advertising.** If you look in the classified section of some newspapers and magazines you will often see adverts seeking participants for television shows ('Young single parents needed for documentary'). A similar approach is often used to recruit a pool of potential subjects to study.
- **Exploiting existing customer bases.** If you work for a telecom network operator, or can work with one, as many of the handset developers do, the recruiting task can be easier in many ways. You already have a pool (perhaps 'ocean', given the number) of committed users – the customers. You also have a fair deal of information about them, including the type of mobile they own, the contract they subscribe to (which can tell you things such as whether they perceive themselves as heavy or light users, and more leisure or business oriented), and their call and service history.
- **Reviewing customer accounts.** This can locate target users. For example, if you're interested in new services to build on communication cultures seen in SMS, it would be a good idea to select people who are already heavy users of texting, but also to include some light users, to understand why they do not find the activity attractive and how extra services may better meet their requirements. Indeed, account log analysis might even provide wisdom without your having to speak to the customers, as we'll see in Section 5.3.4.
- **Releasing 'prototypes'.** Where you're designing for the mass market (as is often the case for mobile services), it's very difficult to predict who will actually end up using the innovation; you may not know completely until the product ships (Grudin, 1991). Companies can release products, in relatively small numbers, to help understand the market and users. Recruiting people who buy into these saleable 'prototypes' can help refine the product for the larger market.
- **Using colleagues.** When looking for people, don't overlook your own organization. Remember that even within hi-tech companies, there's a whole range of 'ordinary', non-technology focused people – accountants, marketers, cleaners, and so on. You are more likely to be able to persuade these sorts of people to help and you will be able to get more access to them. Of course, the downside with this approach is that the subjects may just be too positive about the services, not just because they want to please a fellow worker but because they are too company-focused to see the problems, or they may feel hesitant about being critical of the organization that employs them. Simply relying on in-house users is dangerous; you need to combine the approach with off-the-street subjects too.
- **Endorsements.** For those super-informants, the exceptional types, look to see who is talked about and listened to. They may be in your target user group or be people who are leading the thinking in the area you are interested in – so, if you are keen to understand gamers you could approach both a champion player and a market analyst who has written about trends. Tracking blogs, websites, industry newspapers and conferences are all useful for locating these kinds of informant. (See the *Resources* section at the back of the book for some pointers.)

As you find people who appear suitable, you will also have to make the study prospect attractive to the subjects themselves. Persuading people to answer questions from a clipboard or take part in a quick, five-minute design exercise might be relatively easy, but the more you ask of your subjects,

TABLE 5.1

Methods of identifying people to study

Method	Pros	Cons	Use
Selecting people 'off the street'	Can pick people actually in situation under investigation. Can observe some of potential participants' behavior before approach is made. Fast exposure to many potentials. Quick responses.	Time intensive – many rebuffs likely. Self-selection is a problem – certain types of people more willing to talk than others.	Short, focused surveys. Getting impressions of population profile to help recruitment for more extensive study.
Advertising	Can reach broad numbers of potential respondents. Can target user groups through advert placement (relevant types of magazine, website, etc.).	Can be expensive. Self-selection is a problem.	Focus-group style discussions. Profile gathering to assist in selection of people to study in more depth.
Existing customers	Large amount of profile data already exists. Easy incentives to participants (e.g. reduced call costs).	Can overlook needs of non-customers who might adopt important 'disruptive technologies' (see Chapter 3).	Widely useful, from large survey-type data gathering to in-depth interviews with individuals.
Employees of own organization	Compliant and accessible subjects.	Subjects too subjective or reticent to criticize.	Widely useful, from large survey-type data gathering to in-depth interviews with individuals.
Referral	Much known about subjects. Source of high-authority individuals.	Availability of subjects may be low (or at high cost).	Gathering of emerging trends; broad, 'big-picture' insights.

the larger the incentive you will have to offer. So, a focus-group style session may provide travel expenses, convivial company and some refreshments; while users you wish to shadow or question over weeks or months will need some substantial incentive, such as payment or provision of services: "if you take part in our study, we'll give you free mobile calls for two months". Using people from your own organization may be cheaper, but you should not expect to have free access to employees outside their working hours.

If you do offer incentives, be aware of the side-effects: benefits may bias the pool of people you attract (the sorts of people motivated by the payments may not accurately represent your real target group); and subjects may be inclined to offer only positive comments in an attempt to please you, the paymaster.

As good informants are hard to find, you should work to foster your relationships with the ones you identify for both the short term (the full development period for the product you are currently working on) and the long run (for future projects you may work on). Police forces, of course, have long seen the value in such associations. Their informants are judged by the results they produce, the criminals they help convict; similarly, if informants help lead you to winning designs, keep close to them in the future.

5.3 TOP TECHNIQUES FOR UNDERSTANDING PEOPLE

Read the reports of mobile-type projects in any of the many journals and conference proceedings, and you will see a clear pattern in the way researchers and developers go about discovering useful things from the people they are studying. The recipe to getting inspired or informed goes something like this:

- Carry out field studies – spend as much time as possible in the users' context. Be both in their world while at the same time retaining an objective, questioning perspective. Record as much of what is going on as possible – take a field notebook, camera, recording device and the like. As well as watching, do some semi-structured interviewing, *in situ*.
- Provide your informants with ways to self-report: give them diaries to fill in, devices to capture their thoughts, telephone numbers to call and leave messages on, disposable cameras to snap important parts of days, and so on.
- Carry out follow-up interviews away from the scene; bring groups in for focus-group discussions.
- Analyze your observations using insight and experience to arrive at useful design-guiding accounts and other artifacts (like analyses that show the structure of a set of activities the user carries out).

This recipe has been used, of course, in developing conventional, non-mobile applications. For emerging systems like mobiles and ubiquitous computing devices, the basic ingredients are being supplemented with what we call 'creatively engaging approaches'. As we will see in Section 5.3.6, these include involving actors to play out mobile use in real situations and providing your informants with 'probes' to help them to reflect and think about their situation.

Many of the reports we analyzed were from researchers who do not have the sort of time pressures seen in commercial product development. Their aim is to gain fundamental understanding about the motivations and behavior of the people. Their investigations are characterized by long, intensive periods in the field and a strong use of theoretical tools to help guide both the observations and the analysis; consequently, a high degree of training and skill is employed.

However, there is also a sizable number of studies which have clearly been carried out using more applied approaches, leading to interesting issues being exposed and innovative designs. Often reports of these studies allude to 'ethnographically inspired' approaches, by which the researchers mean they spent time in the field and gathered observations in some ways.

So, if you're an industry-based interaction designer, don't be put off by the 'pure' study methods seen in long-term research, but be encouraged by the results achieved by the faster, less formal approaches. The nature of commercial environments means you are going to have to use techniques that are directed in some way (such as *contextual inquiry* – see Section 5.3.2) and that fit well with time and budget constraints (see Section 5.3.4 on discount methods).

BOX 5.1 THE ESSENCE OF ETHNOGRAPHICALLY INSPIRED APPROACHES

When people use the term 'ethnographic methods', the detail of what they mean can vary drastically. It's worth being reminded, then, of an early definition of what interactive system ethnographers do:

In ethnographic studies, the investigator attempts to be as unobtrusive as possible, finding a group of people already engaged in some interesting behavior. Most critically, the ethnographer adopts the position of uninformed outsider whose job it is to understand as much as possible about the 'natives' from their own point of view. All else flows from this basic precept:

- *the need to use a range of methods including intensive observation, in-depth interviewing, participation in cultural activities, and simply hanging about, watching and learning as events unfold;*
- *the holistic perspective, in which everything – belief systems, rituals, institutions, artefacts, texts, etc. – is grist for the analytical mill; and immersion in the field situation.* (Monk *et al.*, 1993) ■

5.3.1 OBSERVING

My field site was a UK national daily newspaper. I had gone there to explore what 'information gathering' meant in the context of journalism. And I was doing this for a very explicit purpose, that of informing the design of future technologies to support such activities. Like many ethnographers, having made the decision to go into the field I was unsure about what to do when I got there. To complicate matters, I came from a background in computing and human–computer interaction studies and therefore was taking a particular information technology-biased set of preconceptions and inclinations into the field with me. (Catriona Macaulay in Kaptelinin *et al.*, 1999)

Expert ethnographers, often with a sociology-style background, speak about being immersed in the field, of being aware of everything, of a highly tuned sensitivity that can pick up on slight nuances.

But for many, like Catriona Macaulay, quoted above, field study observations can be a daunting, overwhelming experience. While it's obvious that it's a good idea to observe, what exactly do you do when you're there? Without a framework you could spend a long time in the field with little to show. In this section, we'll outline the methods you can employ and two important facets to be alert to: action and context.

Methods

These naturalistic observations are all about seeing the action in its setting. To this end, the emphasis is on capturing as much of the detail as possible, and this involves taking notes, drawing quick sketches, photographing, and making audio and video recordings.

You have to decide on how intrusive your investigations are going to be and the degree of awareness your subjects have of the study itself. In terms of intrusion, it is possible to simply be a bystander, on the margins of the action, not intruding at all (see Box 5.2). Alternatively, you could interrupt and question people about their actions.

The subjects you watch can be complete strangers, oblivious to your study, or people who have agreed to participate and are aware of the purposes of the investigation. There are many benefits of having such 'tame' subjects, like getting access to them over longer periods and being able to follow up observation findings by interviewing them. It is essential too, though, to catch some subjects unawares. This way you will be able to reduce problems that come when people know they are being watched, which include changing what they would normally do, and acting in a self-conscious way.

BOX 5.2 INVESTIGATION METHODS CASE STUDY 1

Focus on participant awareness: Quiet Calls prototype (Nelson *et al.*, 2001)

Context

A study to understand and design for the way people manage private calls in public situations.

Study methods

- Field observations in public places – notes were made of visible actions by mobile phone users, recording information about what they were doing when making or receiving calls, and how they managed these calls. Reactions of people around callers were also observed – what is the impact of mobile use on others?
- Interviews – 16 frequent mobile callers were asked about their use and attitudes toward public calls.
- Anectodal evidence – investigators asked colleagues, acquaintances and people they met in public places to give eye-witness examples of calling behavior. ➤

During field observations, the users were not directly approached (i.e., there was no intrusion) and were not aware they were being studied. Investigators went to places where public conversations happened – restaurants, waiting areas, etc. – and used two methods to provide both breadth and depth to their data:

- Detailed area observation. Two observers noted all phone use over a 30–60 minute period.
- Ten-minute slice. One or two observers, *in situ* for exactly 10 minutes, noted all phone use.

What insights did these methods provide?

- Many people are 'on call' and have to keep their phones on in public. Calls could be business or more personal, such as being available if their child minder needs to contact them.
- Basic mobile call services do not give enough information to the receiver to assess whether to answer a call. Caller line identity, for example, does not indicate the urgency of the call.
- On answering a call in public, people often move to a more secluded place to protect their privacy.
- During calls, interruptions frequently occur – such as an airport announcement – which can cause the mobile user to disengage from the conversation. The person at the other end of the call may be confused, not being aware of the interruption.

What design solution was proposed?

The Quiet Calls prototype is a mobile phone-like device with three additional buttons, each generating a spoken utterance:

- **Engage**: puts the caller 'on hold' while giving the user time to get themselves to a more conversation-conducive location. Pushing the button generates utterances such as "Hello, Matt will be right there, just going somewhere private".
- **Listen**: lets the caller know they are being listened to. Pushing generates, for instance, "Matt is in a meeting and cannot talk, but he is listening".
- **Disengage**: defers call for later. Pushing generates speech like "I think we should talk about this later".

Imagine, then, you're in a business meeting when a call comes through. You pick up the phone and press the 'listen' button; the caller hears "I can't talk but go ahead, I'm listening". The caller mentions an important commercial development and you decide to leave the room to follow up, so you press the 'engage' button and the caller hears "Hold on, just going somewhere private". ■

Before embarking on any observations, make sure you have thought about the ethical and legal issues associated with people-watching as well as the use of any data you gather. The sorts of concern to consider center on the way you are going to record and later use information (in many countries there are laws constraining certain types of recording and data storage, for instance), and the effects on the participants (will they feel comfortable with what you are doing?). Where you need to question or closely observe someone, make them aware of what you are doing and how the information you gather will be used, and then get their informed consent.

A quick, simple, ethical check is to ask yourself whether you would feel happy being treated in the ways planned for the study. It is also advisable to set up a more formal ethical review process in your team to audit the study plans and make suggestions to ensure the integrity of the process.

EXERCISE 5.2 STUDY ETHICS

Your client company has just introduced mobile email appliances to many of its employees. You have been asked to study the impact of these devices on collaboration and communication. A report will be presented to senior management.

- What study methods might you use?
- What ethical issues are involved and how might you accommodate them?

Comments: initially, you might interview people in a number of job roles to identify users to study further. Next, you could shadow the selected people over one or more working days, noting their use of the device and other means of communicating. It may also be possible to get access to copies of communications sent and received via the device (although this would obviously have to be handled very sensitively). These investigations should also be supplemented with follow-up interviews.

A significant ethical problem will be that participants' anonymity will be difficult to protect, especially if a manager selects the initial set of study subjects or the organization is small. At the very least, you would have to try to ensure that any comments you reported were as unattributable as possible. Without such assurances, the cooperation of the subjects is likely to be minimal.

A further ethical concern is the likelihood that during the study you will encounter people who are not part of your consenting sample. For example, while shadowing an informant during their working day, their colleague might come for a meeting. There has to be a clear and unembarrassing way for any party to signal that they would prefer you to withdraw. A useful model here is the participation of trainee doctors in medical consultations: the normal practice is for the regular physician to introduce the student and to ask the patient whether they are happy with them sitting in. ■

Identifying Values, Goals and Actions

A sure way to fail as you design a mobile service is to overlook the importance of value. A service's interaction design might have great usability and be sensitive to the context it is used within, but the user might still reject it with remarks like "so what?" and "it's not worth buying or learning to use".

Understanding 'value' involves both exploring what users hold dear – the things in life that motivate them and give them a sense of fulfillment, for instance – and what contributes to a significant sense of added value in a new product. If you cannot clearly express the value proposition – why should people adopt this? – for a proposal, you should tear it up and start again.

People demonstrate what they value by the things they do – if someone values their family and friends, they may seek out diverse ways of keeping in touch. Their economic behavior – what they are willing to pay for something – may also give clues (Cockton, 2004).

Behavior can be characterized in terms of goals and actions, with the former being what a person wishes to achieve, and the latter the steps they take in trying to do so. In design, the goals of interest are practical, accomplishable ones, which can be attained within a short timeframe (think minutes, hours or days rather than years).

When simply observing, all you see are the actions people carry out, and the situations they are carried out within; from these you may be able deduce some of their goals. Indeed, sometimes, goal-spotting can be fairly easy. If you saw a person in an airport checking the arrival and departure board, looking at their watch and then asking an official a question, what would you think? They are aiming either to catch a flight or to meet someone. Or what about watching a group of friends outside a restaurant? They are chatting while looking at the menu, one of them checks the time, and their conversation continues. Their goal is probably to have a meal together and they are matching up constraints of preferred cuisine, cost and the amount of time they have before perhaps needing to be elsewhere.

But things are not always so straightforward. What would you think if you saw someone on the train reading the TV guide on the back of their newspaper, and then sending a text message? What are they doing? They might be recommending a program, but the communication might be entirely unrelated to TV. But if a few minutes later, they receive a message, read it, look again at the TV guide and send another message, you have more evidence. Be alert, then, for the sequences and timing of actions to help clarify what is going on.

BOX 5.3 TREND-SPOTTING, TREND FORMING

An interview with Elise Levanto, Senior Manager, Consumer Vision, Nokia

MJ: What's the role of the Consumer Vision work at Nokia?

EL: We aim to uncover what the world is really about and how things are changing. These are mega-trends and not just short-term fads; and the concerns are 'big-picture' – security, demographics, environmental and the like. ➤

MJ: To what extent is the kind of work trend-forming rather than trend-spotting?

EL: Clearly, there is a role for showing consumers possibilities. It is hard to quantify but perhaps 60% of our work is trend-spotting.

MJ: So how do you spot these trends?

EL: We commission consultancies around the world to look into issues and we also travel ourselves to see what's happening.

MJ: Do you focus on any particular type of person for these sorts of study?

EL: Yes, the 'young minded' which make up say 20% of the population. These are not just the 'young', but people of all ages who are extrovert and social; they are open-minded, curious, inventive and want to explore new things. We feel these people are doing things now that will become mainstream. The 80% might not do exactly what this group is doing, but the essence of what these pioneers are involved in may be seen distilled in a future mass market.

MJ: As you study these groups, what changes are you seeing in people's views of technology?

EL: People are still positive about computing technology – they still believe it can make lives better; but they are more pragmatic, realizing its limitations.

MJ: . . . and what about the broader values? What will be important in the next five years or so?

EL: A move away from individualism, towards community; a post-materialist, more 'spiritual' outlook. ■

Understanding Context

There has been a lot of research activity and some significant commercial developments in producing mobiles that use contextual information. So, the *Pick Me Up* prototype shows how a mobile phone might learn characteristics of its owner's hand tremor and continue to ring until it is picked up by that individual (Strachan and Murray-Smith, 2004); and traffic updates, for instance, are routinely tailored for the location the user finds themselves in.

These systems sense the context and make choices for the user. In a way, though, all mobile services need to be 'context aware', or perhaps 'context accommodating'. That is, you need to design in situation-sensitive ways. A large clock in a station hall as people hurry by is context accommodating; a tiny one placed at eye-level is not.

While it is now taken for granted that a person's behavior is influenced and mediated through the context, this was not always the case. As Lucy Suchman explains in *Plans and Situated Actions* (Suchman, 1987), in early attempts at understanding human intelligence there was an emphasis on planning, driven by the belief that people achieve their goals by first working out all the steps for success, in a rational, logical way, all in the head, as it were, only then executing the plan in the world itself.

In contrast to this perspective on goals and actions, Suchman showed that human behavior can be understood only in the "... context of particular, concrete circumstances" (p. viii), that the plans people make are not set in stone, but rather "... are best viewed as a weak resource for what is primarily ad hoc activity" (p. ix).

But what things make up this situation? Context is, as Paul Dourish notes, 'a slippery notion' to define (Dourish, 2004). He gives two perspectives on what it is, the first being the conventional, easily understood one that he calls 'representational'. Here, context is a well-defined, distinct backdrop to the action. From this standpoint, the situation you observe can be encoded – you can describe the environment's characteristics, as this definition, quoted by Dourish, notes:

Context encompasses more than just the user's location, because other things of interest are also mobile and changing. Context includes lighting, noise level, network connectivity, communication costs, communication bandwidth and even the social situation, e.g., whether you are with your manager or co-worker. (Schilit *et al.*, 1994)

As a starting point for understanding context, simply noting down its features is useful but may not give a full account of what's important or sift out the irrelevant. In Dourish's view, context is dynamic – 'interactional' – and our eyes should be not solely on 'what it is, but on what it does'. From this perspective, activity is not just influenced by context; it helps define it too, the true context emerging through activity. So, when observing, don't resort solely to a snapshot approach, but look at how the elements of context become more or less relevant and meaningful to the user as they carry out their activities.

In interaction terms, there are three aspects of the situation that are always worth tracking: tools, documents, and emotional setting.

- **Tools.** These are objects that embody – that is, hold within them – a specific purpose and a way of acting, a practice. Working out how the tools to hand shape the way someone behaves can be crucial in designing systems that improve or extend current approaches.
- **Documents.** Documents are not just the conventional, letter-sized page-based ones we might envisage. A more inspiring, broader definition that captures the dynamic relationships people have with documents is given by David Levy, a computer scientist turned calligrapher:

  What are documents? They are, quite simply, talking things. They are bits of the material world – clay, stone, animal skin plant fiber, sand – that we've imbued with the ability to speak. (Levy, 2001)

  So, in the mobile case, cash till receipts we get when buying, street signs, pavements marked up with strange symbols – the WAR chalks – indicating WiFi access points, and instructions we've scribbled down, should all be noted.
- **Emotional setting.** Emotions can drive our actions, and what we do and think can certainly affect the way we feel. Consider your day so far. When were you relaxed, calm or joyful? When were you sad, angry or fearful? Were the emotions related to a specific activity or location and did any technologies have a role? Designs should accommodate the emotional characteristics of

the users and their contexts. When watching people, you can describe the emotional setting along spectrums of arousal (calmness through to excitement) and valence (negative/positive). So, for example, someone can have a low arousal level and be negative (and therefore apathetic); or, if they are highly aroused in a negative way, they will be exhibiting aggressive behaviors. Body language – from postures to gestures – and the volume and tone of conversations give a lot of cues.

BOX 5.4 EMOTIONAL RESPONSES AND MOBILE MUSIC PLAYERS

Emotional needs can help shape designs; conversely, designers need to understand the impact of their designs on a user's emotions. Consider, then, the following two emotion-centered mobile studies.

1. Accommodating emotional needs: music player concept (Zimmerman, 2003)
The 'Spinner' player is designed for young males, allowing them to create playlists and store them on acrylic rods (Color Plate 5). These rods are 'jammed' into the device, reflecting the designers' aims to accommodate the 'in your face' attitudes of many young males, allowing them to express their desire for power and control.

Incidentally, it's worth noting that the tangible rod design for storing digital media is similar to a suggestion for the long-term storage of important SMS messages, which involves decorated memory sticks that can be stored in attractive holders (Berg *et al.*, 2003). In both cases, the design proposal aims at giving a meaningful, evocative shape and form to the formless, invisible data.

2. Impact on emotions: listening to background music while using a pocket computer (Kallinen, 2004)
Pocket computers usually provide a sophisticated digital music player in addition to other tools, such as web browsers. Kari Kallinen carried out a study to assess the emotional impact of music played through headphones to users while they read news stories. The results showed that the music had a positive effect in a number of ways:

- Music increased pleasure and reduced boredom.
- It led users to feel that the media they were experiencing was more socially rich, meaning they felt more engaged with it.
- It led to overall higher user satisfaction.
- It decreased the likelihood of being distracted.

The study also looked at any differences in response in relation to personality types. Participants were given personality tests before taking part in the study to assess their degree of impulsiveness and sensation-seeking. The results indicated that some ➤

responses depended on type – for example, impulsive sensation-seekers were more relaxed when listening to the music than their less spontaneous, calmer counterparts.

Some implications of the work for mobile service providers are that audio tracks to supplement visual content might lead to richer user experiences but, to accommodate different character types, users should be provided with ways of controlling this supplementary medium. ■

5.3.2 ENQUIRING

During observations, in the main, your aim is to be more or less unobtrusive. While the process can lead to a rich set of insights, its open nature can sometimes lead to long periods with little to show. To complement it, more directed, structured techniques are often deployed. Two widely used ones are the contextual inquiry and artifact walkthrough.

Contextual Inquiry

What's your role as you go into the field? It is possible see yourself as the expert, metaphorically white-coated and equipped with a clipboard to study your subjects. In contrast, in proposing contextual inquiry, Hugh Beyer and Karen Holtzblatt argue for a much more humble attitude (Beyer and Holtzblatt, 1995). They suggest the designer should see the relationship as one of an apprentice (the designer) with the master (the person being studied).

In their method, the designer attempts to understand the users by interacting with them while and where activities are actually performed. This contrasts with say a standard interview where the user is plucked out of their environment to discuss their behaviors. There are several benefits arising out of this in-situ interviewing. The people you interview won't theorize, generalize or over-emphasize aspects of their experience – all explanations are grounded in, and open to question through, the activity itself.

The inquiries usually follow this pattern:

1. The designer watches while the participant begins some activity.
2. The designer then interrupts to question the reasons behind a particular practice.
3. Then the participant begins to provide a commentary, explaining while doing, like a master craftsman reflecting on their creative process.

You'll probably have to study someone doing an activity several times to understand it fully. Repeated exposure to the situation – preferably with a number of different 'masters' – will also allow the patterns and systems to emerge from the details of doing. The method was developed for workplace settings, but it can be used when people are on the move and in non-work settings, too. So, for example, it has been used in the home environment, with people being observed when going about their daily routines, leading to a mobile phone prototype for controlling lighting, heating and the like (Figure 5.1) (Koskela and Väänänen-Vainio-Mattila, 2004). The situation might change, the investigator sitting on a car seat or couch rather than an office chair, but the method can still be valuable.

FIGURE 5.1

Home control mobile phone prototype developed through contextual inquiry-style investigations (adapted from Koskela and Väänänen-Vainio-Mattila, 2004)

BOX 5.5 INVESTIGATION METHODS CASE STUDY 2

Focus on interviews: Collaboration among mobile workers (Gutwin and Pinelle, 2003)

Context

Many mobile workers are only loosely coupled with co-workers: that is, they work mainly on their own with a high degree of autonomy, occasionally collaborating with others. This study looked at a group of these types of people – seven home healthcare workers involved in community patient care.

Study methods

- Interviews – three rounds of interviews were carried out, each interview lasting around 1 to 1.5 hours.
  - Round 1: informal interviews, discussing general organizational issues and work patterns.
  - Round 2: focused on how the workers used information in their jobs. Discussions involved talking through the documents created and referred to.
  - Round 3: Follow-up interview to explore the complex issues arising from the previous two rounds.
- Field studies – around 60 hours of field studies were performed. Participants were followed over complete days, including during car journeys to visit patients and while in patients' homes. ➤

What insights did these methods provide?

- During work, people left 'traces' of their activity in the shared workplaces, that other workers could detect and make use of, e.g. notes for others left in the base office or with the patients themselves.
- Low-effort and low-cost methods of communication between group members were preferred.
- Synchronized communication was difficult so was kept to a minimum. The participants preferred the flexibility that asynchronous communication enabled (e.g. leaving messages for others to pick up later).

What design solutions were proposed?

Healthcare givers often visit the same places as co-workers – a patient's home, a medical center – but at different times. Geographically based mobile messaging, such as in the *GeoNotes* prototype (Espinoza *et al.*, 2001), could be used to allow workers to post messages in the places they visit. However, this is likely to be too cumbersome for the already busy clinicians. A stripped-down version of this approach might be useful, however: when a worker visits a location the mobile system could automatically post a simple marker giving their identity and time of visit; the worker could also choose to add additional context information selected from a list of predefined categories (e.g. purpose of visit – check-up, response to patient call, etc.). These tags would be available to other workers when they come to the same location.

Mobile services that provide information about the whereabouts and availability of co-workers would also be useful helpful in coordinating communications and meetings. This might involve mobile access to shared schedules and diaries. ■

Artifact Walkthroughs

Much activity, especially when it is work-based, bustles around documents: people search for, peruse, create, edit, present, discuss and destroy them. Getting people to explain the life of a document, stepping through its creation and use, can give a good sense of the flow and major components of a process.

As an example, consider the lab-books used by scientists. These are vital paper resources where users record all the details of their experiments and findings. Giving scientists mobile, tablet-sized PCs as a replacement could lead to many benefits, such as faster, computer-supported, analysis and sharing of findings (Schraefel *et al.*, 2004). To understand the role of the lab-book, a designer might watch as notes are made, ask questions about the purpose of the jottings, and when an alternative medium – such as a scrap of paper – is used, enquire why the lab-book was usurped.

5.3.3 DIARY STUDIES

Many times you just can't be with your participants when interesting things happen. Partly this is due to a lack of resources – spending 24 hours over several weeks is just not feasible; but clearly there are also issues of intrusion and privacy. A diary study is a self-reporting technique that helps fill in the gaps when you cannot observe. The information you get in the diaries can give a valuable, alternative perspective to your objective one. In writing the entries, a participant can be given the opportunity to reflect on their experience, without the pressure or influences they might feel when being observed. See Figure 5.2.

Self-reporting methods, though, are less controllable – ensuring participants complete entries at appropriate times is difficult – and highly selective, with participants attempting to make useful, helpful, coherent descriptions of their experience. The results, then, are edited versions – edited in the sense that they are synopses and have a viewpoint – of the real experience. However, their subjectivity should not be dismissed or seen as less valuable; you could consider why a participant emphasizes certain aspects and leaves out others: ask what story they're trying to tell you, and why.

To carry out the study, you provide your participants with a way of recording their entries (a paper journal, for instance), and give them instructions on the sorts of observation you're interested in, the period over which the diary should be kept, and the frequency of entries you would like.

- **Types of observation.** Questions can be broad, "Since the last entry, what activities have you seen people doing while traveling?", or more focused, "Since the last entry, what problems, if any, have you had while using the mobile information services on your phone?". It's worth asking for both free-form entries as well as answers to structured questions (multiple choice, rating, etc.).
- **Period of use.** Leaving a diary with a participant for seven days is usually sufficient; far fewer days will probably lead to a too-sparse set of data to be able to see patterns; too many more and you will begin to be overwhelmed. Choose a period that covers times when you expect significant activities to occur. So, if you're interested in work–home differences, provide the diary from say a Thursday morning to a Wednesday evening.
- **Frequency of entry.** Being unspecific, such as saying "Write about your experiences of accessing your email each day", will result in a poor return. To try to maximize the likelihood of a participant making regular entries, give them a routine that's easy to remember and follow. This might take the form of specified points in an activity (e.g. at the start, midway and end of a commuter journey), or whenever they take a break each day, or at regular intervals (e.g. on the hour), or when something interesting or critical happens.

For mobile studies it is particularly important to make sure the recording media is lightweight, in two senses:

- It should be small and not cumbersome – participants need to be able to carry it around comfortably and use it in situations were there might be limited space (sometimes none, making note-writing difficult) and when other people are present (so writing entries should not draw attention to the participant but should allow them to capture their points with some privacy). In terms of a paper-based approach, a small notebook is far more appropriate than a large journal.
- It should also provide for lightweight entry – quick, easy ways of making entries are preferred over time-consuming ones.

(a) SMS text (Gritner, R. E. and Eldridge, M. 2003) © 2003 ACM, Inc. Reprinted by permission

ID No.	Date	Time	Sent by phone (P) or Internet (I)	Reply to other rec'd msg? If yes, give ID	Sent to?	Your physical location	Briefly describe content	Why did you send a Text Message instead of phoning, emailing, etc.?	Length (letters or lines of text)	List any abbreviations, shorthands, etc. in message	Did it lead to a phone conversation, meeting, etc? If yes, explain.
S5	22	20:05	P	R7	Nikki	Still eating a meal at dining table.	I said I'd meet her at the pub soon.	Because she sent me a text message from the pub, so I couldn't phone or email her!	2 lines	V. = very	Meeting. I met her at the pub, like she wanted.
S6	23	10:55	P	R8	Lizzie	Sitting up in bed at home.	I said I wasn't going shopping, I had homework to do etc.~	I was in bed-so I didn't want her to know that!	4 lines	2day = Today Gr8 = Great :) = Smiley face.	No.

(b) activity report (a, b, adapted from Reiman 1993) Categories: fill in at end of day

Date: *friday* 6/6
ID : *3*
Activity: Fill in Every Half Hour

		moving	In public	Using your mobile	txting	Using Instant messaging	emailing	Web access	chatting	Carrying out a transaction
0730-0800	*Walk to station, get newspaper, get coffee, read bit of newspaper, text friend about meeting at 5*	X	X	X	X					X
0800-0830	*On train–read newspaper. Check listings for cinema for weekend*	X	X							
0830-0900	*Arrive station go to underground tube; pick up free paper on way. Sit on tube and read paper for 10 mins. Walk to work; post letters.*	X	X							X
0900-0930	*Scan emails–see what day will bring! See who else is in work by looking at instant message status. Get coffee and chat with couple of the guys.*					X	X		X	
0930-1000	*Answer the bossese mail question. Get ready for 10 briefing; print out notes and put some stuff on handheld.*			X		X	X	X		

(c) Eureka report

Eureka Report.

When you come across a problem using your mobile and then solve the problem, fill in one of these reports

Date and time: *Sat 11*

Your id: *7*

What where you trying to do when problem occurred, where were you and how did you know there was a problem:

Trying to send a videoclip to wife. At son's football match. Device kept saying "err 3".

How did you solve the problem:

_ Read the manual
_ Asked a colleague/ friend
✓ Phoned the helpline
_ Went to mobile dealer
_ Used help on device
✓ Tried various functions until worked

So what was the problem?

Didn't have enough credit in my pay-as-go account to send the data! Can't interpret geeky messages

FIGURE 5.2

Examples of paper-based diary study log sheets

Simple paper diaries can be used for mobile studies, but there are opportunities for the technologies themselves to play a more active role. The *Experience Sampling Method*, for example, uses pagers to interrupt participants and ask them questions throughout a study period (Csikszentmihalyi, 1991).

The criterion of light weight can be met well by having participants use a phone to file entries. One possibility is to have subjects call up a diary telephone line, as Palen and Salzman (2002) did. In their studies they tried two things:

- In an open-ended qualitative study of novice mobile phone owners, they gave 19 participants a list of issues they wanted feedback on and asked them to call whenever they wanted to make a comment relating to these. Each time they called they were paid $1.
- In a large-scale, focused investigation, Palen and Salzman tracked 200 novices during their first year of owning a mobile phone. When they rang the diary-line, they were asked a series of structured questions which they answered by speaking, completing each entry by pressing the pound (hash) key.

More structured approaches are possible, too, using speech recognition or push-key answers. In these cases, the data – possibly from many hundreds of diarists – can be analyzed automatically.

As it becomes more widely available, push-to-talk mobile telephony – where a single button press connects to the diary line – reduces the entry-making burden even further, and other technologies like multimedia messaging are enabling participants to relate their experiences in additional ways (see Box 5.6).

BOX 5.6 INVESTIGATION METHODS CASE STUDY 3

Focus on using technology to capture data: Employing mobile video and images to record user experience (Isomursu *et al.*, 2004)

Context

A study of two context-aware PDA applications. The first involved a location-aware map, showing the user their location and nearby landmarks. The second application delivered advertisements to the handheld depending on location and user profile. ➤

Study methods

- 'Experience clips' – participants were sent out in pairs, one using the PDA applications, the other recording the experiences using a mobile phone equipped with video capabilities. This cameraperson was asked to take as many clips as possible of the application user's experience, focusing on their reactions as they interacted with the services.
- Interviews – on returning from the field, the pairs of participants were questioned about their experiences.

- Video clips were transcribed and analyzed in conjunction with interview material.

What insights did these methods provide?

- The video clips were effective in capturing emotional impact. As well as spontaneous reactions, users acted out their feelings using exaggerated gestures and facial expressions; one clip, for instance, showed a participant using the PDA stylus to stab aggressively at the device's screen.
- Critical weaknesses relating to the usefulness and usability of the applications were also identified:
  - In the map application, users' ability to orientate themselves would have been enhanced if the service had access to directional information (using a device such as an electronic compass).
  - The context-sensitive advertisements used in the trial only gave information about local shops. The users were disappointed – mobile intrusions should have more value, notifying the user, for instance, of special offers. ■

The programmable capabilities of mobile phones mean that interactive diary entry making is also viable. 'Mobile Probes' (Hulkko *et al.*, 2004), for example, is a phone-based technique that prompts participants to make entries and leads them through a set of questions (see Figure 5.3).

FIGURE 5.3

'Mobile Probes' mobile phone application

However entries are made, it's normal practice to follow up the activity with interviews. These should be done while the study is in progress. You might, for example, review someone's entries at the end of each day. This sort of regular, routine follow-up allows experiences to be discussed while still fresh, encourages the participant to make entries (motivated by the knowledge of an impending meeting), and helps solve logistical problems – such as how to operate the recording media – in a timely way. The interviews can consider more than just the specific entries – the diaries act as an effective artifact for talking around the issues.

5.3.4 DISCOUNT METHODS

Mobile product life-cycles can be extremely rapid; however much you might wish to gain a full understanding of users' needs, if you want to influence the design you will have to find efficient ways of providing input to the development team. To do this, you might consider techniques that reduce the effort needed either to gather information or to analyze it once collected.

Some of the methods already described, such as contextual inquiry and diary studies, are discount methods: contextual inquiry takes some of the characteristics of an ethnographic approach, short-circuiting the time spent in the field by using the context to structure an interview style of interrogation; while diary studies are efficient by virtue of outsourcing the observation work to the participants themselves.

Several other approaches can be tried – the first three we present below are more ethnographic in nature than contextual inquiry but are still designed for quick results; the fourth takes the delegation of data gathering to an extreme, by mining insights from automatically generated logs of users' activities.

Ethnography-lite

Pure ethnography is a bit like casting a large net into the ocean, slowly trawling and eventually bringing it up to see what emerges. Sometimes there are only minnows. In contrast, some 'ethnography-lite' techniques are more like fly-fishing – you take a well-chosen piece of bait, and tools with more precision, and you go to fruitful-looking spots.

The 'Quick-and-dirty' approach, for example, involves carrying out a series of short, focused studies in the field (Hughes *et al.*, 1994). As an investigator, you start by asking yourself which situations are going to provide you with the greatest level of strategically useful information – that is, which would be the ones you would study in more depth, time permitting. For each of these study settings, the aim is to tease out the major factors that might affect the acceptability or usability of any proposed changes.

These investigations can be done, then, in the style of a pilot study, the time savings coming from having no follow-up larger-scale observation. Alternatively, the results can be used to target the more involved, costly ethnographic investigations.

'Rapid ethnography' techniques also narrow the 'wide-angle research lens' seen with standard ethnographic approaches (Millen, 2000). The careful choice of informants that we described earlier is one way of making the most of the time you have in the field. David Millen, who coined the phrase, suggests other efficiency measures, including:

- Choosing a useful time period to sample – be strategic, being there when things are likely to happen.
- Involving more than one researcher. While this seems more expensive on the face of it, it may save time in the long run by cutting down on the number of repeat visits needed, or on

problems arising from misguided conclusions that a single observer may draw. With more than one person, you can split up and cover different parts of a large site, or look out for different things (relationships or use of artifacts, say).

BOX 5.7

USING A HANDHELD IN OBSERVATIONAL STUDIES (Spinuzzi, 2003)

Field studies involve much effort, from organizing appointments through to transcribing the large amounts of data gathered. Clay Spinuzzi suggests using a handheld computer to improve the investigation's efficiency. Data can be entered using preformatted forms, designed in a way that allows for on-site initial coding and categorization of observations. The PDA can also capture and store images (both still and video) as well as record audio. PDA data analysis tools can similarly be used on the fly, helping the investigator to draw some inferences to direct the ongoing study while they are still in the field.

On returning from the study sites, the amount of transcription and coding is reduced and the data is in a form that can be quickly shared, electronically, with other team members.

Although this advice might be helpful, it is worth remembering that field studies often involve frenetic, intense work on the part of the designer. Current handhelds often require frustratingly high levels of effort, so using a mobile might reduce your effectiveness. Perhaps someone will design a note-taking device that will better meet field requirements? ■

Auto-ethnography

A technique that blurs the distinction between subject and investigator is what has been called a personal ethnography or auto-ethnography. Here the subject both records observations about their experience, as in a diary study, and is also asked to reflect and make sense of it, to create an account, themselves.

Subjects can find it difficult to adopt an ethnographic attitude; to help them understand the purpose and process of the observation, consider asking them to first observe a friend or colleague. The account from this 'training' observation may uncover relevant issues in itself. In our experience, people are often enthusiastic about being involved – they are motivated by finding out more about themselves.

BOX 5.8

AUTO-ETHNOGRAPHY AND PORTABLE MUSIC PLAYERS (Cunningham *et al.*, 2004)

Ten people were asked to perform an auto-ethnography of their own physical music collection (CDs, tapes and so on). A number of aspects of interest were outlined ➤

for them to consider, focusing on the way they organized and accessed items along with the different situations in which they used the music. These amateur ethnographers were encouraged to take photos, make sketches and annotate these to explain their insights. In addition they performed a similar ethnography of a friend's collection, with particular emphasis on accounting for the differences between this and their own.

A number of interesting findings emerged, including:

- Collections are visible and 'on display'. People are conscious of what their stacks of CDs say about them; some participants spoke about hiding or making more prominent parts of their collection in order to give the right impression to visitors. The tangible qualities of the collection – from the artwork to the packaging – are important.
- Emergent organizations. Periodically, people would put some effort into organizing their collections (by genre or artist, for instance) but over time, this would break down and the organization would reflect usage (e.g., piles of recently played CDs stacked together near a music player).
- Thrash–discard–revive cycle. New albums or tracks are initially used heavily, then listeners tire of the music and move on to something else. However, older parts of the collection experience a renaissance periodically.
- Rich perspectives on music types. As well as classifying by standard features like genre and artist, people also spoke of thinking about music in terms of location and purpose ('party music', 'music for my car', etc.).

In terms of digital portable music player design, these findings suggest a number of enhancements:

- Improve the evocativeness of the interfaces by giving access to artwork. So, the photo viewing features seen in the likes of the iPod could be repurposed more extensively to show artist images, etc.
- Help manage the thrash–discard–revive cycle. Many players give access to recently played tracks; but what about highlighting once popular but long unheard pieces?
- Allow users to add their own meta-data to customize they way they perceive their collection. At the same time, recognize that the amount of effort people wish to put into labeling and organizing their collection is not high – here there's the potential of using automatically gathered data (e.g. location sensing to label music in terms of place of use). ■

Online Enquiry

Ethnographers are, as we have seen, keen to go to the places where subjects spend their time. 'Online' is now a place which many inhabit for significant periods; this is particularly the case with young people, with their desire to be connected via chat, gaming and the like. It seems sensible, then, to observe what is going on in places like chat groups, bulletin boards and multiplayer games.

Sociologists have for many years done this sort of research work, analyzing online forum text postings in attempts to understand both online and offline social phenomena and to track the ways technology is changing society. They have also used electronic communications – email, instant messaging and bulletin boards – to interview subjects.

If you do try these methods, then the ethical audit we mentioned earlier becomes especially important (see Section 5.3.1). There's a lot of scope for an investigation to become derailed morally. Even though the material you analyze – say, bulletin board postings – may be publicly accessible over the Internet, the people who wrote the entries may feel very uncomfortable with the notion that their thoughts were being picked over and presented during a design process. Making contact and chatting with participants electronically can be equally questionable, especially in the light of the dangers posed by ill-intentioned adults wishing to communicate with children.

A Nokia-funded project used web material to help them understand the potential of mobile online communities (Isomursu *et al.*, 2003). Their target was 12–15 year olds – early adopters, they believed, of such forums. As case material for the investigation, they turned to a very popular online activity for girls of that age group in Finland at the time of the study: virtual horse stable management. Members of a stable would write stories about their imaginary horses and participate in discussions around these animals.

A content analysis of the postings to these websites helped the team identify the type of activity a mobile prototype might support and gave them issues to raise in subsequent interviews with girls. The interviewees were not recruited over the web, due to ethical concerns such as those we've already mentioned, but through contacts – friends and family of the investigation team.

However, the interviews were disappointing. The investigators came across a not untypical problem in interviewing, more marked in younger respondents: subjects having difficulties in articulating their feelings ("I don't know" was one expansive reply) or in uttering more than banalities ("It's OK", said another). To try to overcome their difficulties of expression, the team made a further use of online resources, building their own virtual stable for participants to use. The subjects were also invited to post comments about the *PonyCam* handheld prototype designed to keep members in touch with their stable when away from their home computer.

Log Analysis

People's television watching habits and use of online media have long been tracked by analysis organizations, providing content providers and advertisers with detailed information.

Such logging techniques have also been put to use to analyze mobile activities. In one trial, an Internet service provider (ISP) offered 13 households the use of a wireless tablet-sized device (McClarad and Somers, 2000). During a seven-week trial, as well as ethnographic-type observations, a program on each tablet tracked the activity types and durations, capturing the start and stop time for each application launched, along with the window captions. Despite the mobile being always connected, they found that for 45% of the time, people were using standalone applications (like games); mobile system use, that is, should not be equated with online system use. The sorts of websites popular via the tablet also gave a clue to how mobile use might fit into everyday activities: the frequently accessed content included radio (audio being streamed) and easily browsable content (such as news). The technology was being used in a way that allowed people to do more than one thing at a time – listening while doing house chores, or reading from it as they might from a magazine while half-watching television or chatting, for example.

Simple statistics on use, as in this case, are helpful, but log analysis can also call on a more sophisticated repertoire of data-mining techniques. These methods have been used for conventional website analysis – identifying common paths through the data for instance – and can similarly be applied to logs of mobile content access.

An ambitious and sophisticated foray into this sort of logging and analysis is being carried out by Nathan Eagle and Alex Pentland at the MIT Media Lab (Eagle and Pentland, 2006). One hundred smartphones have been given out to Media Lab and Sloan Business School students. In addition to logging the phone status and application use, and network operator cell tower proximities, software on the device uses Bluetooth to regularly discover and store the identifications of other Bluetooth systems nearby. 'Bluedars' – Bluetooth sensors – dotted around the users' environments are also used to track the movements of participants.

Again, the simple data is revealing –80% of usage is simply the 'phone' application; of the remaining 20% the alarm clock accounts for 3% (but requires 10 keystrokes to access!) and the photo application is popular; but more sophisticated features like the music player and web browsing have a low priority.

More involved mathematics are being used to see whether elements of social and organizational activities and structures can be identified. The results are promising and potential applications are suggested. For instance, the patterns of when a colleague bumps into another could be used to suggest future 'spontaneous' meetings; and clusters of regular association might be spotted and used as an additional measure of trust between users for mobile peer-to-peer systems.

5.3.5 FOCUS GROUPS

Imagine you are looking down from the corner of a room, with your fly-on-the-wall view. You see a group of five people comfortably sitting on mauve-covered chairs around a coffee table. They are eating finger food, glasses of juice in hand, and in animated discussion. Amidst the group sits a facilitator, skillfully guiding the discussion in an affable way.

What you've just witnessed is a typical focus-group session. It's a technique widely used in marketing to discuss brands, pricing and the like, which has found its way into interactive system development where people are asked to discuss topics – say how they spend their commute time – or to talk around issues found in earlier field studies (see Box 5.9).

BOX 5.9 INVESTIGATION METHODS CASE STUDY 4

Focus on focus groups: *Hummingbird – an interpersonal awareness device* (Weilenmann, 2001)

Context

A study aimed at understanding how a group of ski instructors would use the Hummingbird technology – the device makes a humming sound when another instructor is within 100 meters. ➤

Study methods

- Ethnographic field study – of 16 ski instructors, eight were given the device. For seven days and six nights, the investigators lived with the instructors, participating in most activities. They recorded observations and noted conversations. This data was organized into categories to assist in steering the later focus group discussions.
- Focus groups – two sessions were performed, one with Hummingbird users, the other with people from the non-user group. The user group discussions were led primarily by the users themselves as they animatedly talked about their experiences with the technology. In contrast, in the non-user group, a more structured question and answer format had to be used. Conversations were later transcribed and coded (noting pauses, etc.), and a content analysis was carried out to classify the different types of comment.

What insights did these methods provide?

While it may seem quite an esoteric application, the study gives some interesting general pointers into how people might negotiate the use of new, group-based technologies; that is, how the norms of use form. Unlike, say, the technology of the static workplace, with mobiles people have to agree on when and where the devices should be used.

In the study, negotiation progressed in two ways:

- Through actions – users would make others aware that they were carrying the device and actively using it by doing things like placing it on the table when out at a restaurant or changing the batteries while standing in a group.
- Through chatting – group members talked about how they felt about using the technology in different contexts (on the slopes, i.e. at work, and when off-duty).

The investigation also demonstrated further social factors associated with mobile technologies – people were willing to help each other understand and operate the device and encouraged each other to keep the devices switched on.

What implications are there for design in general?

Designs should promote social use. First, they should be flexible enough to accommodate etiquettes that develop (e.g., configurable by users to limit the intrusiveness of a device). Second, they should be amenable to the helpful approaches of others. If the way of interacting with a device or service is not consistent with that seen in others, it will be hard for a well-meaning friend or colleague to assist.

Functional prototypes as used here can be effective in teasing out the social dynamics that need to be addressed. ■

Although widely used in industry, there has been some concern about the efficacy of the method. A panel of experts at a human–computer interaction conference offered different takes on its validity as a method (Rosenbaum *et al.*, 2002). There are some obvious dangers such as groupthink – when everybody unanimously agrees, with no dissent. The pleasant, comfortable setting also makes it difficult for people to be disagreeable; they want to please the facilitator and others, and being opinionated could make them feel like the party bore. For these reasons, one of the panelists suggested that in terms of new systems the method is best used for brainstorming possibilities rather than critiquing concepts.

Bringing people out of their context, as focus groups and interviews in the investigators' workplace do, changes the relationship between the designer and the participants. As Michael Muller puts it, in his position statement for the panel, these approaches "tend to extract or mine knowledge rather than engage them as partners with their own skill and knowledge".

As he notes, though, there have been modifications to the basic focus-group format to bring elements of context back into the discussion. One such method is the 'usability roundtable' used by the Lotus software team in developing productivity applications (spreadsheets, workflow products and so on) (Butler, 1996). In their focus group situations, participants are asked to bring in samples of the artifacts and data they use in the course of their activities. Then they are given the opportunity to explain their work, using software tools as necessary. In the mobile case, there might be a number of mobile situations that you cannot get access to: in these cases, simulating the context – even to the limited degree seen here – would help.

5.3.6 CREATIVELY ENGAGING METHODS

The methods we've encountered up to this point are effective at exposing the *status quo*: the things subjects are engaged in and hold dear. Clearly, this present-day knowledge can be vital in designing future services. Interested in extending mobile photo facilities? Watching friends joke and tell stories as they pass photos around over a coffee will point you in the right direction.

But the techniques have limitations. First, people's values are often well hidden: you may be with your participants for extended periods of time just to gain a chink of understanding into what drives them, but when you ask people to talk about what is important to them, they might not be able to articulate these touchstones that are so essential in judging proposed designs. Then there are the difficulties of assessing how both values and behavior might reconfigure in the face of technological developments.

To overcome these obstacles, a number of methods have emerged which can be used to shed light on the inner life of the people being studied as well as to explore how novel technologies might be adopted and appropriated. All of these approaches share the quality of engaging the participants creatively. By allowing subjects to express themselves in personal, playful ways, the hope is that the bits of the subconscious wiring that make people what they are, will show themselves.

Probes

Like astronomic or surgical probes, we left them behind when we had gone and waited for them to return fragmentary data over time. (Gaver *et al.*, 1999)

Probes are data capture tools, given to participants or placed in their environment. As people engage with them, being intrigued and inspired, they record experiences and thoughts for the designers to reflect upon.

One type, *cultural probes* (Gaver *et al.*, 1999), are packages of materials designed to provoke and question informants over time, in a piecemeal fashion – participants provide bits of the jigsaw we talked about at the start of this chapter, bit-by-bit, by returning items from the probe in their own time and terms. In putting together a probe, a range of different types of media and question should be included, both to account for differences in how people prefer to express themselves and to encourage an encompassing perspective. In one study, for example, the probes included:

- Postcards with an image on one side, and on the back a question for the informants such as "Tell us about your favorite device", to ponder
- Maps and a set of small sticky colored dots for participants to mark out places where they would go to daydream or be alone
- A disposable camera with a list of image requests printed on the back, such as "photograph something boring"
- Photo album and media diary for participants to tell their story, giving glimpses of the way they see themselves and their preferences and use of different media.

Each of these items was given to the subjects in a way that made it easy for them to send back to the investigators, with packages and postage stamps provided. Participants make use of a probe item, pop it in a package, and post it.

An interesting side-effect of the approach, noted by its inventors, is the leisurely reflection it allows designers to undertake – in a fragmentary way, each day's post might bring several new items to consider; this is in stark contrast with the potentially mentally straining task typically faced in assessing the slough of data brought back by the designers themselves.

Not all probes are as low-tech as postcards and photo albums. The *mobile probes* we met in Section 5.3.3 are an example of how technology might be used to help gather up information. What have been termed *technology probes*, though, give technology an even more active role in examining a user's needs (Hutchinson *et al.*, 2003). Here, prototypes are installed and people's behavior with and around them are studied. Now, this may sound like the standard design practice of evaluating a prototype in context; however, these pieces of technology are not designed to meet a specific need, tightly providing a constrained set of services; rather, they facilitate a basic activity – such as communication – in a way that is very simple for the user to operate and also highly accommodating of their whims.

To understand this style of the approach, take an investigation of how families might communicate through novel technologies. Two probes were installed in participants' homes: the *messageprobe* and the *videoprobe*. The first was a tablet-type PC, placed in high-traffic areas of the homes (kitchens, hallways and the like), which users could write on with a stylus, leaving messages and doodles for others in the same house or in a different location altogether. The interface also supported synchronous use and a zoomable control so that users could look at an overview of all the jottings. Interaction with the videoprobe was even more basic: when the device detected a constant image over a short period (through, for example, someone standing in front of it), the picture was recorded and transmitted for display on a connected probe's screen in another location, the image fading over time.

These deployments were studied by automatically logging their use in conjunction with interviews and workshops with the participants. From these activities, the investigators were able to define two important family-communication 'needs': the role of games and fun, and the priority of systems to support coordination between people who live in different places.

These technology probes can elicit ways of acting that just would not be seen by conventional methods. Imagine you were looking into how people use maps and geographical information. You might visit their home and find an atlas on a bookshelf; taking it down, you ask the owner to talk through the reasons they might consult it. They provide you with an interesting set of scenarios, ranging from the task-centered ("When I need to find a route") to curiosity-driven ones ("I wonder what the geography of this region is"). But what about "I wanted to reminisce about the place where I proposed to my girlfriend"? The atlas probably would not mediate such expressions. An extreme example of the technology probe approach, the *drift table* (Gaver *et al.*, 2004), set out to garner these types of reaction. The probe looked like a coffee table, low and elegant, but with a viewport in its center. Peering into it, participants could see an extremely high-resolution animated aerial view of the British Isles, as if from a hot-air balloon. By placing weights around the tables – books, coffee cups, indeed whatever was to hand – participants could control the direction the view moved toward, although the movement was purposefully very slow. As well as highlighting romantic, esoteric uses, the tables installed demonstrated how fun relationships between people and technology can form.

Dramatization

Highly professional, video dramatizations – or 'envisionments' – have long been used by consumer electronics companies both to promote future technologies and as talking-points for consumers to provide comment on, often in focus groups. The problem with these, though, is that participants are well trained, through movie-going, to suspend critical judgment; the danger is that they see the presentations as just another sci-fi episode, disjunct from their reality. Furthermore, as in the cinema, they cannot interact with the characters or change the outcomes of the scenarios.

Instead of cinema, it has been suggested that a more useful model is interactive, experimental theater – where there are live actors, props and audience participation. These sorts of elements can be put together as a means to provide what's been called an 'ethnography of the future' (Iacucci *et al.*, 2000).

One such technique is the *Focus Troupe* (Sato and Salvador, 1999). Ideas are explored in a focus-group style setting but instead of being given formal presentations to comment on, or questions to discuss, participants take part in theater.

- The first 6–10 minutes are taken up by actors performing an opening scene showing new technology in use.
- Next come monologues from the actors, one on the positives, the second on possibilities presented by the technology, and the third highlighting the negatives.
- After each monologue, there are discussions involving the audience, designers and actors.

The basic technique can be deployed with many twists. Participants can direct the scenes, calling the shots and even freezing the action, and scenes can be repeated with different emotional emphases.

In these pieces of drama, the technology is made visible by props and these need to be chosen carefully. One way of doing this is to provide the actors with a number of possibilities for each scene from which to choose – say a selection between a wristwatch-type device, a handheld computer, a pen and a sensor – and then getting them along with the audience to explore the potential functions supported by the choices (Howard *et al.*, 2002).

BOX 5.10 INVESTIGATION METHODS CASE STUDY 5

Using a 'magic thing' in understanding user needs (Kuutti *et al.*, 2002)

Context

Studies to understand future use of mobiles by observing exchange students as they live and work in a foreign country.

Study methods

- Simple information gathering, e.g. diary of week (to assess sorts of daily activity participants performed).
- Interview to talk about daily activities and identify scenarios where mobiles may be useful.
- Situated participative enactment of scenarios:
  - Provide participant with very simple, non-functional, future device, the 'magic thing'.
  - Designer follows participant during everyday activities and walks through potential uses of the 'magic thing' in realistic contexts; participants also encouraged to use the 'magic thing' spontaneously. This process is described by its developers as analogous to jazz – the designer and participant play off each other as they creatively consider applications and issues.
  - Field studies recorded via notes and sketches.

Examples of design concepts explored using the techniques

- *Friend finder* – the 'magic thing' was attached to a student's bike to notify them of friend who might be along their route.
- *Language translator* – to help a visitor make sense of a foreign environment.
- *Shopping assistant* – 'magic thing' to keep track of locations of shops visited and price comparisons. ■

While these techniques appear promising in encouraging users to think and express themselves creatively, and the interactivity promotes constructive critiques, they have several features that might reduce the generalizability of the findings:

- Participants can face the same problems as in video presentations of not relating what they are seeing to the everyday circumstances. One adjustment to the technique to ground the action in reality is to perform the scenes in the actual situations they relate to – the street, a café, a commuter train and so on.

- Actors are trained to manipulate emotion, controlling responses while appearing as natural characters. To resolve this, use of non-professional actors – the participants themselves – might be considered, but their lack of acting skill could lead to a stilted, uninspiring performance.
- It's well known that the specifics of any sort of prototype – including the props – will greatly influence the types of comment participants make. Getting the audience and actors to discuss and negotiate form and function can reduce the designed-in bias that's possible in over-constrained, over-specified designer-presented props.

5.4 MAKING SENSE OF OBSERVATIONS

Investigators return each day from the field, bags stuffed with notepads and sketchbooks, photocopies of documents, and video and audio recordings. Their minds are full of memories of events and impressions. These are the results of being immersed in the users' lives.

With all this rich data, the challenge is to sift and filter it to find central features – explanations – to help make sense of the activity being studied as well as an overview of how everything fits together. This process of making sense involves several tasks and can be driven by a number of alternative analysis perspectives.

5.4.1 ACTIVITIES

As you gather observations you will have to transform these into forms which make them more open to analysis (transcribe); construct a framework of understanding (categorize and organize); produce an account of the essence of the situation under study (reflect and interpret); and communicate your findings (i.e. make them consumable for later stages of design).

- **Transcribing.** Roughly written notes need to be made legible and audio/videotapes are typed up into transcripts for more efficient analysis. In moving from the speech/image recordings to documents, try to retain as much of the information as possible, including details of non-speech aspects such as sighs, pauses and body language as well as contextual information (e.g., "Participant pauses while approaching busy road junction").
- **Categorizing and organizing.** As you review both the source materials and transcripts, themes and trends will hopefully emerge from the data. For you to be able to do this pattern-recognition task efficiently, you have to be able to abstract away from all the detail. A way of doing this is to identify how observations relate to each other – that is, you form a view of the distinct categories the data falls into and label the observations appropriately.
- **Reflecting and interpreting.** Whatever way you organize the data, the eventual aim is to explain what you saw in terms of fundamental aspects of the activity, context and people you are studying. In doing this, you should also carefully critique and circumscribe your accounts so that anyone else who reads them knows the extent to which they can generalize from them.
- **Making consumable.** Whatever the level of the study, be it a strategic long-term one that aims at finding some fundamental understanding of mobile behavior, or a more application-oriented study around a particular set of goals and activities, the work is wasted unless the results are put in

a form that can be operationalized. This seems obvious, but there is a basic tension between the work of the user-understanding stage and the system design activities.

On the last point, the design-time job is to come up with a 'system' – something that systematizes, abstracting from the 'mess' and specifics. Meanwhile, detail, of course, is the very driver of ethnographic-type studies we have been discussing. How, then, can the messiness of user studies feed into design (Hughes *et al.*, 1997)? Suggestions include using collaborative computer-based tools to encourage sharing of materials between the field investigators and the rest of the design team and ensuring a tighter integration between the studies and design activities themselves (such as using design issues to prompt additional field studies).

However, there's an argument too for thinking about designs which are less prescribing, less systematic – ones that do not completely try to clean up the rich picture but which can accommodate the complexity, variety and ambiguity of how people might use mobile devices, allowing users to adapt (or even program) the device to suit their needs (Gaver *et al.*, 2003). Consider the iPod, again. When the designers set out to produce a music player, did they imagine that someone would write a program to allow users to view web pages and other recently viewed content on it? Or that a new way of audio broadcasting, *podcasting*, would be facilitated?

These four activities are not really discrete, of course: several additional categorizations will emerge as you reflect on and interpret the data, for instance. It can be helpful, as in all stages in the design process where there is uncertainty, to pilot or prototype – take samples of the data, and perform an analysis to evaluate the usefulness of your transcribing, coding and categorization approach.

Remember, too, that when you are in the field you are not a simple recorder of events. The purpose is not to passively gather as much as possible, as if cramming for a final examination. While you're there, you should take with you some starting questions that can be adjusted in the light of what you find, the normal pattern being to iteratively gather and analyze observations in an integrated way as the study progresses.

5.4.2 ANALYSIS PERSPECTIVES

As you begin the process of accounting for what you see, both while still in the field and away from it in more reflective mode, the type of analysis perspective you bring will strongly influence what you produce.

It is common, particularly among commercial designers, to take a fairly informal approach. By 'informal' we don't mean a sloppy or unprofessional one, rather one not driven by a theory. This method is characterized by accounts that present highlights of the observations, including patterns, and that are peppered with quotations and anecdotes from the field.

More formal analysis techniques also exist, developed to give ways of looking at the data, providing a vocabulary and structure to help make sense of it. Some of these have emerged from the discipline of cognitive psychology where the aim is to account for observations in terms of human mental processes; others are derived from sociology where the perspective is somewhat wider. Our aim here is not to go into any depth for all the methods but to give an impression of what they involve and can offer to designers.

Task Analysis Perspectives

Analyzing activities in terms of the groups or structures they form is widely practiced and there are lots of variants. Hierarchical Task Analysis (HTA), for instance, is a technique that defines a user's goal in a top-down fashion as a series of actions, each decomposed into a further series of sub-actions and so on. The structure dictates the underlying sequence of actions performed during the activity, but additional flow information can be captured in a plan that specifies repetitions and choices. Figure 5.4 shows an example analysis of buying a book in a bookstore.

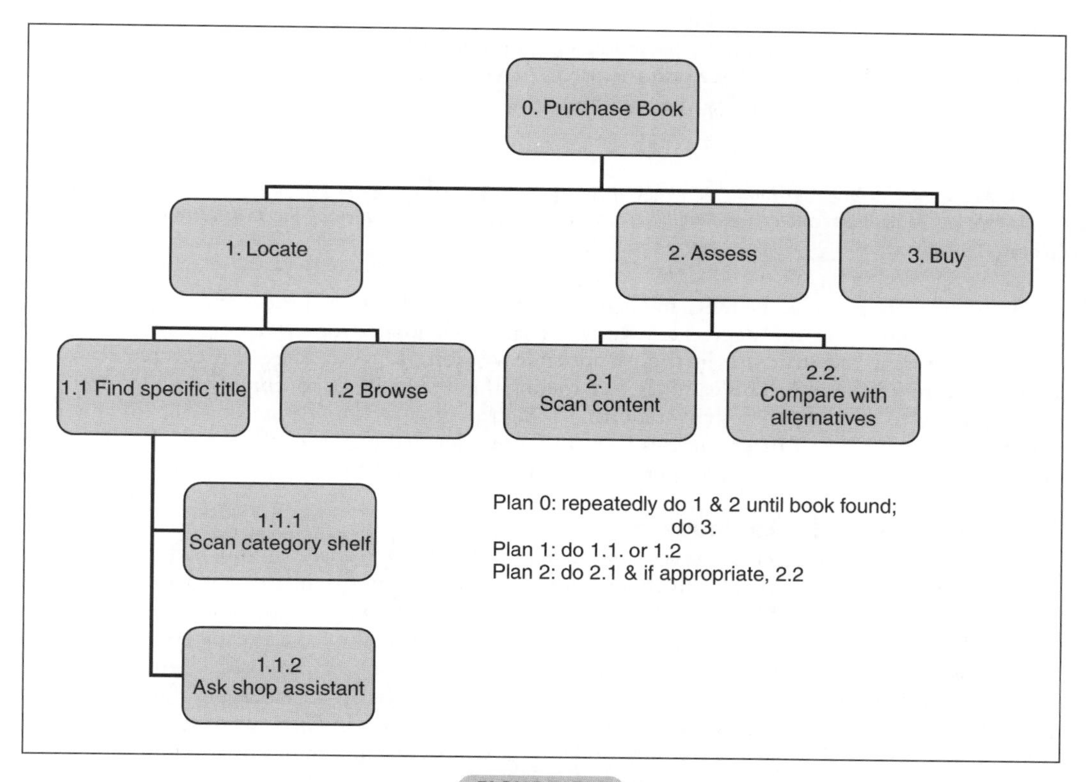

FIGURE 5.4

Hierarchical Task Analysis of purchasing a book

EXERCISE 5.3 DIGITAL AND PHYSICAL INTEGRATION – SUPPORTING BOOK BUYING USING A MOBILE DEVICE

Refer to the hierarchical task analysis in Figure 5.4. How could a mobile be used in conjunction with a bookstore to enhance a reader's book buying experiences?

Comments: think about how the mobile might be used both in the bookstore and before and after a visit. ■

Then, there is GOMS – Goals, Operators, Methods and Selections – which is similar to HTA but grounded more in an understanding of human information processing. Using it involves representing how goals are achieved by carrying out methods, which are themselves made up of groups of actions, the operators. At some points in an activity, more than one method might be applicable, so selection rules define how the choice is made.

Analyses in all of the forms can be presented either graphically, using structure charts, or textually, where a pseudocode style of description is used. As you might see, these task analysis approaches promote quite a systematic, almost mechanistic, perspective. Indeed, one form of GOMS has been described in this way:

A GOMS model in program form is analogous to a parameterized computer program. The methods take any admissible set of task parameters and will execute the corresponding instance of the task correctly. (John and Kieras, 1996)

There are a number of benefits in seeing the action in this raw, procedural way. Almost at a glance, by looking at the degree to which a chart is elaborated or the amount of indentation needed to present the structure in the pseudocode version, you can assess the complexity of an activity, locating its source. This can help in targeting the design effort, to simplify an over-complex procedure, or to support an activity requiring a high degree of knowledge or skill, for instance. Another important use of these analyses is during more detailed phases of design, so the groupings of actions, for example, can suggest potential menu structuring for functions in the final application.

Sociologically Based Techniques

To supplement the engineering style of perspective seen in task analysis, you may also want to consider tools that have emerged from sociology. A popular approach, then, is to use *Grounded Theory* (Glasser and Strauss, 1967). This, as its name so concisely suggests, is about coming up with a 'theory' (an understanding) that accounts for the observed data. We have already come across two of the essential elements of the approach. First, there's the notion of purposeful sampling, where participants are selected in a way that will help shed further light on an emerging theory. Say you notice there appear to be two types of mobile information users: *on-liners*, who do much of their access while connected, and *off-liners*, who prefer to download batches of information for offline use. Proceeding in a purposeful sampling way, you would then try to find participants from both these categories, as well as others who exhibit a more mixed pattern of use, for further study. Coding and categorizing the data is also a very prominent part of the method.

Another approach, *Activity Theory* (Nardi, 1996), is not really a method but a lens through which to look at the observations, its viewpoint defined by five principles (Kaptelinin *et al.*, 1999):

- **Hierarchical structure.** As with the task analysis, behavior is seen as being motivated by goals that can be understood in terms of successively refined actions.
- **Object-orientedness.** That is, activities are all about things, including people. Objects can be described in terms of diverse sets of properties – from physical attributes to cultural phenomena.
- **Internalization and externalization.** Behavior needs to be understood in terms of the user's internal world – their thinking, knowledge and how these processes and information are learnt (for example, repeated practice internalizes how to perform a task). Understanding the external world of knowledge, resources and actions is also critical (so, for instance, knowledge to hand, in an easily accessible external form, means a person does not have to internalize it).

- **Mediation.** Tools people use in their activities. These can be physical ones (such as a computer program) or intellectual ones (such as strategies for thinking through a problem).
- **Development.** There's a strong notion in the approach that the way people behave evolves over time.

This framework can provide useful broad provocations for the design team, leading to questions like "Have we really understood the importance of this tool?" and "What are the social influences on the use of this set of objects?". In terms of a more focused, practical deployment, a checklist has also been developed that can be used simply and quickly in the field. This gives questions to ask in relation to the principles (see Table 5.2).

TABLE 5.2

Adapted questions from *The Activity Checklist* (Kaptelinin *et al.*, 1999)

These are starting points to be kept in mind while in the field and are grouped in relation to four of the principles of activity theory; the fifth principle (mediation – concerning tools) is addressed in many of the questions

Means/ends

- Who is using or will use the proposed technology?
- What are the goals and subgoals they are trying to achieve?
- What are the criteria for judging success/failure of goals?
- What troubleshooting strategies and techniques are used?
- What constraints are imposed by the goals on the choice and use of technologies?
- What potential conflicts exist between goals?
- What potential conflicts exist between the goals and goals associated with other technologies/activities?
- How are conflicts resolved?

Environment

- What other tools are available to users?
- How might other tools integrate with the new technology?
- What level of access do users have to necessary tools?
- What degree of sharing is involved with tools?
- What is the spatial layout and temporal organization of the environment?
- How is work divided up? Think about synchronous and asynchronous work between different locations.
- What are the rules, norms and procedures regulating social interaction and coordination related to the use of the technology?

TABLE 5.2

(continued)

Learning/cognition/articulation

- What parts of the user's actions are to be learnt and internalized?
- What knowledge about the technology remains 'in the world'?
- How much time and effort is needed to master new operations?
- How much self-monitoring and reflection goes on with the users?
- How well are users supported in terms of being able to describe the problems they have with the tools?
- What strategies and procedures exist to allow users to help each other when problems happen?

Development

- What effects might the proposed technology have on the way activities are carried out?
- What are users' attitudes toward the proposed technology (e.g. resistance) and how might these change over time?
- What new goals might become attainable after the technology is implemented?

5.5 PERSONAS AND SCENARIOS

Look at the two images in Figure 5.5. One will be familiar to anyone involved in software development, the other to those interested in art. The first image is a use-case diagram and uses the notation of the hugely popular Unified Modeling Language (UML). As you can see, there are stick people – these are users, playing a particular role – and ovals, the use-cases, which represent the interactions a user needs to have with the system to achieve a goal. The aim is to clearly and simply show the relationships the user will have with the system.

The second diagram also shows a person in action but this time the notation is that of Leonardo Da Vinci. Notice the detail in the facial expression, the sense of movement in the horse. Leonardo captures the essence of the man he was studying as well as the activity of riding a horse.

Now we are not saying that you should forget about UML and use-cases; these sorts of systematic, system-focused approaches are essential in communicating the functions of the system to programmers and, later, maintainers of the system. However, these need to come further down the development process track, when the characteristics and needs of the user are more clearly known.

In terms of making sense of the observations from the field studies, tend toward the Leonardo rather than the UML – that is, look to presenting detail, specifics and richly. Two twin tools that are really very helpful in this respect are personas and scenarios.

5.5.1 PERSONAS

Look again at the Leonardo sketch. You can almost feel the determination of the person whose profile is sketched, getting a sense of their character. The excitement and fear of the rider is equally palpable – he seems a young person, in perhaps a first attempt to master a dangerous and exhilarating sport. These images believably communicate reality. They do this because the genius of Da Vinci was the way he keenly focused his eye on what was around him – his people and their actions came from the situations he encountered rather than simply from his imagination.

Personas, introduced by Alan Cooper – a leading usability consultant and 'father' of the programming language Visual Basic – present users not as stick people, anonymous, abstract figures, but rather as fully fleshed out, Leonardo-style characters. They have names, families, interests and even pets. They lives are shaped through past experiences and future goals and aspirations.

Personas can be developed from the data gathered through the various techniques we have discussed in this chapter. A persona is not a description of one specific individual but rather is the quintessence of a particular type of user. That is, you might end up with several personas for the system you are developing.

Table 5.3 gives a palette of possibilities that you might use as you paint your persona pictures. What socioeconomic background does this person come from? What might they be heard saying? What are they aiming for in life?

Bringing personas to life can be fun as well as effective. The aim is to make the characters seem as real as possible to the design team. In a Microsoft use of the approach (Pruitt and Grudin, 2003), a number of engaging ways of communicating personas to the development team were used: persona posters were displayed around the developers' offices, and they produced mouse-pads and even squeeze balls printed with persona details.

What the personas do, then, is to succinctly encapsulate the important features of the people who will end up using the system. Developers don't then have to resort to thinking about abstract 'users', or worse, think about themselves as 'typical' users – they have a real user to look in the eye throughout the process.

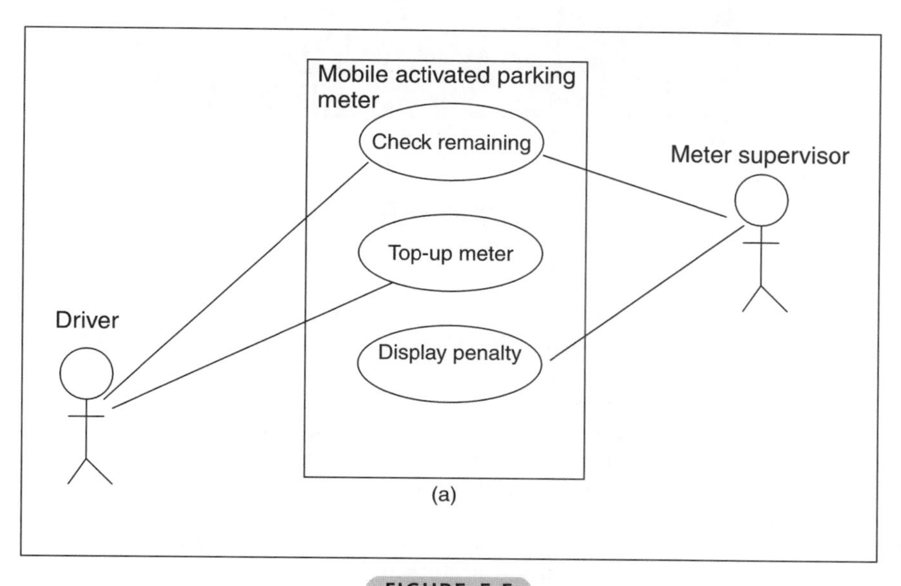

FIGURE 5.5

UML and Da Vinci

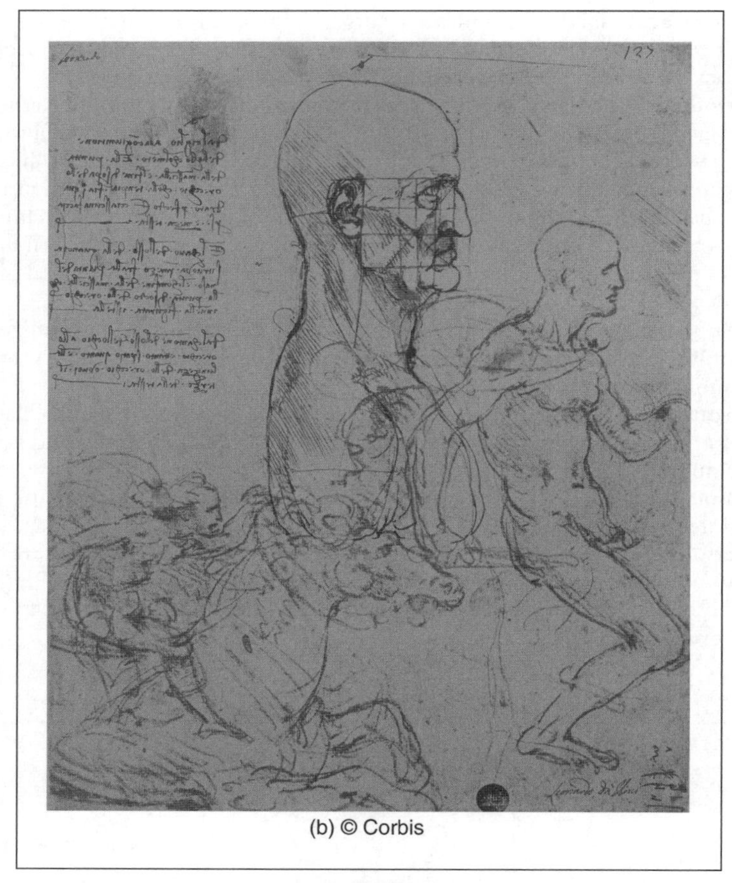

(b) © Corbis

FIGURE 5.5
(*continued*)

Successful soap-operas, films and theaters often have endearing and enduring characters whom the audience can relate to – whom they really care about; that's what you're seeking to produce when you shape your personas.

As designs are proposed, personas can be used to check them against. Pruitt and Grudin (2003), for example, show how new features in software can be evaluated with a feature–persona matrix, as illustrated in Table 5.4. For each feature and persona type, a score is given, from 2 (meaning 'loves and needs it', i.e. very useful) to -1 ('harmed by the feature'). The weights indicate the relative importance of the persona to the market.

Personas can help to inspire as well as evaluate designs. In terms of inspiration, then, if you have a persona that is playful, adventurous and wants to experiment, the sorts of service and form of presenting this might be quite distinct from those produced for a persona who is orderly, conservative and more serious in their outlook.

TABLE 5.3

Persona template (adapted from Pruitt and Grudin, 2003)

- Overview – describe the persona in a nutshell: character, background, work and family.
- A Day in the Life – step through the persona's typical day.
- Work Activities – give the persona's job description and frequently performed tasks.
- Household and Leisure Activities – describe the persona's regular social/sport commitments, chores, and any special events the persona is involved in.
- Goals, Fears and Aspirations – describe what the persona might tell a life-coach or therapist about his work and wider life.
- Computer Skills, Knowledge and Abilities – specify the persona's computing experience and the sort of devices used.
- Market Size and Influence – specify the proportion of your client's or company's customer base this persona represents.
- Demographic Attributes – give the main demographic information (socioeconomic grouping, financial profile, etc.) for the persona.
- Technology Attributes – describe the persona's use of consumer electronic and computing devices.
- Technology Attitudes – early-adopter, trend-setter, geek or technophobe? Describe the persona's attitudes toward technology – current and potential developments.
- Communicating – explain how the persona keeps in touch with people.
- International (Cultural) Considerations – describe any cultural-specific aspects of the persona.
- Quotes – give some typical examples of the things the persona might say.
- References – specify the source documents from field studies that you used to build the persona.

In both thinking up designs and evaluating them, a useful mnemonic to keep in mind is WWxD, where *x* is the name of your persona – it's shorthand for "what would x do?". How would they behave in certain situations, how would they react to the way you are asking them to interact with a system?

5.5.2 SCENARIOS

We're familiar with scenarios from our early childhood:

There was once a sweet little maid who lived with her father and mother in a pretty little cottage at the edge of the village. At the further end of the wood was another pretty cottage and in it lived her grandmother.

Everybody loved this little girl; her grandmother perhaps loved her most of all and gave her a great many pretty things. Once she gave her a red cloak with a hood which she always wore, so people called her Little Red Riding Hood.

TABLE 5.4

Feature–persona matrix example for a mobile, small-screen document viewer/editor (inspired by Pruitt and Grudin, 2003)

The weight indicates the relative importance of the persona to the business. Feature scores range from 2 (very useful) to -1 (harms user).

	Persona 1 Ben (general manager)	Persona 2 Clare (academic)	Persona 3 Freddy (home user)	Weighted sum
Weight	60	30	10	
Feature 1: Reading draft	2	2	1	190
Feature 2: Marking sections for revision	1	2	0	120
Feature 3: Editing	0	1	−1	20

One morning Little Red Riding Hood's mother said, "Put on your things and go to see your grandmother. She has been ill; take along this basket for her. I have put in it eggs, butter and cake, and other dainties."

It was a bright and sunny morning. Red Riding Hood was so happy that at first she wanted to dance through the wood. All around her grew pretty wild flowers which she loved so well and she stopped to pick a bunch for her grandmother.

(from the Project Gutenberg eBook of Little Red Riding Hood, www.gutenberg.org/dirs/1/1/5/9/11592/11592-h/11592-h.htm)

While personas present the characters in a detailed, human way, the aim of scenarios is to do the same thing in terms of the actions these characters carry out. As Jack Carroll puts it, "Scenarios are stories. They are stories about people and their activities." (Carroll, 2000)

They are not long, drawn-out narratives, though; not epics but vignettes – focused pieces of action where one or more characters – your personas – attempt to achieve a specific goal. And, just as we can use a template to help create personas, there are series of features that can help put scenarios together, filled in from the data in observations, as Carroll details:

- **Setting.** This is the starting circumstances for the story. Remember the fables you heard when a child; they always started 'Once upon a time . . .' and went on to tell you where the action was set. Just as these opening words in the story above help place yourself in Little Red Riding Hood's world and moment, so should the setting of the scenarios you write.
- **Actors.** The extract from Little Red Riding Hood, above, also lays out the key players. Scenarios can be written without reference to specific personas but it is better to include them.
- **Goals or objectives.** What do the personas want to achieve in the situation?

- **Actions or events.** Here, you detail the steps the persona takes in trying to achieve their objectives.

From your observations you are likely to produce a good number of scenarios. Analyzing these can help to identify problems or key opportunities for introducing a new system or modifying an existing one. Here, then, is an example scenario that encapsulates the experience of lecturing to large classes, which we created after watching a number of lecturers at work:

Jane is halfway through a lecture on New Zealand culture; she's speaking to 200 first-year students. Now she wants to see what they think about one of the issues she has just talked about. She asks them to raise their hands to make a point, but is disappointed when no one responds. Next, she asks them to chat in pairs to discuss the question and after a few minutes asks again for volunteers to raise their hands to say what they discussed; again the response is slow and low.

It is possible, too, to use scenarios in a prescriptive way; that is as a vehicle for portraying a vision for a future product or service. Take, for example, this scenario we produced while thinking of how mobile systems might help the lecturers we watched in the earlier observations (Jones and Marsden, 2004):

Dr Monday begins her lecture on advanced linguistic analysis to 300 first-year students. ''Before we go any further, are there any questions about last week's topic? Send me a text now from your mobile phone to 444.'' After a minute, Dr Monday checks the computer display and sees there are 25 questions listed in the order they arrived; she can reorder the list alphabetically and by size of message as well. She selects one of the questions to answer.

Later in the lecture, Dr Monday wants to test the students' understanding of 'focus'. ''Here's a quick quiz'', she says. ''If you think focus is related to the subject, text 1 to 444; if you think it is related to the topic, text 2; and if you think it is related to the verb, text 3 to 444.'' Moments later, Dr Monday can display a bar chart showing the students what the most popular choice was. ''Most of you are wrong'', she says, wryly; ''the correct answer is 2 – the topic.''

Several times in the lecture, Dr Monday asks the students to text their current 'happiness level': ''send a text message to 444 now to show how well you understand the lecture so far'', she says. ''Enter H followed by a number from 0 to 9 where 0 is the worst.'' She can view the changing level of 'happiness' over time as a line graph.

After the lecture, she returns to her office and can access all the questions sent by students; she can also review the bar charts for each multiple-choice question, and see the 'worm' trace plotted over time. All this information helps her review the lecture content and plan for next week's session.

BOX 5.11 MOBILE SCENARIO: INTEGRATING MOBILE DEVICES AND INTERACTIVE TELEVISION

In one project we were involved in, the aim was to explore how a mobile device might be used in conjunction with digital interactive television. From the fieldwork, ➤

which involved watching users and talking to experts involved in interactive TV design, scenarios were developed to highlight problematic issues in current use of TV along with others to illustrate design proposals. We reproduce an example of the latter here (Turner, 2004).

- Problems addressed:
  - Knowing which programs of interest are scheduled to be broadcast
  - Recommending a television program to a friend.
- Envisaged system use:
  - Recommending a television program to a friend
  - Recording a program of interest using a Personal Video Recorder (PVR).

Tom's friend Lucy enjoys watching the same sort of history programs as Tom. Lucy is a little more organized than Tom and will usually check the television listings to see if there is anything on during the week that might be of interest. If she sees something that looks interesting she will usually email Tom to let him know.

While looking through the television listings for the week, Lucy happens to notice a documentary about Mary Queen of Scots that she thinks Tom would also like to see. They both studied the Tudor period and like to see how this period of history is presented on television. The program is on BBC3 at 9.00 pm on Tuesday. Getting her mobile phone out, she launches the TV highlights application. She selects 'Find Program' and enters the program name. The system returns a list of programs with that name and Lucy selects the program on BBC3 on Tuesday night.

Information about the program is displayed and Lucy selects 'Recommend Program'. She selects Tom from her list of buddies and in the text field enters a short message for Tom. The system asks Lucy to confirm that she wants to recommend this program to Tom, and she does so.

Tom's mobile phone beeps, indicating that he has received a new message. An alert pops up informing him that he has been recommended a TV highlight. He can tell that this has come from Lucy because the system has matched up her number in his address book. He selects the alert and a screen pops up showing information about the program. The program looks interesting, so Tom selects 'Record this Program'.

He's not sure whether he will be in on Tuesday night, so he wants to make sure that he doesn't miss the show. The program gets added to the 'to be recorded' list for Tom's PVR. Tom writes a quick message back to Lucy to thank her and selects 'Send'.

The system asks Tom whether he'd be interested in receiving details of other programs like this. He selects 'yes' and can see that 'History Documentaries' has been added to his list of favorite types of programs. ■

SUMMARY

The methods discussed in this chapter are about finding out what matters. What are the users' values and why do they hold them? What activities are performed and how are they carried out? How does the situation constrain and facilitate these behaviors?

The answers to these sorts of question are used to identify additional applications of mobile technology as well as working out the best ways to meet market opportunities identified earlier. The range of functions required and the forms they might be delivered in can be addressed.

As in most things in interaction design, work in understanding users involves applying a mix of tools and techniques; some have scientific roots (such as the data-mining log analysis), others artistic ones (such as the cultural probes).

Mobile service investigations differ from those for conventional application development in at least three ways. First, there needs to be greater reliance on user self-reporting techniques to compensate for the more limited opportunities for first-hand investigator observations. Second, in many situations, design is considering unconventional, unfamiliar juxtapositions of computing technology and everyday life along with novel interaction methods. For these reasons, greater effort is needed to engage users creatively in the articulation of their requirements. Finally, product development life-cycles lead to an increased pragmatic emphasis on discount methods.

Data from all the user-understanding methods has to be transcribed, categorized, analyzed and structured in order to draw out the key elements and issues. We've reviewed several approaches and highlighted the popular, practical methods of personas and scenarios.

WORKSHOP QUESTIONS

- Before the workshop session, talk with three people who work in 'mobile' environments: a coffee barista, a street newspaper vendor, a train station official, for instance. Ask them what questions they get asked by members of the public. In the workshop, relate their responses to the contexts and discuss potential mobile services suggested by the observations. What issues are there in terms of location and other context awareness?
- Write a program to log elements of your computing activity during a typical day. For example, record all the web pages you access, or generate a prompt at random intervals that asks you to write a brief description of what you are doing. If you don't want to write a program, use your mobile phone and look at the text messages you've sent or photos you've taken over a period of say a week. During the workshop, discuss issues relating to the logging process and outcomes and think about any patterns or insights the data gives you.
- Ask a colleague to talk you through the artifacts on their mobile – the calendar appointments, images, text notes, music and so on. Get them to explain where they were and what they were doing when they created the document, its purpose and subsequent use. Swap roles and repeat the process. What opportunities for new or improved services can you identify?

DESIGNER TIPS

- *Check your field impressions with people who spend much of their time on location – flower-stall workers, newspaper stand vendors and the like. Ask them what they see and hear, too.*
- *Read blogs relating to mobile life and technology; engage in the debate by posting comments and contact the writers directly to provoke their opinions.*
- *Typical and 'average' users are of course important. But look out for those people who are doing intriguing things with the technology – appropriating and subverting it. Seek out interesting-looking activities and people who are in mobile contexts but who are not using mobile technology – someone sketching in the town square, a local community action group meeting in a café, etc.*
- *Use focus groups mainly with users in brainstorming phases, to inspire designs. Be wary of using the input to inform detailed design.*
- *Think about how you might mine your company's or client's customer service usage logs. What future bits of mobile 'meta-data' might you find useful if it was automatically logged? Talk with engineer colleagues about capturing such data.*
- *When developing personas and scenarios, be aware of the temptation to exaggerate or fantasize. If these artifacts are to have any credibility with software engineering colleagues, they must emerge mainly from the facts rather than speculations. Provide background documents with the field data as a support.*

CHAPTER 6
PROTOTYPES

OVERVIEW

6.1. Introduction
6.2. What is a prototype?
6.3. Different prototypes for different purposes
6.4. Low-fidelity
6.5. Higher-fidelity
6.6. Finishing the process
6.7. Issues in prototyping
6.8. A final note on development

KEY POINTS

- Prototypes provide common and unambiguous communication for multi-disciplinary development teams.
- Low-fidelity prototypes support the possibility of having the end-users become part of the design team – 'Participatory Design'.
- Prototype creation requires compromises in time to create the prototype (hi-fidelity vs low-fidelity) and the functionality of the prototype (vertical vs horizontal).
- Mobile prototypes often need to be evaluated over a long period of time, so must be robust.

6.1 INTRODUCTION

The goal of this chapter is to give you the tools to turn your ideas into something resembling finished software. This will involve the creation of prototypes.

In the words of Scott Jenson (Jenson, 2002), prototyping is a way to 'fail fast', his rationale being that if we fail enough times, then eventually we will get it right. No matter how good the designer, it is unlikely that their first design will fulfill all the varied user, engineering and esthetic requirements. Designers need to communicate these ideas to the various members of the team (and the end-users) in order for them to critique and comment on the design. The designer then alters the design and opens it up for another round of critique. And so on.

At some point the design phase ends and it becomes necessary to commit to a final design. The success of the final design will depend a lot on how many cycles of critique were completed. Using prototypes is a great way to ensure that you get the most out of design cycles.

6.2 WHAT IS A PROTOTYPE?

When you see the word 'prototype', what image does it bring to mind: experimental spacecraft, scale model, buggy software ...? Software developers almost always associate the term prototype with pre-release software, as there are various RAD (Rapid Application Development) software development methodologies that talk about iteratively developing software prototypes until they become final products. For artists or designers, it is usual to think of a prototype as being a rough pencil and paper sketch of the final artifact's appearance.

Although there are no hard and fast rules about what a prototype is, the crucial thing is that it lets you express a design idea as quickly as possible. So, for programmers, it is easier to create an interface skeleton in Visual Basic than sketch the equivalent interface using pencil and paper. Artists, on the other hand, need not learn a programming language to create a prototype.

6.3 DIFFERENT PROTOTYPES FOR DIFFERENT PURPOSES

We can create prototypes for almost any design using a wide variety of materials and technology. Due to this diverse nature, it is important to understand the differences between various types of prototype and the value in building each different type.

One common way to differentiate prototypes is according to how closely they resemble the appearance of the final artifact. Prototypes which do resemble the final product are referred to as 'high-fidelity' and those which do not are referred to as 'low-fidelity'. It is worth noting that this notion of 'appearance' relates to the user's perception and not that of, say, the software developer. For example, we may have a software prototype which contains code to be used in the final product, but looks nothing like the final version – this would be low-fidelity as that is the user's perception.

Obviously prototypes do not always fall neatly in the low-fidelity/high-fidelity classification. Instead, it is more useful to think of a scale starting with, say, paper sketches at one end and beta release systems at the other. In the next section we will discuss a number of prototyping techniques starting with low-fidelity and working our way to high-fidelity prototypes. Along the way, we will consider why each technique is useful and what you might expect to gain by building that type of prototype. As a brief rule of thumb, however, low-fidelity prototypes are more easily created and should therefore be used earlier in the design process before exact details are known. As the design process matures, so should the fidelity of the prototype.

6.4 LOW-FIDELITY

6.4.1 SELF-CHECKING

We've all had experiences where something makes perfect sense in our minds, but when we try to explain it to someone else, all sorts of embarrassing mistakes and flaws begin to surface. "It seemed like a good idea at the time" does not really cut it in interface design.

Prototyping is a good way of working through ideas, promoting, rejecting and refining them. Therefore, designers will often make low-fidelity prototypes for themselves to see whether their ideas make sense before discussing them with others on the team. The most famous example of this in mobile computing is Jeff Hawkin, who carried a piece of wood around in his shirt pocket to act as a surrogate for a PalmPilot (Bergman and Haitani, 2000). Sounds crazy, but it worked for him and the PalmPilot went on to succeed in a market of notable failures (not least, the Apple Newton).

A much more common form of low-fidelity prototyping is sketching an interface. By committing ideas to paper, designers are able to see how their interface might look: how many buttons are

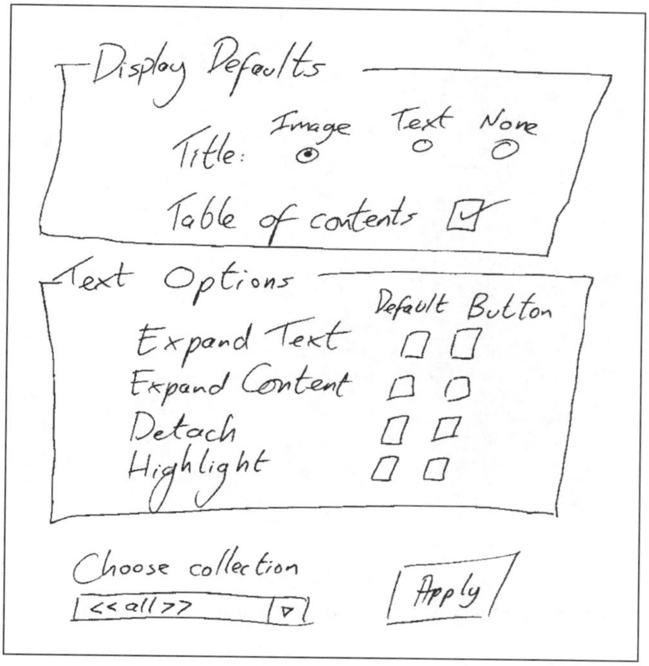

FIGURE 6.1

A sketch from the design process which created an interface to the Greenstone digital library which allows content to be deployed on mobile handsets

required, what warning lights and displays are needed to give feedback, etc. Figure 6.1 is a sketch showing the interface to a digital library system for mobile handsets. After some shuffling of components, making design compromises along the way, the interface contains the key elements which allow the user to interact with the underlying functionality.

As an alternative for those of us who find sketching a chore, we tend to use Post-it notes for each interface element, which can then be moved around without redrawing from scratch. In Figure 6.2, you can see the same interface created using Post-its on a whiteboard.

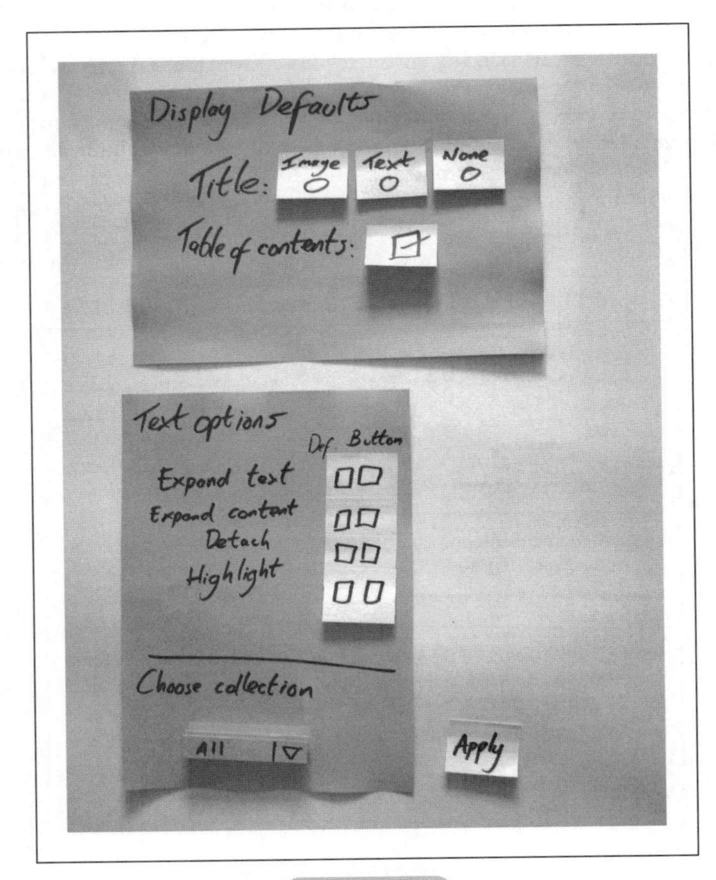

FIGURE 6.2

The same interface, but using Post-it notes on a whiteboard

Another key, but less obvious, benefit of prototyping is the time it gives to reflect on a design idea in isolation from implementation issues. When struck by a design idea, there is a tendency, among programmers at least, to code up the idea, developing the design in tandem with the code. Often this leads to premature commitment to a half-baked design idea. I am guilty of this myself, and wasted about three months of programming time when developing the ideas for the new menu structure discussed in Chapter 8. In my rush to create a functioning handset, I glossed over design considerations and made some arbitrary decisions, such as the number of lines of text the menu should display. For example, had I taken the time to sketch out the interface before committing to code, I would have realized that I needed to use the bottom line of the screen to display the number and not use it to display further menu options. Again, it seemed like a good idea at the time.

6.4.2 COMMUNICATING WITH OTHERS

Just before we were married, my wife and I went on a course to help us prepare for married life. One exercise we undertook required one of us to describe an image and the other to sketch it based on the verbal instructions. It was one of the hardest things we've ever had to do – speech is the wrong medium to convey visual information. I believed I was following her instructions implicitly, but I ended up with a completely different shape.

For interaction and interface designers, the same holds true. I've sat at design meetings and discussed an interface with the programming team. I leave the meeting feeling confident that I've accurately conveyed my ideas and the programmers leave convinced that they too understand exactly what I want. When the demonstration rolls around, however, it is clear that the meeting was a waste of time.

EXERCISE 6.1 PORTABLE MP3 PLAYER – SPECIFICATION

Here is the specification for a portable MP3 player. The YAMP MP3 device will have the following features:

- Play, Pause, Next Track, Previous Track, Forward, Rewind
- Give status about track name, track length and battery status
- Should fit comfortably in pocket.

Read through the specification and sketch a low-fidelity prototype that conforms to the specification. Now, show the specification (but not your sketch) to someone else and have them sketch it. Regardless of how many people you do this with, it is unlikely that any two sketches will be identical. Unless you use prototypes early on in the design phase, a lot of ambiguity is going to creep in. ■

Obviously, the best way to convey a visual design is to draw it. Many people are embarrassed by their sketches and hence reticent to show them to others. This is missing the point. The idea of an initial sketch is to convey abstract ideas, not give a look and feel for a final product.

A sketch of the interface is the first point in communicating a design idea with the rest of the development team. In particular, we have found that the combination of whiteboard and Post-its is very empowering. With paper and pen, of necessity, one person is in control and acts as a filter for updates to the design. With a large shared surface and independently movable controls, all members of the team feel empowered to make changes to the design.

6.4.3 INTERACTION PROTOTYPING

Having sketched the layout of the interface, it's time to give some consideration to how someone will interact with the device. For this, we bring in to play the earlier work on scenarios. Scenarios allow designers to dry-run their ideas on the paper sketches provided. In Figure 6.3, you can see a prototype system we used for one scenario in the digital library application, sliding the appropriate 'screen' into position on the handset.

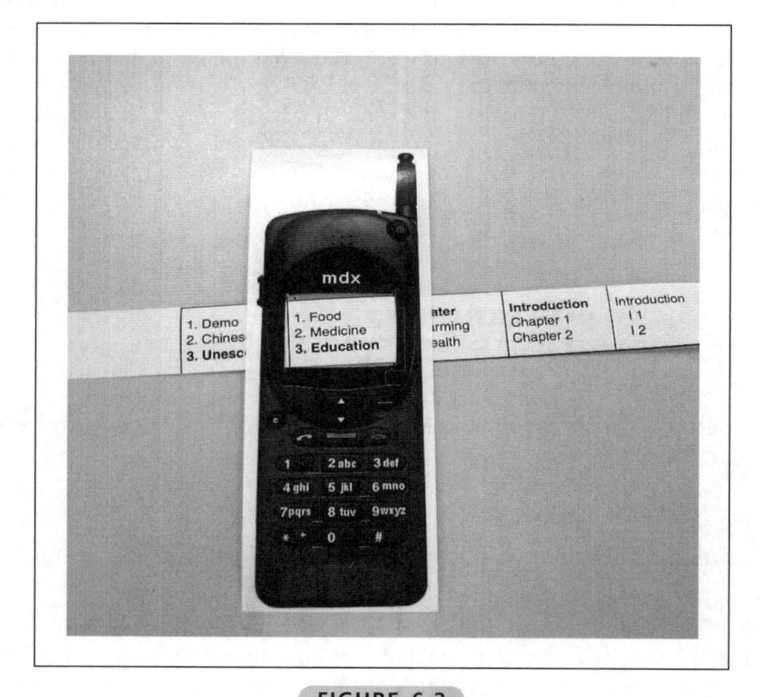

FIGURE 6.3

A scenario being tested by moving the correct screen into position in response to user selection

Working through scenarios is similar to a technique called storyboarding which is used in the movie industry. The basic idea is that a series of sketches are drawn to show the steps required in interacting with the interface design. Note that although storyboarding is based in film, we have adapted it to take in ideas from state-charts to enhance the representation. For example, in Figure 6.4, the items down the left are separated by a dotted line which means that they are present on all screens. As we all understand state-charts, this works well for our group, but you may want to develop your own conventions. (We would, however, recommend you learn about state-charts as they are fantastically useful for designing any interactive system. A good place to start is Horrocks' excellent book (Horrocks, 1999).)

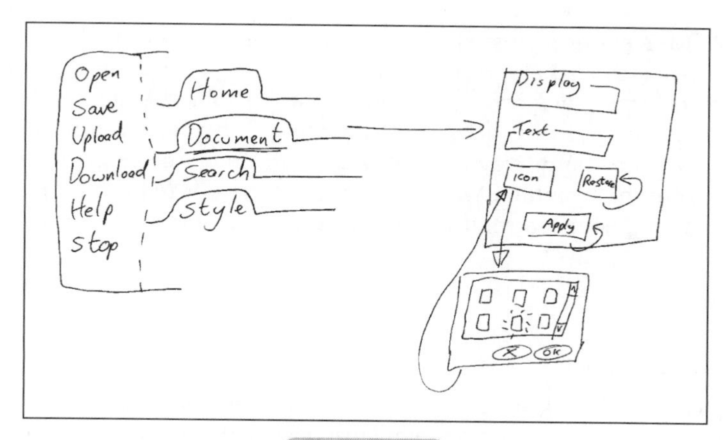

FIGURE 6.4

Here, the effect of each button on a screen can be seen. The items on the left are accessible at any time

The main limitation of storyboarding is its linear nature. Storyboards are constructed to accommodate a fixed set of sequential interactions. Of course, we know that interacting with computers rarely follows this model. Often users wish to explore and will take unforeseen paths through an interface. Therefore, as in Figure 6.4, we have shown possible paths through the interface, rather than examining one particular path through the software.

To support this type of interaction, we have adapted slideshow software. A package such as PowerPoint allows a number of screens to be joined in a nonlinear way. Each sample screen becomes a slide and clicking on a button causes a transition to the next screen in the appropriate sequence.

There are obviously more powerful tools one might use for this role, such as Flash or even video editing tools. In fact, systems such as SILK (Landay and Myers, 1995) use a digitizer to allow users to sketch directly into the computer and then link together the sketched screens to prototype screen flows. Our experience, however, has been that more advanced tools require too great an effort for most designers to learn. Slideshow applications, however, are taught to most students entering tertiary education as a matter of course. The simple 'branching' type interaction they support has proven more than sufficient for this level of prototype.

If you don't want to go so far as to use PowerPoint, it is of course possible for one of the design team to play at being the computer and show the appropriate screen at the appropriate time. Within the HCI community, this is known as a Wizard of Oz prototype, where a human is used to simulate the part of a perfect computer. Usually, Wizard of Oz techniques are used to simulate artificial intelligence solutions or speech recognition – Gould and colleagues pioneered this approach with a 'listening typewriter' back in 1983 (Gould *et al.*, 1983).

EXERCISE 6.2 PORTABLE MP3 PLAYER – FURTHER TASKS

For the YAMP MP3 player discussed in the last exercise, sketch out what will happen to the display when each of the buttons is pushed. Now, try your design with three target users, swapping the screens corresponding to the buttons they push (Wizard of Oz). Chances are you will find this tricky and frustrating (so will the user). Now repeat the exercise, but creating the display using PowerPoint. Create each screen as a slide and link together with the hyperlink feature. Sure, this is harder to do the first time you try it, but now that you have learnt, it is going to save you a lot of time and frustration in future. ■

6.4.4 EMPOWERING USERS

In the next chapter we will look at how functional prototypes (and final systems) can be evaluated with real users. However, we need not wait until that stage of development; we can, in fact, employ users to be part of the design team.

This is formally known as 'participatory design', where selected members from the end-user community develop the design along with programmers, interaction designers and the rest of the development team. Participatory design has a long history and comes in many forms. One of the most popular is PICTIVE (Muller, 1991). Based on low-fidelity prototyping, PICTIVE consists of a kit containing plastic versions of common interface widgets which the participants arrange on a shared surface (usually a horizontal whiteboard) until they reach a consensus of how the interface should appear. The shared surface is video-recorded throughout the session to provide a design rationale.

As noted in Section 6.4.2 above, the shared surface is a very democratic way of creating an interface by making the elements available to, and understandable by, every person on the design team. If you really care about having input from your users in the design process, this technique is hard to beat.

Another form of participatory design is related to live-action role playing. This technique is perhaps more applicable to mobile computing as it relates to users in their real environments. Essentially, participating users are given some low-fidelity props to act as surrogates for mobile devices (similar to Jeff Hawkin's block of wood) and are filmed using these 'devices' in various work scenarios. In one example (Nilsson *et al.*, 2000), the participant is a worker in a reprocessing plant who needs to monitor flow rate in pipes. The worker has a mobile device which he can use while walking round the factory to gain readings from various valves in the system. The mobile device then shows graphical representations of these values which allow the worker to diagnose problems and monitor performance. Of course, this rather relies on the willingness of the participants to be filmed and to role-play – neither of which come naturally to a lot of people.

In Figure 6.5, the participant is using a polystyrene 'computer' to take readings from cardboard 'sensors' in order to explain his design ideas to the development team.

A Note on Low-fidelity Prototyping

Some of our work has been in virtual reality gaming, where the production costs are prohibitively high. So, before we start designing, programming and modeling, we play a 'cardboard' version of

FIGURE 6.5

A worker enacts a scenario using low-fidelity prototypes of mobile computers and sensors

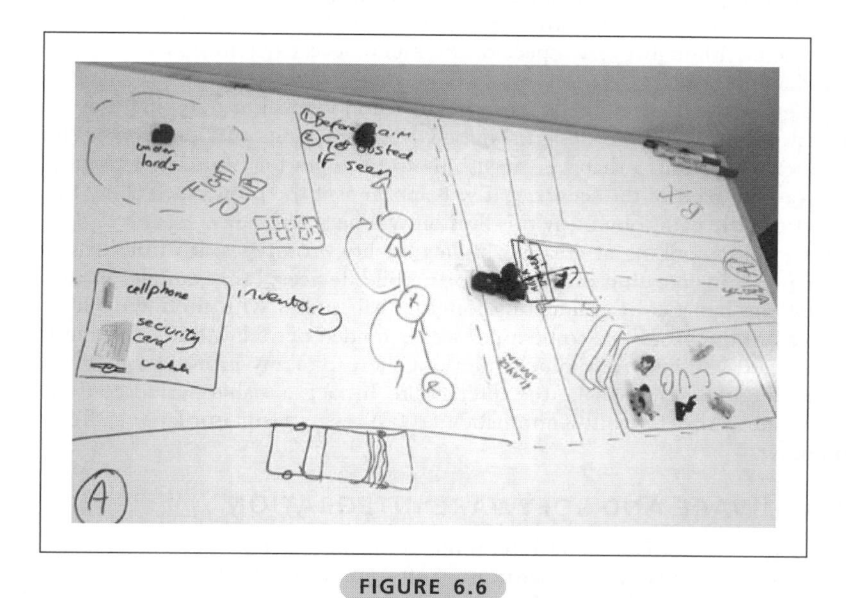

FIGURE 6.6

A low-fidelity prototype of a VR game using pens, paper and plastic figures

the game (see Figure 6.6). Playing in cardboard allows us to decide whether the idea has any merit before taking it to the rest of the team.

When we started using cardboard and paper, the rest of the team were very skeptical about the value of such an approach – virtual reality is a technology-heavy research area. Once they saw how quickly we could refine ideas and empower non-technologists to contribute to the discussion, they realized that cardboard is an essential component in virtual reality. Depending on the culture of the organization you are based in, you may need to do some work before they accept the validity of low-fidelity approaches.

6.5 HIGHER-FIDELITY

6.5.1 DECIDING WHAT TO PROTOTYPE

By the end of the prototyping stages listed above, you should have a clear idea of the basic design and be in a position to draw up a fairly comprehensive list of features. It is then important to see how well the designs support the tasks and scenarios of the target user groups. At this stage of the process, one does not want to implement every feature and screen, so it is essential to determine which aspects of the design are critical and which are not. These critical aspects are then tested in another round of prototyping.

A large part of prototyping is about deciding what to test and what not to test. If you tested everything, then you would be creating a final product and not a prototype. Prototyping, therefore, requires intelligent compromises to be made. One way to think about compromises is in terms of horizontal and vertical prototypes. Horizontal prototypes show as much of the functionality as possible, but none of the functions are active. Vertical prototypes, on the other hand, are designed to test one particular part of the functionality of the device. In the case of the cellular handset design (Chapter 8), we created a vertical prototype which tested the ease with which menu commands could be accessed. Although every aspect of the menu access system was implemented, activating the functions had no effect.

In order to guide the trade-off between horizontal and vertical prototyping, it is worth returning to the original scenarios for the design. Nielsen (1993) suggests that prototypes should primarily support the user scenarios, so that we can use the prototypes for future user testing. So, provided the user sticks to the path of the scenario, it will appear as if the prototype is fully functional. If the user wanders from the path, obviously this illusion will be shattered.

As we move on to looking at creating higher-fidelity prototypes, it's time to start focusing on the particular needs for creating prototypes for mobile devices. For example, in the next chapter, we will discuss the benefits of conducting longitudinal studies with mobile devices. Longitudinal studies will require the prototype to be used over extended periods – one study ran for over a year (Petersen *et al.*, 2002). This pretty much rules out the use of any prototype which relies on using a human to play computer and fake the interaction. In fact, a viable period could be as little as a few hours. In their study, Liu and Khooshabeh (2003) report facilitator fatigue after a few hours of playing computer.

6.5.2 HARDWARE AND SOFTWARE INTEGRATION

Prototypes for mobile devices create interesting compromises not found in other devices due to the close integration of software and hardware. Software prototypes for desktop computers can rely on the fact that the input and output hardware is fairly standard (monitor, screen, keyboard, etc.), allowing the prototyper to focus on software issues alone. With mobile devices, the hardware is often very specialist and optimized to the application. In an ideal world, the hardware would be complete and the software tested on the platform. However, in reality, the hardware and software are highly interdependent and developed in tandem – think of designing the interaction for an iPod without the scroll wheel hardware available. Sadly, due to the costs involved, the hardware iteration cycles are much slower than those for software. This means that the software prototypes have to be developed on hardware that is completely different from the deployment platform.

Another reason for using different hardware is the performance characteristics of the processor and memory of the mobile device. If you're developing an application for a device slated for release in a year's time, then current devices will obviously not have the processing or memory resources available at release time. This effect is much more pronounced for mobile systems than for desktop systems; most current applications do not use anything like the full capability of the available processor. This is not the case with current mobile devices – the form factor, and other issues such as battery life, mean that processor speed and hardware resources are at a premium.

So how do you prototype software for hardware that doesn't exist?

PC-based

The simplest solution is to develop the software on a desktop PC using a software emulator. Many development systems come with a variety of emulators (see Figure 6.7). For programmers used to working in a tool such as Visual Studio, this can be a very easy and natural progression. To help programmers migrate to the mobile platform, Microsoft and Sun use subsets of their desktop APIs rather than force programmers to learn completely new libraries. So, for example, Microsoft PocketPC and Mobile devices carry a subset of the .net APIs in Flash-ROM. Not only does this reduce development time, but by using ROM, the libraries do not take up valuable volatile storage space.

A further benefit of this subset approach is that it better supports evolutionary prototyping (more on this later) and gives the programmer a clearer idea of what is possible on the target platform.

For many programmers, the approach outlined above may be overkill. Perhaps the interface they're building is not sufficiently complex to warrant learning the intricacies of the API subset. Or perhaps they're creating an interface with a completely different look and feel than that currently supported on a standard emulator. One approach we've used in these instances is to create what is essentially an interactive photograph. Figure 6.8 shows a prototype we used to evaluate the alternative menu system in Chapter 8. It's a Java applet (we wanted people to have access to it on the Internet) where invisible buttons are overlaid on the various keys and buttons present on the scanned photograph. We've reused this code for various prototypes we have built, so the initial effort has more than paid off.

One great benefit of developing this way is the separation between the application logic and the interface code. In the case of the new menu scheme, we wanted to check the underlying algorithm first to see whether it was possible to structure functions according to the scheme we had developed. We therefore created this structure in Java. Once it worked, we could simply wrap a simple presentation layer around the object to facilitate the user testing. Once that was complete, we could then use the same code for the final product. Sadly, the interface never made it to market, but that's a different story.

Please note that it was not possible for us to test the interaction with the new menu scheme using paper prototyping – it would be impossible for the Wizard of Oz computer to keep up with the user interactions. This was also the case with the photo browser we discuss in Chapter 10 – there is simply no way we could re-create this effect in paper.

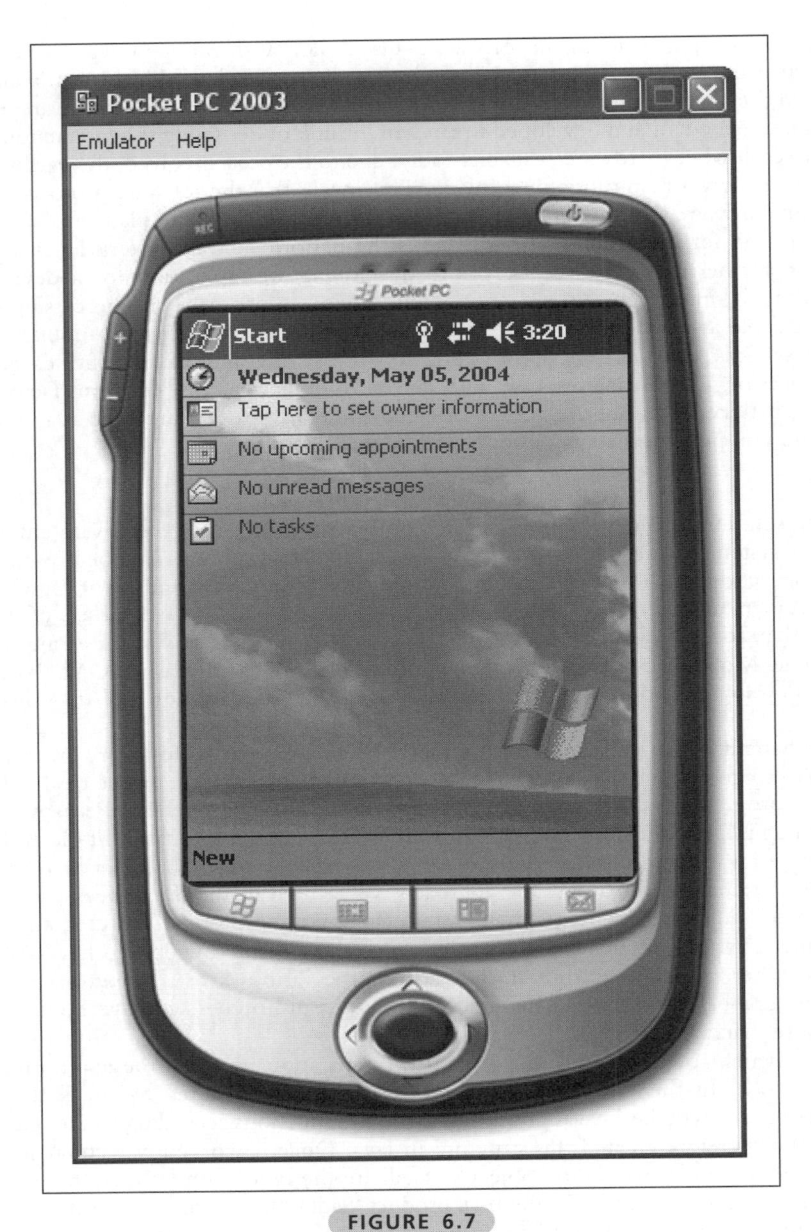

FIGURE 6.7

A screenshot of the PocketPC device emulator in Microsoft Visual Studio

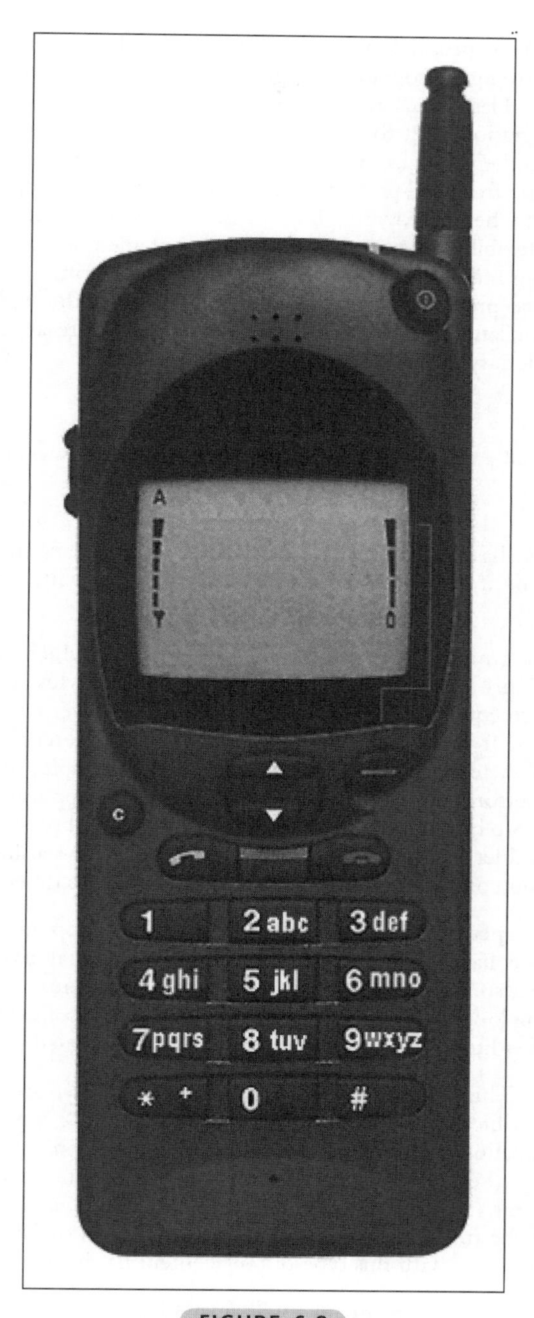

FIGURE 6.8
A screenshot of our Java-based emulator

For designers with limited programming experience, using Java or .net is not a viable option. Rather than using a full-strength programming tool, designers may choose to use more traditional prototyping tools, such as Flash, and create their own mobile prototype. While Flash and similar tools provide a good migration path for those who are familiar with image-editing software and want to add interaction to their designs, there are some pitfalls. Chief among these is the problem of extracting application logic from the prototype. Code in this type of scripting tool tends to evolve organically, which is great when prototyping but hopeless for use in the final system. Our experience has shown us that even flexibility starts to be lost for any sustained development cycle – over time, the patching and changing makes the prototype more and more brittle. If you want to use one of these tools, you should be prepared to throw your code away at the end of the prototype stage and start anew in another language for final implementation. (More about this when we discuss evolutionary and revolutionary prototyping.)

Pitfalls

Developing on PCs has all sorts of benefits as discussed above. However, there are a number of things to be aware of:

1. **Keyboards.** The PC has a great big keyboard which makes data entry rapid. This can skew the value of user testing if you are investigating an application which is reliant on a lot of text entry.
2. **Mice.** Most PCs use a mouse as a pointing device, a device which is almost never found on a mobile computer. This function is often replicated with a stylus or trackpad. Anyone who claims these devices are equivalent to a mouse has obviously never tried dragging and dropping on a mobile computer. It may be possible to skip over this difference if the application is not too reliant on the characteristics of the input device – for example, there is little difference in clicking a cellphone button with a finger or a mouse. For other applications, such as handwriting recognition, or the photo browser in Chapter 10, the input modality is crucial. It may be possible to fake this using a Tablet PC or pen input device like a touch-sensitive tablet, but be careful that any evaluation you conduct is not skewed by these hardware differences.
3. **Portability.** Desktop personal computers usually live on desktops and cannot be easily moved around. It is therefore hard to mimic real-world situations that users of mobile computers will encounter – direct sunlight on the screen, noisy environments, etc. Also, we run into the problem of conducting longitudinal or contextually based evaluations. Mobile computing is, after all, mobile and it makes little sense to conduct only laboratory-based evaluations.
4. **Weirdo hardware.** This is really the converse of problem 2 above. In this case, the mobile device has hardware which is not available on the desktop PC. Jog-wheels, thumb scanners, even Bluetooth connections are rare on most desktop systems. It's possible to cover for these inadequacies, however. (For example, we use a Griffin PowerMate – `www.griffin.com` – as a jog-wheel replacement.) Again, it should be noted that these devices will inevitably be different from those found on the final hardware of the system. Caution should be exercised in drawing conclusions from prototypes with this type of replacement hardware.
5. **Performance.** Desktop PC performance will always be faster than that of mobile computers. Make sure that it is possible to execute your application on the target hardware.

Using a General Mobile Platform

To overcome the problems listed above, with the possible exception of problem 4, one can use an existing mobile device or platform to develop prototypes.

A device such as the HP iPAQ 5550 has ample computing resources (400 MHz XScale processor, 128 Mb of RAM) and connectivity (802.11b, infrared, Bluetooth and an optional cellular jacket). This device also has a variety of text input modes and a high-resolution touch screen.

There are fewer high-level software prototyping tools available for mobile computing platforms than for desktop machines, due to the relative market size (a version of Flash is available for PocketPC, however). If you're going to create a software prototype for a mobile device, almost certainly you'll have to do some programming in a language such as C# or Java. To help programmers get up to speed, there exist multi-platform APIs such as Microsoft's .net or Sun's J2ME. In each case, the mobile platform represents a subset of the full desktop API, so that programmers can transfer more easily between platforms.

If you do decide to prototype on the iPAQ or similar PDA, we would recommend that you write all your code for the target device from the outset and not try to shoehorn code from a PC onto a mobile device. On one project we tried to migrate some J2SE code to an iPAQ. Sadly we could not convert to J2ME as we used libraries reliant on SE. We then tried a variety of JVM (SE) implementations and even converted the iPAQ to run Linux at one point. Eventually, after a month of tinkering and the purchase of a 1 Gb memory card, the application ran (very slowly). After rewriting the code from scratch for the .net compact framework, the same application runs smoothly, even without the extra memory.

Some quite advanced interfaces have been implemented using these standard devices. Brewster *et al.* (2003) report using an iPAQ as part of a personal spatialized sound archive. Part of the work involved the creation of algorithms which allowed the iPAQ to recognize, and act on, certain gestures. For example, to turn up the volume of the music, the user drags their finger in clockwise circles on the screen.

One new alternative to using a general mobile platform is reported by Nam and Lee (2003). Here they use a specially constructed, but non-functional, model of the final product (think of the cellphone handsets they have on display in shops). The only functionality it has are a few buttons linked back to a desktop PC. Onto the screen of the device is projected the software component generated by the same desktop PC. The user can move the device around, as it is tracked, and the computer ensures that the screen output is mapped onto the correct part of the hardware model (see Figure 6.9). This work is still at the preliminary stage and it remains to be seen whether there are benefits from this system that cannot be found using other, less technically expensive approaches.

Using a Specialist Platform

For some mobile applications, it's essential to have the correct hardware and software available – problem 4 from the above list. Sometimes it's possible to mock-up the hardware functionality from existing components. This was done to great effect in the Peephole project (Yee, 2003) which relied on tracking the position of a PDA in three-dimensional space. Rather than construct a device containing the necessary hardware, the researcher simply attached the PDA to a series of cables which were, in turn, connected to a desktop mouse (see Figure 6.10). As the user moved the PDA, the cables tugged the mice and the movements were relayed to a PC. The design appears somewhat 'Heath-Robinson', but allowed the researcher to gage the effectiveness of the interplay between the software and hardware.

When developing the Handspring Treo, the team built a general-purpose testing rig they called the 'Buck' (see Figure 6.11) (Pering, 2002). This consists of the Treo keyboard hooked up to

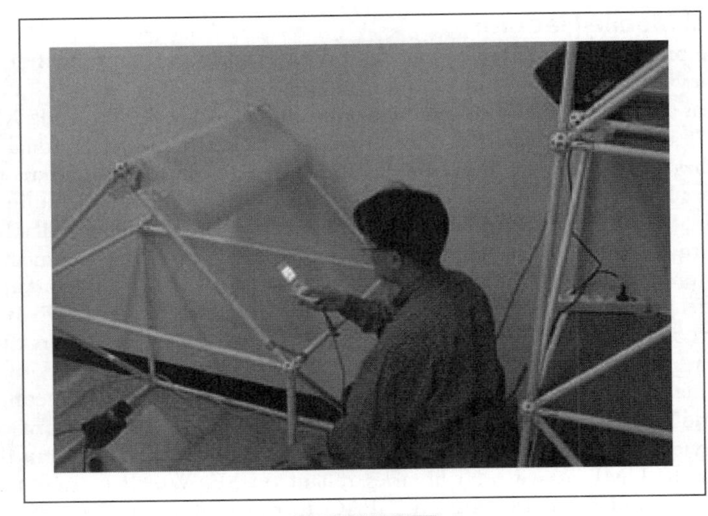

FIGURE 6.9

The participant holds a prototype device while a camera on the floor in front of the chair tacks the prototype's position, allowing the projector (on the shelf above and behind the participant) to project the desired output onto the prototype's screen

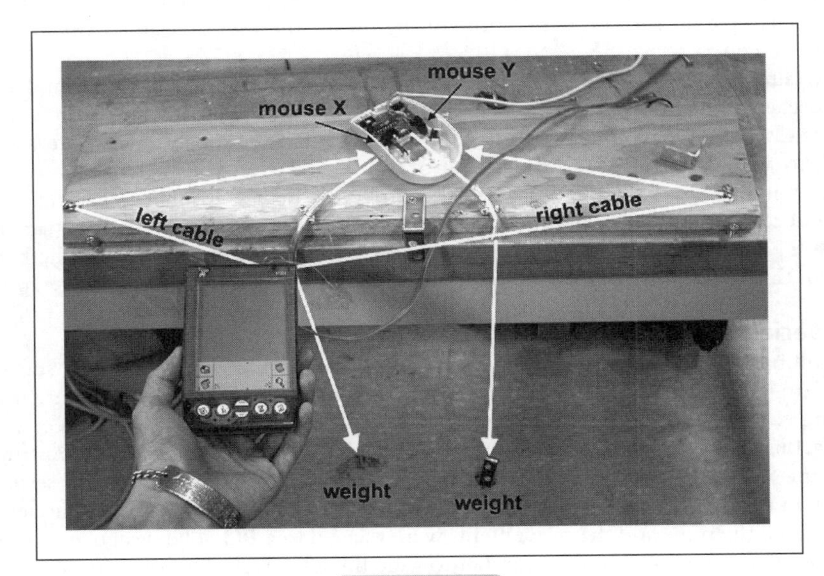

FIGURE 6.10

The cables attached to the mouse wheels allow the PDA to be tracked in two-dimensional space a standard laptop. The laptop was used as an output device and to execute the software being evaluated. In order to evaluate the software properly, it was essential to see how well users could interact using the small keyboard. The design team felt that the rewards from the effort of creating custom hardware were worthwhile as they caught interaction issues that would not have appeared any other way.

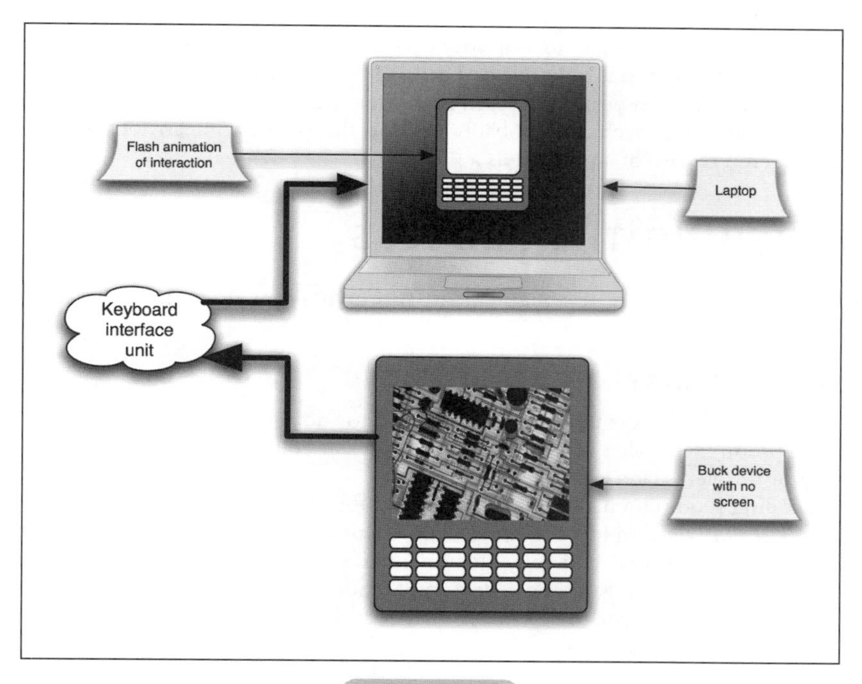

FIGURE 6.11

The Buck is used to capture key presses on the small keyboard, which are passed on to the laptop running the prototype software

One drawback of the Buck is that is it not mobile, which means that it will only provide data on how people react to the device when stationary. This means that the design team could miss out on a lot of useful data, under-utilizing the potential of the prototype. Another team which built a custom mobile prototype is reported by Brown and Weilenmann (2003). Here the team was building a location awareness device for ski instructors. One big change they noticed when deploying the prototype, which would never have been detected in the laboratory, is that the cold weather of the ski slope meant that the battery life was insufficient to make the device useful.

Using Version 1.0

Dray & Associates highlight the problems created by the close software–hardware ties when trying to evaluate prototypes of the Tablet PC (Dray and Siegel, 2002). This represents an entirely new category of product and, while the normal tests had been conducted with earlier prototypes, there remained the problem of whether or not anyone would actually use the device. One alternative would have been to release the product and see what happened. Should reaction be unfavorable, then no matter how much the product was improved, it was unlikely to be a commercial success. Another alternative was to use the beta prototype to gather data. Using the prototype with the usual beta testers is unacceptable as they are hardly typical users. Testing the beta prototype in the field with target users will also cause problems, as the unreliability of the system will skew their attitude towards it.

In the end, the team deemed it so important to have user feedback on the design that they completed the product in full, but only released it to 47 chosen evaluators. The feedback from these users was analyzed, and the first version released to the general public was actually the second version. While this is a laudable approach, it's probably beyond the financial means of most companies to use a fully engineered release of a product as a prototype.

6.6 FINISHING THE PROCESS

Having made all the effort to create a high-fidelity prototype, how does one move from prototype to product?

6.6.1 EVOLUTIONARY

After putting in a lot of effort, one might be tempted to 'tidy up' the prototype code and release that as the final product – evolve it to a higher plane. It's a seductive route but, like all seductions, can lead to major problems later on.

Firstly, the coding requirements for prototyping and for product are vastly different. Prototyping should support fast fail; we should be making rapid changes to our code. For release-quality code, every change must be checked and fully documented – not exactly 'fast'. Another requirement for product code is that of performance. Prototype code is optimized for alteration but not for performance. It was primarily for these reasons that Fred Brooks concluded that it was cheaper by far to throw away prototypes and rewrite the product from scratch (Brooks, 1975).

6.6.2 REVOLUTIONARY

The alternative to evolution then is revolution, where the prototype is discarded and the final product is developed afresh. Unsurprisingly, this is also known as 'throwaway' prototyping. To avoid temptation, one could force the prototyping team to work using tools that will not produce code for the final deployment platform, as advocated by Schach (2002). Of course, one need not abandon all the effort put into the prototype. It may be possible to reuse elements in the final product. Typical examples would be:

- **User interface layout.** If the prototype was created using an interface building tool such as VisualStudio, one could simply remove the associated code but keep the interface forms intact.
- **Vertical prototypes.** Key functional interaction, such as that developed in stage 3 of the process described in Section 6.6.3 below, could be reused in the final implementation.
- **Prototype as specification.** The image of revolutionary prototyping is that the prototype is discarded, never to be looked at again. This is clearly not the case, as the prototype needs to

inform the construction of a requirements specification for final development. Alternatively, the prototype can *become* the specification. This is the approach adopted by the Windows 95 team (Sullivan, 1996), who found that the creation of a separate specification document slowed down the iterative cycle. While this led to problems in communicating their ideas to external groups, the benefits were felt to be more important.

6.6.3 PROCESS

Over the years we've been creating mobile prototypes, our ideas of how to prototype have gone through a number of iterations. While we've always used paper, in the early days of mobile computing there were no emulators or toolkits. Instead, there were many hours of typing code directly into Psions and Newtons, worrying about memory constraints and then losing all the code because the cable to the power supply fell out. Currently, our prototypes are developed according to the following process:

1. **Paper.** We use paper to sketch out initial ideas primarily to support discussion within the design team. People feel free to doodle over designs and chop and change them around. When the changes become very frequent, we transfer key design elements onto Post-it notes and move them around on a whiteboard. Once everyone on the team has agreed on a design, we take digital camera shots of that design and then draw it out using a tool like Visio or PowerPoint. (Remember to use a camera with a high mega-pixel count if you're photographing a whiteboard; those Post-it notes can be hard to read later on.) Over time, we've collected together a kit which we keep in a large box with a portable whiteboard for everyone in our lab to use. Although people keep pilfering from it, usually it contains the following items:
    - Whiteboard makers (multicolored)
    - As many different sizes of Post-it notes as possible (the small 1.5 × 2 inch are most useful)
    - Lego bricks
    - Card for making custom shapes, as well as adhesive tape (single- and double-sided), scissors and craft knife.
2. **Digital screens.** The neater versions of the screenshots are then placed in PowerPoint and linked together to show how the interface would support different tasks. PowerPoint doesn't support group editing very well but, as we said earlier, it's known by everyone on the design team, so can be changed by anyone who wishes to share an idea.
3. **Vertical functionality prototype.** At this point we commit our ideas to code. Because we work in computer science departments, this tends to happen in a full-strength implementation language rather than, say, Flash. The other reason to use full development systems is that often we have no idea whether the solution we're proposing can be implemented at all. Therefore, we identify the most technically challenging aspect of the design and try to build a vertical prototype to test that concept. Assuming it is possible, we move on to the next stage.
4. **Scenario prototype.** Having built the functionality, we then implement enough of the user interface to allow the prototype to support the core usage scenarios. There are two reasons for this: to allow us to do some testing with trial users, and to get funding for tests with real users. Being academics, our work is supported by external funding bodies or companies. We've found

that it's essential to have a working proof-of-concept when making an approach for funding, especially to commercial organizations.

5. **Handheld deployment.** Assuming someone is interested in supporting the project, we build our final prototype on a mobile device of some kind for more user testing. The scenario prototype is usually built on a desktop machine and allows us to conduct lab-based testing. The mobile computer allows us to perform contextual and longitudinal studies. If we've developed stage 4 using a multi-platform toolkit, then it may be that the code on the handheld requires little or no alteration. The tricky part is the logistics of running an evaluation with multiple handsets given to multiple people in multiple locations over multiple days. We will deal with these problems directly in the next chapter, so don't worry yet.

Usually, it's at this stage that our development process stops. As researchers in academic departments, we're usually required to show the validity of our ideas but not to develop them into full products. Often prototypes are used for the sole purpose of conveying an idea – architectural building prototypes serve no other purpose than to convey an idea of a building from the architect's mind to the customer's bank account.

For comparison purposes, however, outlined below is the prototyping process followed by Handspring, as reported in *Interactions* (Pering, 2002). The paper describes the prototyping process of the Treo from original concept to final product.

1. **Paper.** Again, Handspring's prototyping process begins with paper prototypes. Due to the multi-disciplinary nature of their design teams, they see paper prototypes as the 'lingua franca' for design communication. Individual screen sketches are created and then joined using arrows (the arrows originate from buttons and show the screen that appears when the button is clicked). These screens are then used for expert evaluation.
2. **Screen prototypes.** This stage is very similar to our stage 2. Here, the screen sketches are linked using a PowerPoint presentation in order to track task and scenario completion.
3. **Buck prototyping.** To resolve complex design issues, Flash prototypes are created and then deployed for user testing in the Buck test rig. This shows up a major difference between our process and that of a commercial company. Presumably Handspring do not need to conduct technical feasibility tests as they themselves have designed the target platform and therefore know what the hardware and operating system are capable of. They can therefore skip our stage 3. Buck prototyping is thus very similar to our stage 4 and is where real user testing takes place.
4. **Alpha.** Here the software is developed and deployed on fully functional hardware. Although not strictly a prototype, the alpha devices are used by company staff for everyday use. From this internal user testing, information is fed back to the design team and the appropriate changes are made.

The process summary is therefore

- 1–2: Paper in, digital images out. For design team

- 2–3: Digital images in, PowerPoint out. For design team
- 3–4: PowerPoint in, interactive code out. For design team, users and funders.

Ethics

If you're developing a prototype mobile system for a longitudinal evaluation, then you have a responsibility to make it as robust as possible. I speak from personal experience on this. I once developed a phone application for my PDA. This required me to use a large PDA in an even larger GSM jacket as my cellphone for the best part of a year. The phone was cumbersome, crashed mid-conversation and lost many SMS messages. The experience was intensely frustrating and I eventually abandoned the project before subjecting any other users to the system. Mobile devices are a lot more invasive than desktop systems. If you're going to invade someone else's life, we suggest you try it yourself first.

6.7 ISSUES IN PROTOTYPING

We've presented you with a number of techniques for prototyping and discussed why they might be useful in the process of interface design. To help you decide when to use a given technique and to give you a better understanding of the compromises involved, the key issues are presented in Table 6.1, summarizing the article by Rettig (1994) in *Communications of the ACM*, and are then discussed.

TABLE 6.1

Key issues in prototyping

Type	Advantages	Disadvantages
Low-fidelity	• Less time • Lower cost • Evaluate multiple concepts • Useful for communication • Address screen layout issues	• Little use for usability test • Navigation and flow limitations • Facilitator driven • Poor detail in specification
High-fidelity	• Partial functionality • Interactive • User-driven • Clearly defined navigation scheme • Use for exploration and test • Marketing tool	• Creation time-consuming • Inefficient for proof-of-concept • Blinds users to major representational flaws • Users may think prototype is 'real'

EXERCISE 6.3 PORTABLE MP3 PLAYER – PROJECT PLAN

Returning to the YAMP project for the final time, draw up a project plan for turning the initial PowerPoint prototype into a final product. Use one of the processes above and discuss the prototypes you would need at each stage and what aspects of the final system these prototypes would allow you to explore. Finally, speculate about how you would go about testing these prototypes with real users – we shall cover this in more detail in the next chapter. ■

6.7.1 SOME CONSIDERATIONS

Cues to Users

To users, well-drawn interfaces imply that the design must be approaching finality and hence they feel less likely to suggest design changes. This is crucial for architects showing building designs to clients. Figure 6.12 is taken from Schumann *et al.* (1996) and shows a system which generates sketches from exact CAD models. So, if you would like your users to suggest changes to a software prototype, it may be worth sketching the interface on paper before showing it to users.

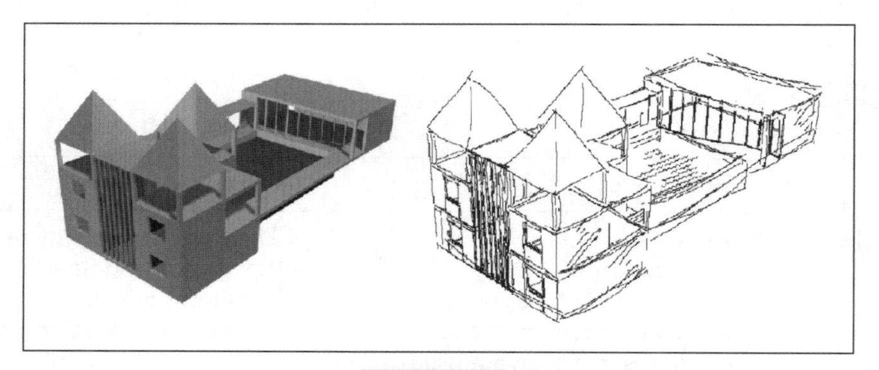

FIGURE 6.12

The 'sketch' on the right is automatically generated from the volumetric model on the left

Misleading Expectations

One of the criticisms of high-level prototyping is that it leads to unreal expectations of how close the product is to completion. Users and clients see a seemingly working demonstration and wonder why it will take so long to implement the final version. This can be very frustrating for the development team as the expectation placed on them is much higher. Less scrupulous people have, of course, used high-fidelity prototypes to their advantage in trying to convince some other party that the promised software is almost complete.

Project Constraints

Most projects run to a particular schedule within a particular budget. Obviously, low-fidelity prototyping will be a lot cheaper, and provide more design iterations, than high-fidelity. If high-fidelity prototyping is required, say for user testing, then it may be more strategic to go for a vertical prototype.

So far as time constraints are concerned, prototyping has two key drawbacks: it's fun and you're never finished. Often our projects have become locked into endless debates and cycles of prototypes, usually because we cannot agree on a design compromise and wish to test it on real users. We suggest that before you start prototyping, you pick a cut-off point and stick to it. Furthermore, creating prototypes is fun, whether this be drawing a low-fidelity sketch or finishing an accurate screen representation in Photoshop – within our research group, this disease is known as Photoshop-itis, where a whole day is spent altering the appearance of a few pixels not discernible to anyone but the designer.

Communication

Low-fidelity prototyping is a great way for the designer to communicate ideas to others, but the lack of fidelity also means there is room for ambiguities to creep in. This is not always desired, but can lead to opportunistic design ideas and leaves the designer some degree of flexibility. Creating a high-fidelity prototype removes the ambiguity, but the investment involved in creating the prototype makes the designer loath to change anything.

For communicating a design idea, or flow of interaction, low-fidelity is great. For a specification which developers can follow, you need high-fidelity.

Evaluation

We deal with evaluation extensively in the next chapter. For the purposes of this discussion, it is worth noting that it is impossible to do any user evaluation with a low-fidelity prototype. While participatory design is great for getting ideas from users, the reliance on a Wizard-of-Oz means that the evaluations cannot be objective. For usability testing and gaging user reaction to a system, high-fidelity prototypes are required. One warning with high-fidelity is that the prototype is unlikely to have the response time of the optimized final system. Make sure that these response times can be factored out of your experiments.

6.8 A FINAL NOTE ON DEVELOPMENT

Although written by people with a background in computer science, this is a book primarily about interaction design and not about programming. However, when the time comes to convert your prototype into a functioning device or application, there are a number of considerations unique to mobile computing which should be taken into account:

- **Computer performance.** In case you hadn't noticed, mobile devices tend to be smaller than desktop systems. This means smaller components inside the device, which means much fewer computing resources both in terms of processor and memory. This is exacerbated for the processor which is usually clocked more slowly to preserve battery power. Also, don't assume that a mobile device treats all memory in the same way. If your application is larger than the memory available on, say, a PDA, don't assume that you can insert a memory card to overcome the problem. Most PDAs treat memory cards as secondary storage (due to their slow speed) and this memory is not available for execution space.

- **Power.** Mobile devices have limited power. You can do a lot to overcome this problem by writing your application to use the machine's resources in an intelligent way. For example, if your target device has a hard disk, pre-load as much data as you can from it, then shut down the disk.
- **Different contexts.** Most mobile computing devices have mechanisms for exchanging data. This can be a fairly simple type of exchange, say between a PC and an MP3 player. However, as more devices become equipped with wireless connectivity and users acquire more than one computer, the synchronization issues become very complex. We have yet to see a convincing solution to this wider problem, so cannot offer advice other than to be very careful when figuring out how data should be shared and how to guarantee its integrity.

SUMMARY

No designer is perfect – every design will have flaws. The fastest way to get rid of those flaws is to show the design to as many target users as possible. The most effective way to show a design is to create a prototype. We have discussed different forms of prototype from low-fidelity, paper-based sketches through to complex pieces of software written for specialist hardware. We have also looked at some of the challenges that arise from prototyping mobile applications and why this is much harder than prototyping desktop applications. Finally, we looked at two processes which can be followed to translate an initial idea into a fully-fledged piece of software.

WORKSHOP QUESTIONS

- If you're familiar with any software engineering methodologies, discuss where prototyping might take place within that methodology.
- Can you think of a project where evolutionary prototyping is preferable to revolutionary prototyping?
- What do you think would prevent people from developing prototypes?
- Write down the first words that come into your mind when you read the word 'prototype'

DESIGNER TIPS

- *When creating initial prototypes, it's a lot better to use a whiteboard and give everyone a pen than have a single person sketching on paper.*

- *Programmers and engineers can be skeptical of using whiteboards (too low-tech) but persevere; once they have used them, the benefits are obvious.*
- *PowerPoint is a great way to create a prototype interface which can provide interactivity through its hyperlink.*
- *When building a high-fidelity prototype, be careful of scripting systems like Flash or HyperCard as the code logic can become buried. If possible, prototype in a system where the interface and functionality are easily separated.*
- *Don't be lured into testing prototype software only on desktop PCs; there are many reasons why the results will not hold true for the final device.*
- *Users are often intimidated by prototype designs that have obviously been created on computer; they are less likely to suggest changes than when shown something that has been sketched.*
- *Be warned that prototyping is fun and can consume all available time unless it is properly managed.*

CHAPTER 7
EVALUATION

OVERVIEW

7.1. Introduction
7.2. Classifying evaluation
7.3. 'Quick And Dirty'
7.4. Conceptual model extraction
7.5. Direct observation
7.6. Interviews
7.7. Questionnaires
7.8. Non-user methods
7.9. Experimental evaluation
7.10. Considering context – evaluating mobile systems
7.11. Complementary evaluation
7.12. Conclusion

KEY POINTS

- Evaluation is an essential part of the design process.
- Choosing the correct evaluation technique depends on the type of results required, user availability and equipment availability.
- As they can be used in different contexts, evaluating mobile systems is more complicated than evaluating desktop-based systems.
- At present, methods for the effective evaluation of mobile systems are an open question but a mixture of laboratory and context trials is recommended.

7.1 INTRODUCTION

Evaluation is about humility. No matter how good you think your design ideas are, there will always be something you didn't consider – users are just so ingenious at doing what you didn't expect them to do (see Figure 7.1).

FIGURE 7.1

Users doing the unexpected with technology

Within the field of human–computer interaction there exist many approaches to evaluating systems. Mostly, these have been adapted from social science and psychology to fit the constraints of a technology development process – we have already discussed ethnography, a technique adapted from sociology and social anthropology. In this chapter we will look at other techniques, paying particular attention to how they may be applied in the mobile context.

There are many excellent books looking at different evaluation techniques. One of the most comprehensive is *Interaction Design* (Preece *et al.*, 2002), which also covers the more practical aspects of applying the techniques and their relative strengths and weaknesses. However, we're not interested in studying evaluation for its own sake. Instead we shall look at how evaluation can be applied in the design process.

Furthermore, the evaluation of mobile systems is different from that of desktop computers. We shall examine why mobile systems are different and which desktop evaluation techniques apply in the mobile context.

7.2 CLASSIFYING EVALUATION

It is important to evaluate your work as soon, and as often, as constraints allow. In Chapter 5 we looked at ethnographic techniques, some of which are designed to evaluate design ideas by observing real users in a real context. In this chapter, we are interested in evaluating actual designs,

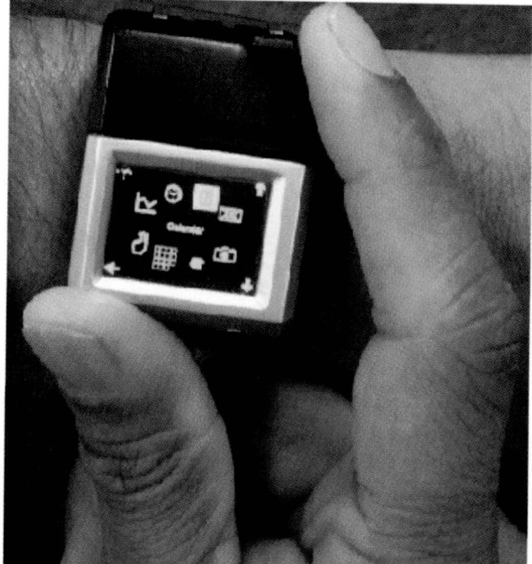

PLATE 1

The diverse mobile world

From top left to bottom right: Thad Starner and the eyeglass output device (Starner, 2003); MediaCup (coffee cup with sensors and communication technologies embedded in base) (Gellerson *et al.*, 2002); the IBM wristwatch device (Raghunath and Narayanaswami, 2002); and Nokia's 770 Internet tablet

PLATE 2

OK/Cancel

PLATE 3

Graceful degradation

PLATE 4

Xerox Parc Tab

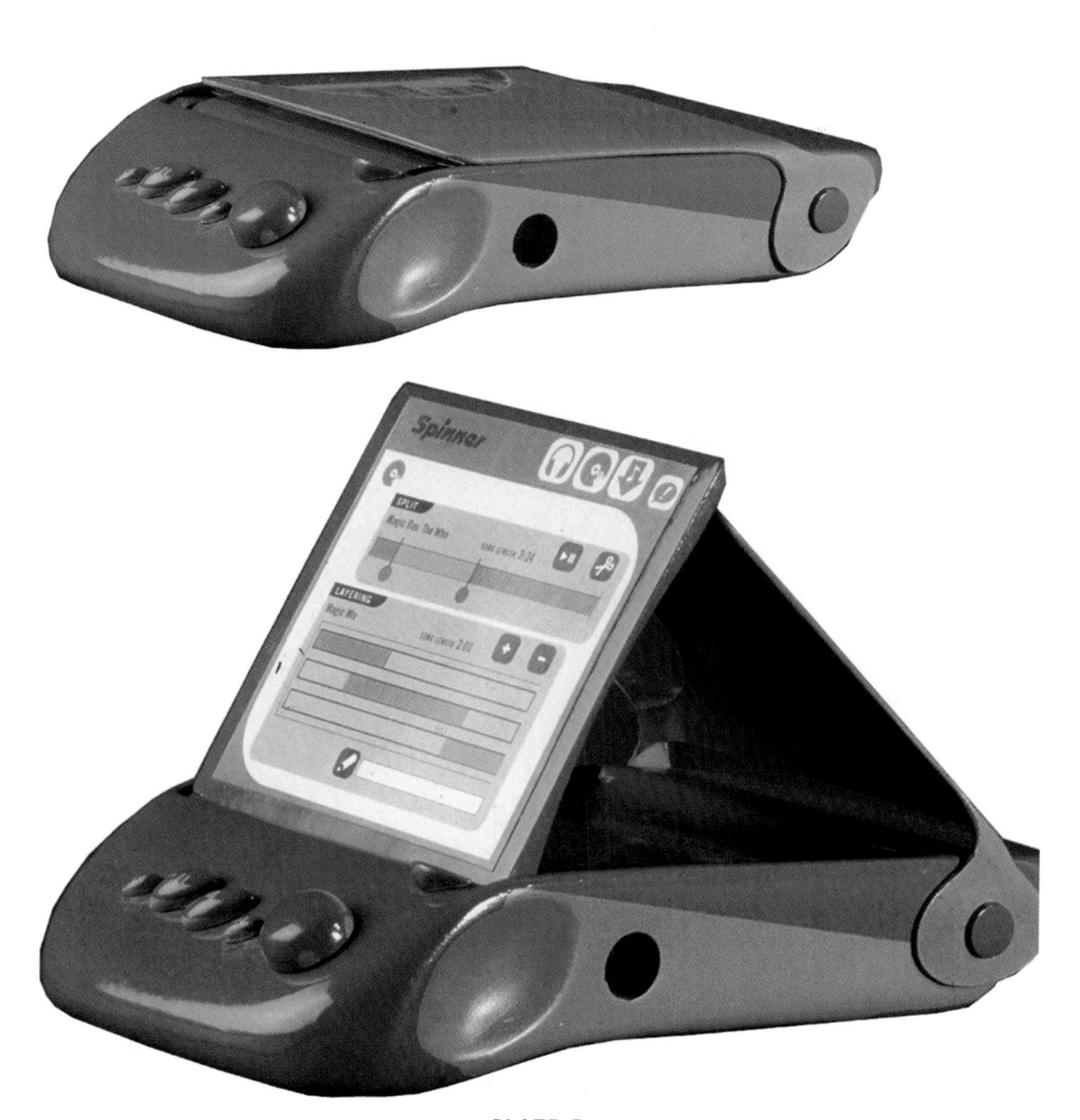

PLATE 5

The 'Spinner' music player prototype

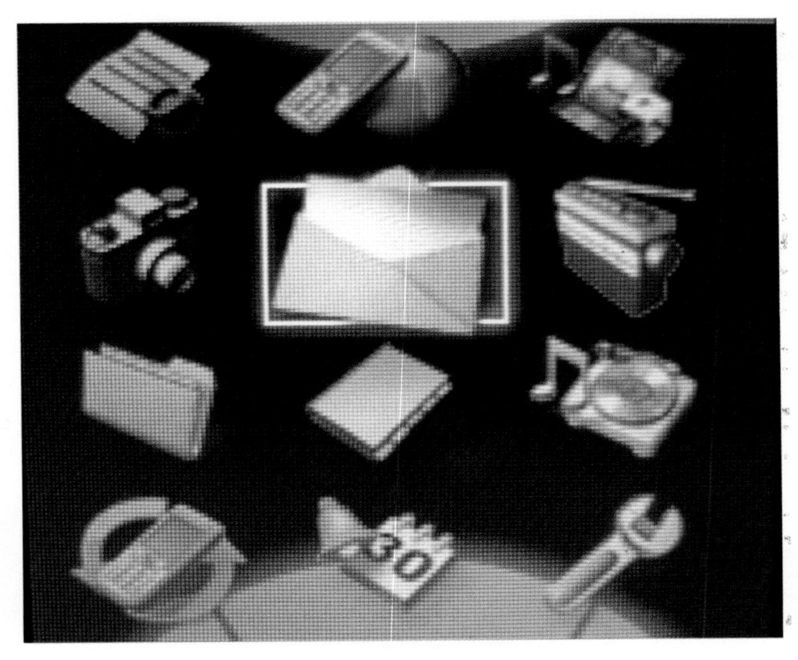

PLATE 6

K700 depicts all twelve main menu items as icons

PLATE 7

The top-left-most image represents the original image. Subsequent images frame the portions of the original which the algorithm thinks are interesting

PLATE 8

A basket woven from telephone trunk cable

rather than design ideas. To evaluate actual designs, we need the design to be available in some concrete form – the prototypes discussed in the previous chapter. This chapter will therefore follow the structure of the last, starting out with how to evaluate low-fidelity prototypes and ending up with conducting scientifically rigorous evaluations of high-fidelity prototypes.

Besides the fidelity of the prototype involved in the evaluation, there are other factors to consider when selecting an evaluation technique:

- **On whom?** You might think that all evaluations will require the participation of the end-users; this is not so. Sometimes evaluation will not involve users at all and may be conducted by usability experts instead. Alternatively, you may not be able to recruit actual end-users and simply use a surrogate end-user.
- **Where?** Again, many evaluations take place in a controlled laboratory environment, but this is not so common with mobile systems. Sometimes evaluations will take place in a user's place of work, or even in an outdoor context.
- **Results.** Different evaluation types will inform the design process in different ways. This can range from purely anecdotal descriptions to help form initial ideas, through to complex statistical analysis giving quantitative proof of how good a system is.

To aid your decision on which is most appropriate, each evaluation technique we present will be described in terms of the dimensions listed above.

7.3 'QUICK AND DIRTY'

Conducted by: End-users
Equipment: Low-fidelity prototype
Results: Anecdotal and unstructured
Where: Informal setting

The first evaluations you will conduct are on the initial design ideas themselves. As such, the goal is to get rapid, broad-brush feedback on the design, rather than painstakingly explore a design space. This type of evaluation is essentially a form of ethnography, which goes under the unfortunate name 'Quick and Dirty' (Hughes *et al.*, 1995). This is to distinguish it from the more formal types of ethnography discussed in Chapter 5.

To conduct this type of evaluation, you should meet with end-users informally and simply ask them what they think of the design. Show them the prototype and jot down any ideas or concerns they have. In our research, we talk about this type of evaluation as a brain-damage check – in design meetings we can get carried away and this type of rapid user test makes sure that our ideas are sensible and relevant.

7.4 CONCEPTUAL MODEL EXTRACTION

Conducted by: End-users
Equipment: An interface sketch
Results: Qualitative
Where: Controlled setting

Mobile computing opens the opportunity to develop entirely new types of application for which users will have no precedent. This is daunting to the interface designer, as it is not possible to exploit familiar metaphors and ideas which the user may be comfortable with already. The goal of this technique is to extract how users interpret a completely new interface, given their existing mental models of how interfaces should work.

For example, when developing the first digital cameras for HP, Dray & Associates had to conduct considerable conceptual model extractions, as most consumers had no idea what a digital camera could do. They used low-fidelity prototypes of the screen on the camera and asked users what they thought the symbols were for. Most were clear, apart from the icon in Figure 7.2(a) – one person suggested it was a mode for taking pictures of skyscrapers! It was, of course, the icon to show how many pictures had been taken (placed on a stack). Eventually, the design team struck upon the idea of having a 'messy stack' as seen in Figure 7.2(b). It was soon discovered that the new symbol unambiguously triggered the correct mental model of a stack of photographs.

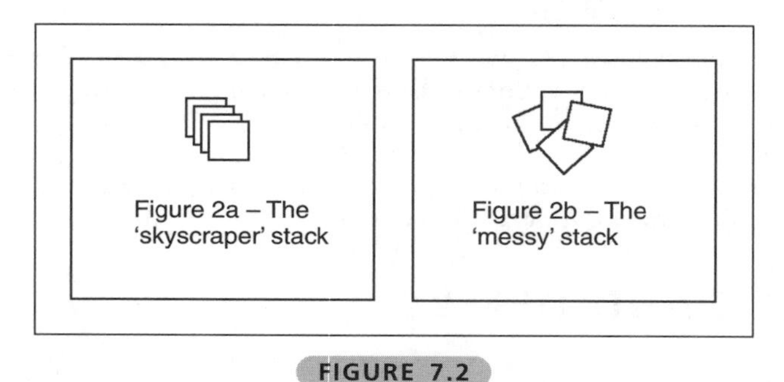

FIGURE 7.2

Conceptual model extraction for digital camera icons

EXERCISE 7.1 CONCEPTUAL MODEL EXTRACTION

It's interesting to see how something that is abundantly obvious to you can confuse others. Take an iconic menu you are familiar with, perhaps the root menu on your cellular handset. (If you don't have access to such a menu, use one of the images of menus in Chapter 8.) Print or photograph that menu and show it to someone not familiar with the interface. Explain where the menu is taken from and have them explain the meaning of each icon on the screen. Chances are they will not be able to interpret them first time off.

Just as an aside, our research group often debates the worth of a conceptual model extraction. The argument against it is that understanding a symbol or icon is not so important, as once the association is learnt, it doesn't really matter what symbol is used. Do you think this is a valid argument? ■

7.5 DIRECT OBSERVATION

Conducted by: End-users
Equipment: An interactive prototype
Results: Qualitative
Where: Controlled setting

Another way to evaluate an interface is to watch people using it. This is hardly a stunning insight, but it turns out to be trickier than might be suspected. To illustrate this point, imagine the following situation:

You sit the user down with the prototype, asking them to complete some task to see how they perform. The user starts by clicking on what looks to you to be a random sequence of buttons, but seems to make perfect sense to the user. You become agitated (''What is this person thinking?''). You start to think about how to change the interface and are startled by a sudden noise as the computer crashes. What happened? How did the user do that? You were so lost in thought you didn't notice what happened. Now you are angry with yourself and the user for crashing your prototype. The user reacts badly and loses self-confidence. When the prototype restarts, the user is loath to click anything and defers to you, asking what they should do next. Eventually the session is abandoned as a failure.

This is clearly a pathological example, but illustrates some key points that need to be addressed in any observation, namely:

- How to find out what the user is thinking without interrupting their flow
- How to record observations
- How to stop yourself biasing the evaluation
- How to make sure that the user has a pleasant experience and does not feel that they are little better than a lab rat.

7.5.1 FINDING OUT WHAT USERS ARE THINKING

Essentially we want the users to verbalize what they are thinking as they complete the tasks. One solution to this might be to ask the user to speak aloud what they are thinking throughout the period of the evaluation. This technique is called *think-aloud* and was developed by Erikson and Simon (1985). Unfortunately, there are two key problems with speaking aloud in this way: firstly, it's embarrassing, and secondly, most people forget to speak after a while.

BOX 7.1 THINKING ALOUD

To have some idea of just how hard it is to 'think aloud', try this experiment. The next time you drive your car, speak aloud the driving decisions and maneuvers you're ➤

making as if to a driving instructor in the seat beside you. (You may have done this already, since the technique is common to many driving examinations throughout the world.) As you start to speak, you're very self-conscious. It's embarrassing to be telling the world these mundane thoughts. (Thankfully, due to the advent of cellular phones, you can reduce the embarrassment by placing some headphones in your ears, whereupon other drivers will think you're talking on a hands-free kit.) Then, after a while, you will simply forget to speak. Something will happen, something that requires your full attention, and when you've finished dealing with that, you will default to your natural behavior and forget to speak out loud. ■

To overcome these problems, a form of think-aloud called *constructive interaction* has been developed (Nielsen and Mack, 1994). In this instance, two users work through the task at the computer simultaneously. As they need to communicate their ideas with each other, talking about what they are thinking becomes a perfectly natural task. A variation on this technique replaces one of the real users with a trained facilitator who continually challenges the real user, asking them to explain their actions more fully. This variant, however, leaves the evaluation open to biasing by the facilitator, and it is probably safer to stick with two real users.

7.5.2 HOW TO RECORD OBSERVATIONS

Really, the first question to ask yourself is not how, but what – what is it you want recorded? Is it important to see the user's face or would audio alone suffice? Perhaps you are watching for a very specific event, in which case is it sufficient to keep a simple tally? In most circumstances, observers opt for video almost by default.

Reasons for Video

The main reason to take a video recording is not so much to capture the user's face, but rather to capture what they are doing on screen. Often the user is interacting with the software too rapidly to understand their actions during the experiment session. Recording the output from the screen allows you to go back and analyze what happened after the event. The screen analysis can be augmented by an audio recording of what the user is saying (assuming you are employing some think-aloud protocol) or possibly by a recording of the user's face to give some indication of their emotional state.

In our research group, we have a portable system which allows us to record the output from the screen (via a gizmo called a scan converter) and the user's face (using a standard camcorder). These two signals are then mixed together (using a mixer with picture-in-picture capability as in Figure 7.3) so that they can be viewed simultaneously.

While some evaluations will require this type of observation, we would urge you to avoid it if possible. Watching hours of video containing nothing but mouse movements rapidly becomes very tedious. Instead of recording events from the video after the fact, decide beforehand what type of events you wish to monitor and take note of these during the experiment – see the section below on coding sheets. This is not to say that video recording should be disregarded altogether. For instance, selected parts of the video can still be used to help jog the user's memory in any subsequent interviews, or to show interesting findings to the rest of the design team.

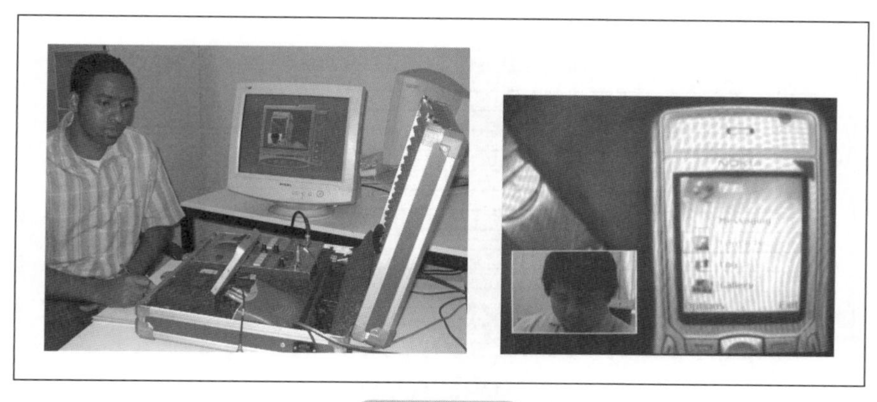

FIGURE 7.3

Left: the researcher looking for events from a mixture of signals incorporating (on the right) the mobile device screen and the video camera

Note Taking

A much less technical approach to recording events in an observational experiment is to use a pen and paper to take notes. Note taking in its simplest form consists of writing a description of what is happening as it happens. The major drawback of this method is that the observer must take their eye off the subject in order to record the event, and may miss something while writing. One may overcome this problem through training to write without looking at the paper, but it still may not be possible to write quickly enough to record every event. Alternatively, you can have a team of people making records which can be correlated at the end of the session. This solution is expensive, however, in terms of paying observers and also in time spent in correlating results. Fortunately this type of note taking is only really needed for pure ethnographic observations, where the observers have no idea of what they are looking for and it is only after the observations have finished that it becomes clear what the important events are. For most evaluations, the researchers have some idea of what they are looking for before the observations occur. For example, one might be interested in how many times users need to refer to the help system. To record this, the observer need only make a tick for each occurrence. Usually, observers are watching for more than one event, so they draw up a coding sheet which consists of a number of columns, where one column represents each event they are watching for. Observers can then place ticks in the relevant column, or write down the time when each event occurred. A typical coding sheet is shown in Figure 7.4. If you are going to do some observations, then it is still worth learning how to write without looking at a page as, no matter how good your coding sheet is, users are bound to do something unforeseen which you wish to record.

Recently, software versions of coding sheets have become available for PDAs. Observers can configure the software before the experiments start, where the PDA screen shows one button per target event. When the event occurs, the observer taps the button and the PDA records the event, along with the time when it occurred. At the end of the experiment, the results can be automatically uploaded to a PC for the data analysis phase. The only downside to using a PDA is that it's difficult to make unstructured notes – it's probably easier to bring a sheet of paper along with the PDA rather than trying to train yourself to be able to enter text reliably on a PDA without looking at the screen.

Time	Help button	Ask for help	Undo	Apply to all	Check design decision	Open new editor
0:00						
0:01						—
0:02						
0:03				—		
0:04					—	
0:05			—			—
0:06						
0:07					—	
0:08	—					
0:09						
0:10						
0:11		—				
0:12						

FIGURE 7.4

Coding sheet for usage of a graph editor

Automatic Logging

The best option of all is to have the prototype automatically log all interaction by the user. This way, your work during the experiment is greatly reduced and there is less chance of your inadvertently biasing the experiment (see the next section). Obviously this will only work on a hardware prototype capable of recording the interaction. This was certainly an issue for us in conducting some of our evaluation on rich media browsing (see Chapter 10) as we were pushing the computing resources of the PDA to the very limit. The time taken for the device to update the log file was too much of an overhead.

Assuming that the hardware is up to the task, some thought should be given to which events you are interested in recording. If you have access to the source code of the software you are evaluating, then it becomes possible to create a customized log containing just those events you are interested in. Thinking about our earlier example of recording when the help system is accessed; we could modify the code for the 'Help' button so that it wrote a time value to a log file on the computer. If you do not have access to source, then the next best solution is to run some form of spyware which records every event the user generates. Just as with observing on paper, having the computer record every event means that a lot of time is wasted at the end of the experiment sifting out the relevant information. (Actually, there are specialist pieces of software such as Theme – `http://www.patternvision.com/` – which use AI (Artificial Intelligence) techniques to spot patterns in observational data and help point out correlated events. It is our opinion, however, that this type of software should only be used as a last resort, as it is not always easy to detect which correlations are relevant to the experiment and which are not.)

Integrating Note Taking

To aid in the results analysis phase of an experiment, there is software available to synchronize the recorded notes with the video of the screen and user. This greatly reduces the effort of reconciling data from a number of sources. If the notes are to be integrated, then they must obviously be captured or translated to digital format. As early as 1989, Wendy Mackay described a system called EVA (Mackay, 1989) which allowed users to view a video feed and annotate it with notes – observers created a button for each event type they were interested in before observation started, and then clicked the relevant button during evaluation. More recent systems, such as the Observer from Noldus, allow the integration of data, including notations taken on PDAs.

7.5.3 HOW TO NOT BIAS THE EXPERIMENT

Despite the supposed dispassionate nature of scientific research, we're all human and keen to see our designs succeed. Users also try to produce the result they believe the experimenters are looking for – this ranges from mild forms, such as the Halo Effect (Thorndike, 1920), through to the alarming results of Milgram (1974), where subjects willingly electrocuted people at the request of the experimenter. (Don't worry – the experiment was designed to see how far subjects would go in obeying an authority figure when taking part in an experiment. The person being electrocuted was actually an actor and the subjects were asked to apply increasing amounts of current. The experiment measured when people would stop administering the current.)

You could attempt to hide your feelings and make sure you presented the evaluation in such a way as to give no clue about what is expected of the user. Even better, one could hire a dispassionate facilitator to run the evaluation in your stead. However, even if we do manage to completely mask our feelings, or use a dispassionate facilitator, the mere act of observation changes subjects' behavior. This was first discovered as part of an experiment at the Hawthorne Plant of the Western Electric Company which was keen to investigate the effects of employee productivity in an office where the environmental factors were altered – different lighting, humidity levels, etc., were tested. The puzzling thing was that no matter how the environmental factors were altered, productivity improved. After some investigation, the team discovered that the subjects had become dispirited in their work and perceived themselves as unimportant to the company. However, the researchers' interest in their work gave them the perception that their work was important, so their productivity increased!

Therefore, when conducting an observation, one should withdraw from the subject as far as possible, but not so far that is no longer possible to make worthwhile observations. If expenses allow, camcorders and scan converters can be used to facilitate remote observation. In fact, one need not go to that much expense. We have conducted remote observation experiments using a monitor splitter lead (this attaches at the back of the PC and drives two monitors simultaneously) and a microphone on a very long lead.

7.5.4 HAPPY USERS

Most people react negatively to being observed – they become self-conscious and lose confidence. This is clearly undesirable.

Before inviting anyone to take part in an observation, it should be made abundantly clear that it is the system you are testing and not their performance. You should explain what will happen, what will be expected of the user and how much time it will take. Only then should you ask them to take part. If the user is willing, it is a good idea to draw up a participant consent form. Ours is based on that used by Dray & Associates (Dray, 2001) and contains the following headings:

- **Purpose of study**. What you are doing and why.
- **Information you will collect**. Explaining what will be recorded and, most importantly, what will happen to that information afterwards – users would be upset to see some of their more hapless moments recorded on video and made freely available on the Internet. You could state that you may use anonymized video or audio to show to your manager or display at a technical conference.
- **Non-disclosure**. The system you are asking the user to interact with may be commercially sensitive and require protection.

- **Freedom to withdraw**. Allow people to pull out or request a break at any time.
- **Questions**. State that the user may ask questions at any time.
- **Payment**. Normally users are paid for participation of this nature. The amount is up to you, but you should tell them explicitly up-front what this amount will be.

With reference to the problem of user-biasing discussed above, there are issues around how much should be revealed to the subjects about the true nature of the experiment. Quoting Milgram's experiment again (Milgram, 1974), his results would obviously have been meaningless had he told the subjects that they were not actually electrocuting the actor. However, are the results from this work worth the emotional trauma experienced by the subjects? A more recent example from mobile computing is reported in Jakob Nielsen's Alertbox column (Nielsen, 2004). In this instance, researchers were keen to see why mobile phones were so annoying. They had two actors hold a conversation in a place such as a restaurant or train station, after which researchers interviewed bystanders to see whether they were annoyed. The experimenters then repeated the process, but this time using only one actor speaking their half of the original conversation into a cellular handset. The researchers discovered that hearing half a conversation is more annoying than hearing a full conversation but, again, was this result worth inconveniencing the bystanders?

Most universities and research institutions have an ethics committee which determines whether the value of an experiment's results outweigh the inconvenience to the subjects. This approach started in medical faculties where the issue is, literally, life and death, but is now accepted practice with any group conducting experiments on people. So before you rush headlong into user evaluations, check whether the institution you study at or work for has such a policy.

7.6 INTERVIEWS

Conducted by: End-users
Equipment: An interactive prototype
Results: Qualitative
Where: Controlled setting

Interviewing is a common technique for getting users to reflect on their experience in their own words. This can be less expensive than ethnographic observation, as the design team need only record and review a few hours' worth of interview material as opposed to what could be days' worth of recorded observations. As with other forms of evaluation which require direct interaction with the user, the value of the session depends a lot on the quality of the interviewer. A good interviewer will be able to put the interviewee at ease, let them express their point of view without being influenced, and be able to detect and follow up on any interesting points made in the course of conversation. Furthermore, a good interviewer can build trusted relationships with the subjects, thus easing the way to conduct further interviews. Whilst experienced interviewers will naturally direct the questioning to pursue the most interesting issues, it may be worth creating a script of questions for those interviewers with less experience.

Conducting interviews as an alternative to observation can lead to information being missed. People are fantastically bad at explaining and deconstructing how they achieve a given task. Tasks that are repeated frequently are chunked together and become secondary to the user, but may prove vital for a system designer. (Think of changing gear in a manual car. When you started driving, you had to think about the clutch, accelerator and gearshift separately, requiring a lot of concentration. Once you had learned to drive, gear changing became a single action, allowing you to do it while changing radio channels and chatting to a passenger.)

From our experience, interviews have greatest value when conducted in conjunction with some form of observation, either ethnographic or laboratory based. Often in observation you will see the subject perform some action which seems incredibly strange to you, but makes perfect sense to them. Asking the users about that incident can lead to very interesting insights into where their mental model diverges from yours – see Box 7.2.

BOX 7.2 **'THE LONG WAY ROUND'**

When conducting the experiments for the new menu interface described in Chapter 8, one user ignored the rapid access system of the new handset completely and simply scrolled to the desired function using the down arrow. In one instance this took 74 key presses! (As we were using key presses as a metric to evaluate the efficacy of the new system, this was very worrying.) At the end of the experiment, we interviewed the user and asked why they had adopted this strategy when it was clearly slower than using the numeric keys. He replied that using the down arrow he did not have to think about what key to press next – although slower in terms of key presses it was guaranteed to arrive at the desired option (eventually). Relying solely on the video recording of the session, we would never have had this insight. ■

7.7 QUESTIONNAIRES

Conducted by: End-users
Equipment: An interactive prototype & questionnaire
Results: Qualitative & Quantitative
Where: Anywhere

Another popular technique for garnering user opinion is the questionnaire. This technique is popular as it has the potential to reach a very wide audience, is cheap to administer and can be analyzed rapidly. Of course, it can never be as flexible as an interview and requires a lot of effort to design, especially if the user is completing it with no external help. Designing a good questionnaire is a complicated process, especially if the results are to be reliable.

There are a number of standard questionnaires for conducting interface evaluations. One of the most popular is QUIS – Questionnaire for User Interaction Satisfaction (`http://www.lap.umd.edu/QUIS/`) – developed and refined by the Human–Computer Interaction Lab at the University of Maryland. Many more can be found at Gary Perlman's site (`http://www.acm.org/~perlman/question.html`) (Perlman, 1998), but none are designed specifically for evaluating mobile systems. This almost begs mobile interaction researchers to create their own questionnaires, but this task can be a lot more complex than it first appears.

At the outset, one must be very clear exactly what you want to find out. Do not simply include questions just in case they may be useful – this will end up wasting your time and the time of the respondents. Also remember that you will need to ask the respondent some information about themselves. Again, this should be limited to just what you need to know about them (e.g. experience of similar systems, age, visual acuity, etc.) but avoid personal questions that have no benefit to your research (e.g. do you really need to know their name?).

Once you know what you want to ask, you need to pose the questions in a way that is unambiguous to all possible respondents. This is no small task. There are a number of standard forms of questions that one might employ to help guard against ambiguity and increase the value of the data. These include:

- Open-ended, e.g. "Did you enjoy using the system?"
  - These are the least formal and are an invitation for the respondent to give an unstructured opinion. The responses to this type of question can be interesting, but are obviously hard to analyze.
- Scalar, e.g. "I was able to enter text easily: Disagree 1 2 3 4 5 Agree"
  - This is an example of a Likert scale, which offers a more quantitative way of assessing a respondent's opinion or attitude than can be achieved through an open-ended question. Typically these scales have five to seven options, but ranges from three to nine options are not unknown.
  - One form of scalar questions are semantic scales, which let a respondent decide where their opinion lies between two diametrically opposed views, e.g.
    Happy - - - - - - - - Sad
- Multi-choice, e.g. "What base would you like on your pizza? (tick one):
  ☐ Thin ☐ Thick ☐ Cheese rim"
  - This is the simplest form of multi-choice where the user should select one option from a limited list. Of course, in some instances we may want more than one selection, e.g.
    "Please select your pizza toppings by ticking appropriate boxes:
    ☐ Tuna ☐ Chicken ☐ Corn ☐ Brie ☐ Cheddar"
  - Sometimes, we may want to know more about the choices people select, in which case we can introduce ranking, e.g.
    "Please select your pizza toppings by writing '1' in the box
    beside your favorite topping, '2' beside your next-favorite, etc.:
    ☐ Tuna ☐ Chicken ☐ Corn ☐ Brie ☐ Cheddar"

Having told you how to design your own questionnaire, we must now caution you against it. Two key problems are:

- **Reliability**. Can you guarantee that the questionnaire will give the same results when completed by similar types of people?
- **Validity**. Are you sure that the questions you set are measuring the effect you think they are measuring? Can you be sure that the respondents are interpreting the questions the way you intended them to?

There is a lot to be said on the topic of questionnaire design which falls outside the scope of this book. For a full discussion on the pros and cons of using questionnaires in usability evaluation, try reading Jurek Kirakowski's thoughtful discussion (`www.ucc.ie/hfrg/resources/qfaq1.html`). If you're keen to develop your own questionnaire, then books such as that by Anastasi (1982) give very detailed accounts of how to produce questionnaires that give rigorous results.

7.8 NON-USER METHODS

Testing with real users is expensive and time-consuming. This has led to the development of user-less user testing. It may seem counter-intuitive, but research in disciplines such as psychology gives us insight into how the human mind works. We can therefore predict how any human would react to an interface without having actual users present. Consequently, this type of evaluation is often called 'predictive'.

7.8.1 HEURISTIC EVALUATION

Conducted by: Usability experts
Equipment: An interactive prototype
Results: Qualitative and quantitative – usually a ranked list of problems
Where: Controlled setting

Heuristic Evaluation is a technique created by Jakob Nielsen (Nielsen, 1994) as a way of structuring expert evaluation of an interface. The basic idea is that the experience of interface designers is distilled into a number of design heuristics against which the interface is evaluated by a usability expert. Nielsen proposed the following 10 general heuristics, found on his website (`http://www.useit.com/papers/heuristic/heuristic_list.html`):

1. **Visibility of system status**. The system should always keep users informed about what is going on, through appropriate feedback within a reasonable time.
2. **Match between system and real world**. The system should speak the users' language, with words, phrases and concepts familiar to the user, rather than system-oriented terms. Follow real-world conventions, making information appear in a natural and logical order.
3. **User control and freedom**. Users often choose system functions by mistake and will need a clearly marked 'emergency exit' to leave the unwanted state without having to go through an extended dialog. Support undo and redo.
4. **Consistency and standards**. Users should not have to wonder whether different words, situations, or actions mean the same thing. Follow platform conventions.
5. **Error prevention**. Even better than good error messages is a careful design which prevents a problem from occurring in the first place.
6. **Recognition rather than recall**. Make objects, actions, and options visible. The user should not have to remember information from one part of the dialog to another. Instructions for use of the system should be visible or easily retrievable whenever appropriate.
7. **Flexibility and efficiency of use**. Accelerators – unseen by the novice user – may often speed up the interaction for the expert user such that the system can cater for both inexperienced and experienced users. Allow users to tailor frequent actions.

8. **Esthetic and minimalist design**. Dialogs should not contain information which is irrelevant or rarely needed. Every extra unit of information in a dialog competes with the relevant units of information and diminishes their relative visibility.

9. **Help users recognize, diagnose, and recover from errors**. Error messages should be expressed in plain language (no codes), precisely indicate the problem, and constructively suggest a solution.

10. **Help and documentation**. Even though it is better if the system can be used without documentation, it may be necessary to provide help and documentation. Any such information should be easy to search, focused on the user's task, list concrete steps to be carried out, and not be too large.

Ideally, there would be at least five experts to conduct independent heuristic evaluations of the interface. Each expert compiles a list of ranked usability problems, paying attention to the issues of the *frequency* of the problem (common or rare), the *impact* on the users (can they overcome it easily?), and the *persistence* of the problem (will the problem crop up in multiple situations or is it quite localized?).

Having conducted quite a few of these evaluations ourselves, one has to be careful in how the findings are reported. As heuristic evaluation is designed to discover faults in the design (and not laud its positive aspects), the output from the process can be interpreted by the designers as an assassination of their work. To balance this, we suggest that when you spot a problem, you also suggest a solution. Being creative in this way can change the tone of the report, making it more palatable and causing less alienation from the designers. Also, as someone who has received these reports on their cherished designs, we appreciate it when the evaluator lists which particular heuristic is being violated, to show that the assessment is based on a rational evaluation and not personal opinion. If you are concerned about how to pitch an evaluation and manage your relation with the design team, Marine's article 'Pardon me, but your baby is ugly . . .' (Marine, 2002) offers some further hints on how to defuse any personal feelings by keeping the evaluation focused on the wider context and not on the designer's decisions.

One problem, noted by Nielsen and others, is that these general heuristics may not be appropriate for every class of interface. In their book *Interaction Design*, Preece *et al.* (2002) note that there is, as yet, no accepted list of heuristics for evaluating mobile devices. Some work (Vetere *et al.*, 2003) has been started in this direction, using ideas from CSCW to provide heuristics which evaluate the contextual dimensions of mobile applications. Developing these heuristics for a domain as new as mobile computing is a large task. The first set of heuristics for assessing desktop systems (Smith and Mosier, 1986) was based on 944 evaluations! As we have seen from Beck's work into evaluating mobile systems (Beck *et al.*, 2003), mobile computing has some way to go before we can form heuristics from this depth of experience.

Another form of expert evaluation is cognitive walkthrough. In this instance, the expert evaluator will walk-through a particular task, seeing if the user's goals can be met by the information and functionality provided by the interface. One variation on cognitive walkthrough is 'contextual walkthrough' as proposed by Po (2003). Po proposes that the cognitive walkthrough be conducted in the same conditions as those experienced by the end-user (hence the 'contextual walkthrough' title). While the idea is sound, Po found no significant difference between conducting the cognitive walkthrough in the lab or in the end-user context. However, it should be noted that this result was based on a single study and further work may prove the validity of the approach. Alternatively, it may be the case that any benefit to the evaluators in terms of being located in the target context may be undone by the distractions of the same context.

There are other forms of expert evaluations, such as consistency and standards inspection. We will not dwell on these as they have little application to mobile computing at the present time. (Both methods compare new interfaces to accepted standards or conventions, neither of which exists for mobile systems as yet.)

7.8.2 NO PEOPLE WHATSOEVER

Conducted by: Theoretical model
Equipment: A formal specification of the interaction characteristics of the device
Results: Quantitative
Where: Anywhere

Building on cognitive psychology research, some HCI evaluation techniques dispense entirely with the user and rely on an idealized model of how people think. Early successes in this field include GOMS (Goals, Operators, Methods and Selectors) which is able to predict interaction problems for expert users conducting limited tasks (Card *et al.*, 1983). GOMS is a very simplified model, but even a model as simple as KLM (Keystroke Level Model) (Dix *et al.*, 1998) can yield interesting results – KLM simply looks at the time taken to find, select and press interface buttons. In fact, we used a very simple keypress-count type of evaluation for pre-testing our ideas for the menu replacement system in Chapter 8. This helped us accept and reject designs, before investing the effort in creating the final interactive prototype for user testing.

One criticism of these models is that they don't take into account anything other than expert users in limited situations (a typical example would be ATM usage). For mobile computing, this type of simplified evaluation is never going to have much relevance. Fortunately, as cognitive psychology has evolved over the years, so have the models of how humans work and interact with their environment. In particular, connectionist models show great promise in predicting how context will affect user performance. One example of this is through the work of Nunez (2002) to show how environmental factors in the real world affect a user's sense of 'presence' within a virtual environment. From observational experiments, Nunez builds a cognitive model that shows which factors would increase presence (e.g. reading a book on the subject of the VE before entering it) and which would detract from it (e.g. lack of ambient sound). While the model may be too complex for many designers to use directly, it should help predict what types of evaluation are useful and what types of incident to watch for during evaluation. Sadly, this work is at too early a stage to have much impact outside the rather specialist research community.

7.9 EXPERIMENTAL EVALUATION

Having arrived at the stage of an interactive prototype, it's time to ask whether your system offers any improvement on those that have gone before. Users may rave about the system subjectively, but does it offer any functional advantage? Can you give some quantitative measure of just how much 'better' your system is?

Shneiderman (1998) describes this type of evaluation as a 'controlled psychologically oriented' experiment. Others call it simply 'experimental evaluation' (Preece *et al.*, 2002; Dix *et al.*, 1998). Regardless, the underlying idea is to bring the rigors of the scientific method to the field of interface evaluations.

The scientific method is a standard adopted across all experimental science disciplines to determine objective truth, i.e. a truth that is independent of any prejudices, biases or belief structure. The practical outworking of this lofty statement is a process for conducting experiments to ensure that the results are as accurate as they possibly can be. This process is detailed below, along with an example from our research to help clarify the issues.

Experimental Process
Conducted by: End-users
Equipment: Interactive Prototype
Results: Quantitative and scientifically rigorous
Where: Usually laboratory based

7.9.1 HYPOTHESIS

Before you can do any type of experiment, you have to think about the term 'better'. In what sense is your system better? Take the example of a new form of text entry for a PDA. Is it better in that it allows users to enter text more quickly? Or is it less error prone than previous methods?

Let's say that we're interested in the time it takes users to enter text – we're not so concerned about accuracy, as the primary application will be sending short messages to friends. Time now becomes our *dependent* variable, in other words, time is the value we are trying to measure (less time means a 'better' solution). If all we do, however, is simply measure how long it takes users to enter data, we have not learnt very much. Instead, we want to know whether our system is faster than existing ones, and therefore we need to record the time it takes users to enter text with our system as compared to some other system. As we can change which system to give to a user, the system becomes an *independent* variable – we are free to choose it at will. So we can now run an experiment in which we manipulate the independent variable (system) to see what effect it produces in the value of the dependent variable (time).

We've just described the simplest type of experiment possible, where there is one independent and one dependent variable. If we wish to increase the number of independent variables, then the experiment will rapidly become more complex. Returning to our example, we might want to measure each system under outdoor and indoor conditions. This means that we need to conduct four separate sets of experiment: System A inside, System A outside, System B inside and System B outside. The complexity grows geometrically and experiments rapidly become unmanageable.

Increasing the dependent variables simply means that we measure some other factor for each user. (For example, we may wish to use a questionnaire to measure each user's subjective experience of the system.) In this instance, the measurement adds little to the complexity of the experiment, but may mean that it will take longer for the subject to complete the session.

Having thought about the variables in your experiment, it is now time to state the objective of your experiment in terms of these variables. This is important, as the results from the experiment must be testable in a clearly defined way, so that there is no ambiguity about what you are measuring and what that measurement will mean. Normally, this statement is known as a *hypothesis* and takes the form of a prediction about the impact that changes in the independent variable will have on the dependent variable. In our case, that might read something like "Subjects will be able to input text more quickly using system A than using system B."

Having formulated the hypothesis, we now have to think a little about the statistical analysis that we conduct at the end of the experiment. The goal of this analysis is to state (with varying degrees of certainty) whether or not the altering of the independent variables did indeed influence the result. Thanks to the wacky world of statistics, the best way to prove the hypothesis correct is to disprove the opposite of the hypothesis! The opposite of the hypothesis is called the *null hypothesis*. For example, the null hypothesis for our example would state that the users of both systems will take the same time to enter text. So, if the results of the analysis do indeed show that there is a difference in time between the two systems, we can reject the null hypothesis. This means that the original hypothesis was correct.

If you're starting to get nervous about these statistical terms and have no interest in conducting your own analysis, please don't worry. The point of this discussion is to provide you with enough knowledge so that you can converse with statisticians and interpret the answers they give you. If you're interested in conducting your own analysis, then books such as Howell (2001) provide an excellent introduction.

Designing sensible hypotheses with testable results can be a challenge. Even after many years of experience in this type of testing, we still present our experimental designs to the rest of our research group. Inevitably there is some factor we forgot to take into account, or some flaw in the design which we had overlooked. Psychologists, more so than pure statisticians, are especially good at this type of experimentation and evaluation. For that reason, our research group at the University of Cape Town employs two consultant psychologists to help us with the design and analysis of this type of evaluation.

7.9.2 THE USERS

We've managed to tighten up on the definition of what it means for a system to be 'better' but have yet to think about the subjects who will take part in the experiment. In many research papers, the researchers follow the path of least resistance and recruit students from whichever faculty or organization the researchers are based in. This makes perfect sense for the researchers, especially academics, as students are readily available at little cost (free food is often enough to entice them) and can be coerced into taking part in the experiment as part of their course requirements. However, unless the system you're building is aimed at students, this is a terrible idea.

In order for your evaluation to hold any weight, it's essential that the subjects you recruit for your experiment are representative of your target user group. They should have the same age profile, similar levels of literacy, and similar amounts of exposure to computer technology. Returning to our example of text entry on a PDA, we should be testing our system with typical PDA users – busy executives needing to manage large amounts of information. And here we see precisely why recruiting students for experiments is so seductive – busy executives would need a large financial incentive to make it worth their while to set time aside and participate in an experiment. I used to work for a marketing research group which ran various focus groups for new products and would recruit users to match a specific profile. This was highly specialized work which we would often have to outsource to recruitment agencies. When one has paid the bill for the recruitment agency and paid the participants a commensurate amount for their time, this rapidly becomes an expensive process. (Just as a word of warning, it may look as though a marketing focus group is the same as an evaluation, but the goals of each group are very different. Marketing agencies can certainly help with recruiting subjects, but you're better off running the sessions yourself. Siegel (2001) has written a thorough account of the benefits and pitfalls of using marketing agencies as part of the evaluation process.)

So, having decided on who you need, the next question is how many subjects you need. Some people, looking for an easy escape, will latch on to the work of Nielsen (2000b) which seems to suggest that five users are sufficient. However, this interpretation confuses quantitative scientific experimentation with the heuristic testing we discussed before. In heuristic testing, we're simply looking at user performance whilst interacting with the target system. In scientific experimentation, we're testing new ideas and adding to knowledge in a quantitative, rigorous way. So Nielsen's argument is that five people are sufficient to reveal the majority of problems in a given interface. (Actually, it's worth noting that a lot of people are cross with Nielsen and his five-user rule (Bevan *et al.*, 2003). The debate still rumbles on for now, so please use the rule with caution.) If, on the other hand, you're running an experiment to prove your hypothesis is true, you need many more than five users.

Dipping our toe into the murky waters of statistics once more, we discover that we need sufficient data to make sure that the results we measured did not happen by chance. In this case, data equates to users. For example, if we recruited only one person, the effect we observed may be down to some strange character trait of that particular user. If we have two users, then it's less likely that two people will share the same strange character trait, so our results become more reliable, and so on. Depending on the statistical measure you use, the number of subjects you need will vary. However, if you don't wish to wade further to determine an exact number, using 10 people per condition is a good rule of thumb (Dix *et al.*, 1998). (A condition relates back to the independent variable story. If we did a direct comparison of system A and system B, we would need 10 people for each system, i.e. 20 subjects. If we were interested in performance outside as well as inside, then we now have four conditions – system A inside and out, system B inside and out – and 40 subjects! This could be alarming, but we will shortly see how clever experimental design allows us to reuse the same person in more than one condition, cutting down on the number of actual people we need to recruit.)

One final note on selecting users for mobile computing evaluations is that for evaluation of cellular handsets, the potential user group is so large and diverse that it may not be possible to find a sample that is representative of the user population. Unless a large budget is available, other forms of user evaluation may be more appropriate.

7.9.3 TASKS

So, we have the question we want answered and we have the subjects to help answer that question, but what are the subjects actually going to do? Every observational experiment of this nature requires the subjects to perform some task with the interface. This can be whimsical, highly structured, or downright boring. The important thing is that the tasks chosen for the experiment should be representative of those in the real world. For example, when designing the tasks for our text entry system, we could pick our favorite novel and have the subject type in a selected paragraph. This might be fun, but it's unlikely that anyone will ever want to write a novel using a PDA. Instead, a better task could be constructed by collecting existing (non-private) notes from other PDA users and collating these into a task list.

Besides being representative, tasks should not bias the experiment one way or the other. For example, if one of our text entry systems was particularly fast at selecting non-alphabetic characters, we could bias the experiment in favor of that system by picking messages with lots of punctuation or numbers in them. This issue of biasing was particularly difficult for us to counter when running the experiment described in Chapter 8.

7.9.4 EXPERIMENT DESIGN

Having derived the tasks, you next need to consider how to allocate users to the various conditions. Let us return to the simplest form of our experiment, where we are interested in the time taken to enter text using system A as opposed to system B. Should we, for instance, have 10 users enter text first with system A and then with system B? Statistically this would be valid as we have data for 10 users in each condition. Experimentally, however, this arrangement would cause all sorts of problems. For example, as the users worked with system A, they would become more skillful at text entry so that the times for text entry with system B would be much lower – regardless of system, performance for the second half of the experiment would be improved. Or, it may be the case that fatigue comes into play and the second system is always the slowest. This is called a *learning effect*, where the order in which users are exposed to conditions affects the final result.

In order to counter the learning effect, there are two things we can do. The first of these is to recruit 20 people and allocate 10 to each condition. In this way, we can be sure that there is no learning effect, as the users only ever see one system. Technically, this is known as a *between-groups* experiment. While it removes the learning effect, between-group experiments require more subjects (in this case, twice as many). Also, one must take extra care of how subjects are distributed between the groups – each group should be a representative sample of the user population.

An alternative to between-group studies are *within-group* studies. Here, users are exposed to more than one condition. To counter the learning effects discussed earlier, however, the order in which the conditions are presented is different for different users. So we would take 10 users, five of whom would use system A first and the other five system B first. Within-group studies have the benefit that you need to recruit fewer people and you have exactly the same user profile for each condition.

Let's say we decide on a within-group experiment for our simple evaluation of systems A and B. We then wish to extend the experiment with the indoor and outdoor comparison. If we remain with the within-group experiment, we now have four conditions which must be randomized. This results in 16 possible orders in which conditions may be presented (A outside, A inside, B outside, B inside; A outside, A inside, B inside, B outside; etc.). Is this a problem? Well, we might possibly recruit six more people so that we have one subject for each possible ordering. However, we're now expecting each subject to complete tasks in four different conditions. This could take a long time, which is unfair to the subjects in two ways: firstly to expect them to spend so long completing the experiment, and secondly, the longer the experiment takes each subject to complete, the more we risk invalidating the results due to subject fatigue.

One common solution to this problem is to use a combination of within and between studies. So, for the experiment above, we could recruit 20 people, 10 of whom would be allocated to do evaluations outside and 10 inside. For each group of 10, five would use system A first and five system B first. Alternatively, it's just as valid to allocate 10 people to system A and 10 to system B, then have five people from each group start outside and five start inside. Either way, these arrangements give you a good compromise – you need recruit only half the people needed for a pure between-groups study and you won't overburden your subjects.

Finally, one should also be aware that learning effects may occur with the order in which tasks are presented to the user. If the tasks are placed in the same order for every user, then it is possible that the order affects the final result. For example, if one of the text entry systems uses previous input to predict future input, the order of the tasks may be critical to the performance of the prediction algorithm. An easy fix to this problem would be to present the tasks in a random order for every subject.

7.9.5 CONDUCTING EXPERIMENTS

Experiments of this nature are usually conducted in a usability lab in isolation from the experimenter. All the rules we discussed above for conducting informal evaluations apply here: how to record observations, how not to bias the outcome, and how to treat your subjects. Also, this type of evaluation can be accompanied by some form of post-experiment questionnaire or interview to give qualitative insight, along with the quantitative result.

7.9.6 EXPERIMENTAL RESULTS

As we stated earlier, the purpose of the experiment is to gain a quantitative insight into how much 'better' a system is. Please note that all the statistical analysis tells us is how confident we can be that the observed effect is down to the independent variables and not random chance. The statistics do not say whether the system is truly better. For example, in the text entry example, the analysis may tell us that we can be 95% certain (for statisticians, anything less is random chance) that users of system A take less time to enter text than users of system B. Great! However, the statistics do not say how much faster. The difference may be as little as 1 millisecond! So, while your results are significant in a scientific sense, they may have little practical impact.

7.10 CONSIDERING CONTEXT – EVALUATING MOBILE SYSTEMS

When evaluating a desktop system, the process is simplified by the fact that, chances are, the situation in which the system will be deployed (an office somewhere) is the same situation in which the usability evaluation will take place (an office somewhere). Even if the computer is to be employed in some other context (an air traffic control center, say), the system will remain in that context once deployed.

For mobile devices, the context will always be changing. Furthermore, it is not just the environmental context that changes, but the social and technological ones too. This has profound consequences for evaluation, as the device should really be evaluated in each likely context of use.

BOX 7.3 WHAT IS CONTEXT?

Dix *et al.* (2000) divide context in a very similar way, but split technology context into 'infrastructure' (network, etc.) and 'system' (other devices, etc.). Their context taxonomy is aimed at informing and inspiring design. For our work in evaluation, we have not found this extra subdivision to be particularly useful. ■

7.10.1 PHYSICAL CONTEXT

For physical context, we need to overcome the problem of observing how the device is being used and, if we are able to observe, the associated problem of recording those observations. One way we have been able to record on-screen interaction is to use the Remote Display Control for PocketPC (a free download from Microsoft). This broadcasts the on-screen image of a PDA across a WiFi network. So, provided the PDA stays within network range, it is possible to capture user interactions. Any interesting parts of the screen capture can then be replayed to the user to elicit comments as part of the post-evaluation debrief. An alternative for cellular handsets, which are currently not able to broadcast on-screen interaction, is to use custom video cameras, such as the Mobile Device camera provided by Noldus (see Figure 7.5). This can hardly be described as unobtrusive, but does at least allow the designers to see what is happening on screen. (Chances are

FIGURE 7.5

The mobile device observation camera

the designers have a better view of the screen than the user.) Using technologies like these, we can then deploy users in a particular physical context (e.g. in a poorly lit, noisy environment) and see how well they are able to perform with the device.

For example, to assess the impact of their mobile shopping mall guide, one research group recreated a floor of a shopping mall within their building (Bohnenberger *et al.*, 2002). Although they didn't recreate the store interiors, they recreated navigational constraints of a mall to see whether the guide was of value.

7.10.2 TECHNOLOGICAL CONTEXT

By technological context, we mean the context of the technology available to the user of the mobile application. Usually, this will refer to the networks available, but may also refer to other resources, such as the availability of external monitors, keyboards, etc. This is especially relevant when conducting evaluations of prototypes which use technologies other than those deployed in the final product. This problem was discussed at length in Chapter 6, looking, in particular, at the Buck used to mimic the technology of the Handspring Treo. When conducting evaluations, one must be sure that the evaluations conducted with the prototype technology still hold for the technology used in the final device.

One problem not discussed in Chapter 6 is assessing the impact that different network technologies can have on mobile applications. For whatever reasons, it may not be possible to conduct evaluations using the network infrastructure available to the end-user. In our research, we've built a number of applications for cellular handsets. However, we cannot afford the exorbitant fees charged by the cellular networks, so we fake the network using our WiFi infrastructure. Of course, the bandwidth of such a network is much higher than that offered by cellular networks, which may give unreal expectations about the final system performance. This cuts both ways, as one system we tested using this technique failed because the bandwidth was too high! The network was pushing data packets to the device which crashed because it could not process the data quickly enough. If we had used a cellular network, it would have run perfectly well.

Another insight we've had in switching applications from WiFi to cellular networks is that user enthusiasm drops off when they are required to part with their own money for network access. A good example of this is the text-worm system we developed which allowed university students to SMS their lecturer during the course of a lecture session (Jones and Marsden, 2004). Students were willing to pay for the SMSs during the first few sessions, but cost considerations meant that usage rapidly dropped off. As technology develops to provide us with devices which support both GSM and WiFi networks (see Box 7.4), it may be the case that this type of project becomes viable.

BOX 7.4 CHEAPER WIRELESS ACCESS

There is currently a move by handset manufacturers to produce handsets which can roam between WiMax, WiFi and GSM networks. This is an interesting development as it makes perfect sense for the handset manufacturers, but there is no incentive for the networks to provide these handsets to customers as it will inevitably decrease their traffic. ■

7.10.3 SOCIAL CONTEXT

Social context can be a lot trickier to engineer than the physical or technological context. In fact, engineering a social context is tantamount to an oxymoron – "Ok, Mr Smith, can you please feel frustrated for 10 minutes whilst using the device, and then feel relaxed and try the task again." This is why ethnography, and other longitudinal study techniques, like diaries, are essential for evaluating mobile devices within social contexts – which is why we spent so long on the topic in Chapter 5.

Not only is it essential to evaluate ideas you think will work in a social context (just in case nobody likes them), it's also worth testing crazy ideas that fail every other test just because they may make sense socially (SMS springs to mind here).

EXERCISE 7.2 UPDATED HEURISTICS

Having just read the section on context, flick back to Section 7.8.1 on heuristic evaluation. Read through the list of heuristics presented there and, based on your understanding of context, add some more heuristics for mobile devices to the list. While you are at it, are there any heuristics in the original list you think should be removed or deleted? ■

7.10.4 OTHER CONTEXTS

So far, we've discussed three forms of context: physical, technological and social. There are many other ways to think about context which may be more helpful in the evaluation (and design) of mobile devices. Dey (2001), for example, looks at several classifications of context and proposes that context may be defined as information that can be used to determine the situation of an entity. Entities are defined as objects, places or people that are relevant to the interaction between a user and an application, including the user and the application. This is a great way to define context for thinking about how an application should fit into a context, but reduces a rich environment to a meager set of interactions between artifacts. Just be careful not to get locked into a mindset of thinking about the technology first and the users second (take a look at Box 7.5), or thinking that the context is more important than the user – Jameson (2001) has some ideas about how to model users and context in a complementary way.

BOX 7.5 CONTEXT AWARENESS

One of our colleagues, Professor Edwin Blake, was asked to create a computer vision system which could recognize the tracks of animals in a game reserve. The thinking was that the computer could process the image and infer the context from cues such as GPS location, time of day, type of foliage nearby, shape of print, etc. – a solution know as 'context awareness'. Not only is this a mammoth piece of computation, but it ignores the fact that the park employs very skilled trackers who are able to read the context instantaneously. So, rather than build an application which would never be as good as a human at reading context, he did some ethnography of the situation and discovered that he could use computers to aid the trackers with recording their insights into context. The result of the project was a GPS-enabled PDA which allowed the trackers to log their observations more accurately than before and ➤

upload these to a central park management system. By seeing context as an artifact of technology, it is unlikely this system would ever have been built.

Part of our research philosophy is that 'people know best about people'. So while we support context-aware computing to the extent that the computer knows things unambiguously (e.g. time and location), we steer clear of other forms of context awareness (e.g. user's mood or animal behavior). ■

7.11 COMPLEMENTARY EVALUATION

So, if we have to evaluate mobile systems, can we use the techniques developed for desktop systems, or do we abandon them in favor of those that take into account the changing context? Sadly, it would seem that both types of testing are essential for mobile systems.

The value of both types of evaluation is highlighted in Brewster's research (Brewster, 2002). He was developing a system for mobile devices which used non-speech sounds to improve accuracy of selecting on-screen buttons. After conducting initial trials in a laboratory, he discovered that sound augmentation did indeed increase the usability of the buttons for data entry tasks. To test this in context, he repeated the experiment, the only difference being that the subjects had to walk along a path outside while completing the tasks. While the augmented system still outperformed the control system, there was a significant reduction in the amount of data entered (32% less).

This research shows us two things:

- Lab-based evaluations can predict performance of an interface 'in-context'.
- Context-neutral testing provides only partial evaluation information – it's not a replacement for testing in context.

From this, one might be tempted to infer that contextual testing is sufficient; after all, the laboratory testing only replicated the finding of testing in context. However, there is still value in laboratory-based testing.

In all scientific disciplines, laboratory testing has been used to provide a controlled environment within which the researcher can isolate the effect of different variables on the test subject. This still holds true in the development of mobile computing. At the outset of the research, the designer uses context-neutral evaluation techniques to assess the impact of design decisions before introducing new variables in the form of a dynamic context. Having optimized the design so far as possible, testing can then begin in the target context.

Another reason for adopting this approach is purely pragmatic: it's a lot cheaper to conduct context-neutral evaluation. Better to sort out any problems using relatively inexpensive studies than arranging the logistics required for contextual testing.

Finally, it's worth noting that mobile computing is a relatively new discipline. A consequence of this is that there is no widely agreed method for conducting evaluation studies. This is highlighted by Beck *et al.* (2003), who conducted a survey of major mobile HCI publications between 1996 and 2002. They discovered that of 114 papers, only 50 had some evaluation component. Of those 50, most used evaluation techniques developed for desktop systems. Work like that of Brewster (2002) is extremely rare.

Having said that, one should not be too quick to dismiss the evaluation techniques used to evaluate interfaces in static (constant context) devices. Our approach, and that of Brewster, is to use these standard static techniques early in the design process and then conduct contextual evaluation only when the standard techniques have yielded a positive outcome.

7.12 CONCLUSION

As we stated at the start of the chapter, we've taken a pragmatic approach to evaluation techniques, as we believe this will provide the greatest value. If your evaluation requirements lie outside the techniques we discussed, or you're not sure which technique to use, there are many resources available to help you. One of the best places to start is the CHARM website (`http://www.otal.umd.edu/charm/`) provided by Ben Shneiderman's research group, which lists all the major evaluation methods and links to the relevant resources. Almost any textbook in HCI will discuss some of these evaluation methods – of these, Preece *et al.* (2002) does the best job. The classic text in this field, however, is a collection of papers edited by Nielsen and Mack (1994) which remains the standard to date.

To a large extent, evaluating mobile systems remains an open question. As Abowd and Mynatt (2000) noted, "we see relatively little published from an evaluation or end-user perspective in the ubicomp community." For them, evaluation remains one of the major challenges for mobile computing systems. This is a sentiment echoed by Banavar and Bernstein (2002) who state that "... the development of effective methods for testing and evaluating the usage scenarios enabled by pervasive applications is an important area that needs more attention from researchers." So don't be put off that you may not be doing the 'correct' sort of evaluation; for the time being, no one is completely sure what a 'correct' evaluation of a mobile system really is.

SUMMARY

In this chapter we have selected those evaluation methods that have proven the most useful to us in evaluating mobile systems. We have also categorized these techniques and given guidelines on when each technique is most appropriate. However, we do not aim to be the definitive guide on how to conduct evaluations of interactive systems. Rather, we strive to give you an overview of the methods, where they fit in and how they might be used. If you are interested in following up on a specific method, there are links in the resources section. What we have tried to do is point out the added challenges of evaluating a mobile system and why evaluations developed for desktop systems may fall short.

WORKSHOP QUESTIONS

- Think about how you would feel to be observed using technology over a long period. Bearing this in mind, draw up a sample consent form for experiment participants, based on that outlined in Section 7.5.4.

- Do you think it is possible to conduct user evaluations without actual users? To what extent, then, are non-user techniques useful?
- Do you think scientific experiments have any place in the scheme of commercial product development?

DESIGNER TIPS

- *It may seem like a good idea to design your own evaluation questionnaire, but this is a subtle art best left to experts.*
- *Unless you're an expert in statistics already, it is much easier to use a psychologist to help you design an experiment and perform the final statistical analysis.*
- *Heuristic evaluation is very popular, especially with commercial clients, as it's quick and doesn't require actual users. However, until some effective mobile heuristics are developed, it's a potentially flawed way to evaluate mobile systems.*
- *Don't be seduced by context-aware computing – computers can know about physical and technological contexts, but not social context.*

PART III
DESIGN GALLERY – DIRECTIONS AND GUIDELINES

CHAPTER 8	**CONTROLLING COMPLEX FUNCTIONS**	**223**
CHAPTER 9	**INFORMATION ACCESS**	**247**
CHAPTER 10	**BEYOND TEXT – USING IMAGES ON MOBILE DEVICES**	**289**
CHAPTER 11	**IMPACTING THE COMMUNITY; IMPACTING THE WORLD**	**315**

CHAPTER 8
CONTROLLING COMPLEX FUNCTIONS

OVERVIEW

8.1. Introduction
8.2. Menus and memory
8.3. Hierarchical menus
8.4. Icons
8.5. Manuals
8.6. No menus?
8.7. More complex menus
8.8. Some concluding thoughts

KEY POINTS

- As the computational power of mobile devices increases, it is increasingly important to find more efficient and intuitive ways of accessing functionality.
- Menus have been used on cellular handsets almost universally, yet often these menus have not been optimized for the smaller screen.
- There are many ways of accessing functions that, depending on the application, are much better than menus.
- Many interfaces borrow ideas from desktop computers, but fail to properly consider the constraints of the mobile platform when making the translation.
- Using manuals with an interface may decrease the likelihood that a user is able to complete a given task.

8.1 INTRODUCTION

Alan Cooper has a recurrent anti-joke in his book *The Inmates are Running the Asylum* (Cooper, 1999) which goes as follows:

Q. What do you get when you cross a car with a computer?

A. A computer!

Q. What do you get when you cross a telephone with a computer?

A. A computer!

His point is that computer technology is so invasive, all other aspects of the product tend to disappear. He argues that computers should be used to enhance some activity, not replace it. We have been arguing a similar point for mobile technologies; they should be used to augment human behavior, rather than modifying it.

When the first mobile phones appeared, there was little chance of computer technology getting in the way, as most of the electronics were dedicated to getting the handset to function, i.e. send and receive calls. The first commercially available cellular handset, released in 1984 by Motorola, was the DynaTAC 8000X. Besides the numeric keys, there was also a group of buttons on the handset which provided direct access to each 'feature' of the handset – some nine features in total. There is a button to set the volume, a button to turn the handset off, and so on.

As it became possible to build more complex circuits on smaller amounts of silicon, handset features increased to the point where it was impossible to have one-button-per-feature interfaces, so an alternative solution was sought. Almost universally, that solution was the menu.

8.2 MENUS AND MEMORY

We know that menus are easy to use as they facilitate recognition rather than recall – what we mean by this is that the human brain is better at recognizing some object in the outside word than recalling something from memory. For example, you can probably recognize the Coca-Cola logo, but would be hard pressed to describe it in any detail. Using a menu, the user can see all the available options and then select the one most appropriate to the task they are trying to achieve – they recognize the command name on the screen rather then recalling the exact word from memory. On the small screen, however, the user cannot see all the options at once, but has to scroll from option to option (often one at a time). This reintroduces the recall problem, as the user will need to remember the options as they scroll off the screen.

Other research in human memory (Miller, 1956) tells us that our short-term memories can hold only seven (plus or minus two) items simultaneously. If the screen displays only one item at a time and the menu is longer than seven entries, then the user is likely to forget the first option they saw by the time they reach the end of the menu (see Box 8.1).

BOX 8.1 INFINITELY LONG MENUS

Some cellular handsets display only one item at a time. When combined with looping menus (where the first menu item is re-shown when the user scrolls off the bottom of the menu) this can be a real problem, as users are not aware that they have passed the bottom of the list. Users become caught in what seems to them an endless list of options. Although you may find it hard to believe, we have video footage from one of our studies where a subject sat for two minutes scrolling through the top-level menu, never realizing that they were constantly re-reading items that had scrolled past before! ■

We've asserted that having menus on a small screen causes problems, but just how bad is the effect? Swierenga (1990) carried out research to consider the impact of reducing the size of the display to a menu system. Display size was gradually decreased, forcing users to scroll more and more. Although users' performance in terms of time to select an option increased as the display size dropped, the impact was not dramatic. Things became much worse, however, when the display was reduced to a single line. Not only was the time taken to select an item disproportionately increased, selection errors were also greatly increased. So, handsets which display more than one option at a time (ideally three or more) have similar performance characteristics to large-screen systems. However, a device which displays only one option at a time will be disproportionately more difficult to use. It would seem that cellular handset designers are unaware of this research, as they persist in producing handsets which display only one option at a time. While some handsets are so small that they could support only a single-line screen, others have a large screen capable of displaying multiple options, yet choose not to do so.

8.3 HIERARCHICAL MENUS

One way to overcome the length of menus is to use hierarchical menus, where selecting a menu option can reveal a new menu. While this overcomes the problem of overloading short-term memory with too many commands, it places a new burden on the user, namely forcing them to remember a function's location in a two-dimensional navigational structure.

8.3.1 LEARNING STRUCTURE

Research by Paap (1988) shows that when users eventually become familiar with the menu structure, they can rapidly find the item they are looking for; those unfamiliar with the structure, however, often struggle to achieve the task they embarked on. When a menu expert uses a handset, they are able to perform 'identity mapping' whereby they know the name of the option they want and rapidly scan the screen text until they find it. Therefore, menu usage, even on a small screen, does not present an insurmountable problem.

Novice users engage in a slower form of searching called 'class-inclusion'. In this instance, users must make decisions about the higher-level menu categories to decide whether their target function is contained within a particular sub-menu. For example, users must decide whether the function to alter the ring volume is to be found in the 'Settings' menu or the 'Tones' menu. Clearly this type of categorization by the designer (who understands the handset's functionality) can prove problematic to a naive user. When it is not possible for the user to see all the available options (due to reduced screen size), determining the correct class becomes even more difficult – there is extra cognitive load in remembering the previous (currently invisible) classifications.

Assuming the user has navigated to the correct sub-menu, they must perform an 'equivalence' search. In this instance the user knows what needs to be done, but does not know the exact phrase used to represent that option. Again, altering the volume of the ring could be described as 'Ring Volume', 'Volume of Ring', 'Tone Amplitude', etc., and requires the user to match their concept with the options presented. Once more, the cognitive load is increased through being forced to recall invisible options rather than compare them directly on the screen. Clearly something must be done to improve menu usage for the new user.

8.3.2 IMPROVING CLASSIFICATION

Often, when users eventually find a function they were searching for on a handset, they are baffled as to why the designer chose to put it where they did: "Ring volume obviously goes in the Phone Settings menu, not in the Ring Tone menu!". One might be tempted to think that search time could be decreased by improving the categorizations used in the menu classification, perhaps using novices to classify items in a way they feel is appropriate. Although no research specific to cellular handset menus has been conducted, this approach has been attempted in other menu-based systems with little success. For example, in one experiment reported by Lee *et al.* (1984), even when great care was taken in choosing meaningful classifications, users of systems mis-categorized options between 39% and 50% of the time. The evidence from these experiments leads us to believe that it is impossible to produce an ideal classification system for all users. Of course, once we learn a particular classification then using the handset becomes much easier. This may explain why, say, Nokia users claim their handsets are easier to use than other makes, and Sony-Ericsson users claim exactly the same thing.

Another question to ask, then, is how many classifications are appropriate? This question has been asked before in terms of breadth versus depth trade-offs – is it better to provide a wide range of classifications for comparison at the root, or to provide few initial classifications to limit user choice? Initial research conducted by Miller (1981) and Lee and MacGregor (1985) show that wide and shallow trees are more desirable than the narrow and deep variety. More recent research (Norman and Chin, 1988) refines this notion to show that concave structures are actually better – i.e. it is important to have a wide choice of options at the root menu and at the final level of menu structure, but intermediate levels should have a restricted choice. Most menus on mobile devices do indeed follow this scheme.

EXERCISE 8.1 CLASSIFICATION IS A PERSONAL THING

Using a cellular handset manual, or the handset itself, write out a list of all the features on your handset – just the functions (e.g. Set Language), not the menu names ➤

(e.g. Settings). Once you have the list, put each function on a separate piece of paper, give them to someone who has not used the original handset, and ask them to group the functions into likely groupings. Once they have completed the task, record their result and give the pieces of paper to someone else to complete the task. We would speculate that no matter how many people you get to complete the task, they will all come up with a different classification. ■

8.3.3 CONTEXT INFORMATION

For novices using a menu, it is essential that they are provided with some form of feedback about where they are within the structure in order to navigate successfully. The limited screen resources of the cellular handset make this a much more difficult task than with desktop-based menu systems. Given that some of the handsets we have seen nest menus up to five levels deep, the problem of navigation becomes all the more complicated.

Some handsets do provide a lot of information about location in a menu structure – not only depth choices, but feedback on the current level (see Figure 8.1). Other handsets, however, show only the most recent category choice (see Figure 8.2).

One vital piece of information which is missing from these visualizations is feedback about which options in the menus are branch nodes (the selection of which will display another menu) or leaf nodes (the selection of which will access a function). From desktop menus we already have an ellipses (or triangle) convention to denote the difference (see Figure 8.3) – leaf nodes have no ellipses beside the name. This type of information is important to novice users exploring a menu structure – they will be more likely to explore the structure if they know their exploration will not affect the handset.

Curiously, the current Symbian user interface guidelines recommend that ellipses are not used in menus since they make menu entries unnecessarily long. It seems as if some manufacturers have a tension between graphic design and user interface design.

8.4 ICONS

One common way to enhance menus is by using icons. Originally, on desktop systems, icons were used to visually represent an object, or function, of the operating system (e.g. an icon to denote a document). Icons were used in menu systems to replace, or augment, text descriptions of functions. Pure replacement of text is rare – it's hard to pick an icon that unambiguously represents a function. More commonly, icons and text are used together in menus to reinforce an idea (see Figure 8.4). Dix (1995) has shown that displaying text and icons together allows the icons to be used in isolation in, say, a toolbar, as the association has been made in the user's mind.

The augmentation of text in menus is common on mobile device menus. For instance, the Nokia menu on the 5110 model displays an icon beside each of the root level menu options, as we see in Figure 8.2.

More recent releases of Nokia handsets include animated versions of these icons. Research conducted on animated icons for desktop systems suggests that they are most useful to explain some action or verb (Baecker *et al.*, 1991). However, of the root level options which have animated

FIGURE 8.1

Here you can see a lot of context information as depicted by the tab bars at the top of the screen

icons, only one option is a verb – Call Divert. Even with this option, the animation adds little to understanding the role of the menu, as it shows an arrow ricocheting off a small picture of the handset. Given the resolution and physical size of the screen on mobile devices, however, the icons can serve to confuse, rather than augment, the user's understanding of a menu item. Rather than helping the user, the icons can be a distraction.

Of course, the screen technology available to mobile devices is constantly improving and many devices are able to display high-resolution color icons. Color Plate 6 shows icons from a Sony-Ericsson K700i handset, considered to be an entry-level device at the time of writing.

Even with the improved screen resolution, it's not clear what these icons add to the understanding of the menu feature. On many handsets, for instance, icons are applied in a seemingly haphazard way. Returning again to the K700, most options under the root options have a small icon beside them (see Figure 8.5(a)). However, those in the connectivity menu do not (see Figure 8.5(b)). One hypothesis might be that those items with an icon have no sub-menu; the designers have found a solution to the ellipses/triangle visualization problem discussed above. Alas, after some investigation

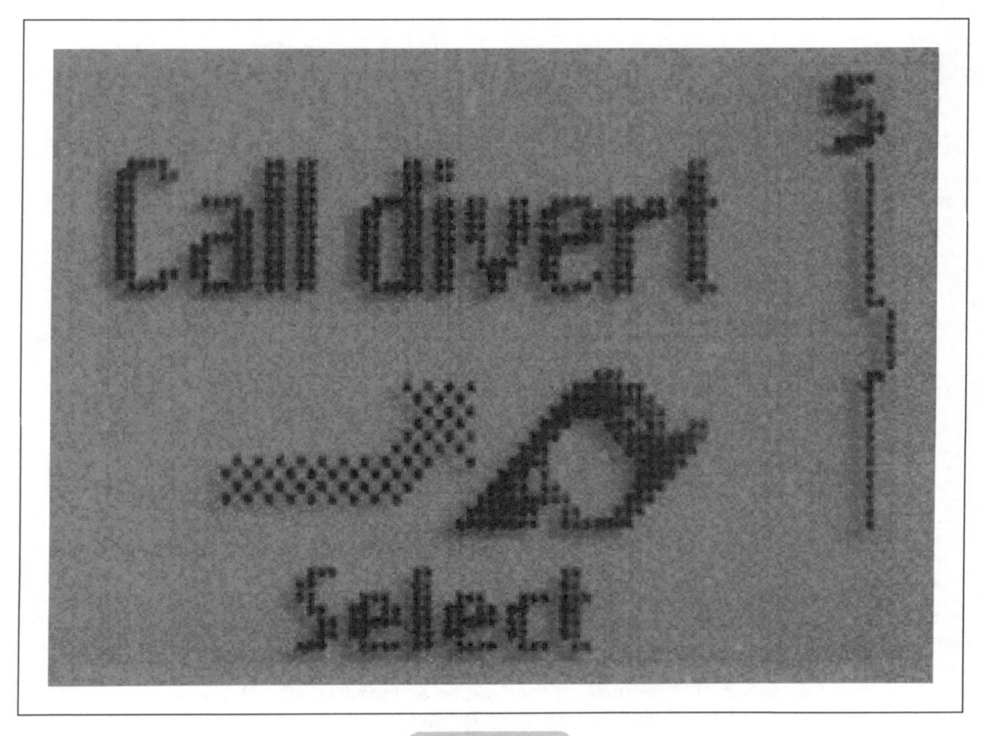

FIGURE 8.2

On this handset, we can see that we are at option 5, but have no idea how many more options are available to us. Please note that the 'bump' in the scroll bar at the side is of constant size and cannot be used to guess how many more options there are

it turns out that this is not the case (e.g. the 'Message:Settings' option has an icon, but has a sub-menu of six items).

This use of smaller icons in sub-menus does echo the use of compact icons in the desktop computer interfaces as seen in Figure 8.4. On closer examination, however, the potential usage of icons in this way is not properly realized for the simple reason that the compact icons rarely appear without the text description. Again returning to the K700, we see that the top of the interface has tabs, each with what appears to be a text-free icon. However, reading down the screen, we see that an entire line of screen space is wasted in explaining the meaning of the icon! For example, the 'General' setting in Figure 8.6 is particularly intractable.

One might argue that it's worth losing a line of screen space, as the tabs at the top of the screen provide the user with better context about where they are in the menu structure – a very laudable goal. If that is the goal, then why do the icons at the top disappear when a sub-option is selected? Furthermore, the use of tabs in the first place should be consistent. After all, a tab is just a way of visualizing a hierarchical structure – why not use it everywhere, rather than in isolated options? It may be that the tabs take up too much screen real-estate to be useful in every menu, but the K700 has menus of three items that are not displayed with tabs.

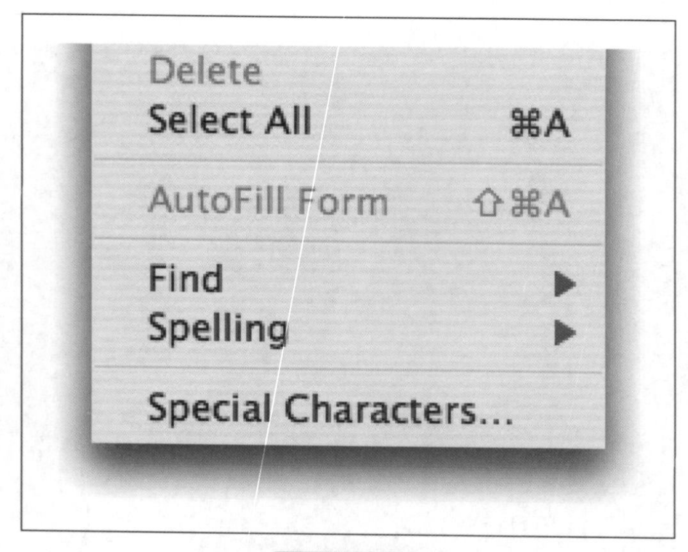

FIGURE 8.3

The triangle beside 'Find' and 'Spelling' shows that another menu will appear when we select either of those options. The ellipses beside 'Special Characters' shows that a dialog box will be opened when that option is selected. We can also deduce that 'Select All' is a function that will be actioned as soon as it is selected, without need for further menus or dialogs

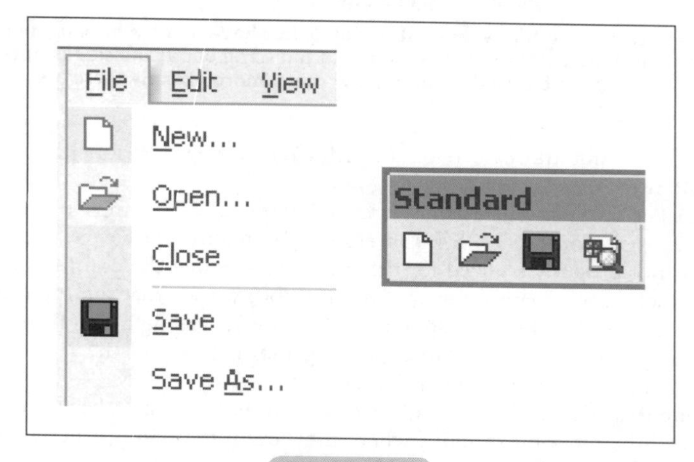

FIGURE 8.4

Left image: a section of the 'File' menu from Microsoft Word. The icons are positioned beside the text to reinforce their meaning. Thus, when the user sees the icon on its own in the standard toolbar, its meaning is clear

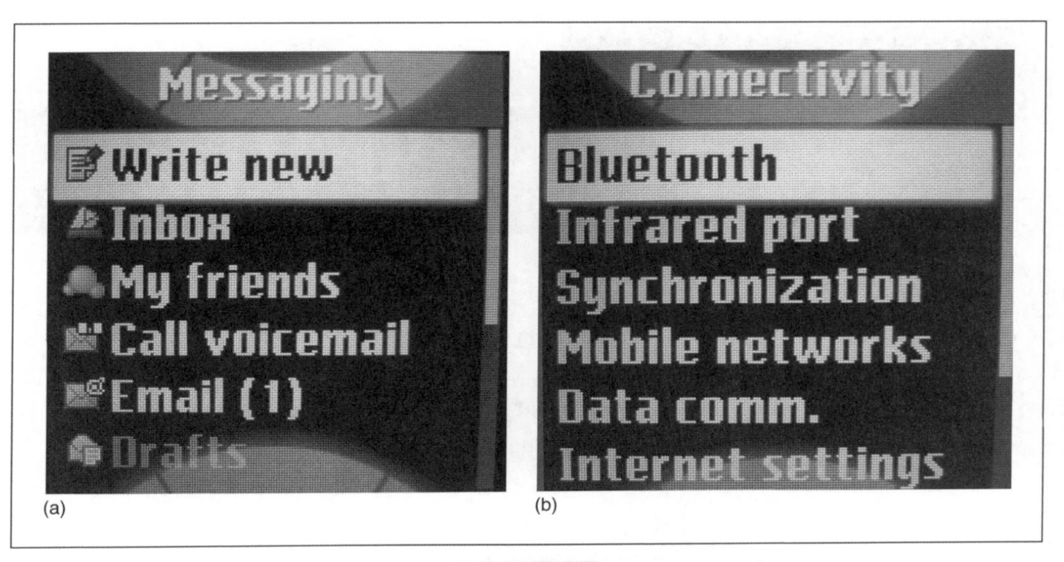

FIGURE 8.5

(a) In this menu, each option has an icon; (b) here the options are described only in text

FIGURE 8.6

Meaningless tab icons on the K700

FIGURE 8.7

Inconsistent symbols used for settings in the menu system of the K700

One final assault on the use of icons in menus is the inconsistent design. Well-designed icons should be created as a set, with common images and glyphs used to represent common ideas. For example, an icon used to represent 'Phone Settings' should look similar to one for 'Message Settings'. On the K700, the two icons used are shown in Figure 8.7. In one, the plus symbol is used to denote the idea of settings, while the other uses the image of tools.

If icons could form a coherent visual language, this would aid the user in understanding the interface functionality. Not only that, but we could greatly improve the usability of the menus through the preservation of context. For example, we could use an envelope icon to denote all messages, a spanner icon to show settings, and an @ symbol to show Internet. If we then saw the screen at the top of Figure 8.8, we would know we had the menu for email settings; the bottom half would be the screen for Internet settings.

EXERCISE 8.2 VISUAL LANGUAGE

Take the pieces of paper you created from the previous exercise and arrange them into what you consider to be logical groupings. Take one of those groups and see if you can create a visual icon language for each function in the group. For example, you might have a 'message' group, so select an icon for that group to serve as the basis for every icon in that group, adding modification glyphs for each function in the group, like the '+' symbol for message settings. Having done this for one of the groups, try it for another. Was it easier this time? How many of the icons you used originally can be reused in the second group? Would it be easier to reclassify the original groups in a way that produced a more coherent visual language? ■

FIGURE 8.8

Creating a visual language for menu structures using icons

Ultimately, as visual entertainment, current icons are highly successful. Some have beautiful animation and can add a whimsical note to what could be a very dull piece of computer equipment. In terms of adding to the usability of the interface, however, they are at best irrelevant, at worst distracting.

8.5 MANUALS

One of the standard answers to poor interface design is to provide users with an extensive manual. Manuals for cellular handsets are really of limited use due to the fact that the manual is usually larger than the device itself. As the point of cellular communication is mobility, it is unlikely that users will carry the manual with the device. Furthermore, research by Youngs (1998) shows that younger users (under 35) are *less* likely to complete a task if they use the manual. Youngs calls this the 'Nintendo effect' and believes that users from this age group are used to playing computer games where the instructions are part of the system itself. Such users, therefore, have not developed the skills to use paper-based and electronic media simultaneously. For users over 35, paper manuals will still prove to be useful.

8.5.1 ONLINE MANUALS

On-screen manuals, however, are more useful to the Nintendo generation. Here, if a user scrolls to a menu option and presses an 'information' button, a description of that option appears on the screen. For example, Lee *et al.* (1984) found that adding extra information to menu options could reduce errors by up to 82%. To date, online help is applied in a seemingly random fashion – help is provided on a per-model basis and is not consistent between the models from a particular manufacturer. As the size of the Nintendo generation increases, we can only recommend that manufacturers take the provision of online help more seriously.

8.5.2 WEBSITE MANUALS

One reason that online help is not provided on the handsets is the lack of screen real-estate. Some manufacturers and service providers have overcome this problem by providing support websites which help users configure and fully exploit the functionality of their handsets. There are a variety of approaches, including training simulators, lists of button presses needed to achieve a desired goal and, most interestingly, an alternative web-based interface, which lets users enter settings on the Internet that are then broadcast to the user's handset. Other manufacturers provide dedicated software for desktop computers which duplicate the functionality of this last solution, allowing users to configure their handset on the desktop machine and upload the setting via Bluetooth.

These are all useful solutions and, perhaps, we are working toward a situation wherein the primary configuration of a mobile device must take place on a desktop machine. The menus on the device, then, become of secondary importance. However, this holds true only if the user has access to a computer or the Internet. As we shall see in the final chapter, this is far from being the case.

So, if we assume that we need to access the functionality of the device using the device itself, are menus the best solution?

8.6 NO MENUS?

Before we launch into a detailed analysis of menu performance, does it really matter? Aren't menus good enough? Can't we get by with things the way they are?

Apparently not – at least, not if you're a cellular service provider. The research presented here was started at the request of a cellular service provider that was concerned with the difficulties experienced by its subscribers when using handsets. The commercial ramifications for the company were twofold:

- They had to set up a call center to handle user queries about the handset.
- They were losing revenue as users could not navigate the menu structures to access the premium services the company provided.

Besides the commercial ramifications on companies, users often suffer frustration when trying to complete tasks using their handsets. For example, despite working in the ICT industry and meeting with highly technology-literate people, I have only once managed to exchange a business card via Bluetooth. Often, I have to hunt for a menu function that I once happened to glance, but can no longer locate. Sounds familiar?

So if menus are causing problems for users and companies alike, what can we replace them with? This next section follows a long research project we undertook to answer that question. Besides providing an answer to the question, we will use it as a case study tying together several of the themes from previous chapters, focusing in particular on the evaluation section.

8.6.1 DATA STRUCTURES

There are lots of different routes one might explore in trying to design a new menu structure; we've already discussed participatory design and ethnographic studies as possible routes. Certainly, for this project, we conducted some ethnographic studies and discovered that people like to do two things with their handsets:

- Go through every function. In an effort to find out what a handset does, a user will attempt to visit every single menu option. This often occurs when someone first buys their handset, or they have quiet time alone.
- Rapidly access a known function. When the user is familiar with the handset's functionality, they want to rapidly access a known function.

From these observations, it's clear that we need to provide support for users who start out as being unaware of the handset's facilities, but who migrate to become expert users in a given subset of the device's functionality.

BOX 8.2 **ONLY TWO USERS**

There is a notion prevalent among software developers that there are two basic types of user: novice and expert. Therefore, software often has a two-tiered interface: a high-level one for novices and a lower-level one for experts. In actuality all users start out as novices and migrate toward being an expert. The likelihood is that they become experts, but only in the parts of the software they need to achieve their own ends. Therefore, software should support user migration rather than providing for static-state novices and experts. For a more complete discussion on these ideas, you should read Alan Cooper's *The Inmates are Running the Asylum* (Cooper, 1999). ■

8.6.2 ALTERNATIVES

Generating completely new ideas for user interfaces is a tricky business. Interface design draws on so many disciplines, it is hard to come up with a design that satisfies all criteria. As computer scientists, however, we can start out by viewing this problem as one of data access, i.e. are current menu structures optimal in supporting users to access data rapidly as well as allowing them to rapidly view every function their handset provides? By 'optimal' we mean the time taken, as measured in key presses, assuming an expert user of the device (an expert is able to memorize the entire menu structure of the handset in their head and therefore does not suffer problems of class-inclusion and equivalence-mapping). Of course, usability is much more subtle than counting key presses, but remember, this is only a starting place for the design, and such approaches have been shown to be successful in predicting good interface designs (Card *et al.*, 1983) – in essence, we are using these metrics as a form of non-user evaluation.

Once we have a design, we are then in a position to conduct tests with real users and to explore these more subtle effects. We can use these non-user evaluation techniques early in the development cycle to quickly disregard failed design alternatives before we move on to the more expensive phase of user testing.

Having critiqued the design of the icons on the K700 interface, let's turn our attention now to Nokia, in particular the 5110. We chose this handset as a reference base as it was hugely successful, is fairly basic in functionality, and represents the core functionality we might expect to find on a modern handset. The 5110 provides 74 functions we may wish to select. To visit every function would require the user to perform 110 key presses. The average number of key presses to access a function is 8.2, with a maximum of 14. These seem like ridiculously high numbers on first inspection, but perhaps it's not possible to do any better.

EXERCISE 8.3 FINGER WORK-OUT

How easy is your handset to use? Have a guess at the average number of key presses needed to access a function on the handset. Also guess how many key presses are required to go through every function in order and how many key presses are needed to access the function furthest from the root menu.

Now, using the manual, or the actual cellular handset, draw out the menu tree for the handset. Calculate the three values above (i.e. average, worst and full list) using the tree. How close was this to your estimate? Did you know your fingers were getting this much exercise? ■

From studies of information retrieval and computer science, we know that the best way to access functions linearly is to store them in an ordered linear list, probably alphabetically. Using the scroll keys on the handset, the user can now start at the first function and scroll to the very last. In terms of supporting initial browsing, it is hard to see how to improve on this interface: access to 74 functions would require only 74 key presses, as opposed to 110 for the existing system. For random access, however, linear lists are problematic. Whereas before it took 8.2 key presses on average to access a given item on the Nokia, the linear list will require 37 key presses! The worst case for accessing an individual function is 74 key presses, as opposed to only 14 on the existing handset. Clearly this is not an optimal solution.

One technique we considered for random access was the use of binary trees. Binary trees are essentially a way of automatically generating a menu structure from an ordered list of options. Because the tree is constructed on strict principles, users are not subjected to the whim of the designer's notion of where menu options belong.

The main difference between binary menus and existing handset menus is that binary menus give you only three choices at each level: choose current, choose option before, or choose option after. So, if you see the option 'Call Barring' on your screen but want 'Cell Info', then you would select 'after' as 'Cell Info' comes alphabetically after 'Call Barring.'

To create a binary tree, you first create an ordered list of all the menu options. Take the middle option from this list and make it the top item in the menu. Imagine we have the numbers 1, 2, 3, 4, 5, 6 and 7 that we wish to put in a menu structure. The middle number in this list is '4' so we would make this the first option the user sees. If the user wishes to select the 'before' button at this

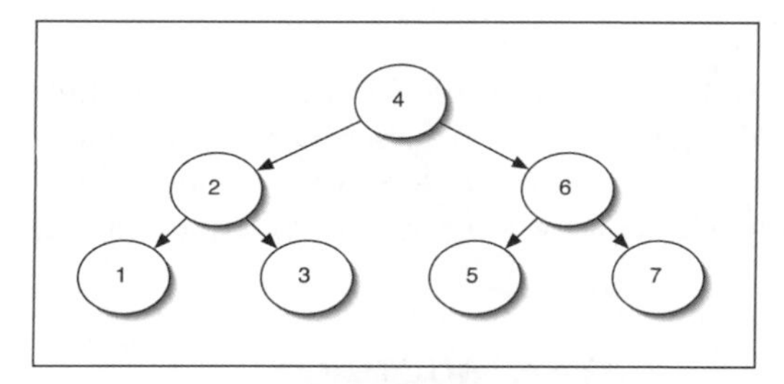

FIGURE 8.9

Binary tree showing how the numbers from 1 to 7 would be distributed, allowing any number to be found after going two levels down into the menu – two key presses. The tree structure will require only one extra key press every time the structure doubles in size. So 16 items need three presses, 32 need four presses, 64 need five key presses, etc

point, they would be shown the option '2'. '2' is selected as it is the middle of the options which come before '4'. Similarly, pressing 'after' at '4' will select the option '6'. The final tree would be as shown in Figure 8.9.

If we apply this process to the 74 options of the Nokia 5110, then we do indeed have a very efficient structure (almost). The average number of key presses drops from 8.2 to 5.4. Furthermore, the worst-case selection requires only seven presses as opposed to the 14 of the existing structure. The cost for all this efficiency? Well, a full traversal of the tree would require 148 key presses!

At this point, we could build a handset that comes with an 'expert' (binary tree) and a 'novice' (linear list) mode, leaving it up to the user to decide which camp they belong to. However, remembering Cooper's point about user migration, we conducted some more research on information storage structures to find one which integrated the benefits of the binary tree and the linear list.

In the end, we settled on a B+Tree structure. We won't conduct a full analysis of B+Trees here, but it's essentially a tree where all the final (function) nodes are joined in a linear list. If you're interested in B+Trees, you can look them up in any database or data structure textbook. Instead, we will present the final interface design which was inspired by the B+Tree.

BOX 8.3 TAKING INSPIRATION FROM COMPUTER SCIENCE

The ideas for the B+Tree interface and the WML interface were both seeded by thinking about these interaction problems from a computer science perspective. This idea comes from one of our colleagues, Harold Thimbleby, who originally proposed the idea in his book (Thimbleby, 1990) and set us thinking down the path which resulted in the ➤

B+Tree interface. Since then, we have used this approach to building other successful interfaces, the most recent being a file browser based on the ideas of relational algebra (Marsden and Cairns, 2004). Even if you are not a computer scientist, we recommend that you read Thimbleby's book for some well-founded design inspiration ideas. ■

8.6.3 DESIGN IDEAS – DATA STRUCTURES

Our final solution exploited the fact that most mobile telephone keypads have up to three alphabetic letters associated with each key. So, on key '1' you can find the letters 'A B C', key '2' has 'D E F', and so on. (Some phones vary in their key allocation, but this is not relevant to our approach.) Users simply had to 'spell out' the function they wished to access by pressing the appropriate numeric keys. Normally, when words are spelt out, the user will press key '1' once to get A, twice to get B, or three times to get C. In our approach, the key is only ever pressed once, and it's allowed to mean A or B or C. Thus there is some initial ambiguity as the user starts to press keys to spell a function name. However, with each key press, the system becomes increasingly certain about the function name the user is attempting to spell.

For example, if the user wished to access 'Call Divert' they would begin by pressing '1' followed by '1' (meaning respectively 'C' and 'A', the first two letters of the function name) and the system would display a scrollable list containing choices such as 'Call Divert', 'Call Identification' and 'Call Barring'. If any other combination of the keys – in this case ABC followed by ABC – also started function names ('Battery Condition'?), they would also be displayed. As soon as the required function appeared in the best-match list it could be selected directly by the user without any further input: the user did not have to spell out the entire function name. To overcome the equivalence search problem, we allowed the words of the function name to be entered in any order: so, for example, Call Divert and Divert Call were both permitted, and the user would probably prefer Divert, since it is unambiguous. Analysis of our solution showed that average search time was reduced from 8.2 to 3.1 key presses!

Besides using the numeric keypad to access the functions, users could also scroll the list using the scroll keys. Providing access in this way supported exploratory behavior as efficiently as possible, effectively flattening the structure down to a linear list – 74 key presses needed to access 74 items. (The software is available for download on the book's website.)

Having designed a solution that was quantitatively better than the existing solution, we still did not know whether users would prefer it to familiar systems. The only way to ensure this is to conduct proper usability experiments, as described in Section 7.10.

8.6.4 EVALUATION VIA EXPERIMENT

The first step in running an experiment is to set hypotheses, requiring us to consider our dependent and independent variables. In this case, the *independent* variable is the system used – either the tree-based handset or the menu-based handset. The *dependent* variable is the time taken to use the interface, where time is measured relatively in key presses and absolutely in seconds. The hypotheses for the experiment are therefore:

1. The tree-based interface would require fewer key presses for function access than an interface based on a traditional menu structure.

2. Users of a tree-based interface would require less time to access a function than users of an interface based on a traditional menu structure.

Remember, however, that the way to prove the hypotheses is to disprove their opposites (null hypotheses) The null hypotheses for the experiment must therefore be stated:

1. There will be no difference in the number of key presses for function access in a tree-based interface than in a traditional menu structure.
2. There will be no difference in time for function access in a tree-based interface than in a traditional menu structure.

Subjects

Subjects consisted of students, academics and administrative staff from our university, as well as some outside participants. As the interface to a cellular handset is not targeted at a specific user group, we went for as wide a range of users as possible. (Sure, there are different handsets marketed at different user groups, but the interface structure is essentially the same.) Subjects were rated on their experience with using cellphone handsets to ensure that we had equal numbers of novices (who had never used a mobile phone) and experts (who were able to change at least one setting on their handset). This was achieved through a pre-experiment interview.

Having only one independent variable (menu type) with two possible options (regular and B+Tree) means that there are only two conditions. Theoretically, 20 subjects would have been sufficient for the experiment, or 10 if we used a within-group study. As we were interested in a wide variety of user types, we actually used 30 subjects and a within-group study, giving us 30 data points for each condition.

Tasks and simulations

Each subject was then given a set of 24 tasks to complete, 12 for each condition. A typical task was "*Your phone's capacity to store numbers is almost at its limit. Check to see how much space you have left.*" The subject would then search for the function which they felt would be used to complete the task.

The order in which the tasks were presented to subjects was randomly reallocated after each subject had completed the experiment. Any given task could have occurred with either the tree-based handset or the menu-based handset. By changing the tasks to be performed on each handset, we ensured that the difficulty experienced in using a given handset was due to the handset itself, not the difficulty of the tasks allocated to that handset.

Furthermore, by having two groups of subjects, it was possible to remove ordering effects by having one group complete their first 12 tasks with the standard simulation and the other group start with the new handset. Subjects then swapped and completed the last 12 tasks using the alternative handset.

The wording of the tasks was carefully chosen so as not to prime subjects and bias them in favor of one particular simulation. For example, the sample task given above does not use the word 'Memory' anywhere, as this may favor the tree simulation which relies on the user entering (Nokia's) keywords. By removing these keywords from the task description, subjects were required to guess what words they should search for.

One of the problems of conducting experiments with mobile devices is that it is often not possible to deploy the software on the device's hardware. In Chapter 6 we looked at various solutions, including Handspring's Buck. In this instance, we created two software simulations to run on a desktop PC. One used the menu structure of the Nokia 5110; the other used the B+Tree. We felt this to be a valid approach as the menu systems did not rely on any specialist hardware of a mobile device (e.g. touch screen and stylus) but required only simple button pushing. Also, by using a software simulation of the 5110 instead of the device itself, we removed any effects introduced by having differing hardware platforms.

Both simulations provided access to exactly the same function list, but the new phone also had some synonyms for function names. Providing too many synonyms could have biased the experiment toward the tree handset, so each function name was allowed a maximum of one synonym to compensate for noun–verb and verb–noun transpositioning – e.g. 'Ringing volume' was also replicated as 'Volume of ring'.

Procedure

Each subject was given a brief (approximately five-minute) explanation of how each handset worked and a demonstration of the type of task they would be expected to perform during the actual experiment. The main purpose of the explanation and demonstration was to ensure familiarity with the computer simulation which required the mouse to press the on-screen buttons. Instruction sheets were also left for the subjects to refer to, should they need reminding of how either simulation worked.

Subjects were told that they would be given a maximum of two minutes to complete the task or they could choose to give up before the two minutes had elapsed. The idea of self-retirement from a task came from some pre-experiments, where it was clear that users could become locked in a loop within the menu structure and would never find the function they sought.

We conducted this experiment before having access to a dedicated usability laboratory, so interaction with the simulation was observed by means of a video splitting cable. This allowed the experimenter to unobtrusively view on a separate monitor what was happening on the subject's screen. The output to this second screen was also video recorded to aid in the post-experiment interviews.

After completing the experiment, subjects were given a brief interview which was intended to extract their subjective opinion about using each handset. Subjects were also ask to supply the words they searched for when using the hash handset. (Rather than attempting a disruptive technique such as think aloud, or interrupting subjects after each task, the video recording of the interaction was used to remind subjects in the post-experiment interviews.)

Analyzing results

The experimental scenarios completed on the new design took, on average, 9.54 key presses to complete, in comparison to the standard design where 16.52 key presses were required. This seems good, but just how good is it? Is it possible that this result occurred by random chance, or is the difference not large enough to be significant?

The only way to answer this question is to conduct a rigorous statistical analysis of the data. As we stated in Section 7.10, conducting this analysis can be a daunting task for those not familiar with statistical techniques. In this case, we employed a psychology graduate student to conduct the analysis for us. The good news for us is that he managed to reject the null hypotheses, which means that the new system was significantly faster than the existing one. For anyone interested in statistics, we used a repeated-measures one-tailed t-test, ($t = 3.4$, $\text{df} = 29$, $p < 0.001$). It turns out that this is a strongly significant result ('$p < 0.001$' means that we are more than 99% sure that the reduced key presses resulted from our new design and not from some other factor).

We also discovered a significant difference in mean times between phone types (again, repeated-measures one-tailed t-test, $t = 1.95$, $df = 29$, $p < 0.03$). The overall mean time for the tree phone is 33.42 seconds as compared to 42.02 seconds for the normal handset. This is a considerable improvement for phone users.

So, the results of this part of the experiment showed us quantitatively that our handset took less time to operate than the existing menu structure. While this is an interesting result, there were other, qualitative, results from the experiment which are just as important.

Observations

The statistics above tell part of the story, but not the whole one. Besides counting key presses and time to complete tasks, we recorded the users' behavior on video and asked them to complete a post-experiment questionnaire. Through either poor design on our part, or a lack of interest by the subjects, the questionnaires did not reveal any particularly astounding revelations. Many users commented that they found our interface strange to begin with (hardly surprising) but liked using it once they understood the idea behind it. Much more interesting were the video-aided interviews.

While conducting the experiments, we would watch our screens in terror as the users would try to do all manner of bizarre things with the interface. (This is a fairly common emotion for anyone who observes user trials, so you'd better get used to it.) One of the most alarming observations was when subjects would simply scroll through the tree linearly until they found the item they were looking for. We feared these continual button presses would skew the final results against our interface. (Given how much better the final statistics were for the new handset, you have to worry about just how many key presses current structures impose on the user.) In the interviews afterwards, the subjects explained that they liked pressing the scroll button repeatedly as they 'knew it would work'. Probing that statement further, we discovered that users would often become lost without hope of escape in the same dead-ends of the menu structure on existing handsets. Using the scroll key on the new handset may be repetitive, but subjects knew they would get to the target function eventually.

Presumably this goes part way to explaining the success of the most popular mobile device interface ever – that of the Apple iPod. The iPod interface has few menus, but many linear lists containing thousands of items. Yet, using the jog-wheel, users are happy to navigate these long lists as they know they will get there in the end. The thought of a menu structure designed for accessing 10 000 functions on a cellular handset is fairly alarming!

Conclusions

From this experiment, we discovered that very simple user modeling can serve as a sound basis for creating new types of improved interface. Basing an interface on a design optimized for a very methodical computer means that users don't need to think so much about the interface, but can proceed with the task in hand. We were able to conduct some quantitative user tests which showed that, for typical tasks, the new handset was much faster to use. Video analysis and interviews with subjects after the experiment showed us that there was an unexpected side-effect of our interface, namely its highly predictable behavior.

You can read more detail on the experiment in Marsden *et al.* (2002). You may be wondering why, if it's so good, our interface is not available on any commercially marketed handset. Well, after completing this experiment, we contacted a patent lawyer who eventually discovered that our ideas were covered by another patent, even though that company had not thought of this particular application. We hope your ideas are more successful!

8.7 MORE COMPLEX MENUS

So far, we've looked at ways of restructuring menu hierarchies (e.g. the binary tree) or eliminating them by flattening the structure into a linear list. But what if we actually increased the complexity of the structure – would it still be possible to create a simplified way of accessing functionality?

Most menu structures are what computer scientists call 'one-to-many'. In other words, one node may have many nodes dangling from it, but the node itself can only be dangled from a single node. The upshot of this in menu design is that a menu may permit the user to select many options, but there is only one way to get to that menu. Returning to the Nokia, the option to change the ringing volume can be in either the 'Phone Settings' menu or the 'Tones' menu, but not in both (see Figure 8.10).

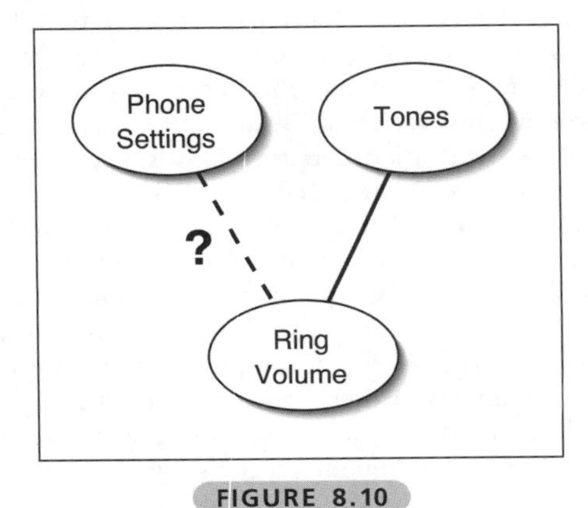

FIGURE 8.10

Perhaps functions should appear under more than one menu

If we were to place it in both places, then the menu would become a many-to-many structure (menus may have many options, and options may be found in many places) and we could, perhaps, eliminate the class-inclusion problems experienced by novice users.

It was the attempt to break free from this type of hierarchical thinking which also motivated Tim Berners-Lee to develop the World Wide Web. He attributes the success of the WWW to its ability to allow information to be joined according to a user's perception (Berners-Lee, 2000), supported by the relative simplicity of HTML which allowed users to restructure any collection of information as they saw fit. Web pages form a very natural and easy to use many-to-many structure. Borrowing from these ideas, we wanted to see whether one could make a viable menu system based on a similar structure.

When we started researching this idea, we came across an interesting observation from the work of Heylar (2000). He was studying the usability of WAP browsers on mobile devices. He noticed that users had trouble changing from the navigation metaphor of the browser (many-to-many) to the navigation metaphor of the handset's menu system (one-to-many). The conclusion we drew from this work was that we should do away with the handset's menu structure and replace it with an interface based on WML pages. This immediately frees the user from

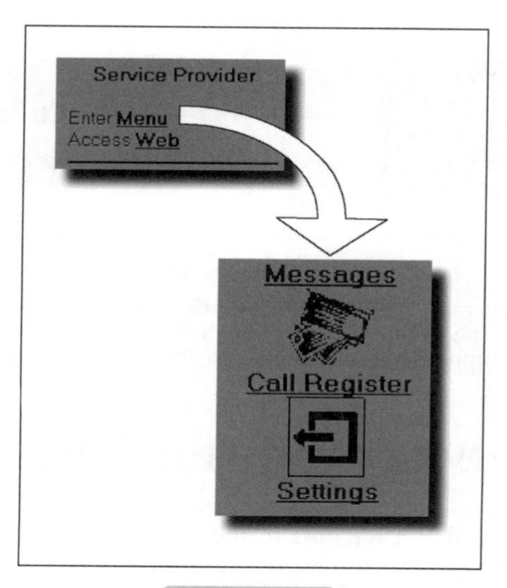

FIGURE 8.11
Initial WAP prototype

learning two separate interfaces and provides a system which they could configure to their own needs.

The simplest way to replace menu systems is to create WML pages which correspond directly to existing structures. We have already built such a system based on the Nokia 5110, as shown in Figure 8.11. This prototype presents the user with a home page providing access to local information, or a remote site. If the user selects 'local information', they are presented with the WML pages replacing the menu system. In this way, the menu becomes just another site accessible through the browser. The only interactional benefit of this prototype, however, is that the navigation keys and paradigm for the menu system are identical to those required for a WML browser.

After some initial user studies, we modified the WML to present as many options as possible on the screen at any one time. We then used indentation to provide the user with context information about their choices (see Figure 8.12). In this way, we have created a system which exploits the work put in to improving hierarchical menus but keeps the navigational benefits of the previous prototype.

Although we conducted user design sessions with the low-fidelity prototypes of this system, it's a lot harder to think of an experiment that would prove this to be a superior system than existing menus – all we're doing is altering the menu's navigation, but not the actual structure of the menu. We could repeat Heylar's experiment with our new system, but we can guarantee we would not see the same usability problems, as the menu system that caused the problems is no longer present.

In our opinion, the only way to really test this system is to conduct a longitudinal study wherein we alter users' cellphones to have the WML-based interface replace the regular menus. As no manufacturer was willing to let us do this, the evaluation will have to wait for another time.

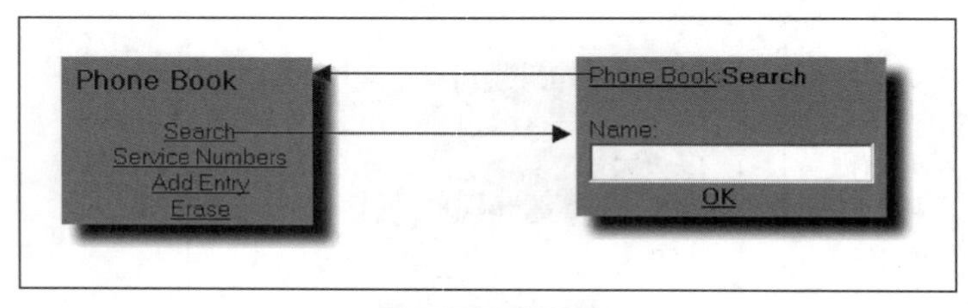

FIGURE 8.12

New WAP prototype with context information at the top of the screen. This information acts like the 'breadcrumbs' found on websites, supporting rapid navigation along a path in the hierarchy

8.8 SOME CONCLUDING THOUGHTS

Originally menus were created as a response to the command-line user interface found on early computer systems – instead of having to remember the exact wording of a command (e.g. 'rm – r *.*' in a Unix system) it is much easier to select the correct option from a list ('Delete All Files'). On desktop computers, as the hardware became more powerful, menu-based interfaces were replaced or subsumed into Graphical User Interfaces (GUIs). Some mobile devices adopt this form of interaction, using a stylus instead of the more traditional mouse.

Due to the relative lack of research in mobile interface design, it is tempting to translate those ideas that work on the large screen directly to the small. This is not a temptation to which we should succumb – translating the end-artifact in a literal way may lose the meaning that underlies the original intent.

We see this type of downsizing a lot in mobile devices. For example, scrollbars are good way of indicating current position in a document. Transplanting these directly to small screens, however, uses too much screen space, so the scrollbar is thinned down. In some cases, this thinning means that users frequently overlook the scrollbar and have no idea there is more content beyond the bottom of the screen.

The idea of blindly taking ideas from desktop computer systems and applying them to mobile devices returns us neatly to Alan Cooper's joke from the start of the chapter:

Q: What do you get when you cross a cellular phone with a computer?

A: A computer!

The only possible justification for reusing design ideas from desktop computers on mobile devices is that users will be familiar with the metaphors from the desktop machine, thus making the mobile device more familiar. This is flawed logic, as many, many more people have used a cellular handset than have ever used a personal computer. Sure, some of the ideas will work, but we have yet to see evidence of anyone rigorously testing the interaction ideas from desktop machines to see whether they are the best solution to an interaction problem on the mobile platform.

SUMMARY

Hierarchical menus seem to have been universally accepted as the only way to permit access to functions on mobile devices. We hope to have shown that hierarchical menus are not the only way to structure these interfaces; in fact, there exist demonstrably better ways to create an interface. While handset interface designers seem to have paid heed to some of the research on menu design, other findings (such as the problems of displaying one line at a time) have sometimes been ignored. As the features of handsets improve, ways are being sought to improve these menus, but the improvements seem to be more in terms of marketing rather than usability.

From our perspective, it seems that this adoption of menus (and then icons in the menus) is merely symptomatic of the inappropriate migration of design elements and metaphors from the desktop PC to the handheld device. The developers creating mobile interfaces are all familiar with desktop PCs, so these elements seem familiar and intuitive. As we shall see in Chapter 11, most users of cellular handsets have never even owned a desktop PC. So arguing that the inappropriateness of a design solution from a PC is outweighed by its familiarity simply holds no currency. It's time we developed device-relevant designs.

WORKSHOP QUESTIONS

- Menus exploit the fact that humans are better at recognizing things in their environment than recalling them from memory. To illustrate this point, have a go at writing down the exact wording of each item in the root menu of your cellular handset. It is unlikely that you will get this correct, yet you can still use your handset. Do you think icons can be used to enhance the recognition of items in a menu?
- We have suggested using a B+Tree as a way of structuring menu items. Can you think of other structures and the benefits and compromises they might bring?

DESIGNER TIPS

- *Scrollbars are fine on a small-screen device, provided the user sees them. If you are keen for your users to scroll on down the screen, then use some visual cue such as displaying only the top half of the last sentence on the screen.*
- *When using looped menus, make sure the user knows that they have been returned to the top of the menu.*
- *Handsets which display more than one option at a time (ideally three or more) have similar performance characteristics to large-screen systems. Displaying one option at a time drastically reduces user performance.*

- *Unless you have a very specific group of end-users, you will never come up with a menu classification system that pleases everyone. The best you can do is copy some widely accepted scheme or de-facto standard.*
- *Menu structures should be concave – provide a lot of options at the top and bottom levels, but few in the middle.*
- *Online help is a good idea for those under 35; paper-based manuals work better for those over 35.*
- *If you provide more than one way to access a function make sure they are complementary (e.g. linear and random access) and don't interfere with each other (e.g. WML browser vs hierarchical menu browser).*

CHAPTER 9
INFORMATION ACCESS

OVERVIEW

9.1. Introduction
9.2. Small-screen impacts
9.3. Designs for browsing
9.4. Improving search
9.5. Mobile information ecologies

KEY POINTS

- Users will want to use mobile devices to access all sorts of information – from emails to novels.
- Designing the interaction with this content involves both detailed screen layout considerations and wider aspects such as the degree of context adaptation and the information servers used.
- Early research on non-mobile, small-screen devices suggests that users will have little trouble when reading or interacting with simple content – short chunks of material with limited navigation content.
- If users try to interact with more complex content which is not adapted for small-screen viewing, usability disasters will occur. Guidelines and presentation techniques can help. These point towards the need to give users effective ways of overviewing and assessing content before having to commit to accessing it in full.
- Mobiles must play their part in the information ecology, fitting in with other devices, network availability and physical resources in the environment. Peer-to-peer approaches offer interesting, novel possibilities.

9.1 INTRODUCTION

With always-on broadband connections commonly found in homes as well as workplaces, piping information into powerful, fully-featured desktop and laptop computers, you could be forgiven for thinking that people have all the access they could ever want to digital resources. Given the opportunities they have when not mobile, why would anyone, in addition to all this, want to use a small device, with limited input and output capabilities to find and read content?

There is, though, a strong information imperative – we are great consumers of information. We hunt and forage for it; sometimes we immerse and wallow ourselves in it, at other times we skip through it lightly, moving from one nugget to the next. You would think that after a day at the office, a day spent intensely at being productive and efficient, commuters would want to do anything but process more information – but a ride on any train or bus will show you how powerful this information seeking urge is: you will see people flicking through magazines and newspapers, and others browsing documents they've encountered during the day.

When mobile, then, users will appreciate access to lots of types of information; sometimes the purposes for and preferred format of the content will be similar to those when using their home and work computers, while at other times it will be quite different.

- Standing in a bookstore, reading the dust jacket of a new book on naval history, Jenny decides to check what other readers have said about it by using her mobile to look up reviews on an online site. She also compares the price; it's a little cheaper from the e-retailer but she wants the book right now so purchases it from the shop, anyhow.
- Having mislaid the directions to a meeting, John needs to use his mobile to look up the address of an office; directions would be helpful too.
- Rosie stores hundreds of emails on her mobile. She's on a train traveling to see a client and just wants to double-check the agenda she proposed a few weeks ago. How will she find and skim-read the notes quickly?
- Nathan works in London and a major natural disaster has just hit his home continent, many thousands of miles away. Whenever he gets a moment, he wants to find more news of the incident in any way he can, be it on his desktop computer or via his mobile device.
- Jason wants to call Paul, an acquaintance, but doesn't have his telephone number. He thinks one of his closer friends will have it in the address books stored on their mobiles. What if his mobile could access these friends' contact lists and give him the number without his having to call them and ask? (Chen *et al.*, 2002)

If you are developing content for mobile access, as well as identifying the information your users will want, you can use the user-understanding, prototyping and evaluation techniques we saw in the second part of the book to figure out how best to deliver it. Some aspects you'll need to find answers for are outlined below; we'll be considering such issues – and interaction designs to address them – throughout this chapter.

- **Simplicity.** Does the user want a short, concise chunk of information or would they appreciate being able to browse more extensively? Often they will want the former – that is, where the content is brief and serves a focused purpose. This brevity might be an intrinsic quality of the information – for example, consider a set of news headlines, product information or directions to a location. Alternatively, it might be a function of a technique used to summarize or overview more complex information, which the user can further peruse if motivated. There will be occasions, however, when the user has the time and inclination to consider longer, structured forms of content (in some countries, for instance, reading novels on mobile phones is a popular activity).

- **Format.** Is the content specifically designed for the mobile? If not, how will it be adapted to be useful and usable on these sorts of platform? Something to consider here, in particular, is the role of carefully selected, grouped information, sometimes called mobile portals or channels.
- **Context.** To what extent is the content they are seeking context-driven? Is the information being accessed very much tied to things like the location or time of access, or is it something that could be sought anywhere, anytime? Location-based services are seen as a highly important form of information provision by mobile developers, but in rushing to produce many types of content that is tailored in this way, there is a danger that other contextual factors or the value of non-context adapted information are underestimated.
- **Source.** Some information will be stored locally on the device, others on remote servers. There's also the possibility of finding information in a peer-to-peer fashion, where other mobiles act as servers of content. Then there are technologies to enable nearby, short-range wireless connections, providing access to localized information servers: a street server could give content on shops in that street, a museum gallery server could give information on pictures in that room, and so on. Users may need to be made aware of the potential sources of content and given control over the information they draw on.
- **Interaction.** How does the user get the information? It can be *pushed* to them, so they are automatically provided with it with very little interaction, or they can actively *pull* it by browsing content listings and the like. Hybrid *push–pull* approaches are possible too, with, for instance, users setting up details of the sorts of information they want to find out about (the *pull* component) and then, when that information becomes available, the system delivering it (the *push* part).

While we will see an example of non-visual presentation via a mobile a little later on, much information will be delivered via the device's screen. That screen, in many handhelds, will be small. Even with the increasing quality of displays, their ability to convey information will remain limited in comparison to those seen in desktop contexts. We begin this chapter, then, by looking at the impact of this reduced screen real-estate for a number of information access tasks.

Two of these fundamental information activities are browsing and searching. Browsing is the process of moving through content, using access paths (such as menus and hyperlinks); searching, on the other hand, is about locating information resources in direct ways – that might mean entering textual search terms or taking a picture of something for the system to use in a search. Browsing, then, is finding things by navigation, and searching is finding things by querying (Furnas and Rauch, 1998). Innovative browse and search schemes have been designed for effective small-screen use; we'll consider a number of these, weighing up their pros and cons.

In Chapter 2, we discussed the idea of information ecologies. That's the notion of people making use of evolving sets of complementary information resources in carrying out their tasks. So, to conclude this chapter, we look in more detail at what this might mean in the mobile context, by considering how a device might be used with other digital and non-digital resources that surround it.

9.2 SMALL-SCREEN IMPACTS

There's a scene in the Walt Disney movie *Aladdin* that encapsulates the challenge facing mobile designers. The genie is demonstrating his enormous potential and power; seconds later, he's bemoaning the limited dimensions of his lamp: ''It's all part and parcel of the whole genie gig: phenomenal cosmic powers, itty bitty living space.''

Small display areas are part and parcel of the whole mobile gig. Table 9.1 compares the display characteristics of a number of mobile devices: a PDA, a PocketPC, a mobile communicator (telephone/PDA) and a mobile phone. The characteristics of a laptop computer and desktop screen are also shown.

Devices A, B and C are sophisticated consumer handheld devices. While resolution and color quality continue to improve, an aspect that will remain a very real constraint is the size of the viewable screen. To remain pocket-portable, the physical dimensions will have to be limited. Increasing the number of pixels packed into these small displays will enhance the user's experience

TABLE 9.1

Display characteristics of example mobiles and conventional, large-screen devices (Jones *et al.*, 2004)

	Device	Display characteristics		
		Resolution (pixels)	Viewable dimensions (inches) (inches)	Colors
A	Palm Tungsten T PDA	320 × 320	2.3 width 2.3 height	16-bit (65 536 colors)
B	Compaq iPAQ 5400 series Pocket PC	240 × 320	2.26 width 3.02 height	16-bit (65 536 colors)
C	Nokia Communicator 9290 Mobile telephone/PDA	640 × 200	4.3 width 1.4 height	12-bit (4096 colors)
D	Nokia 6800 Mobile telephone	128 × 128	(approx.) 1.2 width 1.2 height	12-bit (4096 colors)
E	Apple Titanium Powerbook 15''	1280 × 854 (max.)	(approx.) 12 width 8 height 15.2 diagonal	Millions of colors
F	Philips 202P monitor	2048 × 1536 (max.)	16 width 12 height	Millions of colors

in terms of legibility of text and crispness of images, but tiny pieces of text or graphics, however highly rendered, will not be usable.

BOX 9.1 **FLEXIBLE ORGANIC LIGHT EMITTING DIODE (FOLED) SCREENS**

Will small screens, and their inherent interaction challenges, pass into technological history in the near future? One remarkable, promising innovation that will have an impact on the design of mobile devices is Flexible Organic Light Emitting Diodes (FOLEDs). Whereas today's LEDs are housed within rigid substances, like glass, FOLEDs can be embedded within bendable, rollable materials such as lightweight, thin plastic. Need a large screen? Just unroll one, view the content and roll it back up when you've finished. To further add to the full-screen experience, you could also use a technique like Canesta, where the large keyboard is projected onto any available surface, with finger tracking picking out the keys being 'pressed' (Roeber *et al.*, 2003).

While these sorts of innovations will allow users to enjoy fully featured input and output devices while retaining much of the portability advantages of current mobiles, small screens (and input controls) will continue to dominate the market, at least in the medium-term future. Even when it becomes viable to use FOLEDs pervasively, and this is some way off, there will still be a strong desire for the ultra-portability of smaller screens. Users will continue to prefer devices that can be placed in a shirt pocket, are ready and available at all times with minimal startup or setup costs, and can be operated with one hand. ■

As well as considering screen resolutions, a useful way of understanding the impact of the small-screen factors is to consider the size of physical display relative to standard devices. Devices A, B and C offer only 6–7% of the display area of device E and 3–4% of that of device F. Device D is even more restricted, with 2% and 1% of the display areas of devices E and F respectively.

What we are faced with, then, is a world (wide web, even) of information, presented to the user through a diminutive window. Let's consider the impact of these smaller display areas on user effectiveness. What we will see is that for simple tasks such as reading a bite-sized chunk of text users can cope well; however, as activities become more complex, such as browsing and searching web content, there could be significant problems if careful design is not carried out.

9.2.1 LESSONS FROM THE PAST

Long before the small screens of mobiles, there were other limited display areas that interested human factors researchers. Take automated cash machines. While today's ATMs often have large, colorful screens, some early ones could display only one line of text, sometimes read through a periscope-style viewer. Then, there were electronic devices from photocopiers to sewing machines, all with small LCD displays to present information; many of these types of device, of course, continue to have relatively limited screens.

So during the 1980s and the early part of the 1990s, there were a number of studies looking at the effect on reading times, comprehension and usability of different-sized display areas.

Reading and Comprehension

One of the early studies considered the effect on reading of window heights and line widths (Duchnicky and Kolers, 1983). These researchers found that difficulties arose mainly when the width of the display was reduced, with the full-width display being read 25% faster than the screen which was one-third of the width.

The impact of varying the display height, however, was very much less dramatic. Although very small window sizes (one or two lines, like those seen in early mobile phones, for instance) gave poor performance, a four-line display was only 9% slower than one with 20 lines.

Another experiment provides further evidence of the effect. In this, a smaller screen size also slowed down reading time, but not dramatically. Users were asked to read computer program texts and answer questions (Resiel and Shneiderman, 1987). On a 22-line display this task took 9.2 minutes, while on a 60-line display it was some 15% faster.

Fast reading speed with minimal understanding is, of course, of little use. Again, though, in terms of simple chunks of text with limited navigation possibilities, it seems that users will have few problems in making sense of the information unless the display size is very small (one or two lines high). In the study we've just mentioned, by Duchnicky and Kolers (1983), there were no significant improvements in comprehension when the display height was increased to 20 lines over the four-line display.

In another experiment, participants were presented with a 3500-line text using a 20- and 60-line display window and were asked to read the texts and later summarize the main points (Dillon *et al.*, 1990). This study also found that the comprehension rates on the smaller screen were as good as those on the larger.

What are the implications of all this past research for future mobile devices? Unsurprisingly, reading and using simple textual materials on a small screen will be slower than if a large display is used. However, the experience will be manageable and not so dramatically different from the large-screen case.

The biggest impacts come as the width of the display used for the content is reduced – make sure, then, that you use as much of the horizontal plane as possible for the information itself: menu bars or navigation controls placed in columns, for example, will reduce the overall usability of the system.

User Interaction

Within-page navigation

If the content cannot be displayed within one non-scrolled screen, then obviously the user will have to use mechanisms that allow them to view the remainder. Techniques include scrolling (allowing small, fine-grained movement through the information) and paging (making bigger jumps, hopping from one chunk of the content to the next).

Not being able to see the whole doesn't just potentially mean more effort to sequentially view all the content. Users may also have to scroll or page backward as well as forward through text to orient themselves, the navigation helping them to understand the context of the information being viewed (Dillon *et al.*, 1990). For mobiles, then, keeping the content simple in terms of structure is a must – you don't want your users having to do lots of navigation to understand the material and how to use it.

BOX 9.2 SCROLLING AND SHORT-TERM MEMORY

Remember, human memory includes a limited amount of working storage – that's the short-term memory (STM) – and when capacity is reached, it starts to leak, with items being forgotten. Imagine you are reading a document on a small-screen device. The smaller the screen, the greater the burden you will place on STM to keep track of things you need to note – what you can't see you'll have to remember. Soon, you will forget something you require and will have to either scroll back to find it again, or make a possibly erroneous guess as to what it was (Loel and Albers, 2001). A vicious cycle will be set up: as you become frustrated with having to repeat work, this frustration will further reduce the effectiveness of your cognitive processing. ■

When the web first began to be widely used, scrolling was seen as a usability disaster even on large screens with only 10% of users ever scrolling to view content beyond the bottom of the screen. Having been familiar with interactive systems that presented content in terms of fixed single screenfuls, they just weren't used to the notion. Now, of course, everyone is happy to scroll through a web document (Nielsen, 1997a). A clear lesson for small-screen information architecture is that users need to be prompted and trained in any new form of navigation – in the simplest case, making sure users know they have to scroll is a start.

Let's assume that vertical scrolling is acceptable. To what extent should it be relied on? Whatever the size of display, the answer is not too much – excessive scrolling without some clever visualizations of the content will be tedious and disorienting for the user.

An important factor in assessing the viability of scrolling is the degree of effort needed to control the movement through the content. Consider the WebTV device that displayed web pages on a standard television set. Like today's mobile devices, the amount of information shown within one screen was small compared with standard computers, due to the lower resolution of the TV display and the distance users sat from it. Scrolling through the content required lots of work on the user's part, with many button pushes. Because of this, the design advice for the device was to make sure that each page of information fitted onto a single screen, with no scrolling (Nielsen, 1997b). Now, on some mobiles where scrolling is still a costly activity, presenting information within one or a limited number of screenfuls is also advisable. However, with many mobiles, the scroll control mechanisms are now sophisticated, so the size of the document being displayed within a scrollable page does not need to be so constrained.

Goal-led navigation

Often, in mobile situations, users will be accessing content to achieve a goal; in these cases, they are not reading for reading's pleasure. It is easy to imagine typical goals for handheld users – 'find nearest motel', 'locate the bank with the best exchange rate', and so on. Again, it is useful to turn to some early work on non-mobile systems which can help give clues as to the effect of small screen sizes on these sorts of interaction.

Remember, then, the work we mentioned in the last chapter on menus. There we saw that if users can see only a very small subset of the choices without scrolling, they can become disoriented.

In another set of studies Ben Shneiderman and colleagues carried out a study involving hypertext materials on limited displays. These documents were similar to simple web pages, in that users could interact with the texts, selecting links as they progressed through the task (Shneiderman, 1987). In one trial, two systems were compared: one group of users used a display size that was 18 lines of text in height, whereas the other group had a display capable of showing 34 lines. No significant differences in time to complete the task were recorded.

Any interactivity (like selecting from menus or following links) does, however, require extra effort compared to conventionally sized screens, so consider reducing the amount of navigation for key tasks, whatever the application.

EXERCISE 9.1 WEATHER INFORMATION SERVICE USABILITY PROBLEMS

One mobile, small-screen weather service has the following menu structure:

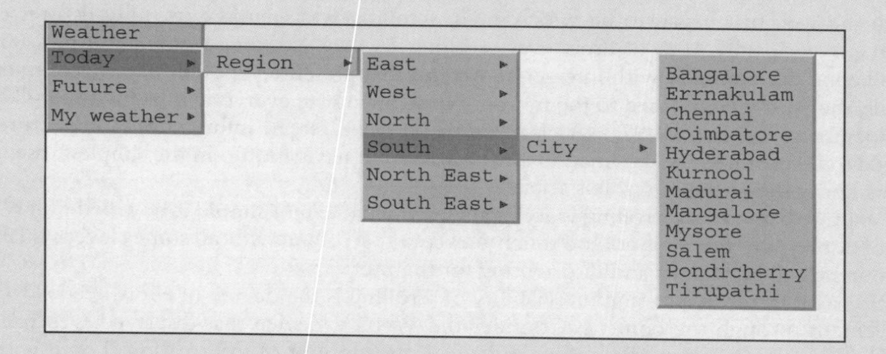

So to find today's weather in a particular location requires two clicks to get to the *Region* selection list, a further three scrolling actions (on average) and two clicks to get to the *City* selection list, and six more scrolling actions (on average) through this to indicate the city of interest. The *My Weather* option is designed as a shortcut and displays the current forecast for the last location viewed; it is dynamically updated each time a new location is accessed from either the *Today* or *Future* options. Discuss potential usability problems of this design and suggest improvements. ■

User Experience

Task performance is one thing, but the way the users feel about the system is also important. It doesn't matter how fast or efficient an information access scheme appears; unless it is enjoyable and pleasant, than you have lost your user.

In one of the studies we mentioned earlier, while there was little impact on performance between the large and small screens, the researchers did see a difference in the users' satisfaction. When they asked participants whether they would like to change the size of their display, of those who said 'yes' the overwhelming majority (75%) were people who were using the small screen. They wanted a bigger display (Dillon *et al.*, 1990).

How can you make your users feel good about accessing information through the small window available? The key to this is designing schemes that make it obvious that you've thought about how best to use the space and control mechanisms at your disposal. The users need to feel you've done as much as you could to shape the presentation into an effective one; if, in contrast, they feel *they* have to put in the effort to make sense of the content, they are likely to become increasingly negative about the service.

9.2.2 IMPACT ON BROWSING COMPLEX CONTENT

The studies we've just looked at used simple textual content, or textual content supplemented with basic navigation such as limited hyperlinks. In addition, the only scrolling users had to do was vertically, up and down the documents.

Today, though, and increasingly in the future, people can and will access far more complex content from their mobiles. Usually this is in the form of web-type information. Browsers on PDAs and many phones allow users to access content specifically designed for these platforms, as well as to view pages that have not been optimized for small-screen presentations.

How do users cope with these sorts of material on a downsized display? To find out we collaborated with Reuters (the international news content provider) to look at how people performed when completing tasks using web materials and a small screen. The content wasn't adjusted in any way – we just used the pages as designed for large-screen viewing (Jones *et al.*, 1999b).

We carried out a controlled, experimental evaluation method of the form discussed in Chapter 7, involving two groups of users. One set of participants had to work with a PDA-sized display similar in dimensions to device B in Table 9.1; the other viewed the materials via a desktop-sized screen.

What we saw was that if people try to use content that makes no concessions to the small-screen context, there will be huge usability problems. In fact, in our case, their ability to browse effectively broke down, and the participants resorted to non-browsing strategies. When we questioned users at the end of the trials, we found that most of them ascribed the failures to the small screen.

Of course, knowing that a system is failing is just the start. As in all interaction design, you have to look in detail at what is going on so that alternative schemes can be explored. So, the next question we asked was what interaction behaviors could have led to this poorer performance?

Participants on the small screen had to put in an enormous amount of effort to navigate within the pages. The number of vertical and horizontal scrolling actions carried out was many times higher than those on the large screens. This painful, high-cost page viewing led participants to be disinclined to browse. Indeed, when we looked at the logs of the pages accessed during tasks, we saw that while the large-screen users followed link after link, exploring areas of the site in a classic browsing way, the small-screen ones cautiously probed the information, with their browse-paths being considerably shorter.

Our small-screen users also showed how unattractive browsing was to them by using the site's search features instead – most of them started every task by using it and employed it twice as many times as the large screen participants. That is, they didn't want to wade through hard-to-navigate material; they wanted a direct answer.

The log analyses we carried out also showed something else interesting. The overlap between the pages viewed by the large-screen users and the small-screen ones was not high. As the former group were the most successful in completing the tasks we set them, it seemed that poorer link choices were being made by the small-screen bound users. Content that was hidden by many scrolls or page clicks was being overlooked.

9.2.3 IMPACT ON SEARCHING

Searching is perhaps the most widely performed computer-based task – we search our email for previously received correspondence, we search the web for anything and everything, and we hunt for photos we've taken and stored on our hard-drives.

Web searching in particular is a hugely popular activity, with some search engines reporting hundreds of millions of user queries every day. On the desktop, then, search systems are seen as useful and the most popular ones as reasonably usable. Given this appeal and the emergence of search engines for mobiles, we carried out a follow-up investigation to the browsing studies, to compare search performance on large screens to that on much smaller devices (Jones *et al.*, 2003a).

We took as our focus the versions of a major search engine aimed at the phone market, which was WAP based, and another designed for handheld PDAs. The sorts of question we wanted to answer were "Does the small screen environment reduce users' effectiveness and, if so, how?" and "Do users alter their searching behavior when using small screens?".

If you're thinking of building a mobile search interface, there are two elements you need to address:

- How to present the search results: as a list? More visually? What summary information do you provide – these are the meta-data or surrogates for the actual content: author, title, keywords?
- How to integrate the task of reviewing the results with accessing the content itself: select from list and display full content, as in conventional search engines? Use a technique like RSVP (see Section 10.4.3) to automatically present results one after the other? Provide roll-overs to show snapshots of content without the user having to navigate to another page (see Figure 9.8 for an example)?

The design choices for the WAP and PDA versions we looked at are shown in Figure 9.1. Search results are presented as a list. Each includes some meta-data about the actual page to help a user make choices about which to explore. In the desktop version, with more space available, additional information including a longer summary is displayed for every result.

When a user clicks on a result in the list, the corresponding page is displayed. Often, in the WAP case, this process involves some additional processing by the search engine. This is because the number of web pages explicitly created for WAP devices is still tiny – Google, for instance, estimates that 5 million of the 8 billion pages they index are WAP-based (Google). So that WAP users can access any page indexed, there has to be a transcoding process, taking the standard web page and breaking it up into a series of smaller, linked WAP pages.

To find out how users might fare with these small-scale versions, we asked a group of participants to use them to complete some tourist-style tasks: they had to find out the opening hours of a major art gallery, for example.

The results of this investigation suggest that trying to use a WAP-type device for search might lead to some very frustrating user experiences: in our case, only 36% of tasks could be completed successfully. The picture is more encouraging for PDA-type devices: our users achieved around 80% of the tasks.

For both the WAP and PDA cases, when the users succeeded they did so quickly, with few interactions with the search engine. When they failed, though, they failed badly. We looked through

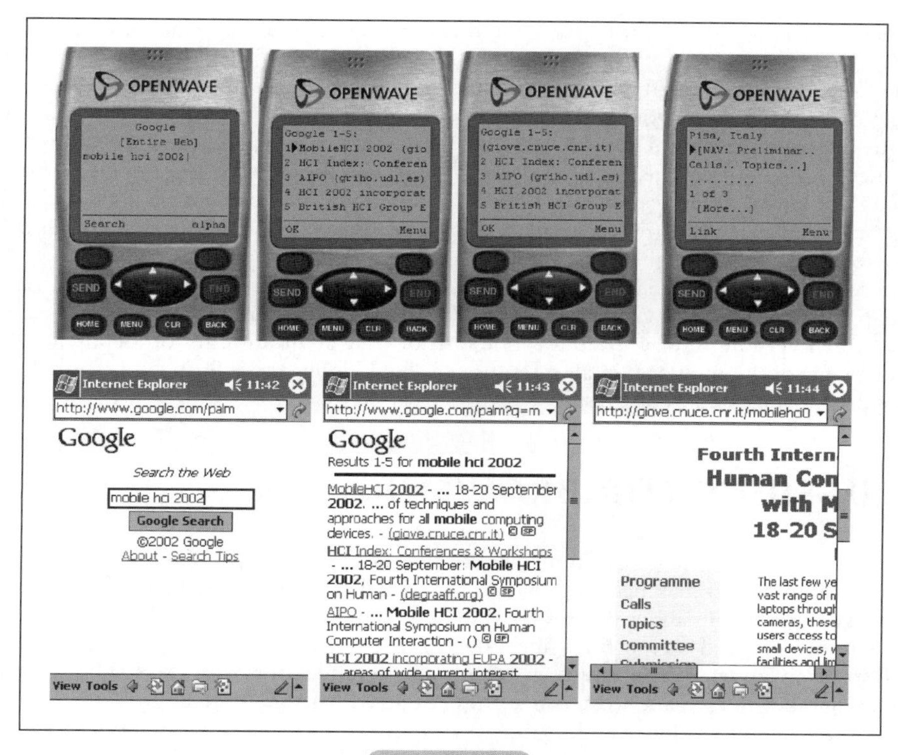

FIGURE 9.1

Using a search engine on a WAP device (top) and a PDA (below). Note that in the WAP case, conventional web pages are split into a series of smaller ones for display

the logs of access and found some explanations for these two distinct patterns of use – quick successes and prolonged, painful failures.

The first thing to note was that small-screen users were making choices from a smaller set. That's because the default small-screen list length was five and that of the large screen 10; in line with other studies, our users rarely went beyond the second page of the results list. So, on average, the large-screen users were selecting from a set of 20 choices, small-screen users from 10.

As with the browsing study, exploring any search result on the WAP or PDA small screen had the potential of involving a very high cost in terms of time and effort. As Figure 9.1 illustrates, finding information within a conventional HTML page, which is being redisplayed on the smaller interface, can be a tedious and frustrating task. A major cause of failure, then, was the great difficulties users had in navigating the site selected from the search result. Most of their wasted time and effort was spent in becoming increasingly lost within the small window.

Failing users also carried out more search engine interactions: they used a greater number of search attempts for each task, browsed more of the search result list pages, and viewed more of the result pages themselves. The impression was of users 'thrashing' to solve the problem. They would carry out an initial search attempt, spend more time scanning the search result outputs, explore a search result, becoming lost and frustrated, and then return to the search engine for another fruitless attempt.

In the unsuccessful cases, often it seems that users were very uncertain about whether a search result they were about to explore was going to be of any use. They then made blind leaps of faith into a usually disappointing unknown.

The successful cases for the WAP and PDA contexts were where the search engine results contained 'obviously' good candidates. These results were the ones where even the limited information about the page (title and web address – URL – for WAP; title, URL and limited summary for PDA) was enough to suggest the page was worth exploring.

When we asked users to indicate the main reasons for their having problems with the search interface, for the small-screen versions the size of the screen was identified as the main culprit. For the large-screen version, display space was not a major issue at all. In terms of identifying the most helpful elements of the interface, in all cases, users valued highly any information that helped them judge the potential usefulness of a result.

9.3 DESIGNS FOR BROWSING

Now we've seen the likely usability problems in browsing and searching content on a mobile device, let's turn our thinking to making things better. First we'll consider browsing again, and then we'll go on to make suggestions about designs for search.

In the studies of small-screen browsing, the content did not accommodate the constraints of limited displays in any way. The results, as we saw, were unpleasant, with users failing to complete tasks, becoming bewildered and frustrated as they struggled with the systems.

If you are a content developer wishing to see your information accessed on mobiles, the message is very clear: you cannot simply expect users to access information designed for the large screen on their small-screen devices. The experience could be awful and users may not tolerate it.

A number of mobile web browsers are emerging that go some way to solving the problems (we'll see some examples in Section 9.3.2). They take standard content, optimized for large screen viewing, and adapt it to make it more palatable for handheld access. Of course, in adapting the content, the way the user experiences the information will be very different from the way originally intended by the designer.

For some content providers, the quality of interactive experience provided by these solutions will be adequate. Information services that are primarily aimed at a large-screen audience, and that expect infrequent visits by mobile users, need little extra design thought, if these sorts of automatic adaptation systems are available to users. If this describes your situation then all you need to do is to make sure that you structure your content so that these bits of rendering software can do a good job (see Section 9.3.2).

But if you are seriously considering delivering material to mobile users, you should not abrogate your responsibilities by relying on the efforts of a third-party. Rather, your aim should be to ensure that the content that leaves your server is in a form that both fits the display restrictions of its destination and has a design that is consistent with the style and image you wish to present.

The next sections will help you think about how to adjust the content design so it makes better sense on the small screen. You'll find some helpful guidelines and also some example presentation techniques that live up to the ideals. When you go to develop mobile content, check your information architecture against the guidelines and be inspired by the examples.

9.3.1 GUIDELINES

Browsing, as we've seen, involves two activities: navigating through the content to find interesting portions, then reading through the material. To support these two tasks effectively on the small screen, the information design should aim to:

- allow users to overview the material at every opportunity;
- promote focused, direct access; and
- reduce scrolling.

Overviews, Overviews, Overviews

Any technique that helps the user quickly grasp as much of the content as possible, to assess the value it might provide to them, is helpful. What you want to avoid is users futilely spending time perusing material that doesn't meet their needs: the goal has to be to allow them to see easily whether the content looks promising, without their having to commit to accessing it fully. The sorts of aspect to consider, then, include the following:

- **Writing style.** It is well established that people read differently on the screen compared with how they do so from paper. One important element of online style is the need for conciseness. For small screens, this advice is even more important. Give the reader exactly what they need, neither more nor less.
- **Summaries.** Structural overviews are useful (think outlines, tables of contents, etc.) and summarized content can be effective too. In the latter case, while the default view of the information should contain the key points, the user should be able to reveal further details if they wish.
- **Skim-reading.** People tend to scan online content. This is a rapid process where the reader is trying to identify the main points, assessing relevance and seeking out content they are interested in. One study, for instance, of desktop web use showed that 79% of users worked in this way; with only 16% reading word by word (Nielsen, 1997b). Scanning can be promoted by structuring information effectively into sections and subsections, as well as highlighting important parts using fonts and other graphical effects. On the small screen, getting the font size, spacing between lines and layout of the information right is even more critical in this respect.

BOX 9.3 **USING KEYPHRASES FOR SMALL-SCREEN SKIM READING** (Jones *et al.*, 2004)

Automatic techniques can pick out the keyphrases in a document text. Once spotted, these can be put to use to help a reader skim the information in various ways. The phrases themselves can be highlighted, as in the example shown in Figure 9.2. Alternatively, the sentences or even paragraphs containing the keyphrases can be brought to the user's attention. ➤

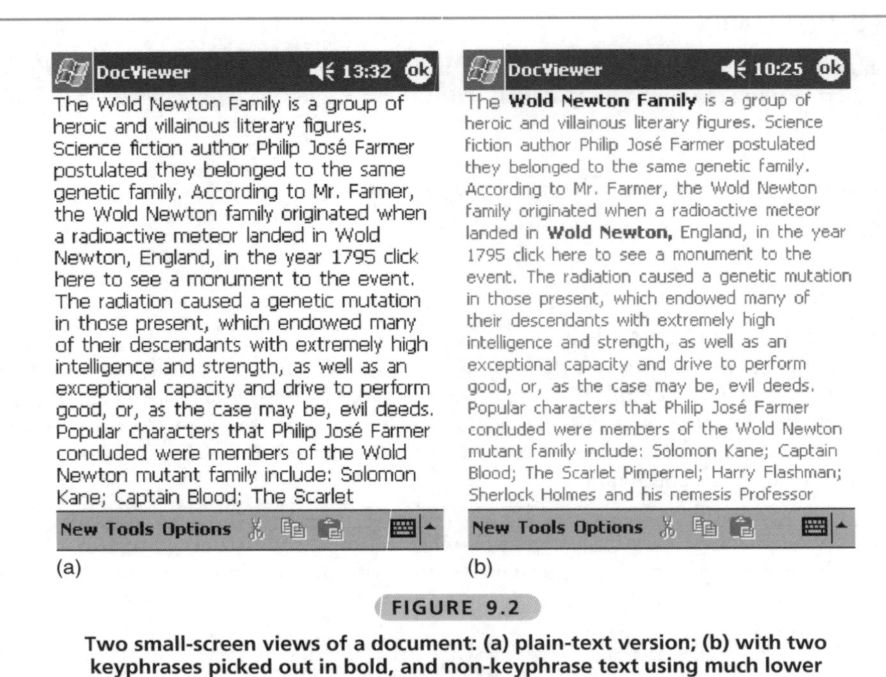

FIGURE 9.2

Two small-screen views of a document: (a) plain-text version; (b) with two keyphrases picked out in bold, and non-keyphrase text using much lower contrast

Keyphrase extractors assign probability scores against every phrase in a document, the value showing how likely the phrase is to be a key one – from 0 (not at all) to 1 (certain). These values can be used to control the degree of highlighting used, the highest scoring portions being heavily emphasized and less likely keyphrases given less prominence. ■

Providing Focused, Direct Access

Small-screen users seem to choose and prefer direct access strategies which will lead them quickly to a piece of content. Handheld information designs should accommodate these preferences. Some possibilities are as follows.

- Use a navigation scheme that allows users to move purposefully toward finding the content they need. A loosely structured tangle of information will not work well on the small screen. A better model to aspire to is one where the user can drill down into the information, moving from overviews to more detail. While the WAP approach to content structuring has been much criticized, one aspect in its favor in this regard is its use of a transaction model: each card (i.e. screen) of information allows a user to carry out a limited set of actions, leading to the next step of either completing a task or locating some content. However, avoid tedious, clunky structuring (see Exercise 9.1 earlier).

- Present users with a small set of paths to content which will allow them to meet the majority of their goals. Whenever one develops content, it is tempting to give access to everything one can; however, this strategy will lead to overwhelmed users. That's not to say that users should be prevented from accessing anything they want (see the discussion on portals later in Section 9.3.3). What you can do is to hide the extra material (consider, for instance, having options like *Other information* and *More on X*).
- Provision of a search mechanism: sites which are to be viewed by handheld users must provide one or more search features.

Reduce Scrolling

It's clear that users will potentially have to carry out far too many scroll actions when using small-screen displays. Such activity will interrupt their primary tasks. Horizontal scrolling should be eliminated entirely – users should never have to involve themselves in the awkward two-dimensional navigation tasks we saw earlier. To reduce the degree of vertical scrolling, you can arrange content in the following sorts of ways:

- Placing navigational features (menu bars, etc.) near the tops of pages in a fixed place.
- Placing the most important information toward the tops of pages.
- Reducing the amount of material on a page; making the content task focused rather than verbose.

9.3.2 SCHEMES

Remember that the purpose of guidelines is twofold. They can provide starting points for design, inspiring the choices you make as you begin thinking about an interaction scheme; and they are a critiquing tool for any prototypes that emerge.

Let's now turn to some example content presentation schemes which aim at improving the user's browsing experience on the small screen. Hopefully, you'll see how these relate to the guidelines we've just presented.

We've classified the different approaches as being 1D, 1.5D and 2D (one-, one and a half- or two-dimensional) in nature. What we are attempting to do by this is to distinguish between the different levels of layout complexity inherent in a scheme – the 1D schemes focus the user's attention simply in a vertical manner, whereas the 2D ones structure the content horizontally as well.

The 1D and 1.5D sorts of scheme are especially relevant to the smaller mobile screens of phones, while the 2D is more suitable for the larger, fully-featured ones seen on the likes of PDAs.

1D Browsing

To visualize this approach, imagine content being presented along a narrow, vertical film-strip. The user starts reading it from the top and can scroll down it and back up using only a simple vertical control.

Take a look at the screenshot shown in Figure 9.3 – how would you convert this into a linear form? A usable approach could involve moving the main navigation bar on the left of the screen to the top of the page, and then, beneath this, placing the content in order of importance, broken up into blocks. You might also want to repeat the main navigation elements at the bottom of the page as well as throughout the document to allow the user to make selections without having to return all the way to the top. An illustration of how this might look on a small screen is shown in Figure 9.4.

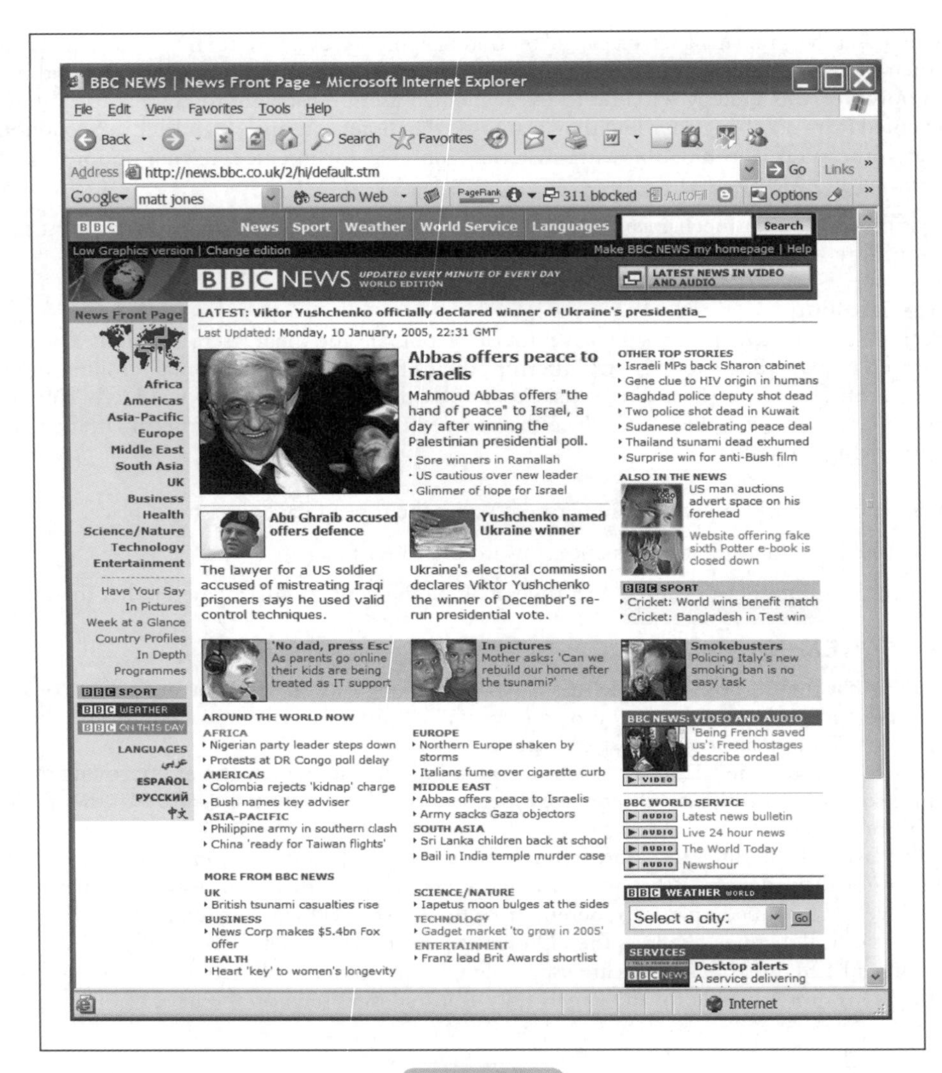

FIGURE 9.3

News website viewed on a large-screen desktop PC

In passing, it's worth noting that this example of a pared-down presentation is the low-graphics version of a popular news website. One reason the provider allows this view of its content is to make it easier for users with limited eyesight to read it. It turns out, though, that other types of impairment – such as a small screen – benefit from the design too. This is another illustration, then, how the universal access thinking we talked about in Chapter 1 can lead to widely applicable designs.

FIGURE 9.4

Low-graphics version of the news website exhibits a linear form, more suitable for small-screen viewing

In the above example, the web design team has explicitly thought out how to re-present their material. There are, though, a number of commercial browsers that automatically do this sort of conversion. One of these is the *Opera* browser for mobiles (Opera); another is *NetFront* from Access which employs the *Smart-Fit Renderer* to turn the content into linear form. Figure 9.5 shows how one example website appears when seen through the Opera lens. These sorts of adaptation systems work by identifying components in the content – menu bars, adverts, etc., – and using some heuristics to place them in a more usable sequence.

While the adaptation is an automatic process, you should not assume that it takes away all the design effort. The tool providers advise content developers to be aware of how their transcoding process works and to design with it in mind. Opera, for instance, suggests that you should check your large-screen web designs to ensure that the following appear:

- A small set of links horizontally at the top of the page
- A further set in a vertical bar on the left of the page
- Subsidiary links in an area on the right of the page.

A design that features just a very long list of links in the left-hand navigation bar would not reproduce well using their rendering algorithm approach – the user would be confronted with having to scroll vertically through this long set of links before getting to any of the content itself.

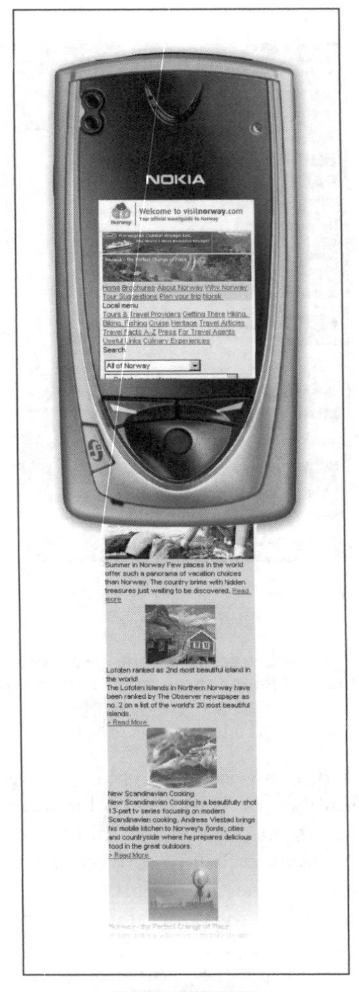

FIGURE 9.5

The Opera mobile browser. Standard web pages are rendered as a vertical film-strip to improve small-screen usability

1.5D Browsing

In the 1D browsing approach, viewing all of a page's content is a simple matter of rolling through the filmstrip. The attractive aspect of this sort of design is that it is easy for a user to grasp how to control the view, and the navigation process places little demands in terms of mental effort.

However, in many cases, where there is a fair deal of content, the process of scrolling through material may take up much user time, as the linear view will fill many screens of the small display.

To cut down on the amount of information presented, you should consider techniques that summarize or hide content. We've termed these 1.5D browsing schemes. As you'll see, with these approaches the information – be it a page or a larger grouping such as a website subsection – is shown to the user using a hierarchical scheme. So, at first, the user sees only an outline of the content, but they can progressively expand their view, seeing more and more detail. We call them 1.5D because, as with the 1D approaches, the basic navigation the user performs is to move linearly through the outlines, but as they expand the content it appears progressively indented along the screen's horizontal axis.

Page-level schemes

Orkut Buyukkokten and the Stanford University Digital Library Lab developed the *PowerBrowser* (Buyukkokten *et al.*, 2000). One of its features is a browsing approach they called *accordion summarization*; just like the musical instrument it is named after, the content can be expanded or contracted to see more or less detail (Buyukkokten *et al.*, 2001a).

It works by first identifying the structural blocks in the page – called *Semantic Textual Units* (STUs). A STU might be a bullet-pointed list of items or set of paragraphs or any of a number of other components the system can recognize, using a rule-of-thumb approach. Like the 1D methods, then, the system parses existing web content and finds its building bricks. Unlike the 1D approaches, though, there's the notion of hierarchical relationships – STUs can be nested within others.

Having extracted the structure of the content, it is then visualized as a hierarchy. STUs are displayed with nesting controls (+, –) that allow a user to expand or contract the view, respectively. Want to see what's within a unit? Click the + control. The approach protects the user from being engulfed with content – they can overview the possibilities and get more details of the interesting-looking portions.

As we earlier mentioned in the section on guidelines, textual summarization methods are also useful in reducing overload and clutter on the small screen. If you want to consider using summary techniques for your own content, there's a wealth of approaches you can take. As a taster, consider the following methods demonstrated in the PowerBrowser. In each case, the user gets more and more information each time they click on a summary icon next to each section of text (Buyukkokten *et al.*, 2001b):

- **Incremental –** present first line of text only, then the first three lines, and finally all of the text.
- **Keyword –** present automatically extracted keywords from text, then the first three lines, and finally all the text.
- **Summary –** present the most important sentence (again automatically extracted from the text), and after a second tap present all the text.
- **Keyword/summary –** hybrid of the keyword and summary methods, presenting keywords, then key sentence and finally, after another click, all the text.

These sorts of method can dramatically reduce the amount of scrolling a user has to carry out. Orkut and his colleagues quantified this by taking a number of web pages and viewing them on a phone and PDA-sized screen. Without summarization, the sites filled between six and 324 screens of the phone and between three and 88 on the PDA. After summarization, this dropped down to 1–6 on the phone and 1–4 on the PDA.

When they compared the performance of their system with another small-screen browser that presented the original content in a linear fashion, they found that with their approach the time to complete tasks was much faster, with the number of scrolling actions being substantially reduced. Of course, the method is dependent on there being a good and meaningful structure in the content; on top of this, if the summarized version of each component poorly expresses the information it contains, it's likely that the user will overlook it, failing to open it up to browse potentially useful material.

PowerBrowser's purpose was to render large-screen designs in a useful way on the small screen. However, the approaches it illustrates are really good pointers to the sorts of methods that can be used when developing content specifically for the smaller displays on mobiles. Look at the content you want to deliver, then, and think about the importance of each part – *does the user need to see this immediately or can we hide it away for them to discover as necessary?* Think back to the news site example in Figure 9.4. On the small screen, headlines could be shown to the user initially. Clicking on the headline link might lead to the full story (displayed on another page), but clicking repeatedly on a summary icon could lead to the content being expanded within the current page.

Site-level schemes

The idea of providing a hierarchical overview can be applied to units of content larger than the single page. Two systems we worked on – *LibTwig* and *WebTwig* – used this approach to give overviews of digital library content and entire websites, respectively.

Looking at the digital library case first, you might not know what a digital library is but you have probably used one, accessing articles such as those referenced in this book, or reading back-issues of a magazine, online. In short, a digital library is the web wearing a suit and tie – that is, the material is more formally classified, organized and structured.

Figure 9.6 shows how LibTwig presents digital library content. Users are shown an overview of the categories of information available to them; each of these can be further explored to view any subcategories. This top-down expansion of the table of contents continues until a list of actual documents is shown; selecting one of these presents the content in all its detail (Buchanan *et al.*, 2002).

In WebTwig, our small-screen web browser, there are no categories and subcategories but, rather, sections and subsections of a site. The browser software works by first crawling through the web content, much as a search engine does when it indexes a site, attempting to work out the structure of the information (Jones *et al.*, 1999a). Then the user is shown an overview of all the content, which they can interactively expand and contract. So, for the news website in Figure 9.3, the WebTwig version would initially show a linear list of headings such as 'Front Page', 'Africa' or 'Americas'; clicking on any of these top-level sections would display the relevant subsections (e.g. 'Nigerian party leader steps down' and 'Protests at Congo Poll Delay' for 'Africa'). The PowerBrowser does a similar job to WebTwig at the site level.

There have been user evaluations of all these three systems which compared performance with the situation when users have to access non-adapted content on the small screen. The results of these studies indicate that users can be faster and more satisfied with the overviews. So, if you have a large amount of information to convey on the small screen, consider using these sorts of dynamic tables-of-content which give users the power to explore the space of possibilities before delving into the detail.

2D Browsing

The 1.5D schemes we've seen need interface elements both to control the interaction and to display the results of a user's action. So, the PowerBrowser has the nesting controls and summary icons, and

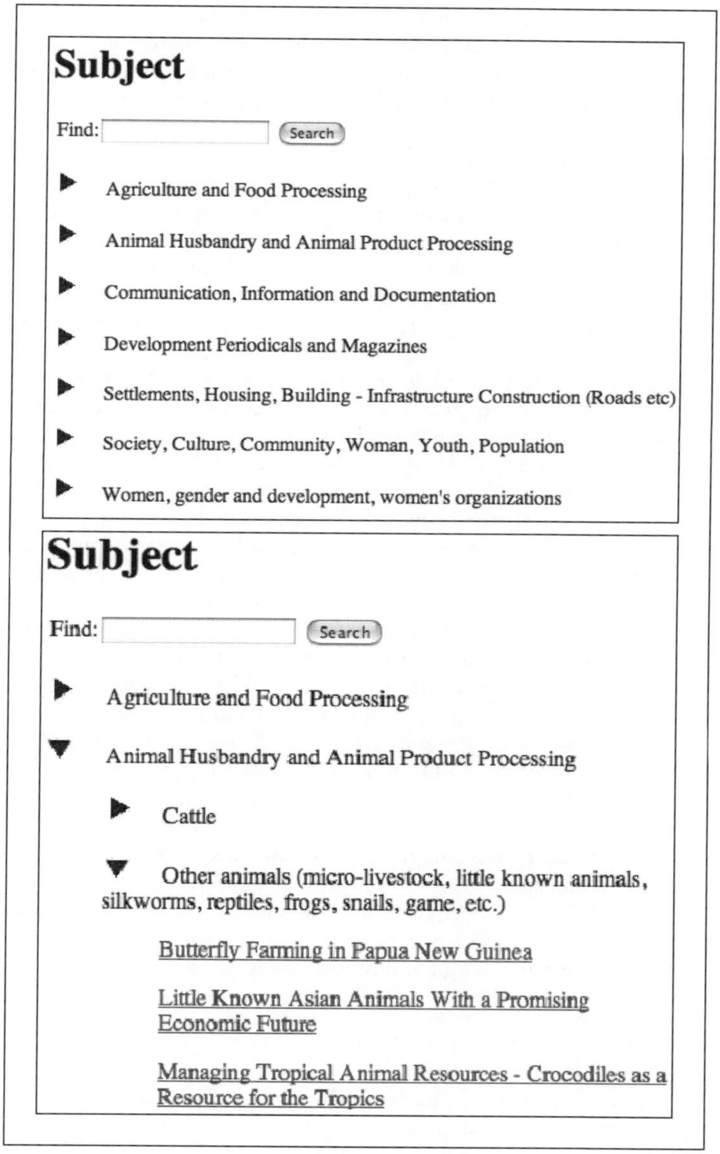

Subject

Find: Search

▶ Agriculture and Food Processing

▶ Animal Husbandry and Animal Product Processing

▶ Communication, Information and Documentation

▶ Development Periodicals and Magazines

▶ Settlements, Housing, Building - Infrastructure Construction (Roads etc)

▶ Society, Culture, Community, Woman, Youth, Population

▶ Women, gender and development, women's organizations

Subject

Find: Search

▶ Agriculture and Food Processing

▼ Animal Husbandry and Animal Product Processing

▶ Cattle

▼ Other animals (micro-livestock, little known animals, silkworms, reptiles, frogs, snails, game, etc.)

Butterfly Farming in Papua New Guinea

Little Known Asian Animals With a Promising Economic Future

Managing Tropical Animal Resources - Crocodiles as a Resource for the Tropics

FIGURE 9.6

LibTwig hierarchical overview of digital library content (Buchanan *et al.*, 2002). User can dynamically expand or contract view to see more or less of content

LibTwig uses node control widgets to expand and contract content. These sorts of items use up valuable screen space. In addition, there's a limit to the degree of overview possible – the font size used for the textual descriptions has to be large enough for the user to be able to read and interact with them.

The 2D techniques we see here, though, use an alternative approach to provide overviews that give access to detail. Instead of being textually oriented, they are visually based, using zooming visualizations.

Increasing and decreasing content magnification is something we're all familiar with on the desktop. Consider looking at a map: if you need to orient a location to its wider surroundings, you can zoom out; similarly, if you want to read the street names in a specific area, you may have to zoom in. Or take document viewing: you can zoom out and scroll through content, and when you see an interesting picture, say, zoom back in to read the surrounding text.

Mobile map and document viewers that use these sorts of zooming will become increasingly popular. In terms of applying the technique to web content access, an early attempt was the WEST browser (Björk *et al.*, 1999). Pages of information (which are cards of a WAP deck) are shown to the user as thumbnail images within a single small screen. One of the pages, the one in focus, is displayed in a larger area. The user can change which page is in focus, and the display is dynamically updated, with the new focus becoming enlarged, and the old reduced. Selecting a page causes a complete zoom in onto the content, allowing it to use up the entire screen area.

The researchers also experimented with summarizing the content shown for each thumbnail: in one mode, the system displayed only the keywords for each page; in another, just the navigation links.

In a limited evaluation of the prototype, users were found to enjoy the approach but took some time to understand how it worked. If you develop any novel schemes for accessing content, you may find that when users first see the system they are puzzled by how to operate it. This in itself is not a sign that the approach is flawed – the issue is whether the mechanism can be explained easily, and once they have understood the method whether they can return, over and over, and use it without having to expend a lot of mental effort in using it. The user's goal is not to gain satisfaction in operating tricky schemes you might provide, but to find and make use of information.

With the increasingly sophisticated graphics processors that are being developed for mobiles, zooming approaches can become more ambitious. The *SmartView* system, developed by researchers at Microsoft, is an example (Milic-Frayling and Sommerer, 2002). Like the 1D and 1.5D browsers we saw earlier, it also depends on finding a page's layout structure; however, instead of then turning it into a linear or a hierarchical view, it goes on to use this knowledge in conjunction with a reduced, full view of the web page.

Figure 9.7 gives you an idea of how the technique operates. Each region identified by the system is highlighted, and when a user selects an area – say a menu bar – they are shown a full-size view of it.

Retaining the original designer's design and presenting it in overview in this sort of way has two main benefits:

- Users might be able to quickly spot areas of interest by recognizing structural landmarks – a main content area, navigation bars and so on.
- There's also the consistency between the way the information looks on the large screen and the mobile counterpart. We have excellent spatial memory abilities, so when we look at a reduced visualization of a web page we've seen previously on the large screen, we may be able to use this knowledge of how the content is organized within the page. Bonnie MacKay saw this effect in action when she tested the GateWay system which is similar to SmartView.

One problem with SmartView, identified by other Microsoft researchers, is that in many cases it is difficult to make out the detail in the parts of a page without zooming in (Baudisch *et al.*, 2004).

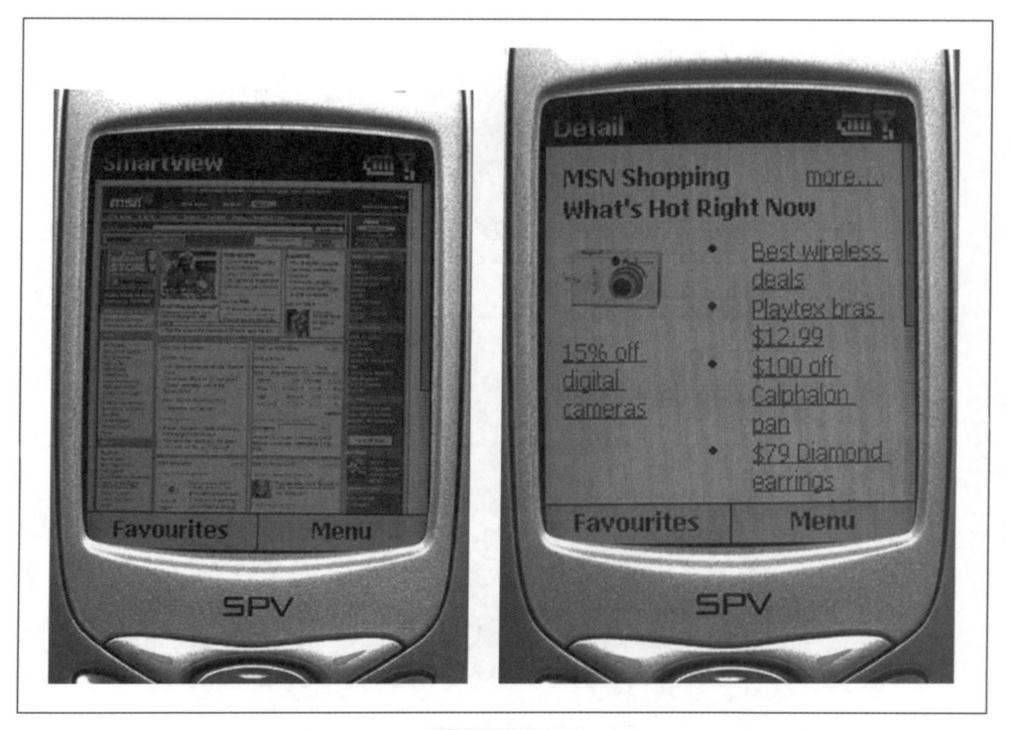

FIGURE 9.7

SmartView browsing techniques (Rodden *et al.* 2003)

Left hand image shows reduced view of complete web page; right hand, the zoomed-in detail of one of its components

This can lead to the user having to 'hunt-and-peck' in their search for the portion of content they want to view: they zoom into one area, find it doesn't contain what they are looking for, return to the overview and repeat this process (perhaps several times) until they find what they need.

The GateWay system reduces this problem by using roll-over boxes to give a preview of the detail (see Figure 9.8) (MacKay *et al.*, 2004). The Microsoft team, though, demonstrate a more radical solution they call *Collapse-to-Zoom* (Baudisch *et al.* 2004). As well as allowing users to zoom into an area of a page, this also gives them the opportunity to strike out areas that don't look interesting to them. If you want to read only the main text, you might remove navigation bars, pictures and adverts, for instance. With each component removed, there's more space for the rest of the content to be redisplayed. After each deletion, the content is reconfigured, the remaining elements filling the display with the removed items being represented as small tabs on the edges of the display (the user can select these if they want the respective content to be added back into the picture).

These 2D techniques and the 1.5D ones tend to use a touchscreen and stylus. The approaches, though, are amenable to other types of control mechanism. Imagine then using a joystick control to navigate between the different sections of a SmartView type presentation; one button click could then activate the zoom-in, and another the return to the overview.

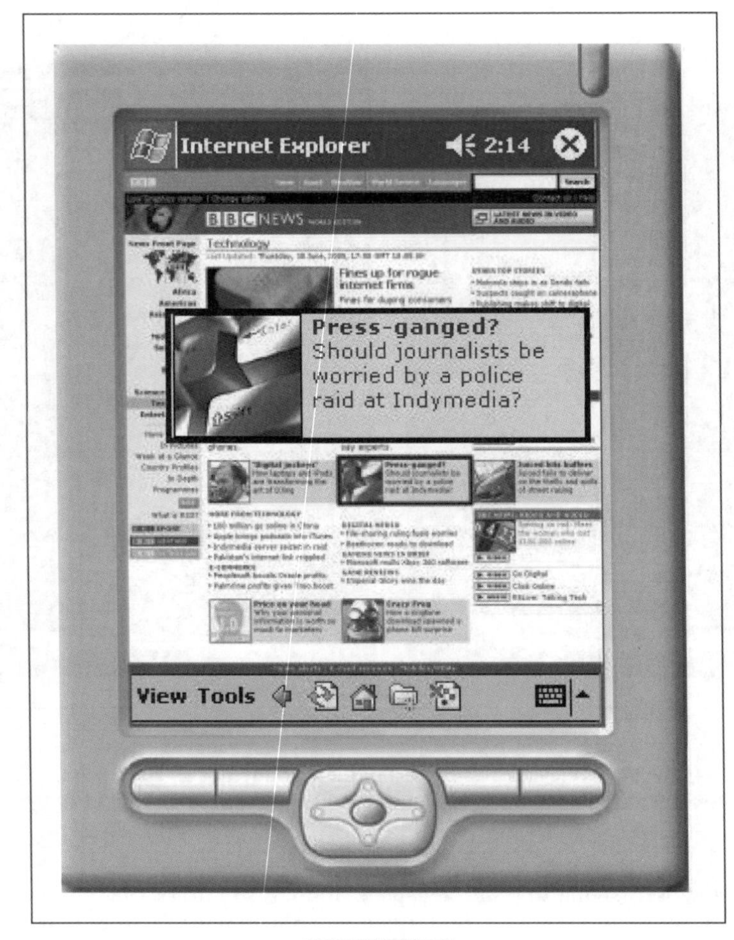

FIGURE 9.8

GateWay browser (MacKay *et al.*, 2004). As in the SmartView system (see Figure 9.7), browser gives visual overview of web page on small screen. Pop-ups act as magnifier lens to give detail

EXERCISE 9.2 WEBSITE REDESIGN

Get a pad of PDA-sized Post-it notes, and create a prototype redesign for a website you're familiar with – your corporate intranet or university site, for instance. Create ➤

a sequence of screen layouts for the main page and a range of the other content and functionality supported by the site.

Comments: first think about the sorts of information users will want when mobile – what can you leave out or de-emphasize in the mobile version? Is there anything missing which would be useful in this new context? Then consider the guidelines and schemes we've been looking at and apply them in your redesign. ■

9.3.3 PACKAGING CONTENT

Many mobile users will want specific types of information or to be able to access particular resources which are important to them. So, they might want to read a news digest, get some sports information and perhaps view entertaining content. In the business context, their goal might be to access information – from product details to company address books – that can support them while they are away from the office.

Recognizing this, there are a number of techniques that can bring sets of content to the user in a consumable way.

Portals

This very common approach involves providing users with a choice of resources via a (usually, at present, not simple) set of menus. Apart from sorting out menu structuring, portal providers need to think about how limited the selection should be. For many providers, their instinct is to establish a 'walled garden' – users can access only the resources placed before them; they cannot stray to locate alternatives, or if they can, the process is complex. Be careful: there is nothing more frustrating for a user than thinking the system is nannying them. A more pleasing approach for users is to complement these 'approved' selections with easy ways for them to find and add additional sources. Give users access to a web search engine, then, and allow them to set up links to their own favorite sites.

Channels

Channels are carefully selected sets of content, with a strong sense of brand, that are automatically updated and brought to the user's device. Instead of the user having to hunt for information, the latest content is pushed to their device. Channel technology had its debut on desktop devices several years ago but the success was very limited – users seemed to prefer the freedom of more interactive information access provided by conventional web browsers. However, the idea looks like a better fit for the mobile market, where the costs – in terms of user effort and bandwidth charges – of extensive browsing seem more of a deterrent.

On the mobile, some channels might contain very limited, focused information, leading to interactions which are more 'glancing' than browsing in nature. A commercial example is illustrated by the wristwatch-style devices, developed by Microsoft, that provide micro-content such as weather forecasts and news headlines. Just as you might steal a glance at your watch to look at the time, you can do the same to get a quick information update. As the Microsoft manager for these technologies, Chris Schneider, notes (Evers, 2003): "This is not for reading the newspaper, but for the micro moments in people's lives, providing perhaps a paragraph of information."

RSS (Really Simple Syndication)

Like most people who use the web, you probably have regular sites you return to, over and over again. Visiting them to see what's new or updated can take up a fair bit of time. What if you could see a summary of all the updates to these sites, conveniently displayed on a single page? That's what RSS is designed for. The scheme works like this: websites publish summaries – called feeds – of their updates, then a piece of software on the user's device (often called a feed-reader or news-aggregator) gets all the summaries from the sites a user subscribes to, and displays a timely digest. Many users then simply read the summaries without visiting the sites themselves, but if they really want more detail they can easily navigate to the content itself. RSS and related schemes are becoming a desktop phenomenon; you can expect to see its popularity rise on mobile devices, too.

9.4 IMPROVING SEARCH

In Section 9.2.3, we saw how users can get into difficulties when using a small-screen device to carry out searches. They can have problems choosing the best search results to pursue and are most effective when there are obvious good leads. If you are designing a mobile search interface, two of your goals should be, therefore:

- to allow users to quickly assess the value of the set of results and to spot any particularly useful hits. If they would be better off trying another set of search terms, they should realize that sooner rather than later; and
- to help them make good decisions about which results to pursue. Go for fully informed interaction – avoid them having to make guesses about possibly useful material.

Let's consider each of these goals, in turn.

9.4.1 ASSESSING SETS OF RESULTS

A simple improvement on the small-screen schemes seen in Section 9.2.3 would be to increase the number of results shown on each page, say from 5 to 10. Because people tend to review only the first couple of results pages produced by a search engine, pages with smaller numbers of items will lead to fewer possibilities being considered. Furthermore, extended page-to-page navigation, as we saw in the browse case, is not something users want to engage in, so displaying more information on each page is beneficial.

A more sophisticated way of helping users to see more results while not overburdening them with navigation activities is, once again, to exploit the power of overviews. Instead of giving users a simple list of search hits, the individual results can be grouped together and the overall topics or categories they fall under can be shown to the user. One system that does just this is the *Scatter/Gather* scheme explored in Cutting *et al.* (1992). Here, similar documents are automatically clustered together. Key terms are then extracted from each cluster and a summary of these terms is displayed. Users can gain an understanding of the topics available by scanning the cluster descriptions.

Computationally neat while the idea is, a problem with automatic clustering is that the descriptions chosen for the clusters can be difficult to interpret. So, a more promising approach is to group documents into pre-existing, meaningful categories. Many search engines already provide browsing of categories to access their content. In Yahoo!, for instance, users can select from top-level categories such as *Entertainment, Government* and *Health*, and browse further subcategories to help them gain an understanding of the sorts of material available.

Susan Dumais – an information retrieval expert responsible for the desktop search innovations at Microsoft – and colleagues illustrated the value of such an approach on conventionally sized displays (Chen and Dumais, 2000). Their system automatically categorizes web search results against an existing hierarchical category structure. In an attempt to make good use of the screen space, the system displays the all-important first page of results in a way that gives an overview of how the results are distributed across the categorical structure. Only a top-level category view is shown, and just the top 20 results are given. The user can expand and contract categories to see more of the hierarchical structure and how the results relate to it, and additional matches can also be displayed on demand. A user study showed that users not only liked the new approach but were 50% faster at finding information than in a simple ranked-list scheme.

BOX 9.4 SEARCH AND THE QWERTY EFFECT

Despite many interesting interface research innovations over the past 10 years, as far as search engines on the large screen go, list presentations still predominate. There seems, then, to be a QWERTY effect. QWERTY keyboards were designed to slow typists down, in the days when physical typewriter mechanisms could cope with only limited typing speeds. Despite many keyboard layout innovations that would potentially improve the typing experience, QWERTY remains. It's hard to overthrow a well-established interaction style. While novel search approaches have made little headway for desktop use, radical designs may be received more readily in the mobile market where conventional ways of presenting information just do not fit. ■

EXERCISE 9.3 SEARCHING FOR EMAIL ON A SMALL-SCREEN DEVICE

Imagine a user with hundreds of emails stored on their mobile device. How would you help them find particular emails?

Comments: on a large screen, a list of search matches which the user can reorder flexibly, sorting by say sender, subject or date received, can be a very effective approach. But on a small screen, where only 5–10 emails are visible and much scrolling is required, this could become unviable. You could make use of the user-defined mail folders (e.g., Meetings, Deliverables, Admin, etc.), presenting the emails that match a query in relation to these. For the items already assigned a folder by the user, this is trivial to do; emails still in the inbox, though, could be automatically classified by comparing their contents with those already classified by the user. The small screen may be big enough to show all the folder labels (and counts of relevant emails held within them) without the user having to scroll. ■

BOX 9.5 SMALL SCREENS AND CATEGORY SEARCH

The LibTwig system we discussed earlier uses a category-based overview approach to show the user the results of their queries. As with browsing, the outline view not only limits the amount of scrolling required to make sense of the search results, but provides context information which might help users make decisions about which alternatives to pursue.

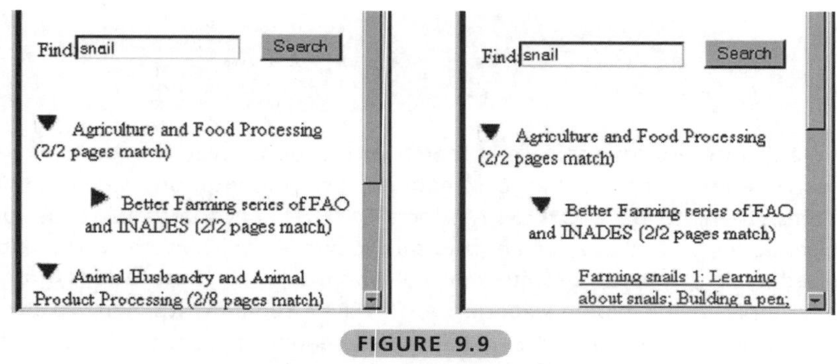

FIGURE 9.9

LibTwig outline view of search results

For example, in Figure 9.9, the user has entered a query 'snail' and is shown there are several top-level categories (including 'Agriculture and Food Processing' and 'Animal Husbandry and Animal Product Processing') that contain 'snail' documents. On expanding the first category, the user sees that two such documents are within the 'Better Farming series of FAO and INADES' subcategory. Finally, on further expanding this subcategory, they are shown the document links themselves (see right-hand screenshot). ■

9.4.2 JUDGING THE VALUE OF INDIVIDUAL RESULTS

What about helping a user decide whether to explore a particular search result? Knowing what topic or category a result relates to, as in the examples above, of course helps in this value assessment. The Cluster Hypothesis says that most 'real' matches to a user's search could be grouped under a common heading; matches that are not in this category are probably less relevant (van Rijsbergen, 1979).

Providing category information, though, is just one of the ways to help users make good choices on the small screen. Another involves making use of keyphrases automatically identified from the candidate documents. Figure 9.10 illustrates the idea: the left-hand display shows a list of search results with the title for each document given for each item. On the right, in contrast, there's the same list of documents but this time each is described by a number of phrases extracted from the

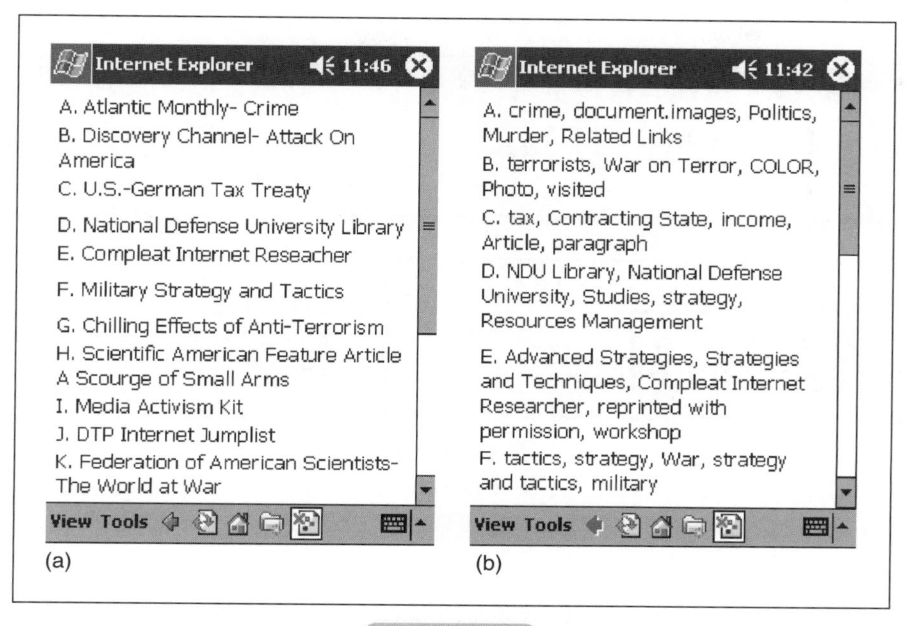

FIGURE 9.10

Search result presentations: (a) titles of documents; (b) keywords extracted from the same documents

documents themselves. In an experiment, this derived presentation was seen to be as effective as the title display in terms of enabling users to work out what a document was about (Jones *et al.*, 2004).

The information conventionally provided for a search result (e.g. the title, URL) could then be advantageously complemented with these sorts of extra item mined from the content. Giving users extra clues about the real content of a hit could guide them more effectively to the documents they actually need. Indeed, information extracted in this way and displayed in the result summaries could provide the answers without the user having to access the source at all, as an SMS search system described in Box 9.6 illustrates.

BOX 9.6 SMS SEARCH (Schusteritsch *et al.*, 2005)

The Google text message search illustrates how text-mining techniques can be used to give users direct answers to their queries. A user sends an SMS message to the Google server containing their query terms and then receives one or more text messages back in return. Each message consists of details extracted from pages aimed at providing the information the user needs. No further interaction is required by the user. ➤

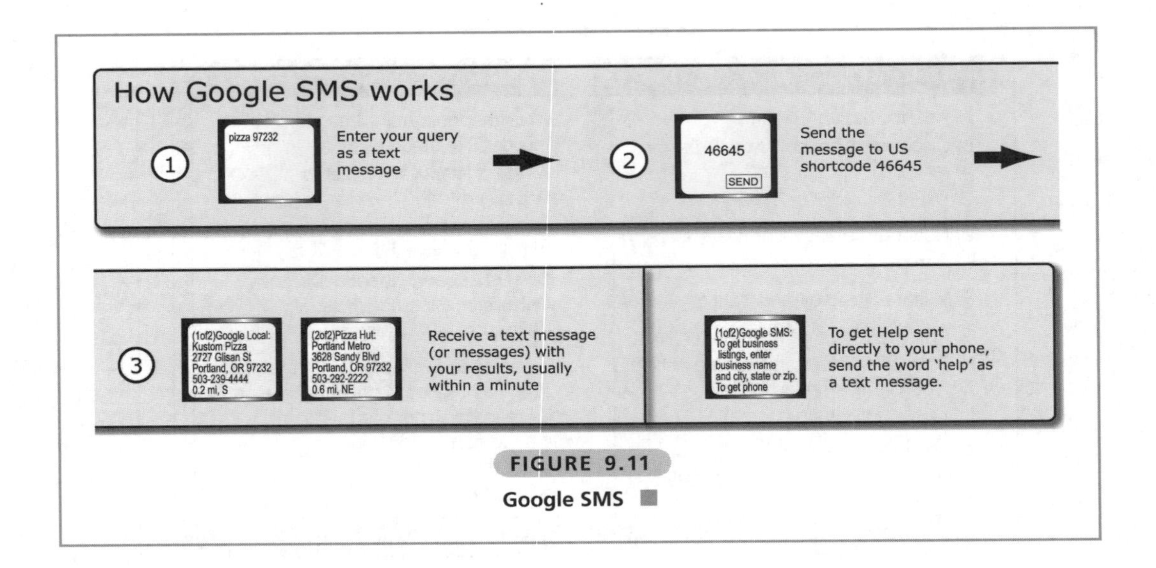

FIGURE 9.11
Google SMS

Keyphrase approaches are useful not just for web-like document search tasks. Summaries of emails could be useful for the small-screen context; see, for instance, *AmikaNow* (AmikaNow). There is also potential for use in managing a user's local mobile information space.

Let's think about that second case – the management of information held on the device itself. Conventional desktop and laptop computers already have vast long-term local storage capabilities (for example, the laptop computer used to write this chapter has a hard disk capacity of 18 Gb). Mobile small-screen devices are also beginning to provide storage for large quantities of local information: it's easy to find PDAs with 1 Gb local storage, and 60 Gb digital music-come-information storage players are also commonplace.

So, people already can carry lots of information with them on their mobile devices. In cases where this includes documents they have created themselves – presentations they are working on, reports they are editing and the like – techniques like the keyphrase one will become more important. That's because it is more likely that the documents on these devices will have 'poor' author-specified titles/descriptors. For example, take a look at the contents of a folder from one of our laptop folders, shown in Figure 9.12. Some titles are obscure (e.g. 'p3-churchill'), general (e.g. 'Overview'), coded (e.g. '30070372') or vague (e.g. 'ideas'). Over time, and in the context of thousands or tens of thousands of documents, the contents of these files might be hard to discern from the titles alone. Additional surrogates such as keyphrases, both while browsing available files and when using the device's search engine, might be essential.

Whatever information you decide to give the user about search results, you should do so as concisely and directly as possible. In the WAP search version considered earlier, only the first few words of each result can be seen at first with, after a delay, horizontal marquee scrolling used to show the remaining portions. A better design might have involved wrapping the full text of every result over several lines on the display, so the user could read the complete titles immediately. When we looked at displaying news headlines for a mobile service, we found that this non-auto-scrolling presentation was more effective than alternatives (see Figure 9.13).

Name	Size	Type	Date Modified
trademarks	1 KB	Text Document	14/06/2005 5:19 p.m.
currentTOCJune05	49 KB	Microsoft Word Docu...	13/06/2005 6:15 p.m.
FullTOC-forcopyedit	51 KB	Microsoft Word Docu...	13/06/2005 5:10 p.m.
mid-for-copyedit	462 KB	EndNote Library	13/06/2005 9:59 a.m.
wordcounts	14 KB	Microsoft Excel Works...	7/06/2005 10:54 a.m.
TechreviewsResponse	41 KB	Microsoft Word Docu...	2/05/2005 1:22 a.m.
mid	458 KB	EndNote Library	15/04/2005 3:03 a.m.
permissions_MID	39 KB	Microsoft Excel Works...	8/03/2005 10:25 p.m.
PERMISSIONSFORM-MID	38 KB	Microsoft Word Docu...	8/03/2005 9:32 p.m.
PERMISSIONSFORM	24 KB	Microsoft Word Docu...	8/03/2005 9:26 p.m.
coveringletter	104 KB	Microsoft Word Docu...	23/02/2005 11:33 p.m.
coverforboxes	24 KB	Microsoft Word Docu...	22/02/2005 7:58 p.m.
Mobile Interaction Design	20 KB	Microsoft Word Docu...	22/02/2005 7:13 a.m.
FullTOC	55 KB	Microsoft Word Docu...	22/02/2005 6:22 a.m.
overviewTOC	34 KB	Microsoft Word Docu...	22/02/2005 6:21 a.m.
Overview	25 KB	Microsoft Word Docu...	17/01/2005 10:19 p.m.
ideas	1 KB	Text Document	29/07/2004 10:32 p.m.
p115-tractinsky-VISUALBEAUTY	803 KB	Adobe Acrobat Docu...	24/02/2004 8:53 a.m.
p3-churchill	832 KB	Adobe Acrobat Docu...	19/01/2004 2:38 a.m.
30070372	337 KB	Adobe Acrobat Docu...	19/01/2004 2:30 a.m.
MIDrethink	28 KB	Microsoft Word Docu...	12/01/2004 4:55 a.m.
~$Drethink	1 KB	Microsoft Word Docu...	12/01/2004 4:55 a.m.
p370-ohshima	478 KB	Adobe Acrobat Docu...	5/01/2004 11:59 p.m.
notsure	370 KB	EndNote Library	1/01/2004 8:36 p.m.

FIGURE 9.12

Contents of a personal folder taken from a laptop

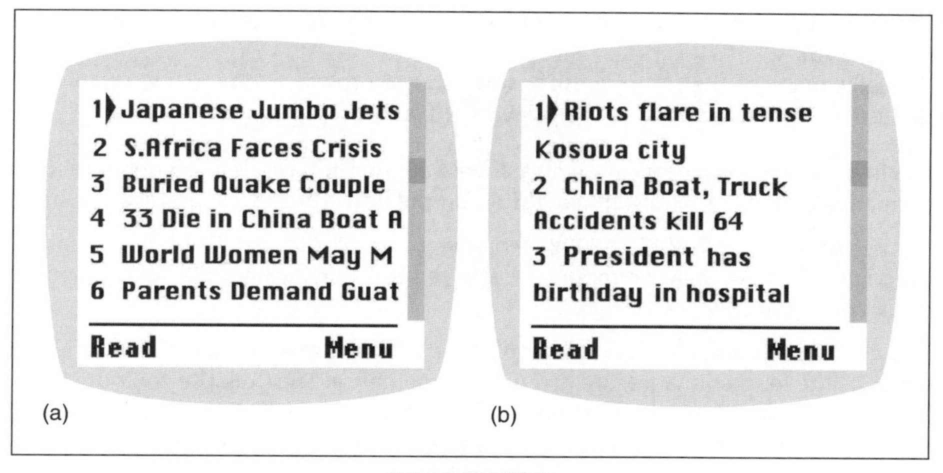

FIGURE 9.13

News headline presentation on the small screen: (a) horizontal, marquee scrolling approach (text moves to left to reveal full headline); (b) complete headlines presented using wrapped text. Second approach was seen to be more effective in user studies (Buchanan *et al.*, 2001)

BOX 9.7 INFORMATION VISUALIZATION AND MOBILES

Information visualization is a well-established discipline (Card *et al.*, 1999). Much work has been put into the use of highly graphical, sophisticated approaches to help the user make sense of vast sets of information. These graphical schemes have been applied to the fields of information retrieval and exploration in an attempt to overcome search and access problems on conventional, large-screen displays. For instance, the *Information Visualizer* allows users to manipulate an animated 3D categorical view of search results (Card *et al.*, 1991). Some visualization schemes may not be appropriate for small-screen devices: even if the display technology can deliver the high resolution required, the available screen space is not necessarily adequate for meaningful presentations and manipulation by the user.

However, adaptations of some of these approaches may be effective. So, if you are a small-screen content developer, it might pay to look at techniques proposed by researchers in this field. Figure 9.14, for example, shows an attempt at using the well-known *Starfield* querying method (Ahlberg and Shneiderman, 1994) on a PalmPilot (Dunlop and Davidson, 2000). The visualization is so called as it represents all the possibilities (perhaps hundreds or thousands) as points on a display space; filters can be applied to refine the set of possibilities to match the user's requirements. In the example, then, the user first selects the type of restaurant they are in interested in, leading to a map with points showing all restaurants; a further price-range filter is applied and this set is reduced.

Actually, many of the techniques for small-screen browse and search we've discussed make use of ideas developed in the infovis field, as these examples illustrate:

- The information visualization mantra: 'overview first-filter-details on demand' (Shneiderman, 1996). Accordion summarization on the PowerBrowser is an instance of this.
- Focus+context (Card *et al.*, 1999), allowing users to see detail while retaining an overview of the content is important. We've seen this in the 1.5D and 2D browsing cases, for example.
- Fish-eye lens (Furnas, 1986): one region of the display is magnified while others, on the edges of the lens, as it were, are given less prominence. The Collapse-to-Zoom browser is an example of this sort of scheme; as elements are removed, remaining portions are emphasized but the deleted components are still available as tabs on the edge of the screen. ➤

FIGURE 9.14

Starfield visualisation on a PDA (Dunlop and Davidson 2000). Restaurants are shown as small squares, their number whittled down after applying a price filter

9.5 MOBILE INFORMATION ECOLOGIES

If you look at the marketing that surrounds many mobile devices and applications, the message appears to be that by buying the product, you'll soon have everything you need in the palm of your hand. The device will deliver every conceivable service and it will always be connected to a high-bandwidth network. The mobile will supercharge your life – helping you to operate efficiently, juggling many tasks, in a fast-paced way.

But a much more realistic, healthy and profitable viewpoint, as we discussed in Chapter 2, is to see that mobiles are just part of a complex ecology within which they have to fit in.

9.5.1 FITTING IN

Mobiles will have to learn to play their part. But what will they have to fit in with?

With Other Devices

For many users, mobiles will not be the sole or even primary way to access digital information. There will be lots of alternatives, from conventional PCs at work and home to digital media centers in the sitting room. Mobiles will be used in conjunction with this ensemble of devices. Simple examples, like shopping mall photo printers that can create prints from images stored in a camera phone, already exist, of course. More elaborate device collaborations are likely if research lab visions come to fruition. Imagine, then, using your mobile as a sort of mouse for a large-screen in-street display – you point and select a particular option on the display by gesturing with your mobile in that direction.

With Physical Resources

People are object-oriented in outlook. Our experience of life is shaped and directed by the things that surround us. We'll use mobiles to capture information around us, using them to help us interrogate and understand our surroundings and to reflect on our experiences. Take a picture of a tourist spot you are standing in front of and a service returns related information (and photos other tourists have taken in the same spot in the past several years).

One technology which will become increasingly important in this linking together of the digital and physical worlds is RFID: tiny chips, secreted within almost any object, and that can wirelessly transmit their content to a scanning device. Scan a product you are thinking of buying, for instance, and receive current bid prices for the same item from an auction website. The Near Field Communication Forum is one group (made up of key industry players) working on standards to enable these sorts of interaction for mobile phones (NFC).

With Network Availability

Traditionally users have had to rely on a single network provider for their mobile connection. Being so locked in can lead to all forms of problems. Now, though, devices are beginning to be fitted with a range of network technologies – WiFi and Bluetooth being the most prominent – that will allow for more flexible information access. In addition, enormous on-board storage capabilities mean that much access will be of information stored locally on the device, and this content may have found its way onto the mobile not via a wireless connection but along a cable attaching it to another computing device such as a desktop PC.

With Varying Paces of Interaction

Think about these two different interactive system experiences: using a search engine on a desktop PC, and watching a television programe on an interactive TV device. In the first case, you will be interacting in a fast, dynamic way – you are in 'sit-forward' mode, eagerly engaging with the system. In the second situation, your mode is 'lean-back'; you are passive or involved in minimal interactions with the TV as the content flows over you. When mobile, the pace users will want to work at as they access and use information will vary. True, oftentimes they will need to interact in an urgent, quick way, but there will be lots of activities that are not time critical and that can be done in a more leisurely fashion.

A nice example of a more relaxed form of interaction is given by Christian Lindholm, one of the leading interaction designers in Nokia, now at Yahoo!, responsible for, amongst other things, their *LifeBlog* system which allows users to organize photos taken using a camera phone. Writing about how he found himself using his mobile, he says:

When I had some 'empty' moments I renamed pictures in LifeBlog, this kind of task takes only a small moment and once it is renamed it is searchable. I have always been of the opinion that the mobile internet strength lies in doing small tasks in idle time. Renaming pictures is a typical one. (Lindholm, 2004)

With the Context

The most obvious way a mobile can made to 'fit in' is to automatically adapt itself to take account of the situation it is being used in. These context-aware systems have been much pursued by research labs over the past decade.

BOX 9.8 NAVIGATION USING MUSIC (Warren *et al.*, 2005)

Personal portable music players are essential pieces of street equipment. While such devices have been available for over a quarter of a century, recently digital versions have emerged. These provide powerful onboard processing and integration with other computing resources via fixed and wireless connections. Commercial services are exploiting these innovations, providing, for instance, mobile online music purchase and graphical information to complement the audio stream.

But what about using them for providing navigation and context awareness by adapting the music the listener is hearing? The *Ontrack* prototype aims to help a pedestrian navigate to a target destination via calm feedback. The concept is illustrated in this use scenario:

Ben is going to meet a friend in a restaurant across town. After alighting from the tram station closest to the restaurant, he puts on his headphones and turns on his portable music player to hear a new song he's just downloaded. At the same time, he turns on the navigate-by-music feature; the restaurant location was copied from the email his friend sent him.

He's fairly certain of the direction to head, and as he moves off, the music playback is clear and strong, at a normal volume and through both headphones. As he ➤

approaches a crossroads, Ben perceives the music shifting slightly to his left, with the volume decreasing. He crosses the road and heads in that direction and the music is now balanced and the volume returns to normal. As he walks further along the street, he notices the music beginning to fade, the volume is decreasing; he looks around and notices he's just walked past his destination.

For a full realization of the concept the mobile has to be able to determine both the location of the user (via GPS) and the way they are orienting themselves using advanced compasses.

In building this system we were focusing on navigation from and to a fixed point, but the approach is applicable in a wide range of route following and target location tasks. For instance, a *tourist service* might guide a listener around an interesting route while they listen to either their own music or a commentary. A *find-a-friend service* could lead the listener to rendezvous with a nearby acquaintance. In a gaming context, these people would be 'targets' as in Crabtree *et al.* (2004); again the audio content – a gaming soundtrack, or communications with other players – could be seamlessly integrated with navigation information. Meanwhile, a *child monitoring system* could act as a reassurance aid: a parent sits in the park, reading their magazine, listening to music as their young children play. The music grows softer as the children move further away; when the volume is at an uncomfortably *low* level, the parent looks up and calls them back. ■

One of the most widely considered contextual factors has been location, where the system can make use of information about where it is in geographical terms or relative to other objects in the environment (see Box 9.8 for one use of location information). If you're thinking about context-based services, though, it might prove valuable to widen your thinking to move from the 'where' and to consider other 'Ws' (Abowd and Mynatt, 2000):

- *Who* – e.g. who else is in the vicinity
- *When* – how the user's needs are related to the passage of time
- *What* and *why* – how users' activities and motivations can be assessed and exploited (though this may be hard to do effectively – be cautious!).

BOX 9.9 WARNING: AUTOMATIC ADAPTATION IS DIFFICULT TO DO SUCCESSFULLY

Second-guessing the user is hard. Many attempts have been tried – from photocopiers that adapt their default settings to reflect the most frequently used print options, to cash machines that give users cash withdrawal options based on the average ➤

of the previous set of transactions – all well intentioned, with the unintended result of frustrated users.

And the frustration continues as mobile designers exhibit their virtuoso skills. A version of the iPod can sense when the headphones are removed from the socket. When this happens, the device automatically pauses the playback. A great feature: the user isn't listening any more, so save power, and when they want to resume listening the track will be in just the right place. The socket is so sensitive, though, that some people's device switches into pause mode at the slightest jiggle of the cable – push the pod into the pocket and it pauses; jog too vigorously and you are in pause mode . . . ■

9.5.2 CASE STUDY: THE LAID-BACK SEARCH TOOL

One mobile-based system that illustrates ecological thinking is the laid-back search scheme (Jones *et al.*, 2003b). It uses a mobile with other types of computing devices to offer a range of information access experiences to the user.

Background Information Seeking

As we have seen, mobile handheld devices can be used to provide *online* search access, and clearly these services may be useful, especially to meet specific, focused and urgent information needs. However, even when the interfaces for these search engines are well adapted for the small screen, these approaches can ask much of the user who has to engage in a cognitively demanding 'foreground' information-seeking process

Sometimes users will find these burdens unhelpful and inappropriate – they don't need immediate, fast responses to their queries; instead they want to carry out the information seeking in, as it were, the background.

Barry Brown and colleagues carried out an interesting diary-style study (Brown *et al.*, 2000) into the types of information people capture during their working day. One of their findings was that people make notes which they follow up on a later occasion or use in some other task, such as document preparation.

So, imagine some situations, like these two, where notes on memo pads, on scraps of paper or in a diary are used to drive future computer-based searching sessions:

- Sitting in a meeting, a colleague makes a brief mention of some competitor's new product. Josh wants to find out more after the meeting.
- Over a cup of coffee, friends Rob and Suzy chat about resorts they might like to visit during their next summer holiday. They make a list of possibilities and want to find out some prices and options later.

Unlike the foreground information seeking, the user doesn't necessarily want to use a search engine immediately, *in situ*. Rather, they want to carry on with the main activity they're involved in (say listening to a colleague).

Brown's work also suggested that information capture tools should help users to organize and make sense of their notes, as well as providing reminders to use these entries in the future. Current background search tools – that's pen-and-paper, really – seem to fall far short of these ideals. Many noted search inspirations are not going to be followed up: firstly, perhaps the bits of paper are lost before the user gets back to their desktop PC; alternatively, when they return to their PC they might not be able to read the scrawling handwriting of their own notes, and even if the notes are legible they may not remember the significance of the proposed search.

Capturing Background Searches

The laid-back search tool was developed to complement conventional online, fast-paced searching with a slower, more reflective scheme. The user enters search terms on an offline handheld computer. They can record simple keyword searches and use the 'advanced search' interface to restrict the scope of the search to a particular website, etc. The handheld application performs a check for duplicate entries and allows the complete set of queries to be viewed and edited.

The handheld, then, gives the user greater support for query noting than when they simply use paper-and-pen. However, as with paper-and-pen, the user's main focus – such as listening to a talk – is not greatly disrupted while their search need is captured. When the first prototype of the system was shown to users, one missing feature they identified was a way of integrating it with the other handheld applications they used regularly. The next prototype, then, provided options to scan all of the user's handheld notes, calendar and task entries and automatically extract words and phrases that have been marked by the user for possible querying. The user can select from the extracted terms and add these to any explicitly entered queries (Jones *et al.*, 2006).

Processing the Captured Queries

When the handheld is reconnected to the PC – by a cradle or wirelessly – all of the queries captured offline are sent to a search engine. For each query, the search engine returns a list of result web pages. Each of these web pages is also retrieved and processed to download the web pages they in turn reference. This 'crawling' process continues recursively to a depth specified by the user. When pages are retrieved, they are copied to the handheld computer, so they can be available offline. In this way, then, the user's searches are guaranteed to be performed, even if the user has forgotten about the exact notes they made, or has no time to do the searches manually.

Using the Search Results

After processing the queries, the results are made available to the user in four ways that differ in terms of the device used to access the information, the need for an Internet connection, and the degree of interactivity involved between the user and the system.

1. **Offline on the handheld computer.** Users can view a list of all the queries recorded – along with the date and time each was input – and access the downloaded cached result sets and associated web pages. Millions of handheld users are already using services such as Avantgo (`www.avantgo.com`) to read web pages offline, or listening to downloaded audio broadcasts via so-called pod casting software; the laid-back approach extends this popular activity to searching.
2. **Online on the handheld computer.** If the user has a wireless connection available, they can access any pages not downloaded during the processing stage, and perform further searches stimulated by the cached results.
3. **Online on a desktop computer.** A purpose-built browser for the desktop allows the user to view the handheld-captured queries, access the result sets produced by these queries, and carry out further searches online, thereby interactively refining the results of the initial queries.

4. **Background, ambient use of search results on the desktop and large interactive displays.** The system makes use of the ideas behind Andruid Kerne's Collage Machine (Kerne, 2000) to display the results of queries gathered via the handheld over time on the desktop or large interactive displays. Images are extracted from the web pages relating to all of the search queries, and are collated together. A user can select any image – for example, by clicking it on the desktop or touching the large-screen display with a pen stylus – and the relevant web page is then displayed. Again, the aim was to explore the benefits of a 'calmer' approach to search that does not demand instant attention.

Related Ecological-minded Mobiles

The laid-back scheme supports people in their background information seeking – in terms of the way they both capture queries and later review these queries and the results. In contrast, other researchers have proposed approaches where the system, rather than the user, works in the background.

For instance, Aridor *et al.* (2001) have demonstrated an offline/online handheld search system that 'pushes' information from a PC-based intelligent agent to a handheld device. This system attempts to use knowledge about what the user is interested in to find content they may later want to view on the handheld.

The XLibris system (Schilit *et al.*, 1999) is a sophisticated mobile electronic document reading support tool. While the user annotates the text with a stylus, the system generates links to additional documents that might interest the reader. This then supports searches focused around documents; the laid-back tool, on the other hand, is about information seeking that arises more widely within the mobile context. Some other systems also looked at such a linking of physical contexts while mobile with later online information access. The InfoPoint (Kohtake *et al.*, 2001), for example, is a handheld device that allows users to capture information from objects tagged with a visual code. This information can be used later for electronic content access when the user returns to their workstation.

The laid-back tool combines different computing devices – the mobile, desktop PC and large displays – in an asynchronous way. That is to say, the devices are used separately, at different times. Ways of combining handhelds and PCs synchronously – together, at the same time – have been creatively considered by Brad Myers and his *Pebbles* project, with applications such as the slideshow commander that allows a user to use their handheld to control a presentation held on a desktop computer (Myers, 2001).

BOX 9.10 IMPROVING SOCIETY THE MOBILE WAY

While many parts of the world take always-on broadband access to the Internet for granted, in other places there are no connections whatsoever. The delayed, batched processing style of information access seen in the laid-back system (Section 9.5.2) can improve this situation, as the *Wizzy Digital Courier* in South Africa illustrates (Lindow, 2004). Children use their school computers to write emails and compose Internet search requests. These are then copied over onto a USB memory stick and transported, possibly by foot, to a central computer miles away, that will process them overnight. At the same time, the results from the previous batch are copied back to the stick and returned to the eagerly awaiting schoolchildren. ■

9.5.3 PEER-TO-PEER SCHEMES

Up to now, the sorts of information access we've been describing have assumed a traditional client–server model. That is, the mobile device – the client – requests information from a server. The relationship, then, is not an equal one, with the mobile being reliant on a centralized infrastructure.

A quite different model – one that gained some notoriety due to its use by millions of people to share music over the Internet – is peer-to-peer (p2p). Here, every device is a server as well as a recipient of information. To understand the approach, consider a file-sharing application of p2p. When a user wants to find a particular file, instead of the request going to just one potential source (as in the client–server model), their device contacts several servers. If any of these can satisfy the request, the quest is complete; however, if the information cannot be found, each of these devices is in turn connected to a number of others so the search can spread outwards along the network.

Techniques are being developed to allow mobiles to act in p2p ways, too. When these become widely available, whole new forms of mobile information access will become possible. Think then of a situation where millions of users in a city are carrying around mobile information servers – devices with enormous storage capacities and the ability to communicate with others in an ad-hoc, spontaneous way.

Let's take a specific example. You are at a major tourist location and want to find out some facts about it. You open up your mobile device, launch a search engine and enter a query. It's likely that other people close by you have a similar need and have already accessed interesting information. So, in a p2p way, the search system could first search this local cache of information. To do this, your mobile would connect to a set of others close by and send requests for information to each of these. These mobiles, in turn, could connect to others near them and propagate your request quickly to many devices in the vicinity.

BOX 9.11 P2P IN TRAFFIC

There are lots of potentially useful services that could be supplied using p2p technology between vehicles – for example, a car heading from the direction you are traveling toward might share data on the traffic situation ahead. There are, though, more esoteric applications being considered. Take, for instance, *Mobile HocMan* (Esbjörnsson *et al.*, 2004). Bikers – who are a social, tribal lot – were used in a study involving mobile devices fitted to their motorcycles. These devices could broadcast biker-authored sound clips and web pages to other users as they passed each other. The aim was to enhance the sense of community and enjoyment in riding. Or, consider the car-to-car game described in Brunnberg (2004). Here, drivers can send virtual electronic pulses, throw virtual sludge and cast spells on each other via wireless LAN connections. ■

SUMMARY

In Chapter 1, we looked at the question of whether mobiles will have a role as information appliances: the answer is *yes*; anyone doubting this only needs to consider the commuters who are reading novels on their phone screens as they journey home from work. Even those not wanting to peruse such extensive content will be interested in accessing shorter, more targeted information – emails, updated blog entries and the like. Research from a pre-mobile era indicates that users will be able to cope with this sort of content on the small screen.

With the advances in mobile technology, from greater network capacities to higher-resolution screens, many content providers will look at how their offerings can be made available to mobile users. In doing this, they will need to adapt their design ideas: content cheaply repurposed for the small screen, with limited accommodation for the new users needs, will fail, badly. Users need to be given ways of assessing and reading content which don't involve excessive scrolling or page-to-page navigation. Automatic techniques from text summarization to zoomable interfaces can help.

In the western world, mobiles will not be the predominant way users access information in the future, though, and designers need to learn how to ensure their services fit in with other resources at the users' disposal. Conventional mobile models (such as client–server and the use of a single network provider) are likely to be complemented with more sophisticated, flexible schemes.

WORKSHOP QUESTIONS

- When you're accessing the web from a conventional, large-screen computer, what are the most frustrating aspects of page design? What do you find most effective? How could these experiences help you if you are designing for the mobile net?
- Show a colleague some example notes you've made recently (say in a seminar or meeting). Discuss the characteristics of these notes and they way you went about making them. Next, look at some of their notes and discuss these. Discuss the sorts of function and forms of interaction you would like to see supported in a mobile note-taking system.
- What information might you want to capture using a mobile device and how could this be used with other computing resources?
- We have mentioned a few potential peer-to-peer mobile applications. Discuss others, writing some scenarios of use. Say why you think these innovations might make the user's life better in some way.

DESIGNER TIPS

- *Browsing and search mechanisms which break with the conventional, desktop experience may be initially harder for users to use. Don't be too quick to write off your innovations: ensure users are given time to understand and play with the scheme. Remember, they've had possibly many years with approaches you're comparing yours with.*
- *Portals and other ways of packaging content are useful. Consider particularly the qualities of channels and RSS. But avoid restricting the user – give them freedom to explore more widely.*
- *Keep track of the research going on in information visualization. This discipline is all about making sense of vast data sets in screens too small to display it all meaningfully. In the mobile case, almost every information space is too big for the small screens involved.*
- *Zooming interfaces can provide an effective and fun experience (see the next chapter for an application to mobile photo browsing).*
- *Start thinking about how your information services can be ecological – how could you use the flexible network connections, capture and storage capabilities that are becoming available?*

CHAPTER 10
BEYOND TEXT – USING IMAGES ON MOBILE DEVICES

OVERVIEW

10.1. Introduction
10.2. Ethnography
10.3. Finding photos
10.4. Browsing photos
10.5. Downscaling case study
10.6. Advanced technology
10.7. What are photos for?
10.8. Looking to the future

KEY POINTS

- Rarely does anyone take the time to organize and annotate photographs; it is likely that this trend will continue for digital photographs.
- Searching photographic collections is hard, more so on smaller screens where less detail is apparent.
- Mobile devices can contain many thousands of images, which requires highly scalable search solutions.
- Besides recording an event or person, a key use of photographs is to maintain social contacts.

- **The introduction of communication devices with imaging has created new types of application (e.g. storytelling) that would not have occurred with camera-and-PC-style digital imaging.**
- **Simultaneous audio and image recording can be used to give new purpose to images or simply to augment the experience of seeing an image.**

10.1 INTRODUCTION

2004 was an important year for mobile computing and photography – it was the year in which camera-phone sales overtook the sales of digital cameras. According to iSuppli (`www.isuppli.com`), 100 million camera-phones were bought in 2004 as opposed to just 20 million digital cameras. As the technology improves, we will, no doubt, have handsets capable of taking multi-megapixel images which are stored on gigabyte-sized long-term storage. It is possible to take images of any aspect of your life and carry these images with you anywhere you take your cellular handset.

The great benefit of camera-phones is that they have communication capabilities at their core, so sharing photographs should be straightforward. Cellular service providers are hoping that Multimedia Messaging Service (MMS) – the standard way to send a picture from a cellular handset – will prove as popular as SMS.

Of course, photographs are only the beginning of rich media content. As 3G becomes widespread, we are starting to see video transmissions, music files and even virtual environments turning up on handsets.

In this chapter, however, we will focus exclusively on static images. There are several reasons for this; most importantly, as camera-phones have been around for a few years now, there is more research relating to their use than any other media type. The approach presented below is equally applicable to other types of rich media, however.

10.2 ETHNOGRAPHY

Rather than rush headlong into the excitement of counting megapixels, it is worth standing back and taking a look at what people do with paper-based photographs. Sure, these new devices will allow people to do things with photographs that were not previously possible: for instance, should we be recording audio along with the photograph? What about text annotations? Cataloging for albums or sharing images with others? However, before we look at any of these advanced features, we need to make sure that the systems we produce now are able to support how users work with photographs currently.

If you have read the earlier chapters of this book, you will know that the way to answer these questions is to conduct some form of ethnography. Fortunately, a lot of work has already gone into analyzing what people do with paper-based photographs and, to a lesser extent, what happens to digital photographs.

10.2.1 WHERE HAVE ALL THE PHOTOGRAPHS GONE?

It would be nice to believe that we are all highly organized beings, who work efficiently and are in control of our lives. How many of us fall into that category, however? When it comes to collections of photographs, how organized would you say you were? Are all your photos neatly annotated and stored in albums, resting on a shelf in chronological order? If photos are not stored in this way, then how do people organize them?

A study undertaken by Frohlich *et al.* (2002) produced some alarming results. They undertook an ethnographic study funded by HP to answer these questions. Essentially, most people do nothing to organize their photographs – the time required to organize them into albums is simply too great. One of the families studied had 20 years' worth of photographs in a drawer under a sofa-bed!

Some people did manage to organize photographs for particular events, such as birthdays or weddings. Unlike the organization of regular photographs, participants were keen to work on these 'special' projects. (One can speculate that, in this instance, the task is creative and the photos are a single part of the wider task; organizing photographs for the sake of having organized photographs is obviously a less attractive task.) So most photographs stay in the packets in which they were returned from the processing laboratory and these packets end up distributed around the house. Besides the problems of organization, users also confessed a tendency to forget the locations and identities of people from older photographs.

Rodden (2002) also conducted an extensive survey of what people do with their photographs. The findings were similar to those in Frohlich's study, with people tending to keep photographs in their original packets and only occasionally making an album of a special event.

So, from our ethnography, we can conclude that any system which relies on users explicitly labeling photographs (or making any other sort of meta-data annotation) is unlikely to succeed. However, it would be great to provide some way of remembering who is in a given photograph.

One aspect unique to Rodden's study was her interest in how people used (or searched) their collections. She discovered that people often searched for an individual photograph. To aid their search, they would remember something about the packet the photograph was in, or would remember a vague point in time when the image was taken. Of course, if images had been moved from packets, or the packets were out of chronological order, these search recollections were useless.

Another class of search activity was finding a group of photographs all containing the same element, usually a particular person. This was often an impossible task and required a full search of the entire collection.

Clearly, from Rodden's research, any application to support digital photography will have to support:

- Searching for an individual image
- Searching for a special event
- Searching for a group of photos containing a common element.

To follow up on these ideas, she asked users what features they would want from photograph software to support these activities.

- The first requirement was for folders which are used to group photographs of a particular event. It is also necessary for the folders to be arranged chronologically.
- A slide show facility was also highly rated as a way to share the images.

- Text annotations were also considered useful, but there was no consensus on how they might be implemented.
- To support searching, users wanted to be able to see all the contents of a folder simultaneously. This should be supported by a rapid-scan facility 'like video fast-forward' to rapidly search the archive.
- Chronological ordering was also considered important, more so than being able to search for a given date (the human sense of time being more relative than absolute).

More importantly were the features users did not value. None of the users (except an art student and an architecture student) wanted to search on image attributes like color and composition. Also, searching for similarity in images was not valued, as users reckoned that similar images would be taken at the same time, so chronological ordering would be sufficient to support this type of search.

10.2.2 DIGITAL ETHNOGRAPHY

If we know what people do with paper-based photographs, what do they do once they are in the digital domain?

Frohlich *et al.* (2002) continued their study on paper-based photography into how people used digital photographs on a PC. Interestingly, they did not see evidence of any organizational scheme on the PCs. They attributed this primarily to the fact that digital photography had not yet replaced paper-based photography; families were simply not prepared to store their most precious memories in something as ephemeral as hard disk data. Instead, the hard disk was used as a dumping ground for images, which were then sifted for forwarding to other friends or family members.

Like Frohlich, Rodden continued her research into the usage of digital images. She discovered that, although users of digital images put no more effort into organizing their photographs than they did with paper-based images – when the camera's memory filled up, the photos were dumped into a folder which may or may not be labeled – they felt that their digital image collections were better organized. Rodden attributes this to having all the images in one place (no more individual packets around the house), in folders (which roughly correspond to events) and in chronological order (generated for-free by the PC file system).

So, bearing in mind that we know people want to search for events, groups and single images, how can we build software to support these activities?

10.3 FINDING PHOTOS

Finding text is easy – Google can search 8 billion web pages for a given phrase in less than a second. This is possible because written language was developed as a concise abstract way of sharing knowledge. Searching photographs this way is impossible, as there is no simple automatic way to extract meaning from the image – you may be able to find an image of your Aunt Lucy rapidly, but your computer doesn't know what Aunt Lucy looks like, or even what an 'aunt' is. The information is implicit, which is of no use to the computer.

To compensate for this lack of explicit information, we can ask the user to annotate each photograph with typed text. Once the annotations are complete, we can then search the text relating to the image. Of course, this scheme will work only if users go to the effort of labeling photographs. While this may happen for professional photographic agencies, we know from Frohlich and Rodden that amateur photographers are unlikely to put in the effort to annotate their photographs.

(This is further exacerbated on mobile devices where text entry is complicated by limited input functionality.) As expected, users did not annotate their digital photographs any more than printed photographs. While a user might label a folder the image is stored in, individual image names remained largely unaltered.

The PhotoFinder system from Kang and Shneiderman (2000) goes some way to alleviating this problem by allowing users to drag 'canned' annotations onto a photograph (see Figure 10.1). These annotations may be taken from the user's address book, so that they can easily label photographic subjects. This solution seems like an ideal way to address the problem of forgetting the names of people in photographs (reported by users in Rodden's study). However, it's not clear how easily this solution will transfer to camera-phones that don't support this type of 'dragging' interaction.

FIGURE 10.1

Dragging an annotation from the box on the left allows members of an image to be tagged with meta-data without any typing

The good news is that meta-data need not be entered explicitly. Mobile devices, and cellular handsets in particular, have meta-data available to them from other sources. We shall investigate the application of these below. Before we do that, it's worth noting that using the image data directly (i.e. the pixel values of the image) is of little benefit in finding images. Rodden *et al.* (2001) found that searching for objects grouped by similar attributes (e.g. a lot of green in the image) was less useful than searching for images arranged around some meta-data category.

10.3.1 META-DATA

The term 'meta-data' refers to data about data, in this case data about photographs. Meta-data is essential in searching for images, as it gives context to an image that is otherwise meaningless to a computer. Below we discuss some of the forms of meta-data that could be used.

Time

As part of the Exif format (Exif, 1998) for storing digital images, digital cameras automatically record the time a photograph is taken. Intuitively, we would expect that ordering photographs according to time would help users locate them. Research from Graham *et al.* (2002) confirms that time does, indeed, help users locate photographs. In fact, it's impossible to find a photo browser that doesn't allow users to order their photograph collection according to time. More sophisticated systems, however, try to automatically extract 'events' from the collection by spotting periods of time when more photographs were taken than usual; for example, Loui and Savakis (2003) report a system that automatically generates digital 'albums' by spotting clusters of photographs taken over a given timeline.

Location Data

One obvious way to search for photographs is according to location. Using a GPS system in conjunction with a digital camera allows us to accurately record where a particular photograph was taken. Toyama *et al.* (2003), for example, report a photo management system which they created to use with GPS-enabled cameras. The accompanying photograph management software allows users to browse their collections on a map showing where each photograph was taken.

Diary Data

Besides being a camera and a phone, camera-phones are also diaries. In other words, they can know where we are at a given time and with whom we'll be meeting. While it's a pain to fill in this type of meta-data for photo-organizing software, many of us are motivated to fill it into a diary as an aid in organizing our lives. So, if we take a photograph when our diary says we are 'Meeting with Aunt Lucy in Darkest Peru', then the handset could automatically attach 'Aunt Lucy' and 'Darkest Peru' as meta-data to the image. To date, we haven't found a system that exploits this type of information.

10.3.2 META-DATA MANAGEMENT

A project from the Helsinki Institute for Information Technology and the University of California at Berkeley has been looking at tying together all these different threads of meta-data and allowing users to review the inferences the system is making (Sarvas *et al.*, 2004). The system automatically records location, time and user data as one might expect, but then compares these readings with values in a central server to see whether any further meta-data is available. The idea is that a lazy user can exploit the efforts of a user willing to enter the meta-data. However, before any inferred data is attached to the image, the photographer is first asked for verification. The process is neatly summarized in Figure 10.2.

10.4 BROWSING PHOTOS

Given the meta-data available, how do we facilitate someone rapidly browsing or searching through thousands of photographs on a screen smaller than the size of a single standard print? Well, from the ethnographies on photographers, time is seen as a key way in which people think about and organize their photographs. Ordering chronologically would therefore seem like a good place to start. (This is fortuitous, as all current digital cameras support time-stamping.) Spatial and other forms of meta-data will all help in locating an image, but should not serve as the primary interface for a general photograph browser.

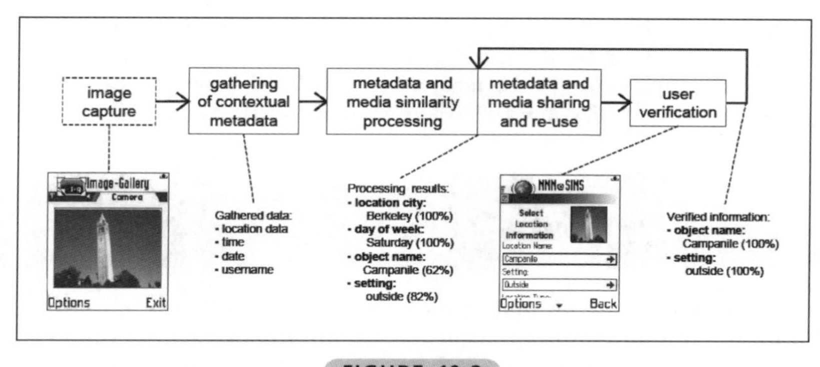

FIGURE 10.2

The process of inferring data from images taken by other people

So having decided that we wish to display images chronologically, how can they be effectively displayed on a small screen?

EXERCISE 10.1 PHOTOGRAPHIC TIMELINES

We know that people think about their collections in terms of time: either absolute time, where day, hours and minutes are provided, or time in terms of a series of events. Given this information, how would you go about designing an interface to a photographic collection on a small screen? Is a simple timeline enough? How would you cluster images? What information do you need to give on screen besides the photographs? ■

10.4.1 TIMELINE

As Harada *et al.* (2004) report, when getting feedback on their timeline system, it is essential to provide the users with a wide context of photographs; showing a few on the screen is insufficient. A naive start would therefore be to shrink all the photos to a smaller size and display as many of them as possible in a grid on the screen. This is, in fact, the approach taken by most contemporary software for mobile devices. The details may vary – the iPod photo has a 5 × 5 grid on a two-inch screen, while ACDSee for PocketPC uses a 3 × 3 grid on a 3.7-inch screen – but the interaction is the same. We shall shortly investigate the effectiveness of this solution.

10.4.2 TREEMAPS

Khella and Bederson (2004) have developed a PocketPC version of the excellent PhotoMesa desktop image browser. The system works by showing a small thumbnail of every image stored on the device, but laid out as a treemap and not in a simple grid. Images are grouped in the treemap depending on the folder in which they are stored. Clicking a group expands the individual images to fill the screen, and selecting a thumbnail expands the thumbnail to a full image. These expansions are smoothly animated to preserve the users' context within the application: in other words each screen is not suddenly replaced with the next, which has been shown to lead to user confusion (Combs and Bederson, 1999). The interface is shown in Figure 10.3.

BOX 10.1 TREEMAPS

Treemaps were developed by Ben Shneiderman as an efficient way of visualizing hierarchical data. This technique has been applied to photographs, stock markets, Usenet groups, hard disks, etc. – in fact, any form of hierarchical data you can think of. There are variations on the technique to optimize it for different application areas, but essentially the visualization attempts to display every data item on screen simultaneously. The size of each item varies depending on the user's criteria – for example, in the stock market visualization, the area used to display information about each individual company is directly proportional to the company's value. A well-designed treemap is an astoundingly effective tool. The potential problem with using them for photographs is that there is no intrinsic 'value' in the photograph to determine the relative size at which the photographs should be displayed.

To find out more about treemaps, check out the following site:
`http://www.cs.umd.edu/hcil/treemap-history/` ■

Sadly, in user tests, the browser did not perform quantitatively better than a standard thumbnail browser (ACDSee in this case). However, users' subjective experience was much more positive, enjoying the zooming aspect of the interface and the treemap layout.

One area for concern with Pocket PhotoMesa is its scalability. The first image in Figure 10.3 shows the interface working with 110 images. The authors concede that the interface will not scale much beyond that, but justify their decision by stating that mobile devices do not have a storage capacity much greater. This may have been true at the time the system was developed, but since that time devices such as the iPod photo have come to market: the iPod can hold 25 000 images!

10.4.3 RSVP

The approach taken by the iPod to managing so many photographs is an interesting blend of solutions. One area where the iPod has always shone is the tight integration between the mobile device, the desktop computer and the online iTunes music store. For the iPod photo, iTunes synchronizes the photos from the user's iPhoto collection (iPhoto is the standard photograph management software for Macintosh OS-X). So, any albums or rolls created in iPhoto appear on the iPod in much the same way as song playlists appear. Selecting a group of photos fills the screen with a 5 × 5 grid of thumbnails. Using the jog wheel, the user can scroll to the desired images as they would on any standard thumbnail browser – rather disappointingly, there is no smooth transition between thumbnail screens to maintain context as one finds in, say, PhotoMesa. Selecting an

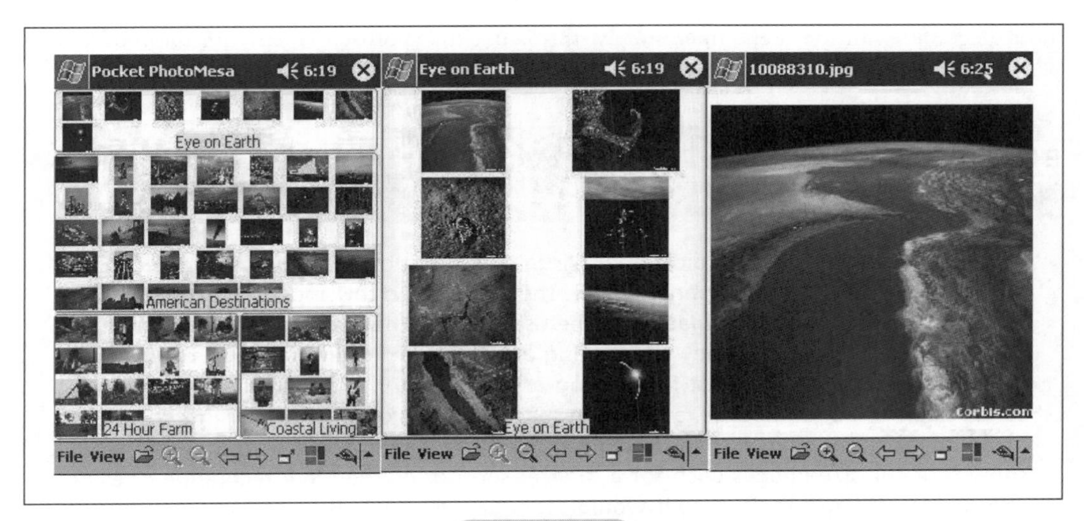

FIGURE 10.3

The PocketPC version of PhotoMesa showing all images simultaneously

individual image, however, allows users to view images according to an RSVP paradigm – turning the scroll wheel scrolls users through full-size images (see Box 10.2).

In an effort to determine how effective an RSVP approach would be in browsing image collections on a variety of devices, Spence *et al.* (2004) conducted a major multi-factor evaluation. They set users the task of identifying a single target image from a collection of 64. Users were presented with images at different rates, on different screen sizes (to simulate a PC screen, a PDA screen and a cellular handset screen) and in different layouts. Their were several significant findings from their experiment:

- Users had great trouble in identifying images properly if they were shown for less than 100 ms.
- Screen size did not affect the task error rate.
- Users preferred mixed-mode presentation.

The first finding was universal across all modes of display – the human visual system cannot parse images properly if they are replaced more often than every tenth of a second. In these experiments, the visualization rate was under the control of the system. With the iPod photo, the user can dynamically alter the presentation rate using the scroll wheel, allowing them to find the presentation rate which best suits their current conditions.

Interesting, for designers of mobile devices, was the finding that the screen size did not effect task performance. It is not clear whether this result was due to the nature of the task chosen by the researchers, but this finding could be seen to support the perceived suitability of RSVP to devices with small screens.

Taking the last point, the researchers in this experiment created a hybrid mode between 'pure' RSVP (one image per screen) and thumbnail presentations (multiple images per screen). They found that a mixed-mode approach of rapidly presenting screens containing four thumbnail images proved most successful with the users. Interestingly, this is not the approach taken with the iPod photo, where the thumbnail mode remains distinct from the RSVP mode.

BOX 10.2 RSVP

RSVP is an acronym for Rapid Serial Visual Presentation, a visualization technique developed by de Bruijn and Spence (2000). The idea behind this approach to visualization is to throw snippets of information at the user to give them an overview of the entire contents of whatever it is they are looking at – think of flicking through the pages of a book in a bookstore or fast-forwarding a video DVD. More formally, the idea is to compress information in time rather than space. In terms of image browsing, this would mean that, rather than display four thumbnails on screen for a second, RSVP would show four full-size images each for a quarter-second. As the RSVP technique does not rely on screen size for efficacy, it would seem like an ideal visualization technique for use on small-screen devices.

RSVP works due to the staggering visual processing capability of our brains. Current estimates by cognitive psychologists, e.g. Zeki (1993), speculate that about half the celebral cortex of all primates is used to process visual information. In computing terms, this is of the order of several gigabits per second. ■

Although the results from RSVP look promising, the results reported were derived from a single task of looking for a target image among 64 possibilities. This is obviously not representative in terms of collection size or task domain (we have already seen that people wish to find events and collections of images containing the same person). We look forward to future studies which investigate the applicability of RSVP to searching large collections of photographs.

10.4.4 SPEED DEPENDENT AUTOMATIC ZOOMING

Another approach to visualization on the small screen is that of SDAZ (Speed Dependent Automatic Zooming) (Igarashi and Hinckley, 2000). Again, this technique was developed for desktop machines but, we believe, it has great potential for mobile devices. It was originally developed by Igarashi and Hinckley to overcome the problems of losing context when working with large documents on PC monitors. Context losses fall into two categories:

- Forcing users to shift focus from the area of interest in the document and the scrollbars at the edge of the screen.
- Having disproportionately large movements in the document for relatively small movements of the scrollbar, which leads to visual blurring.

Of course, these problems are greatly multiplied on small-screen devices, where the amount of screen real-estate not only forces more scrolling, but the size of the scrollbars is greatly reduced. (Having small scroll-bars was a huge usability problem on small screens, as reported in Chapter 8.)

The approach Igarashi and Hinckley took to eliminate these problems was to automatically link the zoom level to the rate at which the document was being scrolled. For example, consider Figure 10.4(a), which shows part of a document at maximum zoom. As the user starts to scroll down the document, the zoom level reduces, as in Figure 10.4(b), so that more of the document is visible on the screen. The subjective effect is like 'flying' over the document, where the faster you scroll the more your altitude increases. (If you're familiar with Grand Theft Auto, a similar mechanism is used to link the map scale to driving speed.) Despite being visually appealing, the results from user evaluations were disappointing. For the tasks set, SDAZ was no better, and occasionally worse, than existing techniques.

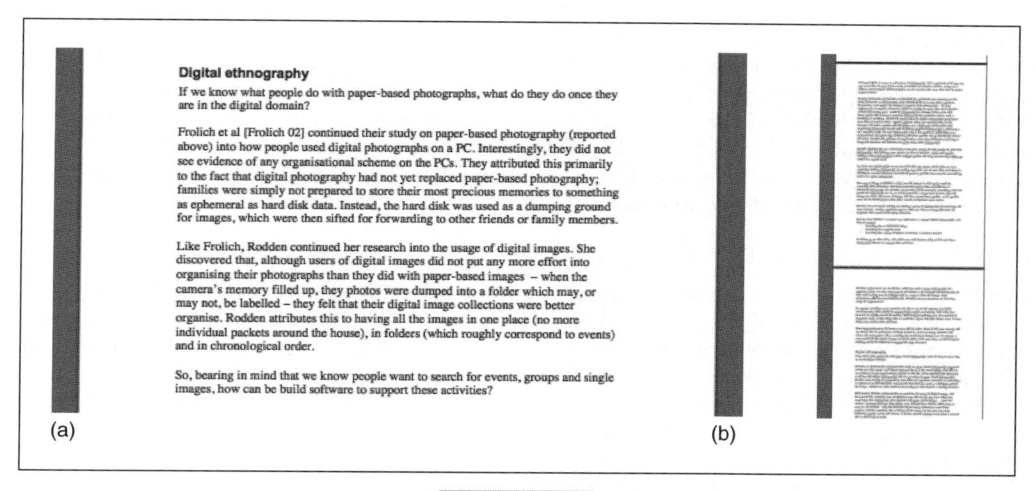

Digital ethnography

If we know what people do with paper-based photographs, what do they do once they are in the digital domain?

Frolich et al [Frolich 02] continued their study on paper-based photography (reported above) into how people used digital photographs on a PC. Interestingly, they did not see evidence of any organisational scheme on the PCs. They attributed this primarily to the fact that digital photography had not yet replaced paper-based photography; families were simply not prepared to store their most precious memories to something as ephemeral as hard disk data. Instead, the hard disk was used as a dumping ground for images, which were then sifted for forwarding to other friends or family members.

Like Frolich, Rodden continued her research into the usage of digital images. She discovered that, although users of digital images did not put any more effort into organising their photographs than they did with paper-based images – when the camera's memory filled up, they photos were dumped into a folder which may, or may not, be labelled – they felt that their digital image collections were better organise. Rodden attributes this to having all the images in one place (no more individual packets around the house), in folders (which roughly correspond to events) and in chronological order.

So, bearing in mind that we know people want to search for events, groups and single images, how can be build software to support these activities?

(a)

(b)

FIGURE 10.4

(a) The document at full zoom; (b) as the user starts to scroll, the zoom level is automatically reduced

Undaunted by this result, Cockburn and Savage (2003) improved on the original SDAZ algorithms, producing a highly responsive system with improved scrolling. They conducted evaluations for two application domains; namely document viewing and map viewing (the first testing vertical scrolling, the second testing vertical and horizontal scrolling). For document scrolling, users were, on average, 22% faster when finding a target text than they were with a commercially available document viewer. For the map application, users were 43% faster. Added to these quantitative measures, qualitative feedback from the users heavily favored the SDAZ techniques.

Given this successful set of results, we were inspired to adapt SDAZ techniques to scrolling through photos on the small screen. At least, that is what we thought we would do. It turns out that we had to think of a lot more than just the screen size. The physical diversity of camera-phones and camera-PDAs is truly staggering. This applies not just to the dimensions of the screen, but also to the physical input mechanisms available: some have touchscreens, others have jog-wheels and some even have tilt-based interfaces. Therefore our final, modified SDAZ algorithm would need to cope with diverse input devices modifying images on a screen that is as little as 5% of the size the algorithm was originally developed for!

We do not claim to have a sure-fire way of converting interaction techniques from desktop to mobile systems – due to the inherent diversity, it is unlikely that a prescriptive technique is possible. However, we will take you through the steps we followed as an example of how one might approach this type of problem.

10.5 DOWNSCALING CASE STUDY

10.5.1 ARRANGING PHOTOS

The first decision we needed to make was the order in which photographs would appear on the screen. We could have a two-dimensional browsing scheme, with photographs laid out in a grid. Alternatively, we could present photographs linearly and stick with one-dimensional scrolling. As the two-dimensional system had proved so dramatically effective in Cockburn and Savage's work, we tried hard to think of a meaningful organizational scheme that would result in a regular grid of photographs. From the ethnographic studies reviewed already, particularly Rodden *et al.* (2001) and Frohlich *et al.* (2002), we knew that most users favored a chronological layout. We therefore produced a one-dimensional SDAZ system, allowing users to scroll vertically through a chronologically ordered list of photographs.

10.5.2 SCREEN SIZE

As we discussed in the prototyping chapter, we always start development of any technique on a desktop machine to see whether our approach is viable. In this instance, we developed in Java to make the most of the Piccolo toolkit developed by Bederson *et al.* (2004) – if you develop interfaces that scroll and zoom, this is an excellent resource. In effect, we replicated Cockburn and Savage's system, but this time limiting ourselves to a standard 240 × 320 PDA-sized display area. Once we had the algorithm working, the next problem we faced was in setting the thresholds for the zooming.

SDAZ has two thresholds, which we will call 'take-off' and 'cruising altitude'. To explain further, when the user is making small scrolling movements of an image, it is not necessary to decrease the zoom level – the desired portion of the document is, obviously, already visible. When the user makes large scrolling movements, then the zoom level should decrease so that the user can have a wider view of the document. The point at which the zoom level starts to decrease is the take-off point. Once 'in the air', the user can continue to increase the scroll rate, which will continue to decrease zoom level. However, the zoom reduction cannot continue unabated, otherwise the document will eventually zoom to a single pixel and disappear. That is why we need to set a cruising altitude, beyond which the user can continue to increase scroll rate but the zoom will remain unaffected.

When setting these for our application we obviously could not naively adopt the values from previous research in desktop systems – the 'take-off' point could be a value greater than the number of pixels on the small screen! In the end, we modified our prototype to allow these thresholds to be set dynamically. This can be seen in Figure 10.5, along with sliders to set initial zoom levels, etc.

With this version of the prototype, we conducted informal evaluations to find default values for the algorithm. The good news is that the settings for a given device seem to be constant across all users – the algorithm does not need to be customized for each individual user.

Once we had default thresholds in place, informal feedback from users was very positive, but most expressed skepticism that the highly graphical approach of SDAZ could be supported on a device as

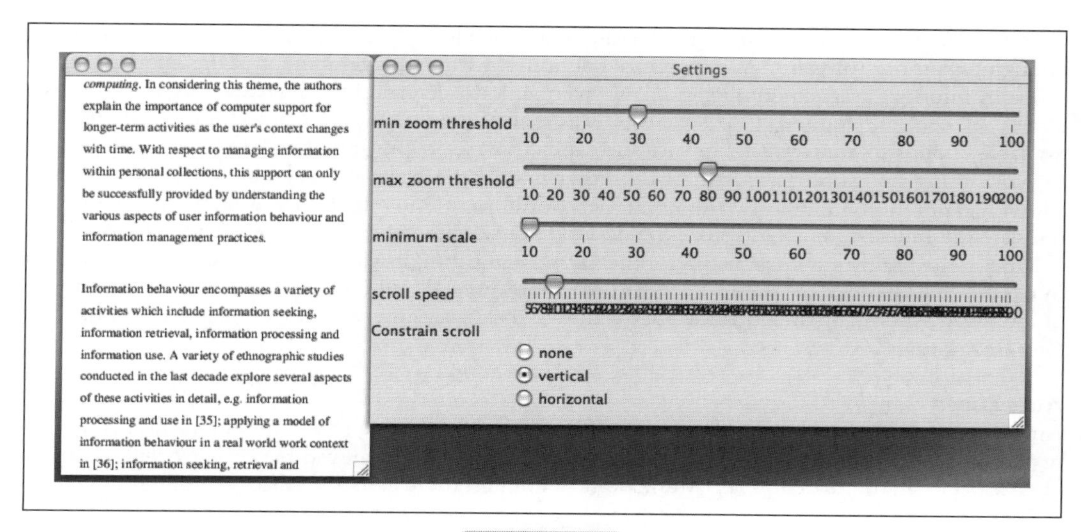

FIGURE 10.5

You can see the sliders which allowed us to tune the thresholds to the smaller screen size

computationally limited as a PDA. This seemed like a valid criticism so, rather than continue with full user evaluations, we decided to see whether it was possible to implement an acceptable version of SDAZ on a PDA.

10.5.3 WRITE ONCE, RUN ANYWHERE

One of the advantages of developing in Java should be that you can deploy the same code on multiple hardware platforms. This is largely true, but we had a problem in that we were using Piccolo Java, which needs J2SE (designed for desktop computers), not J2ME which is more common on mobile devices. Fortunately, we found a version of J2SE for mobile Linux, so set up a PDA running J2SE on top of Linux. However, it turned out that this version of J2SE didn't implement the graphics routines we needed.

We won't bore you with the details, but we could have saved ourselves months if we had planned our prototype strategy more effectively from the outset. In the end, we scrubbed the original code and reimplemented the prototype using .net, making sure the routines we used were also available in the compact framework version. Of course, we could have done this with Java, limiting ourselves to J2ME routines, but Waikato University had just given us the fastest PDA available commercially. This PDA was running PocketPC, so we felt this would give us the best shot at producing a workable implementation. In the end, it took several months' work and some consultation with Microsoft, but the SDAZ photo browser runs smoothly on a standard 5550 iPAQ.

10.5.4 MEANWHILE, BACK WITH THE USERS

Even if it turned out that it was not possible to implement SDAZ on current camera-phones and PDAs, Moore's law means that these devices would eventually provide appropriate levels of computing power. (Moore's law states that the power of processors will double every year. As this law has held true since 1965, we can be fairly confident that cellular handsets will eventually be powerful enough to run our software.) We therefore continued with the development of the interface.

From informal user experimentation, we were able to determine the default thresholds for the screen size. So far, so good. Our next issue was that of input device. Even the most basic handset available supports some way to specify 'up' and 'down', so the modified SDAZ should be able to work using no more than that. At the other end of the scale, camera-PDAs had touchscreens allowing continuous input in two-dimensional coordinates. One might, therefore, be able to directly translate the mouse movements from the desktop SDAZ directly into PDA stylus movements.

Due to the highly graphical nature of the SDAZ algorithm, it was impossible to prototype any of our proposed solutions on paper. Each had to be prototyped and tested using a desktop simulation of the PDA. After many iterations we derived two SDAZ variants, which we called AutoZoom and GestureZoom.

AutoZoom

AutoZoom was the variant developed for minimal specification devices – the interaction is limited to scrolling up and down. The up and down scrolling can be achieved by key, joystick, stylus or even wheel-based interaction. In AutoZoom, scrolling down starts the images scrolling down the

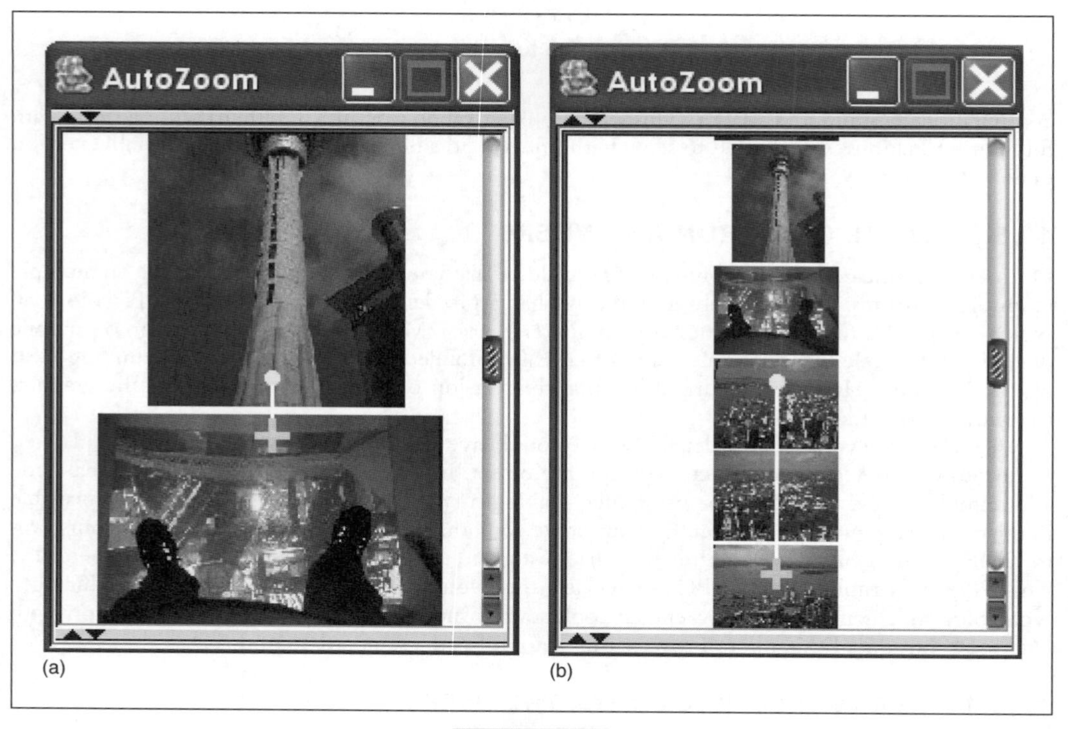

FIGURE 10.6

(a) The user is scrolling and the images are at full zoom; (b) the user is scrolling faster and the image size is diminished

screen, as in Figure 10.6(a). The line that extends from the circle that can be seen in the center of the screen in Figure 10.6(a) represents the current scroll rate. (The cross represents the current position of the stylus on the screen, as these images were taken using a stylus-based version of AutoZoom.) Using key or stylus or wheel, the user can 'grow' this line, as in Figure 10.6(b). Here, we have passed the take-off threshold and the zoom level has decreased. Similarly the line can be shrunk, so the zoom level increases once more.

GestureZoom

GestureZoom was developed for devices which allow two-dimensional input. Similar to AutoZoom, dragging the cursor vertically from the center point of the screen increases scrolling rate in that direction. For GestureZoom, however, zoom level is independent of scroll rate. Instead, zoom level is dictated by the horizontal distance of the cursor from the center of the screen. This is shown in Figure 10.7, where the stylus (represented by the cross) has been placed below and to the right of the central circle. The effect of this is to give a slight reduction in zoom level (proportional to the length of the horizontal line to the right of the circle) and to scroll the images down the screen (at a speed proportional to the length of the vertical line below the circle).

FIGURE 10.7

(a) The user is scrolling and the images are at full zoom; (b) the user is scrolling faster and the image size is diminished

Sadly, a paper description and static images do not do justice to this highly interactive technique. Experientially, it allows users to fly rapidly over their photographs, swooping down for more detail when they spot something of interest. At this point they can descend so the image fills the screen, or soar back up over the photograph landscape. When scrolling at maximum speed and smallest zoom, it is not possible to pick out individual images well, but events are rapidly identifiable due to the similarity in images – as we know from the ethnography, identifying events is an essential user requirement.

At the risk of over-emphasizing a point, you should always conduct user tests as early and as often as possible, no matter how informal. Even if the testers are your friends, exposure to your system, especially over long periods of time, is invaluable. By doing exactly this (installing our system on people's computers and watching them 'play' with it), we discovered two things about GestureZoom and AutoZoom that we would never have picked up, even in formal user testing.

Firstly, we discovered that we needed to add a third threshold to the algorithm! This came about as the size of the photo collections we examined increased. On the small screen, once the cruising altitude has been achieved, it was taking users too long to scroll down their collections. We therefore added a new threshold, beyond which scrolling rate would accelerate. Descriptively, this notion of three thresholds may sound overly complex, but is surprisingly natural in usage.

Our second discovery was the usefulness of the scrollbars (visible in Figures 10.6 and 10.7). The widget set used to develop the application included a scrollbar by default on this type of window. As people played with the application, we realized it provided good feedback on where, roughly, the currently displayed photo fell in the current collection. Also, it provided a very coarse way for users to scroll to a particular part of their photo collections. As Igarashi and Hinckley observed, the scrollbar was too coarse-grained to be used as the only way of scrolling through a photo collection, but worked will in combination with AutoZoom and GestureZoom.

So having conducted informal tests and ironing out the unforeseen issues with this new technique, we proceeded on to full user testing.

10.5.5 USER TESTING

Tasks

Just as Khella and Bederson (2004) had done when testing Pocket PhotoMesa, we wanted to test how the SDAZ variants compared with thumbnail browsers for typical photo-finding tasks. Our experiment therefore had to evaluate three separate systems (Thumbnail, AutoZoom and GestureZoom).

When deciding on the tasks for users to perform, we tested for the tasks identified in the ethnographic studies of Rodden *et al.* (2001) and Frohlich *et al.* (2002), namely:

- Finding events – locating a group of consecutive images related to a well-defined event
- Finding an individual image – locating a single photograph from the entire collection
- Finding a group of images containing a common element – locating a group of non-consecutive images which all share something in common (e.g. identify all photos in which you appear).

One final influence for our evaluation was taken from Cockburn and Savage's original evaluation of the improved SDAZ. In their paper, they tested whether there was any difference in scrolling techniques when scrolling for a distant target or a close target. Therefore, when designing the tasks for locating events and individual images, we ensured that some targets were close to, and others far from, the point of origin – for our purposes, 'far from' is defined as requiring the user to scroll through more than half the total photographs in the collection. Obviously, this distinction of close and distant does not apply to the search for a group of images, as users are expected to scan the entire collection. When searching for individual images, we did make the distinction of asking users to search for images containing large features and small features (in this instance, we defined large as occupying more than an eighth of the image area). Also, we wanted to test whether the size of an event had any bearing on how easy it was to find. We therefore had far and close events which were both large (more than three photographs) and small (three or fewer photographs).

Conditions

By taking into account the three influences described above, our experiment ended up with three independent variables as follows:

1. System type: AutoZoom, GestureZoom and Thumbnail
2. Task target: event, individual image and image group
3. Target distance: close and far (or big and small).

Taking into account the different values for each of the independent variables, we end up with 27 conditions. At 10 users per condition, this would imply 270 users! However, even with some statistical jiggery-pokery, we ended up having to test with 72 users to provide statistically meaningful results. (System type was between-subject, while the other variables were within-subject.) As this is not a chapter on experimental method, we shall spare you the drudgery of the procedural details. You can always read the paper on the experiment (Patel *et al.*, 2004) if you're interested.

Results

The results from our evaluation were very encouraging. To summarize:

- Events
   1. AutoZoom and GestureZoom were better than Thumbnail browsing for finding small events. For events in general, there was no significant benefit from the SDAZ systems.
   2. Far events were found more quickly than close events.
   3. For far events, long events were found more quickly than short events.
- Individual image
   4. AutoZoom was better than Thumbnail browsing for far images.
   5. SDAZ techniques were better for finding images with small features.
   6. Close images were found more quickly than far images.
   7. Images with large features were found more quickly than images with small features.
- Image groups
   8. No interface was proved faster in identifying image groups, though SDAZ-based interfaces provided much more accurate results.

Discussion

Overall, the new systems were just as fast as, and sometimes better than, existing thumbnail browsers. Given that none of the users had seen an SDAZ-based system before taking part in this experiment, the results are particularly encouraging. Taking each result in turn:

1. We speculate that this result is due to the fact that the user has greater control of the scroll rate than with a thumbnail browser. The discrete lurching from screen to screen of thumbnails may result in small events going undetected.
2. This seemingly paradoxical result came about as users assumed that the image would be far away and were keen to start scrolling as quickly as possible.
3. As users scroll further from their origin, their scroll speed increases, which can hide small events.
4. It is not clear why AutoZoom (and not GestureZoom) should be better here, as in every other task they performed identically. We would speculate that this is an anomaly and that SDAZ techniques provide much faster scrolling rates than are possible with thumbnail browsers.
5. SDAZ will allow users to select an appropriate size of image, allowing them to see small features which are hidden in the predetermined image size of the thumbnail browser.
6. This result would have seemed self-evident had we not observed result number 2. Further investigation is need to see why close images are found more easily than close events.
7. This result seems self-evident.
8. When completing these tasks, users scrolled at a uniform rate. Again, it seems that the ability to select a dynamic zoom level allowed users to select a level appropriate to the task.

10.5.6 PLATFORM

Having conducted these experiments, and found such promising results, we were motivated to continue development onto the target hardware platforms and explore other variations. One direct implication from our experiment was that the AutoZoom system (with more simple input needs) was just as good as (and possibly better than) the GestureZoom system. Therefore, we are currently concentrating on AutoZoom.

Currently, AutoZoom is running smoothly on a variety of iPAQs and a Nokia 6600 handset. We are also looking at ways of enhancing AutoZoom, perhaps using semantic zooming techniques involving timelines, as in Harada *et al.* (2004).

The system we developed here is only the first step into photo organization; there are many variants on this system which one might pursue. However, we are convinced it represents a sound, scalable solution to the problems of image searching as identified in the earlier ethnographic studies. Like the developers of RSVP, our solution hinges on human capabilities: specifically, the capacity for rapid image processing and a good understanding of relative time. Other researchers, however, are pursuing solutions based on machine intelligence in order to aid users in finding photographs. These two approaches are not necessarily exclusive and we shall look at some promising avenues currently being explored.

10.6 ADVANCED TECHNOLOGY

One alternative to simply shrinking the image to a thumbnail is to automatically crop the image to an area of interest within the photograph. Of course, it is tricky for the computer to figure out what a human might find interesting. However, there are algorithms which make a reasonable attempt by exploiting knowledge about how the human visual system works. One such algorithm developed specifically for PDAs is reported by Liu *et al.* (2003) (see Color Plate 7). While the approach looks promising, the evaluation in the paper is rather disappointing. Instead of measuring how the cropped photos affected searching and browsing performance, the authors conducted an experiment in which users rated the algorithm's performance in identifying interesting parts of the image. So while the algorithm could find interesting things, we don't know whether it aids humans in image recognition and retrieval – for instance, it may turn out that users remember the overall composition of an image much better than the component key elements. Until such an evaluation is conducted, it would be unwise to adopt this technique – especially as it is currently too computationally expensive to run on a PDA or digital camera.

Another alternative is not to show all the images stored, but rather a single key image to represent a group of similar images. The problem then becomes one of figuring out what distinguishes a key image from other candidates. Research such as that by Savakis *et al.* (2000) and Luo *et al.* (2003) has shown the following factors to be important:

- Colorfulness
- Sharpness
- Format uniqueness (e.g. the only panoramic image in a group)
- Skin area
- People present
- Close-up subject
- Good composition

Analyzing these factors from a sample data set, researchers built a Bayesian network to identify key images (Luo *et al.*, 2003). As an evaluation of the network, they compared the images it selected as 'key' to those selected by humans: 77% of the images selected by the network were in the top three chosen by the user group. This is a fairly impressive result on one level but, again, does not constitute any kind of meaningful result. In their work, these researchers are assuming that a single representative frame is the best way to identify a given event. A better evaluation would have been to simulate some user task, such as finding a particular event, and seeing whether the key image selected could be used to identify an event more quickly than an image chosen at random (or the first one for a given event). Given that the computation required to identify a key image is fairly expensive (too much for current camera-phones or PDAs), it may be that a randomly selected image is *good enough* to represent a group of images.

10.7 WHAT ARE PHOTOS FOR?

Assuming for the moment that we have solved the problems of organizing photos, what do people actually do with them?

The KAN-G framework from Liechti and Ichikawa (2000) suggests that it is primarily to maintain social contacts. Their work is based on ethnographic studies which show that photographs are used within families and social groups to create and build emotional links between members. These links are further strengthened by the ability of the group to give feedback on the images and share reactions to them. One of the inspirations behind their ideas comes from email and SMS ethnographies which show that people often exchange messages with fairly meaningless context just as a way of keeping in touch and maintaining emotional links: sending photos for this purpose allows much more information to be sent for relatively less effort. The ultimate goal of these links is to create a sense of 'affective awareness' – the sense of feeling 'close' to someone.

They suggest that social links can be created in two ways. When we receive a photograph from someone, we feel connected to them; knowing that someone has seen a photograph I sent to them connects me with that person. One consequence of desiring feedback on an image is that users tend to email them to recipients, rather than place them on a website. Emails are a symmetric communication medium which encourages commentary, whereas the web tends to be asymmetric. The mix between using the web and email is analogous to the situation from paper-based photography where we have albums for special events, but the rest of the images float around the house where they can be viewed by anyone who is sufficiently well known to be let into our house.

EXERCISE 10.2 SOCIAL AWARENESS

Given that photographs are used to maintain social contact, design an information appliance for social contact preservation via images. Think particularly about the issues of calm technology, context (social and technical, especially) and which user groups in particular may want a device that does these things. Having thought about all that, how well does a camera-phone fulfill that role? ■

So, returning to the camera-phone, what happens if we think of it as a social link tool, rather than a miniature version of a camera-cum-digital-gallery? Firstly, the device should be able to display images in a 'calm' fashion (see Box 10.3 for a discussion on calm technology) – so the screen saver on my phone should be able to cycle through my MMSs. (This does not really represent a huge change in technology.) More interesting is the ability to show people that you have seen their photograph. At present, this functionality is provided in email and SMS by including the original message as part of the reply. There does not seem to be any handset which supports replying to an MMS by, say, overlaying text on the original image.

BOX 10.3 CALM TECHNOLOGY

The notion of calm technology was first suggested by Weiser and Brown (1997). They were keen to ensure that, as the number of computers around us increases, they do not overly intrude into our lives. At present devices like cellular handsets, PDAs, pagers and computers all attract our attention in fairly invasive and irritating ways. Instead, ➤

Weiser would like to see devices that inform without irritating. One of his key ideas is to have all devices lie in the background of awareness and come into 'center stage' only when they have something urgent to tell us. As an example, think about the helpful balloon and accompanying beep that appear every time you insert your USB drive into a Windows computer. Is it really necessary to announce this and attract your attention every time you insert the drive? Calm technology is an attempt to force designers to consider what information the user should deal with immediately and what information should be left available for the user's convenience. ■

Of course, being mobile, camera-phones can be used to show images to other people when meeting together. Rodden discovered that laptops are an ideal way to show and share photographs, unlike the desktop systems examined by Frohlich. Similarly, the television-out feature on many digital cameras was seen as an ideal way to share images. Using add-on Bluetooth devices, camera-phones already have the ability to display images on a television screen for shared viewing.

The research and ethnographic studies on mobile photography emphasize the value of sharing photographs to improve and maintain relationships. Counts and Fellheimer (2004) built a system for camera-phones which supports what they term 'lightweight' sharing. Identifying that a barrier to sharing is the effort required to make the sharing happen on a mobile device, their system is set up to automatically share photos with a group of friends. To improve social cohesion, the application constantly displays images of group members, and clicking on an individual image reveals the photographs taken by that person. Surprisingly, in the field studies, users were happy to have their images shared indiscriminately – only one user changed their photo-taking habits. Also, recipients were not swamped, as the metaphor for retrieving images was a 'pull' rather than a 'push' based approach like email (calm technology again). In fact, users reported enjoyment at looking through the latest images taken by people in the group. The biggest design flaw reported was the fact that the application supported only one group of people; participants would have liked several groups of friends, at the expense of an extra click in the sharing process. Finally, one excellent extra addition to this system was a client application for PCs. This allowed users to offload and archive data from their device. This notion of online and offline integration is discussed further in Section 9.5.

So, provided the cost of image sharing is not prohibitively high, sharing images from a mobile device does indeed seem to fulfill the aims of maintaining and improving relationships.

One final interesting discussion from Liechti and Ichikawa's work is around video conferencing, a technology which many network providers hope will drive revenue streams. They postulate that annotated photographs may prove to be a more effective (and affective) means of communication than can be achieved with video conferencing. In part, this idea is driven by their observation that static images are still cherished in an age when it is so easy to record video. Again, we do not need more technology, we just need to understand what people want to do with communication media and how to support their social needs.

10.7.1 WHAT ARE WE SHARING?

Given that photo sharing is clearly a popular activity, what is it we are sharing? There is a branch of anthropology called 'visual anthropology' dedicated to answering that question. Obviously there are artistic, scientific and journalistic applications, where the photographs have a well-understood purpose. Less obvious in application is the home photograph. One visual anthropologist, Richard Chalfen, has produced numerous works studying how North Americans and Japanese use home photographs (see more at `www.richardchalfen.com`). Reporting on their work, Liechti and Ichikawa (2000) show that photographs are taken for five main purposes:

- Shared photographs – photographs taken to give to friends
- Household photographs – for framing and display
- Work photography – photos to display at work
- Wallet photography – personal photos to be carried in a wallet or purse
- Tourist photography – photos taken on holiday

These results come from the study of paper-based photography. A study of children using prototype camera-phones in Finland shows that the potential uses of mobile photography are much more diverse (Mäkelä *et al.*, 2000). In this paper, five separate activities are identified:

- Creating stories
- Expressing spirituality – art from photographs
- Expressing affection
- Increasing or maintaining group cohesion
- Conversation support – augmentation with images

Overall, the images were used for expressing emotion or humor. The images were of primary use where sender and receiver were sufficiently aware of each other's lives to make the image meaningful. Within the family context, the exchange of images was seen by older family members as a great way of communicating with their children or grandchildren.

In a later study by Kurvinen (2003), the author analyzes the use of MMS and discovers that message senders will often send 'teasing' images in order to elicit a response from the recipient. The example given is of a message showing a ring on the finger of the sender's hand – he has just become engaged. The recipients then respond with appropriate messages.

The work reported in Bitton *et al.* (2004) represents an interesting approach to studying digital photography. This project sets out to discover how people use a new type of digital camera which records a minute's worth of audio before, and after, an image is taken. The authors go to great lengths not to influence their subjects, so do not show them other users' recordings or give them any ideas of what the camera should be used for. To their credit, the authors evaluate the device in a developing world context to see how people who have low media exposure use the device. Initial observations from their work suggest that image collection falls into one of four main categories:

- **Social glancing.** Essentially the recording is used as a 'conversation piece' around which to build up some social interaction.
- **Caught in activities.** Recordings are used to document activities in a given day. There is no intended audience for these recordings but they simply act as a documentation of the activity.
- **Active documentation.** Here, the user produces a mini-documentary about some aspect of their lives.

- **Intentional disclosures.** In this category, the audio and images are used in a complementary fashion to communicate a specific idea or message.

EXERCISE 10.3 MOBILE BLOGGING

All of the above uses for the audio imaging devices sound plausible, but it is by no means an exhaustive list. The device that was created for the research seems like an ideal mobile blogging device (except that the results are not placed on the web). To start with, consider how design enhancements to the system would allow the device to become a blogging tool. Then, take a look at an existing mobile blog and see how well the posts on that blog fit the four categories given above. It's likely that there are other types of activity not covered here. Is it possible to modify the design of the device so that it supports the new activities as well? ■

10.7.2 USING AUDIO WITH PHOTOGRAPHS

As mentioned at the end of the previous section, one other digital enhancement of photographs is the use of audio recording. Either the audio can be recorded at the time the photograph is taken, or a subsequent recording can be attached to the photograph. The purpose of most audio/photo systems is not to aid in searching (although, with speech recognition, this is a possibility) but to provide more information about a photograph once it is found.

Work by Frohlich and Tallyn (1999) shows that ambient noise recordings taken at capture time can enhance the enjoyment of a photograph. Not only that, but the inclusion of the audio can 'save' a bad photograph – the authors give the example of a poorly lit photograph of a marching band, which was highly valued by the photographer, as the ambient noise and photo together perfectly captured the moment. Interestingly, the ambient noise seemed to act as a memory aid, with subjects talking more about the context of photographs when accompanying audio is recorded.

Here again, we see the benefits of adopting a calm technology by automatically recording audio, whether the photographer ultimately wants it or not. The software Rodden used in her study supported explicit audio annotation, but this was largely unused, even though users requested this feature from the software. One reason for this may be that, as the camera automatically time-stamps images, users considered this to be sufficient annotation.

10.7.3 VIDEO

Video is coming to a mobile computer near you. Either it will appear in the form of a dedicated 'Personal Media Device' where the hard disk contains movies and other video clips, or the movies could be streamed directly to your handset via a wireless network. There are many cellular service providers globally who are hoping you will elect the second option as they struggle to recoup the costs they paid for 3G licenses a few years ago. This is all very well, and technically viable, but will anyone want to watch movies on a small screen? Is video really a mobile technology?

Video on mobile phones has been available in Finland since the second half of 2002. A team from the National Consumer Research Center in Finland investigated how people used this service and integrated it into their lives (Repo *et al.*, 2004). The somewhat unremarkable result of their research was that when on their own, users would watch videos to avoid being bored; when in a group, they would use the video to share an experience together. This second category of sharing a video refers not just to personal video clips, but karaoke videos which a group could sing together. It is not surprising that people wish to use videos as part of a group, but the nature of karaoke is that it relies more on its audio, rather than visual, content. Is it likely that a group of people will sit together and watch, say, a soccer match on a small screen? At the time of writing, this remains an open question.

Again, all the issues we discussed in finding and using photographs apply equally well to video. Like photographs, videos have no content that is meaningful to a computer. Beyond time and possibly location, video has no useful meta-data to aid in a search. In fact, the problem is much worse with video as users would typically have to watch several seconds of video before they could identify what the clip contains. At the moment this problem is not too great as mobile devices have limited memory and cannot contain too many clips. As storage space expands, searching for video clips will become a huge research area.

10.8 LOOKING TO THE FUTURE

With the advent of terabyte disks and miniscule image recorders, the idea of recording one's entire life becomes a possibility. Although we are not big fans of 'context-aware' computing, recording heart rate and galvanic skin response (GSR) could provide ways to rapidly identify those sections of one's life that are 'interesting', be it for positive or negative reasons. Already, systems such as the StartleCam (Healey and Picard, 1998) are designed to record images in response to a change in GSR.

However, this opens up many philosophical questions about what one should record and when you are going to get the time to watch what you have recorded. Some of these issues have already been humorously discussed in Umberto Eco's essay on how to create a 1:1 map (Eco, 1995). With cameras, there is the added recursive problem of recording oneself while watching oneself watching a recording (etc.). Potentially more interesting are the ethical questions raised by recording so much information. How would you feel if your health insurance company could demand a full recording of your life to see how well you ate and how much you exercised?

Even with existing camera-phone technology, a number of interesting ethical problems are created. Obviously there are the invasion-of-privacy issues which have resulted in camera-phones being banned from some public buildings. Before we become carried away with the negative aspects of camera-phones, it should be realized that there are many positive aspects. For instance, it becomes a lot harder to fake a photograph of an event if several hundred witnesses of the same event have their own photographic evidence. Regardless, camera-phones are unlikely to go away due to any ethical constraint. As designers of technology, however, it is our responsibility to help make sure these devices augment society and human activity rather than restrict it.

SUMMARY

Incorporating imaging capabilities on communication devices opens up all sorts of exciting new application possibilities. The crucial thing to remember is that, despite the ➤

marketing, the result is not a camera, but a social awareness and cohesion device. When you start to look at it in those terms, new design ideas become apparent. A lot of ethnography has already been conducted and offers some great insights into how to design new applications and devices.

Having said all that, there are still the major issues of image searching and browsing to be solved. Many approaches have been tried but few have made the successful transition from large to small screen. Until users can effectively search image collections of several thousand photographs to find a target image, there is limited application in allowing them to share images.

WORKSHOP QUESTIONS

- How do you organize your digital photographs? First write down what you think you do, and then go and check your collection to see whether that is what you actually do.
- The evaluation we conducted for the zooming browsers in Section 10.5.5 tested very specific aspects of the interface. What other types of evaluation do you think might have been appropriate and what information might we have missed by conducting so focused a study?
- If you have a camera-phone, go through the images you have taken that are still stored on the device. Can you classify them according to the lists given in Section 10.7.1? Are there any that fall outside this classification?

DESIGNER TIPS

- *Building a photobrowser which requires users to manually input meta-data is unlikely to succeed.*
- *Users tend to think about their collections in terms of time, be that absolute, data-stamped time or relative time, where users recall events and the order in which they occurred.*
- *Mobile devices already have gigabytes of hard disk space. Make sure any photo visualization software you devise can cope with at least 4000 images.*
- *Supporting sharing of images in a rapid way is absolutely critical to the success of a imaging application or device.*
- *Remember that camera + phone ≠ camera. Camera + phone = social awareness and relationship building device.*

CHAPTER 11
IMPACTING THE COMMUNITY; IMPACTING THE WORLD

OVERVIEW

11.1. Introduction
11.2. The digital divide
11.3. Mobiles work
11.4. Planning a project
11.5. That culture thing
11.6. Case studies
11.7. Call to arms

KEY POINTS

- For most of the world, the cellular handset is the only interactive technology they have ever seen.
- Cellular technology is truly democratic, and extremely poor people are willing to make sacrifices in order to have access (some people will buy air-time rather than food with their wages).
- ICT solutions from the developed world which are deployed directly into developing countries almost always fail.
- To adapt solutions to individual countries often requires some quite subtle research, especially when trying to employ cultural dimensions.
- Due to the lack of programmers in developing countries, efforts should be taken to make software 'communitizable'.

11.1 INTRODUCTION

In the early chapters we looked at how mobile technologies have effected societal change. But, in reality, mobile technology is just another facet of a wider technological incursion into most people's lives. As a new phenomenon, it is interesting to study how mobile technology impacts society and how we, as designers and technologists, can create systems which enhance human activity.

However, what if there was no other technology – the only technology you had access to was your mobile phone or your PDA? We are not talking about giving up your laptop for an afternoon, but having no access to any other technology again. Ever.

Worried? Could you survive?

For most people on the planet, this is their daily reality – their only connection to the outside world is a cellular handset.

In the early chapters, we were considering only the part of the world which already had a rich technological infrastructure. Whilst interesting, this accounts for less than half the world's population. In this last chapter, we will look at how mobile technology has swept through the developing world and what can be done to improve the lives of everyone else on the planet.

11.2 THE DIGITAL DIVIDE

There cannot be many people working in ICT who have not heard of the digital divide. There are many definitions, but essentially, it is the notion that the world is divided into those who have access to ICT and those who do not. There is the belief that by giving the have-nots access to resources like digital libraries and the Internet, they will be able to educate themselves and hopefully move out of the poverty trap. Failure to bridge the digital divide will ultimate leave the developing world with even more barriers to compete on the global stage.

One of the potential benefits for developing countries in deploying ICTs is that they can learn from the costly mistakes of the developed world. This 'leapfrogging' can be seen, for example, with cellular networks – for example, no current service provider in the developing world is going to deploy an analog network. Despite the hope and the hype, the successes in bridging the divide are relatively few. Most of the failures stem from a form of technological imperialism, where solutions from the developed world are deployed in developing countries without any consideration for local constraints. Thanks to cellular phone networks, however, we do know that ICTs can succeed spectacularly.

11.3 MOBILES WORK

Where do you think the world's fastest growing mobile market is: South East Asia, Europe or India? Actually, according to the ITU (2004), the African market is growing faster than any other market – 65% growth, with the next closest continent, Asia, experiencing 38% growth. Some 70% of the telephone users in Africa have mobile rather than land-line connections.

Cellular communication is truly a democratic medium in a way that the Internet is not. Studies by the ITU show that there is little correlation between income (as measured in per-capita GDP) and cellular penetration. The Internet penetration in South Africa, the best on the African continent, is only 7.1% of the population, yet cellular penetration is around 50% (in 2005).

11.3.1 THE RISE AND RISE OF MOBILE TECHNOLOGY

Lesson number 4 in the World Bank Institute's 'Ten Lessons for ICT and Education in the Developing World' is 'Loose the Wires' (Hawkins, 2002). The authors relate how fixed-line technology in the developing world can never compete with wireless communications (although they did note that there were problems with monkeys eating cables on the satellite dishes!). Without wireless, the only way to access the Internet, or communicate, is via fixed-line telephony. In most developing countries, telephone lines are only to be found in urban areas, so people have to travel to the urban centers using erratic public transport. One aid worker in Sierra Leone in the 1980s reported "I had to take two days off in order to make a phone call home" (Oxfam, 2005). Even when you get to the town, there is no guaranteeing the telephone service will be working (I worked in Zambia for six months on a contract giving me free telephone calls from the local town – never once did I manage to make a call while I was there, due to network outages). Besides the usual maintenance problems of land-lines, the developing world has its own unique problems which greatly increase the problems of maintaining the network (see Box 11.1).

BOX 11.1 THE REAL REASON WHY TELEPHONE TRUNK CABLE IS BRIGHTLY COLORED

Continuing the theme of analyzing the impacts of technology on society, there is an alarming trend in some developing countries of stealing telephone cables and selling them to tourists! The bright color and thin malleable nature of telephone trunk cable makes it ideal for basket weaving. Within Africa, at least, trunk cable is often 'recycled' in this way. For those who do not have a land-line handset installed, selling the wire to tourists is obviously more useful than having it hanging in the air. While the baskets are beautiful (see Color Plate 8), please make sure they come from a sustainable source before purchasing them. ■

In many countries, wireless access has allowed communication to move out of the urban centers to areas which previously had no coverage. In India, Shyam Telecom has equipped rickshaws with cellular phones and has plans to add laptops with cellular access to the Internet (BBC, 2003). In South Africa, cargo containers are being used to set up land-based public phone operations but connected via the cellular network. This is a particular problem in South Africa, where the apartheid government paid no attention to infrastructure in the townships. These cellular containers allow telephone access to a wide group of people, close to their homes, for minimal cost.

Even for those who do have access to a telephone, their lifestyle may dictate that they are unable to have a permanent address – a large portion of the workforce in developing countries is itinerant. Having a cellular handset means that, regardless of physical location, the owner is always contactable. Furthermore, it's not unusual for a group of casual laborers to purchase a handset between them and use that number as a contact for potential employers.

Obviously, the income to the network providers from this type of user is much lower than in more developed countries, but the network is still used. In particular, SMS usage is high in South Africa, where each subscriber sends, on average, 17 messages per month – the world average is four.

At present, the handsets purchased by the majority of users in developing countries provide basic functionality. If you ever wondered what happened to your old handset that was sent for recycling, chances are it is living on in a developing country somewhere. As better and better handsets trickle through, users in developing countries will start to have fairly advanced computing devices available to them. At last, computing power will be placed within the hands of those who have been denied every other form of access. There exists a window now for us to look at what can be done with these resources to maximize their impact. The next section looks at how to create effective solutions for the developing world and examines some preliminary work we have undertaken.

11.4 PLANNING A PROJECT

A lot of our work has been carried out in conjunction with bridges.org, an NGO looking at digital divide issues. Having worked on many successful developing world ICT projects, they have developed a list of 12 'Real Access' criteria that a project should meet in order to be viable in a developing world context. We will present only a summary here – you can see them in full at the bridges.org website – but it is interesting to look at them and see why mobile technology can succeed where other technologies have failed. If you're planning a project in the developing world, then it's worth taking these factors into account on top of the other factors and development methods we've discussed elsewhere in the book.

Real Access

1. **Physical access to technology.** As most telecenters are located in urban areas, users would need to commute for a day either side of actually using the center. As we have seen, even rural villages can have access to wireless networks, making it a much more appropriate technology. In South Africa, some 97% of the population has access to the cellular network.

2. **Appropriateness of technology.** Again, many desktop-based systems come unstuck on the fact that they need a constant supply of electricity and need to be stored in a cool, secure location. Not only can mobile technology go for several days without being plugged in, their low power drain means they can be recharged from solar cells or clockwork generators.

3. **Affordability of technology.** One of the great things about cellular handsets is that the cost of the hardware is subsidized by the network. This is not going to happen for desktop machines. (Actually, we have used games consoles instead of PCs for some of our work, as hardware costs are subsidized. However, this is only viable in areas with a constant electrical supply.) The handsets are sold at little or no profit in the hopes that revenue will be made through network access. While there is still a cost attached to the device, it is pared to the minimum possible.
4. **Human capacity training.** How much training do people need to use the technology? Again, mobile handset interfaces are familiar to most users in a way that Windows or Linux is not. Building an application which mirrors the menu structure of a cellular interface has a much greater chance of success than one based on a 'standard' desktop GUI.
5. **Locally relevant content and applications.** This is constant across all platforms and comes back to the issue of ethnography and understanding the true needs of your user group.
6. **Integration into daily routines.** Will the technology add an extra burden to the users? Life in developing countries is hard in a way that is difficult for those on the outside to understand – when was the last time you had to carry water into your house for your daily needs? Technology which can be a convenience in the developed world (e.g. an ATM) can be a burden for everyone else (after a bus journey, you discover that the electricity supply is out and you cannot get money – the cost of hiring human tellers is relatively little in the developing world and they are still able to work when the lights go out). Again, mobile technology wins here over any desktop solution.
7. **Socio-cultural factors.** This is dealt with extensively in the next section.
8. **Technology trust.** This point cuts both ways in that users can be nervous about entering personal details into a faceless computer, but also, less sophisticated users may willingly enter details, which leaves them open to all sorts of scams. The decentralized, open nature of the Internet, which increases its popularity in the developed world, can prove a liability for less technically literate users. Like it or not, many users are happier to use the closed cellular networks, which have put huge marketing efforts into building trust, than use the unbranded Internet.
9. **Local economic environment.** Is there any spin-off for the wider community? Well, in this case, any access to the outside world has the potential to help the community. Mobile computers are more likely to succeed at this, for the reasons listed above, than non-mobile systems.
10. **Macro-economic environment.** Are the wider economic factors of the country in line with the project? This may not seem so important, but any ICT development work in a developing country is often viewed as an expensive indulgence (wouldn't the money not have been better spent on water pipes?) and needs to be in line with the government's wider aims for the country as a whole – the project has to work.
11. **Legal and regulatory framework.** Is what you are doing legal? Many developing countries have telecommunication monopolies which have no desire to see competition to their networks. Even worse, some governments are keen to keep the monopoly in place as it simplifies

the process of eavesdropping on their citizens. These monopolies are slow to change and you can find yourself in legislative trouble – for example, VoIP was illegal in South Africa until March 2005.

12. **Political will and public support.** Are the community and the wider populace behind what you are doing? Again, this issue comes back to the researchers' and developers' relationship with the community they are developing for. It can take a long time (usually three years in our experience) to gain the trust of a community to the point that they will give you useful information on the service or application you are trying to develop.

While this list is still evolving, it has been tested in real situations and provides a minimum checklist for any ICT project in the developing world.

EXERCISE 11.1 HOW RELEVANT IS REAL ACCESS?

The list above was developed by a multi-disciplinary team of dedicated people, but not one of them was an expert in interaction design. From what you know of interaction design, how many of the criteria above could be derived from following an interaction design methodology? Which ones would not be picked up, and could interaction design be altered in any way so that they would be addressed? ■

11.5 THAT CULTURE THING

A lot has been written about how to incorporate cultural factors into the design of ICT systems – most of it is collected at `http://www.i18ngurus.com/`. Within the literature, there is research which attempts to classify cultures using abstract dimensions. Foremost among these is the work of Hofstede (1997), who analyzed the culture of hundreds of IBM employees across 53 countries between 1978 and 1983. The result of his work was the following five cultural dimensions which can be used to classify any culture:

- **Power-distance (PDI).** This dimension refers to the power structures within a country. Countries that are low on this scale have fairly flat power structures. Countries scoring highly have rigid hierarchies of power, with clear levels of status.
- **Collectivism vs individualism (IDV).** Individualistic countries tend to emphasize personal goals and assume that everyone can look after themselves. In collectivist countries, governments seek to create a common good and engender harmony; fitting in is critical.
- **Femininity vs masculinity (MAS).** This is an interesting choice of terminology, as Hofstede uses traditional notions of femininity (proclivity to focus on the home, children and nurturing) and masculinity (proclivity to be assertive and competitive) to define where countries lie on this dimension.

- **Uncertainty avoidance (UAI).** Countries react differently to uncertainty. In some cultures, uncertainty is to be avoided and feared. Other cultures embrace uncertainty and see it as an opportunity.
- **Long-term vs short-term orientation (LTO).** Some countries, specifically Asian ones, have been influenced by Confucian philosophies for centuries. This gives these countries a 'long-term' view of life, engendering people with a desire to work patiently, respect the elderly, etc. 'Short-term' countries contain people who are fulfilled through individualism and creative expression.

This work is very seductive to computer scientists as it implies that somehow culture can be quantified. In fact, the paper by Marcus and Gould (2000) includes a table in which the cultures of many countries are scored according to these dimensions (reproduced in Table 11.1). The ultimate goal of this class of research is to allow software designers to work through the various dimensions to assess the likely impact on the target culture of the design they are proposing.

TABLE 11.1

Hofstede's dimensions of culture (Marcus and Gould, 2000)

	PDI		IDV		MAS		UAI		LTO	
	Rank	Score	Rank	Score	Rank	Score	Rank	Score	Rank	Score
Arab countries	7	80	26/27	38	23	53	27	68		
Argentina	35/36	49	22/23	46	20/21	56	10/15	86		
Australia	41	36	2	90	16	61	37	51	15	31
Austria	53	11	18	55	2	79	24/25	70		
Bangladesh									11	40
Belgium	20	65	8	75	22	54	5/6	94		
Brazil	14	69	26/27	38	27	49	21/22	76	6	65
Canada	39	39	4/5	80	24	52	41/42	48	20	23
Chile	24/25	63	38	23	46	28	10/15	86		
China									1	118
Colombia	17	67	49	13	11/12	64	20	80		
Costa Rica	42/44	35	46	15	48/49	21	10/15	86		
Denmark	51	18	9	74	50	16	51	23		
East Africa	21/23	64	33/35	27	39	41	36	52		
Equador	8/9	78	52	8	13/14	63	28	67		
Finland	46	33	17	63	47	26	31/32	59		
France	15/16	68	10/11	71	35/36	43	10/15	86		
Germany (FR)	42/44	35	15	67	9/10	66	29	65	14	31
Great Britain	42/44	35	3	89	9/10	66	47/48	35	18	25
Greece	27/28	60	30	35	18/19	57	1	112		
Guatemala	2/3	95	53	6	43	37	3	101		
Hong Kong	15/16	68	37	25	18/19	57	49/50	27	2	96
India	10/11	77	21	48	20/21	56	45	40	7	61
Indonesia	8/9	78	47/48	14	30/31	46	41/42	48		

TABLE 11.1
(continued)

	PDI		IDV		MAS		UAI		LTO	
	Rank	Score	Rank	Score	Rank	Score	Rank	Score	Rank	Score
Iran	29/30	58	24	41	35/36	43	31/32	59		
Irish Republic	49	28	12	70	7/8	68	47/48	35		
Israel	52	13	19	54	29	47	19	81		
Italy	34	50	7	76	4/5	70	23	75		
Jamaica	37	45	25	39	7/8	68	52	13		
Japan	33	54	22/23	46	1	95	7	92	4	80
Malaysia	1	104	36	26	25/26	50	46	36		
Mexico	5/6	81	32	30	6	69	18	82		
Netherlands	40	38	4/5	80	51	14	35	53	10	44
New Zealand	50	22	6	79	17	58	39/40	49	16	30
Nigeria									22	16
Norway	47/48	31	13	69	52	8	38	50		
Pakistan	32	55	47/48	14	25/26	50	24/25	70	23	0
Panama	2/3	95	51	11	34	44	10/15	86		
Peru	21/23	64	45	16	37/38	42	9	87		
Philippines	4	94	31	32	11/12	64	44	44	21	19
Poland									13	32
Portugal	24/25	63	33/35	27	45	31	2	104		
Salvador	18/19	66	42	19	40	40	5/6	94		
Singapore	13	74	39/41	20	28	48	53	8	9	48
South Africa	35/36	49	16	65	13/14	63	39/40	49		
South Korea	27/28	60	43	18	41	39	16/17	85	5	75
Spain	31	57	20	51	37/38	42	10/15	86		
Sweden	47/48	31	10/11	71	53	5	49/50	29	12	33
Switzerland	45	34	14	68	4/5	70	33	58		
Taiwan	29/30	58	44	17	32/33	45	26	69	3	87
Thailand	21/23	64	39/41	20	44	34	30	64	8	56
Turkey	18/19	66	28	37	23/3	45	16/17	85		
Uruguay	26	61	29	36	42	38	4	100		
USA	38	40	1	91	15	62	43	46	17	29
Venezuela	5/6	81	50	12	3	73	21/22	76		
West Africa	10/11	77	39/41	20	30/31	46	34	54		
Yugoslavia	12	76	33/35	27	48/49	21	8	88		
Zimbabwe									19	25

For abbreviations see text.

EXERCISE 11.2 NAVIGATING THE CULTURAL SPACE

Make an attempt to classify *your* culture on each of the five dimensions above. Now ask a few people you know to do the same thing. Finally, compare your result with the result for your country in Marcus's table. Are there any differences? If so, why do you think those differences arose? ■

This all sounds very laudable but, in our experience at least, has proven fairly fruitless. Besides the ethical issues (see Box 11.2), we have also encountered problems in applying this work directly. Foremost among these is the notion of a 'target culture'. Returning to Marcus and Gould's table, it is impossible to see how a country can have a single culture – most countries comprise more than one distinct cultural group. The notion of a single culture per country is also something Marcus and Gould themselves take issue with. For instance, when considering a software application, we have encountered the situation where the target culture is completely different from the wider social culture. Often the target group of users have been trained in a particular way of working by the computer system to such an extent that it affects other aspects of behavior (see Box 11.3). Also, in some developing countries at least, users would prefer not to use internationalized versions of the software – using English software allows them to practice their English and may provide an opportunity to gain better employment in another country. We have seen attempts to translate open-source software into local languages fall flat for this very reason.

The projects that we have worked on have led us to believe that, once again, the only way to understand a target culture is through direct ethnographic or anthropological means. (It must be stated that we are not experts in analysis of culture and these opinions are based purely on pragmatic experience.)

BOX 11.2 CULTURAL DIMENSIONS – TREAD LIGHTLY

Working in post-apartheid South Africa can be a fantastically positive experience. One reason is the open way in which racial issues are discussed. Taking the lead from initiatives like the Truth and Reconciliation Commission, most of the populace will openly discuss racial issues which lie hidden in other cultures and countries. What rapidly becomes apparent is the way in which diversity is celebrated and any attempt at categorizing an individual by something as arbitrary as race is vilified. Therefore, within some cultures, the paradigm behind work like Hofstede's is questionable – to people in South Africa, it is hauntingly reminiscent of the old apartheid racial classifications. Although this is clearly not the intention of Hofstede's work, and there may be benefits in adopting it, as a group we have chosen to reject any techniques which objectify culture. ■

BOX 11.3 COMMUNICATION IN ENGLISH

One of our colleagues, Marion Walton, was conducting some research into the communication patterns of students using cellular handsets at the University of Cape Town. She discovered that students often communicated in English rather than their home language. For example, one Zulu student would SMS her Zulu-speaking mother in English. When interviewed, the student explained that the design of the handset interface forced her to 'think in English'. ■

The Hofstede dimensions deal with the hidden parts of a culture – the motivations, psychology and values that drive people. Another aspect of cultural analysis is the inspection of the tangible artifacts produced by that culture. For software developers, we are on firmer ground here, as these artifacts can be codified into unambiguous design rules. For example, paper sizes are different across different countries, but each country has an agreed standard set of sizes. Obviously cultural artifacts like address formats, measurement units, etc., would fall under this same category. It almost seems too obvious to state that, for software to succeed in a given country, it must conform to the various standards used in that country – something that most packages do well already.

There is a danger, however, in treating the internationalization of an interface as an exercise in tinkering with icons and formatting strings. In the various projects described below, we have made observations that lead us to conclude that it is essential to understand the visual literacy of the target user group. A person's visual literacy is a measure of their ability to interpret signs and diagrammatic conventions. This ability goes beyond the simple interpretation of single images and relates to how groups of items are interpreted as a whole. At present, most of the research into cultural interpretation of visual interfaces is still at the level of guidelines on culturally appropriate use of colors and icons.

To pick an example from our work, we have found that certain groups of users struggle with the concept of a hierarchy (Walton and Vukovic, 2003). This cropped up in the CyberTracker project and the Mobile Digital Library project. We observed users struggling with navigation in both these systems. Initially we thought this was due to poor choices in designing the hierarchy, so the hierarchy was redrawn in different ways. After some further research, however, it became clear that the issue was not the symbols used to denote the hierarchy, but the whole notion of a hierarchy. To test this idea, we had subjects draw family trees which produced diagrams similar to that shown in Figure 11.1.

Similarly, when we explained the concept of standard hierarchical animal classification (e.g. Reptiles: Snakes: Adders: Puff Adder) to the animal trackers in the Karoo (see next section), they laughed in amazement – "Why would anyone want to do that?".

In summary, then, internationalization guidelines can take you only so far. While they are useful for minor formatting issues, the deeper structures and paradigms on which an interface is built must also be examined.

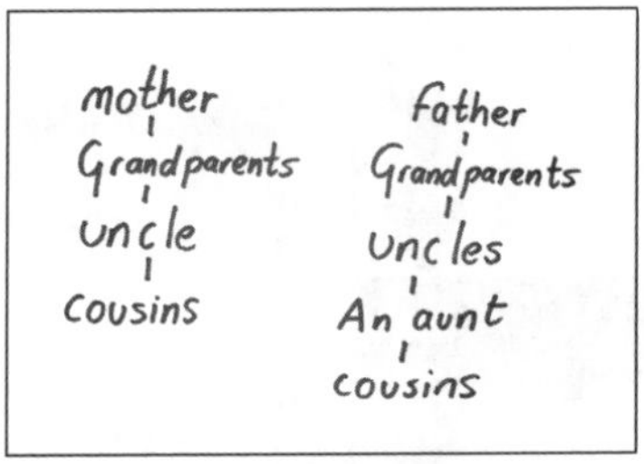

mother
Grandparents
uncle
Cousins

father
Grandparents
Uncles
An aunt
cousins

FIGURE 11.1

The subjects had the concept of a family tree explained to them and were asked to draw a tree for their family. This is among the more sensible responses we received

11.6 CASE STUDIES

11.6.1 EMPOWERING PEOPLE – CYBERTRACKER

One of our colleagues at the University of Cape Town, Edwin Blake, produced one of the first demonstrations of how effective mobile computers could be in the developing world. In this instance, the target user group were animal trackers in the Karoo National Park. These trackers are able to infer all sorts of subtle information from the tracks left by animals moving through the park. Theirs is a rich oral culture which emphasizes an understanding of the environment. Sadly, much of this knowledge cannot be shared with those from outside the culture as the trackers are, to Western cultures at least, effectively illiterate. (Ironically, the trackers see Westerners as illiterate in reading the signs and symbols of the veldt.) Their inability to communicate their knowledge effectively is frustrating for tracker and ranger alike.

Professor Blake, however, realized that the tracker's communication skills are highly visual; the tracker must attach information to the signs left by the animals. Iconic interfaces require the same skills. From this starting point, Professor Blake and his team went on to develop an icon-driven interface for the Apple Newton (this was 1996, after all) which allowed the trackers to record what they had seen by selecting appropriate icons.

Rather than apply any form of cultural dimensions, the team engaged in *Critical Action Research* with the trackers and rangers. This is a methodology whereby the researchers become part of the community with which they are trying to work. The researchers develop ideas about the behavior of the community (in this case, the interpretation of icons) which they write down and reflect back to the community for critique. Inevitably changes will need to be made after the critique, and the cycle is repeated until agreement is reached between researchers and community. To communities wary of outsiders, this can be an ideal way to work together in a sympathetic way.

After several cycles of critical action research, the interface shown in Figure 11.2 was developed. The interface first required the tracker to identify the animal, in this case a klipspringer. Next, activities were selected – the selection of more than one activity had to be supported by the interface.

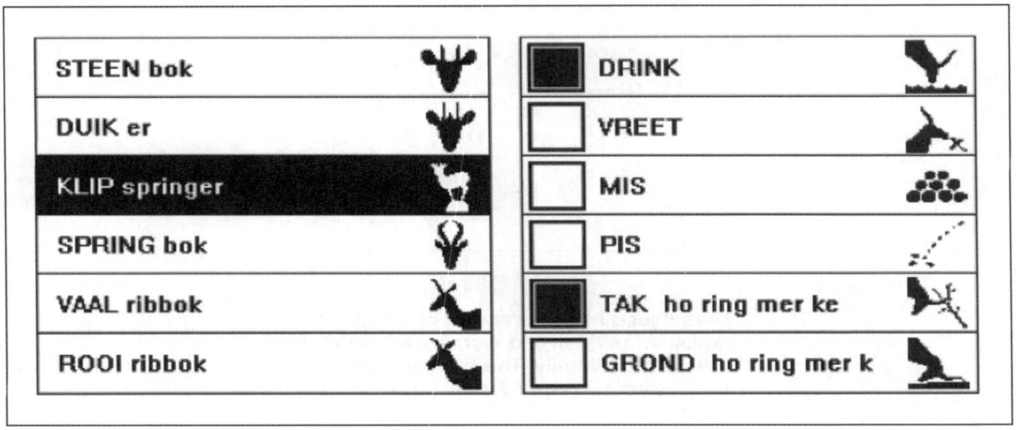

FIGURE 11.2

Iconic interface for the Newton. The screen on the left shows the animal, which is selected first. The screen on the right then appears allowing the tracker to record the activity the animal was engaged in

Everything the system could do was displayed directly on the interface – there were no pop-ups or special modifiers required. One thing you may notice from Figure 11.2 is that the interface has descriptive words beside the icons (the language is Afrikaans, as spoken by the trackers). These words served two purposes: firstly, they could be used as an aid by those trackers who were literate to some degree; secondly, they could be used to help teach the words to the illiterate trackers.

Once the entry is complete, a time stamp and location information (the Newton was connected to a GPS) were added to the recording. This information remains in the device's memory, until it is uploaded to a PC when the tracker returns.

To illustrate the importance of working in this way with the target community, consider the following two discoveries which seem to run contrary to existing research and intuition:

- **Recognition of animal icons**. The trackers paid much more attention to the overall form of an icon than to any single given aspect. For example, when creating the icon for a zebra, the designer assumed that showing stripes would be sufficient, so created a vague animal shape with stripes. This caused confusion with the trackers, some identifying it as a dog, due to the haphazard way in which the silhouette of the animal was drawn. Again the researchers' visual literacy is very different from that of the tracker.
- **Verb icons**. Accepted wisdom has it that icons are better at showing nouns than verbs – after all, how do you show 'broke twigs for small animal to eat leaves' in a grid of 32 × 32 pixels? Yet the trackers seemed to identify the action icons much more readily than they did the animals.

The success of this system can be measured on many levels. It is used in many parks around the world for many purposes – the software was ported to the Palm platform once the Newton prototype was complete. (A version can be downloaded from `http://www.cybertracker.co.za/`.) In the Karoo park, where it was originally deployed, the park management have a wealth of data on rare species, and their behaviors, which was impossible to record before. They can therefore better plan for and manage these animals.

Most importantly, the effect on the trackers has been remarkable. Whereas previously their skills seemed irrelevant, the ability to impart their knowledge has improved their self-esteem and given them an incentive to further improve their skills. Being able to communicate this information outside their culture helps ensure their knowledge will be preserved and valued by future generations.

11.6.2 EDUCATION

At present in sub-Saharan Africa, four out of every 10 children do not attend school (UNESCO, 2002). With the number of children set to increase and the number of teachers decreasing (for various reasons, including HIV/AIDS), clearly something needs to be done to make education delivery more effective and efficient. For all the reasons we have discussed before – poor electricity supply, cost concerns, etc. – mobile computers make an ideal alternative to desktop systems in the classroom.

In an effort to measure the potential impact of mobile computers in primary education in Africa, the Open University in the UK set up Project DEEP – `http://www.open.ac.uk/deep/`. The optimism for mobiles gained from the Real Access criteria certainly seems to be borne out in the DEEP project. Teachers reported that by using laptops and PDAs they were better able to cope with the erratic electricity supply and were able to work at home (ICT usage was not limited to desktop machines at school). Also popular were the camera-enabled PDAs used in the project. Originally intended as a way for teachers to document the DEEP project, students and teachers alike soon started using them as resources for projects and fieldwork. These devices engendered learning and creativity in a way that was not happening with the desktop systems. One teacher on the project wrote "The [handheld] is my companion". Many teachers commented on the unique abilities of the PDAs to be used anywhere and how it opened up new possibilities for learning. Encouraging as it was, the DEEP team were educationalists, so took the technology as a given and saw how it could impact learning. As designers of technology, we are now interested in building systems optimized to developing world education environments.

One project we have completed tackles the problem of providing computing facilities in a developing world university. We were interested to see whether we could build a system which used technology currently available to students (i.e. cellular handsets) that did not require the university to purchase more expensive computer hardware. This resulted in the 'Text Worm' system which allows lecturers to pose questions during a lecture and have the students SMS the answer in real time back to the lecturer's computer – the computer has a mobile handset attached in order to pick up the SMSs (Jones and Marsden, 2004). The system supported multiple-choice type questions (as seen in Figure 11.3), with results being displayed dynamically on a graph, as well as open-ended questions. The system was well received, but there were issues with the cost of SMSs and students abusing the open question system (questions were displayed on a side-screen as they were received, which ultimately proved too distracting).

Considering future handsets, we then developed a system which allows a lecturer to broadcast lecture slides to any device running Windows Mobile. This system allows students to follow a lecture without the need of a data projector (an expensive temperamental item that requires a constant electricity supply) by transmitting individual slides to the client devices. Students are able to annotate the slide using a sticky-note metaphor, as seen in Figure 11.4. At the end of the lecture, the students will have a complete annotated slide deck. These annotations are also shareable independently, so

FIGURE 11.3

The screen on the left shows the question the students must respond to. The screen on the right shows the results in real time as they are received

students can give them to friends. Also, the system supported lecturer polls and open questions, as in Text Worm.

Our system was based on a peer WiFi network between the lecturer's laptop and the client devices. We realized that not all handsets will have WiFi, so we adapted our network infrastructure wherein handsets with both Bluetooth and WiFi could act as bridges for Bluetooth-only devices.

This system may seem trivial to those familiar with campuses that have ample ICT resources. For our students, however, there are immense benefits to being able to share notes and download class materials directly without having to queue at highly oversubscribed computer laboratories. Using our software, teachers can run interactive lessons with students using nothing more than a laptop and smartphones.

11.6.3 COMMUNITIZATION

There is some excellent work currently being undertaken by various NGOs at making information and educational material available to the developing world. Some of these organizations realize that the problem is a little more complex than simply putting the material on the web. The Greenstone software, from the New Zealand Digital Library project, is an excellent example of this approach

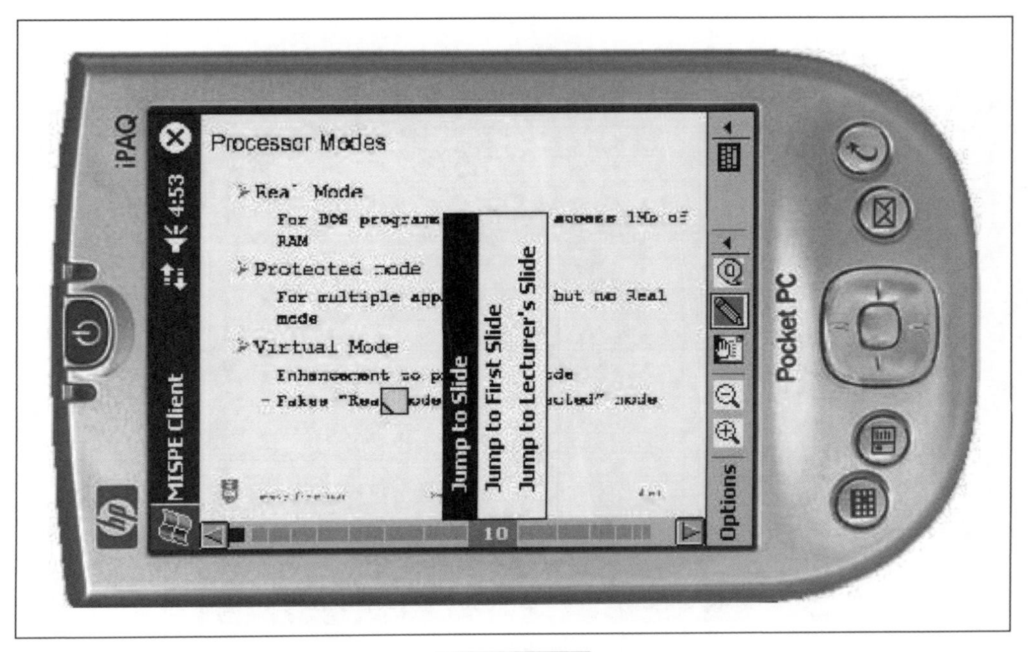

FIGURE 11.4

A yellow sticky-note can be seen on the last line of the slide. Clicking here opens the standard text entry box so the student can annotate the slide

(more information on the project can be found at `http://nzdl.org`). While it can be used to run Internet-based digital libraries, it also allows collections to be stored on CD-ROM. This was a conscious decision as the designers realized that, in the developing world, CD-ROM is a more effective way of distributing information. Furthermore, Greenstone runs on Linux, OS-X and every version of Windows from 3.1 upwards. Currently Greenstone is used to distribute the UNESCO collections of humanitarian information. Of course, we have already made the argument that mobile devices are better than desktop systems in the developing world context, so we developed a proxy for Greenstone that would allow users to access Greenstone collections using nothing more than a device with a WML browser. The project worked well and we have had interest from various organizations about adapting the solution to their needs. As information access from mobile devices has already been dealt with in Chapter 9, we won't debate the issue here. However, one interesting result which we did discover in user testing is that scrollbars are too small to be used as positional feedback in a document – they are fine if the user knows that they need to scroll down the screen, but are too small to give sufficient cues that there is more information to be scrolled to (see Figure 11.5).

The only time users did scroll down is when a line of text was truncated (see Figure 11.6) by the bottom of the screen. In the final version of our system, we forced the scrolling to always have an incomplete line at the bottom of the screen.

Another finding from the usability testing was that users struggled with how the hierarchy of documents was presented: libraries are made from collections, which are made from books, which

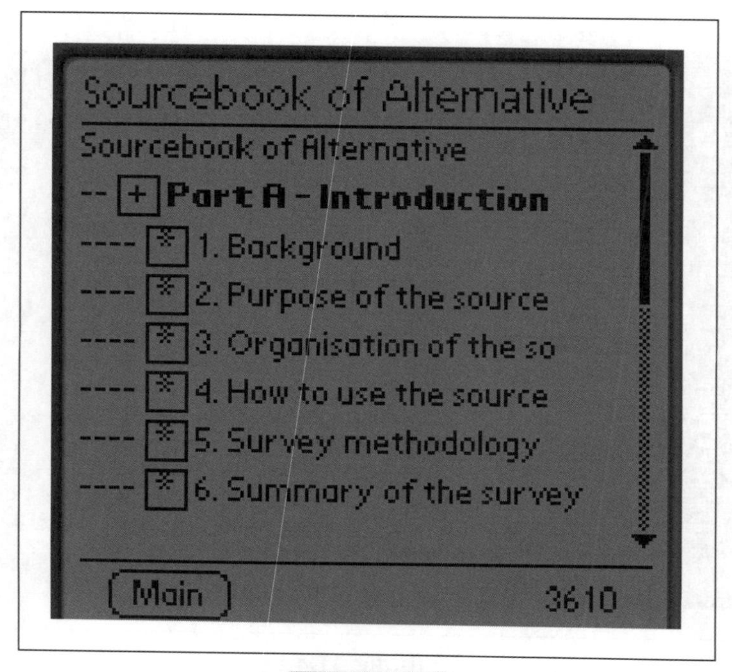

FIGURE 11.5

A seemingly complete list of the contents of the document: being three pixels wide, the scrollbar does not give sufficient feedback for users to scroll on down to see the full list

are made of chapters, which are made of pages. Believing our interface design to be sound, we decided to run the same tests using a standard desktop version of Greenstone and discovered that the same problems were evident. Obviously, users in developing countries are unlikely to have visited a library and so are unfamiliar with terms like 'collection', which are essential to understanding the interface. When this is combined with the result we reported earlier about users having trouble with hierarchies of information, clearly users are going to struggle with information that is stored and queried in this hierarchical way. If we do want people to be able to access this information, then we need to redesign the interface to suit them specifically. But, if we do that, then surely we must redesign the interface for every other group of users that we identify. Clearly there isn't time to do this, so we concluded that it was time to empower users to create their own interfaces.

The Greenstone work, and many similar projects, were presented in the Development Consortium at the CHI 2002 conference. At that consortium, the members agreed that it was necessary to develop interfaces targeted at specific groups of users in developing countries – they too rejected the notion that interfaces can be built using a tool as crude as cultural dimensions. The notion which arose was one of 'communitization' (as opposed to personalization) of software. Software created for user communities in developing countries should have the ability to be customized by a suitable member of that community. The Open Source movement would claim that such customization

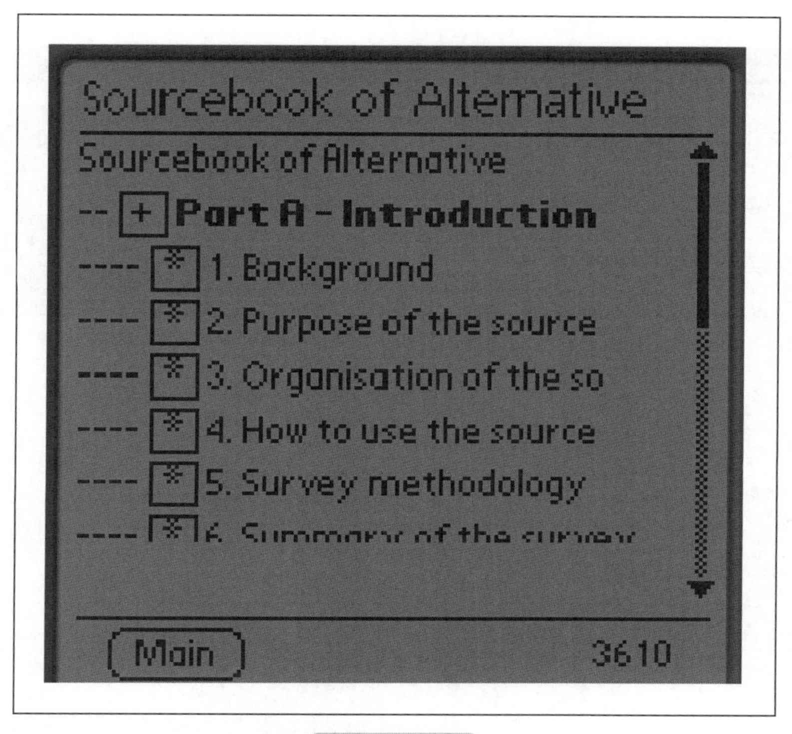

FIGURE 11.6

In this layout, users are much more likely to scroll, as the half-rendered text at the bottom indicates that the full list is not visible

is inherent in open software. That is true, but there are few open source programmers in the communities which we are targeting.

Taking our Greenstone example once again, a suitable community member would be a librarian or school teacher who wanted to make the Greenstone information available to their community in an appropriate way. To support this idea, we created a librarian's interface to Greenstone which lets them customize the appearance of the final interface. This software also has a specific option for creating a layout for mobile devices as well as the desktop version (see Figure 11.7). As Greenstone is open source, we could create this interface ourselves; so whilst open source may not be modifiable by the end-user community, it provides the possibility of modification by sympathetic third-parties.

We have not really fully explored the ideas behind 'communitization' and whether it's really any different from personalization. However, the benefits come from the process of creating software for a community rather than an individual user. In the developing world, where a user is unlikely to have their own PC, creating software for a CC (community computer) is likely to be more successful. Thinking about the community as one that includes users with mobile handsets further improves the chances of success.

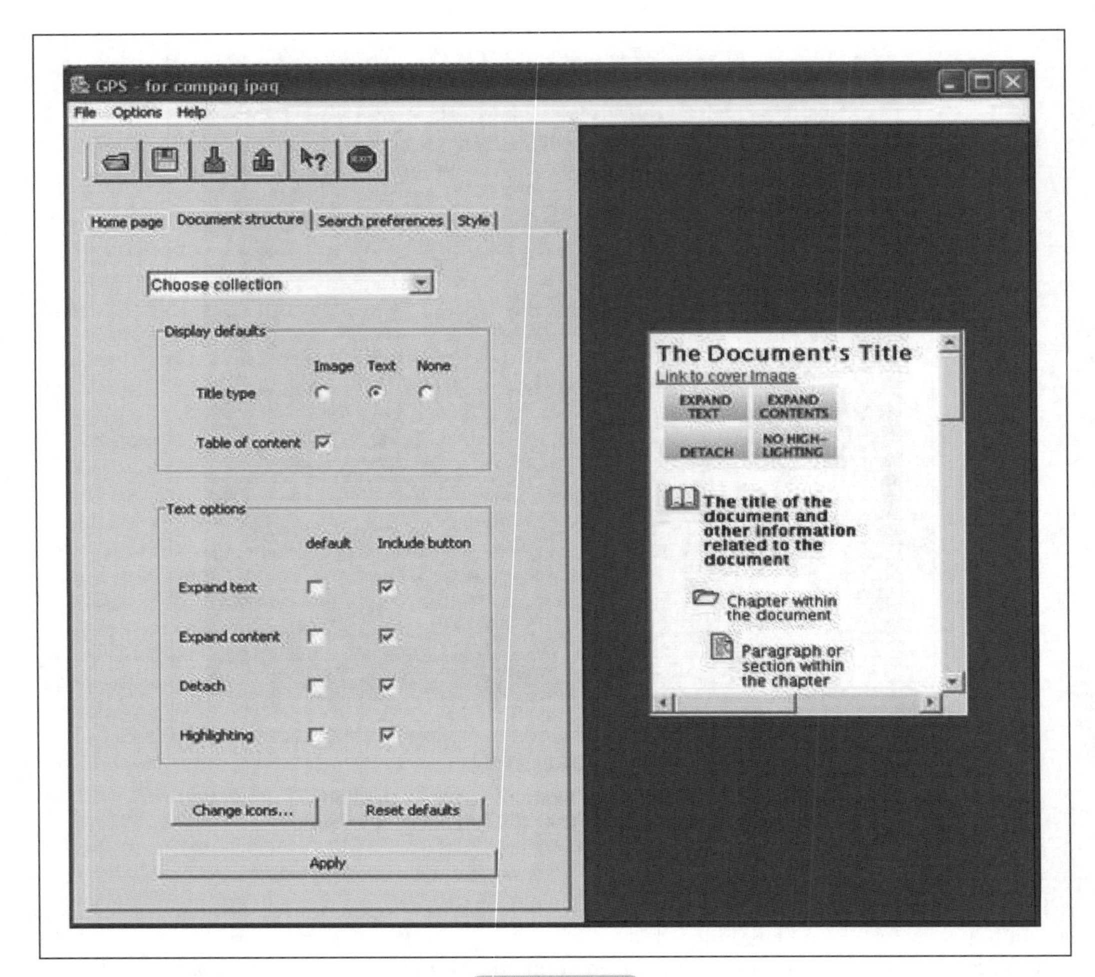

FIGURE 11.7

Digital library design system for a PDA screen. The user selects options on the left, and the screen on the right immediately reflects how those choices will affect the display on the target PDA

EXERCISE 11.3 COMMUNITIZATION

Take a look at the 'Preferences' panel in your favorite piece of software. Given what we have just said about communitization, what else do you think should be added to the panel in order to make the software customizable by a community? ➤

Or, do you think that communitization at this level is not possible and that the Open Standards community should be engaged in order to separate out the presentation layer from all existing forms of software? Is this possible (commercially) or even desirable? ■

11.7 CALL TO ARMS

The projects described in this chapter are just scratching at the surface of how to create mobile technologies with the potential to radically improve the quality of life for huge numbers of people. However, to take the education example, our work and the DEEP project are the only ones looking at how mobile technology can be used for education in developing countries. We would therefore encourage you to get actively involved in creating mobile solutions for the developing world. If you have a project to complete, or are working for a company creating solutions for the developing world, we would urge you to study documents like the Real Access criteria and get involved with the target communities. Maybe it is not too late to undo the future . . .

SUMMARY

Few ICT interventions into developing countries have succeeded; the one exception is cellular technology. For all the reasons we have listed above, and no doubt a lot more beside, cellular technology has the greatest potential to help the greatest number of people. We have been working on a number of disparate projects with a wide community of users in an attempt to understand how interaction design works in a developing world context. So, while methodologies which work closely with people (e.g. Action Research) seem to prosper, theoretical and abstract approaches (e.g. cultural dimensions) have been less successful. Our hope for the future is that more people will start to develop solutions that are sympathetic to the developing world context and we can enhance existing interaction design practice to help close the digital divide.

WORKSHOP QUESTIONS

- The term 'digital divide' is hard to define and has a wider application than the distinction between the developing and the developed world. Do there exist communities of ICT have-nots within your locality? Why is it that they do not have access, and can anything be done to alter the situation?
- Do you think that culture can be measured in dimensions as Hofstede suggests? For your culture, do you think that these dimensions capture useful ideas? Ideas that can be used in interface design?

- Universities in developing countries cannot really afford computers for all their students. How much of what is done at universities already could be successfully migrated to a mobile platform?
- If you have a study break, a sabbatical or a placement to do, we would encourage you to get involved with a project in a developing country – the impact of your work and the personal rewards are greater than anything you will do in countries already saturated with technology.

DESIGNER TIPS

- *Using the visual language of cellular handsets is a good starting point for any interface used in a developing world country.*
- *When creating software for the developing world, be mindful of extra guidelines (such as the Real Access criteria) beyond the usual design heuristics you have used in the developed world.*
- *It may be the case that you do not need to translate your software into local languages for it to succeed. Many users in developing countries welcome the opportunity to practice English.*
- *For Africa at least, be wary of interfaces that rely on users understanding hierarchically classified data – we have found that hierarchies are not a common way of thinking across all cultures.*
- *For highly visual cultures, we have shown that iconic interfaces can be effective.*

RESOURCES

These resources will be updated on the online website supporting the book – see `http://www.wiley.com/go/mobile`

BOOKS

We've found several books to be particularly helpful and inspiring in thinking about interaction design and the specifics of mobile systems. Included in this list of good reads are the following:

- *The Design of Everyday Things* by Donald A. Norman (Basic Books, 1st Basic edition, September 2002). The classic work on usability.
- Two encyclopaedias of HCI knowledge: *Designing the User Interface: Strategies for Effective Human–Computer Interaction* (4th edition) by Ben Shneiderman and Catherine Palisant (Addison Wesley, March 2004); and *Human–Computer Interaction* (3rd edition) by Alan Dix, Janet E. Finlay, Gregory D. Abowd and Russell Beale (Prentice Hall, December 2003).
- *The Invisible Computer: Why Good Products Can Fail, the Personal Computer is So Complex, and Information Appliances are the Solution* by Donald A. Norman (MIT Press, reprint edition, 1999). Presents the argument for information appliances as well as promoting approaches designers can take to make sure their work can be integrated into the commercial development life-cycle.
- *Information Appliances and Beyond: Interaction Design for Consumer Products* edited by Eric Bergman (Morgan Kaufmann, February 2000). A collection of essays discussing mobile and ubiquitous system development – from the PalmPilot to Barney, the interactive toy.
- *Interaction Design: Beyond Human–Computer Interaction* by Jenny Preece, Yvonne Rogers and Helen Sharp (John Wiley & Sons, January 2002). A text of breadth and depth with examples from a wide range of application areas.
- *Mobile Usability – How Nokia Changed the Face of the Mobile Phone* by Christian Lindholm, Turkka Keinonen and Harri Kiljander (McGraw-Hill Professional, June 2003). A collection of essays by Nokia developers and researchers talking about that company's human-centered methods and successes.
- *Prototyping – Paper Prototyping* by Carolyn Snyder (Morgan Kaufmann, 2003). This must be the definitive book on low-fidelity prototyping. It covers every aspect (rationale, technique, application in development process, etc.) in a style that is clear and enjoyable.
- *The Simplicity Shift* by Scott Jenson (Cambridge University Press, November 2002). A short, practical and inspiring approach to consumer electronic interaction design, written by a leading practitioner.

- *User Interface Design* by Harold Thimbleby (ACM Press, September 1990). This book is a truly inspirational read. It is full of deep insights into the problems of user interface design and offers solutions that remain largely untapped. Anyone who is interested in the philosophical and scientific side of solving user interface problems will find this book very satisfying.

MAGAZINES AND JOURNALS

Regularly reading the following will help keep you up to date with what's happening in the mobile and ubiquitous computing field:

- *IEEE Pervasive Computing*. Magazine-style journal with accessible articles, often looking at the field from a technical and technology perspective (see `www.computer.org/pervasive`).
- *International Journal of Personal and Ubiquitous Computing*. All aspects – from the technical to the social – of emerging technology development with a research focus; often has themed issues. Published by Springer (see `www.personal-ubicomp.com`).
- *Communications of the ACM*. The Association of Computing Machinery is the oldest professional computing organization and this is its monthly magazine. It covers topical social policy as well as technical issues of all aspects of computing and is also available online (see `www.acm.org`).
- *Interactions*. Published bi-monthly by the ACM, this is the magazine of the Computer–Human Interaction Special Interest Group. Interesting interaction designs, novel technologies, research updates, written to appeal to both practitioners and researchers (see `www.acm.org/sigchi`).
- *ACM Transactions of Computer Human Interactions (ToCHI)*. Each issue contains a number of substantial articles written by and for expert researchers. Topics cover a broad range of HCI issues (see `www.acm.org/tochi`).

CONFERENCES

Researchers from industry and academia meet throughout each year to present the findings of their latest work. The conferences you might consider attending are listed below. If you cannot go in person, try to get hold of the published proceedings containing the papers discussed.

- *International Symposium on Mobile Devices and Services* (commonly called Mobile HCI). Held usually in September (in Finland in September 2006). The most human-focused of the conferences, looking at mobile and ubiquitous technologies (see `www.mobilehci.org`). Proceedings up until 2005 published by Springer-Verlag (`www.springeronline.org`).
- *Ubicomp*. Held annually, usually in September. Learn about the newest (and sometimes strangest) emerging computing devices, infrastructures and applications (see `www.ubicomp.org`). Proceedings published by Springer-Verlag.
- *Conference on Human Factors in Computing Systems* (commonly called CHI). Takes place every year in April (in Montréal in 2006). The highest rated, best attended (usually 1500 people plus) international conference on human factors.

WEBSITES AND BLOGS

- www.useit.com. Website of Jacob Nielsen, guru of usability. Each month he publishes an article about a usability problem and its solution. Previous posts have included discussions on mobile email, WAP, tablet PCs and the like.
- www.otal.umd.edu/charm. A great resource when choosing which technique to use when evaluating a design. The site contains summaries of most evaluation techniques and helps you assess which is the most appropriate.
- www.jnd.org. Don Norman's website. If you've read through this book you'll have seen Don's name crop up many times. He's one of the seminal thinkers in HCI (and much else!) and is an excellent writer. His website contains interesting articles, drafts of books he's writing and answers to readers questions.
- www.christianlindholm.com. Christian Lindholm is a leading usability specialist at Yahoo! most recently known for his work on LifeBlog.
- www.antimega.com (Chris Heathcote) and www.blackbeltjones.com (Matt Jones – no relation). These two work at Nokia on consumer insights. Their blogs discuss interesting technology and social trends.
- www.engadget.com. A blog that reports rumors and developments concerning all types of consumer electronic gadgets.
- www.nooface.com. Blog tracking user interface innovations with many articles on mobile and ubiquitous computing schemes.
- www.cameraphonereport.com. Alan Reiter's site contains all the latest industry and research developments in the field of camera-phones.
- bridges.org. This site contains case studies of completed ICT projects in the developing world and guidelines for those starting new projects.
- www.digitaldivide.net. A great place to start if you are interested in digital divide issues.

STYLE GUIDES FOR MOBILE DEVELOPERS

We've presented design issues and guidelines in an implementation-free way. If you are a developer, ultimately, of course, you'll have to render designs using a particular interface framework. Books on mobile application development such as those listed below often have sections containing user interface style guides. In addition, operating system providers and handset manufacturers have guidelines available online; some examples are given here and further updates will be placed on the book's website.

- *Programming Microsoft Windows Ce. Net* (3rd edition) by Douglas Boling (Microsoft Press, 2003).
- *Developing Series 60 Applications: A Guide for Symbian OS C++ Developers* (Nokia Mobile Developer) by Leigh Edwards, Richard Barker, Staff of EMCC Software Ltd (Addison-Wesley Professional, March 2004).
- Online style/user interface guides:

- ... for Symbian OS versions can be found at www.symbian.com and www.symbianone.com
- ... for Microsoft PocketPCs, Smartphones, Tablets, etc., available via http://msdn.microsoft.com/mobility/
- Nokia handset usability issues are widely discussed at Nokia's www.forum.nokia.com (see, e.g., http://www.forum.nokia.com/main/1,,200,00.html?topic=Usability)
- Sony Ericsson's developer website includes documents and developer discussions on the user interface: http://developer.sonyericsson.com.

REFERENCES

Most of the work we've referenced is available online via the publishers' websites. The ACM – Association of Computing Machinery – has a search service (`www.acm.org/portal`) that can locate many of the sources. Note, however, that most publishers charge for access. Some authors provide preprint copies of their material, free of charge, on their own websites.

Abowd, G. D. and **Mynatt, E. D.** (2000). Charting past, present, and future research in ubiquitous computing. *ACM Transactions on Computer–Human Interaction* **7**(1): 29–58.

Agar, J. (2004). Learning from the mobile phone. *Journal of the Royal Society of Arts (January)*: 26–27.

Ahlberg, C. and **Shneiderman, B.** (1994). Visual information seeking: tight coupling of dynamic query filters with starfield displays. *Proceedings of the SIGCHI Conference on Human Factors in Computing Systems (CHI '94)*: 313–317, 479–480. ACM Press.

Al-Ubaydli, M. (2003). *Handheld Computers for Doctors*. John Wiley & Sons.

Anastasi, A. (1982). *Psychological Testing* (5th edn). Collier Macmillan.

Anderson, R. (2000a). Conversations with Clement Mok and Jakob Nielsen, and with Bill Buxton and Clifford Nass. *Interactions* **7**(6): 46–80.

Anderson, R. (2000b). Organizational limits to HCI: conversations with Don Norman and Janice Rohn. *Interactions* **7**(3): 36–60.

Andersson, N. (2002). Helping the helpers: Cameo – an information appliance for home care service. *Proceedings of the Second Nordic Conference on Human–Computer Interaction (NordChi)*: 223–226. Aarhus, Denmark. ACM Press.

Aridor, Y., **Carmel, D.**, **Maarek, Y. S.**, **Soffer, A.** and **Lempel, R.** (2001). Knowledge encapsulation for focused search from pervasive devices. *ACM Transactions on Information Systems* **20**(1): 25–46.

Baecker, R., **Small, I.** and **Mander, R.** (1991). Bringing icons to life – Use of familiar things in the design of interfaces. *Proceedings of the SIGCHI Conference on Human Factors in Computing Systems (CHI '91)*: 1–6. ACM Press.

Banavar, G. and **Bernstein, A.** (2002). Software infrastructure and design challenges for ubiquitous computing applications. *Communications of the ACM* **45**(12): 92–96.

Barnes, **S.** and **Huff**, **S. L.** (2003). Rising sun: iMode and the wireless Internet. *Communications of the ACM* **46**(11): 78–84.

Baudisch, **P.** and **Rosenholtz**, **R.** (2003). Halo: a technique for visualizing off-screen objects. *Proceedings of the SIGCHI Conference on Human Factors in Computing Systems (CHI '03)*: 481–488. Fort Lauderdale, FL, USA. ACM Press.

Baudisch, **P.**, **Xie**, **X.**, **Wang**, **C.** and **Ma**, **W. -Y.** (2004). Collapse-to-zoom: viewing web pages on small screen devices by interactively removing irrelevant content. *Proceedings of the 17th Annual ACM Symposium on User Interface Software and Technology (UIST '04)*: 91–94. Sante Fe, NM, USA. ACM Press.

Beck, **E.**, **Christiansen**, **M.**, **Kjeldskov**, **J.**, **Kolbe**, **N.** and **Stage**, **J.** (2003). Experimental evaluation of techniques for usability testing of mobile devices in a laboratory setting. *Proceedings of the International Conference of the Australian Computer–Human Interaction Special Interest Group (OzCHI '03)*. Brisbane, Australia.

Bederson, **B. B.**, **Grosjean**, **J.** and **Meyer**, **J.** (2004). Toolkit design for interactive structured graphics. *IEEE Transactions on Software Engineering* **30**(8): 535–546.

Berg, **S.**, **Taylor**, **A. S.** and **Harper**, **R.** (2003). Mobile phones for the next generation: device designs for teenagers. *Proceedings of the SIGCHI Conference on Human Factors in Computing Systems (CHI '03)*: 443–440. Fort Lauderdale, FL, USA. ACM Press.

Bergman, **E.** and **Haitani**, **R.** (2000). Designing the PalmPilot: a conversation with Rob Haitani, in *Information Appliances and Beyond – Interaction Design for Consumer Products*, **Bergman**, **E.** (ed.): 81–102. Morgan Kaufmann.

Berners-Lee, **T.** (2000). *Weaving the Web: The Original Design and Ultimate Destiny of the World Wide Web*. Harper Business Press.

Bevan, **N.** (2001). International standards for HCI and usability. *International Journal of Human–Computer Studies* **55**(4): 533–552.

Bevan, **N.**, **Barnum**, **C.**, **Cockton**, **G.**, **Nielsen**, **J.**, **Spool**, **J.** and **Wixon**, **D.** (2003). The 'magic number 5': is it enough for web testing? Panel. *Proceedings of the SIGCHI Conference on Human Factors in Computing Systems (CHI '03)*: 698–699. Fort Lauderdale, FL, USA. ACM Press.

Beyer, **H. R.** and **Holtzblatt**, **K.** (1995). Apprenticing with the customer. *Communications of the ACM* **38**(5): 45–52.

Bitton, **J.**, **Agamanolis**, **S.** and **Karau**, **M.** (2004). RAW: conveying minimally-mediated impressions of everyday life with an audio-photographic tool. *Proceedings of the SIGCHI Conference on Human Factors in Computing Systems (CHI '04)*: 495–502. Vienna, Austria. ACM Press.

Björk, S., Holmquist, L. E., Redström, J., Bretan, I., Danielsson, R., Karlgren, J. and **Franzen, K.** (1999). WEST: a Web browser for small terminals. *Proceedings of the 12th Annual ACM Symposium on User Interface Software and Technology*: 187–196. Asheville, NC, USA. ACM Press.

Blattner, M., Sumikawa, D. and **Greenberg, R.** (1989). Earcons and icons: their structure and common design principles. *Human–Computer Interaction* **4**(1): 11–44.

Bødker, S. and **Buur, J.** (2002). The design collaboratorium: a place for usability design. *ACM Transactions on Computer–Human Interaction* **9**(**2**): 152–169.

Bohnenberger, T., Jameson, A., Kruger, A. and **Butz, A.** (2002). Location-aware shopping assistance: evaluation of a decision-theoretic approach. *Proceedings of the 4th International Symposium on Mobile Human–Computer Interaction (Mobile HCI '02), LNCS 2411*: 155–169. Pisa, Italy. Springer.

Brewster, S. (2002). Overcoming the lack of screen space on mobile computers. *Personal and Ubiquitous Computing* **6**(3): 188–205.

Brewster, S., Lumsden, J., Bell, M., Hall, M. and **Tasker, S.** (2003). Multimodal 'eyes-free' interaction techniques for wearable devices. *Proceedings of the SIGCHI Conference on Human Factors in Computing Systems (CHI '03)*: 473–480. Fort Lauderdale, FL, USA. ACM Press.

Brooks, F. (1975). *The Mythical Man Month: Essays on Software Engineering*. Addison-Wesley.

Brown, B. (2002). Studying the use of mobile technology, in *Wireless World – Social and Interactional Aspects of the Mobile Age*, **Brown, B., Green, N.** and **Harper, R.** (eds): 3–14. Springer.

Brown, B., Sellen, A. J. and **O'Hara, K. P.** (2000). A diary study of information capture in working life. *Proceedings of the SIGCHI Conference on Human Factors in Computing Systems (CHI '00)*: 438–445. The Hague, The Netherlands. ACM Press.

Brunnberg, L. (2004). The Road Rager: making use of traffic encounters in a mobile multiplayer game. *Proceedings of the 3rd International Conference on Mobile and Ubiquitous Multimedia. ACM Conference Proceeding Series* ***83***: 33–39. ACM Press.

Buchanan, G., Farrant, S., Jones, M., Thimbleby, H., Marsden, G. and **Pazzani, M.** (2001). Improving mobile internet usability. *Proceedings of the Tenth International Conference on World Wide Web (WWW10)*: 673–680. Hong Kong. ACM Press.

Buchanan, G., Jones, M. and **Marsden, G.** (2002). Exploring small screen digital library access with the Greenstone Digital Library, in *Proceedings of the 6th European Conference on Research and Advanced Technology for Digital Libraries*, **Agosti, M.** and **Thanos, C.** (eds): 583–596. Springer.

Butler, M. B. (1996). Getting to know your user: usability roundtables at Lotus Development. *Interactions* **3**(1): 23–30.

Button, **G.** and **Dourish**, **P.** (1996). Technomethodology: paradoxes and possibilities. *Proceedings of the SIGCHI Conference on Human Factors in Computing Systems (CHI '96)*: 19–26. Vancouver, Canada. ACM Press.

Buyukkokten, **O.**, **Garcia-Molina**, **H.**, **Paepcke**, **A.** and **Winograd**, **T.** (2000). PowerBrowser: efficient web browsing for PDAs. *Proceedings of the SIGCHI Conference on Human Factors in Computing Systems (CHI '00)*: 430–437. The Hague, The Netherlands. ACM Press

Buyukkokten, **O.**, **Garcia-Molina**, **H.** and **Paepcke**, **A.** (2001a). Accordion summarization for end-game browsing on PDAs and cellular phones. *Proceedings of the SIGCHI Conference on Human Factors in Computing Systems (CHI '01)*: 213–220. Seattle, WA, USA. ACM Press.

Buyukkokten, **O.**, **Garcia-Molina**, **H.** and **Paepcke**, **A.** (2001b). Seeing the whole in parts: text summarization for web browsing on handheld devices. *Proceedings of the Tenth International Conference on World Wide Web (WWW10)*: 652–662. Hong Kong. ACM Press.

Card, **S.**, **Moran**, **T.** and **Newell**, **A.** (1983). *The Psychology of Human–Computer Interaction.* Hillsdale, NJ: Erlbaum.

Card, **S. K.**, **Robertson**, **G. G.** and **Mackinlay**, **J. D.** (1991). The Information Visualizer, an information workspace. *Proceedings of the SIGCHI Conference on Human Factors in Computing Systems (CHI '91)*: 181–186. ACM Press.

Card, **S. K.**, **Mackinlay**, **J. D.** and **Shneiderman**, **B.** (eds) (1999). *Readings in Information Visualization – Using Vision to Think.* Morgan Kaufmann.

Carroll, **J. M.** (2000). Five reasons for scenario-based design. *Interacting with Computers* **13**: 43–60.

Ceaparu, **I.**, **Lazar**, **J.**, **Bessiere**, **K.**, **Robinson**, **J.** and **Shneiderman**, **B.** (2004). Determining causes and severity of end-user frustration. *International Journal of Human–Computer Studies* **17**(3): 333–356.

Chen, **H.** and **Dumais**, **S. T.** (2000). Bringing order to the Web: automatically categorizing search results. *Proceedings of the SIGCHI Conference on Human Factors in Computing Systems (CHI '00)*: 145–152. The Hague, The Netherlands. ACM Press.

Chen, **Y.**, **Huang**, **H.**, **Chen**, **M. -F.** and **Rao**, **H.** (2002). IMobile ME: a lightweight mobile service platform for peer-to-peer mobile computing. *Proceedings of the IFIP TC 6/WG 6.4 Workshop on Internet Technologies, Applications and Social Impact*: 199–214. IFIP.

Cheverst, **K.**, **Clarke**, **K.**, **Fitton**, **D.**, **Rouncefield**, **M.**, **Crabtree**, **A.** and **Hemmings**, **T.** (2003). SPAM on the menu: the practical use of remote messaging in community care. *Proceedings of the 2003 Conference on Universal Usability*: 23–29. Vancouver, Canada. ACM Press.

Christensen, **C. M.** (2003). *The Innovator's Dilemma.* HarperBusiness.

Cockburn, **A.** and **Savage**, **J.** (2003). Comparing speed-dependent automatic zooming with traditional scroll, pan, and zoom methods. *People and Computers XVII: Proceedings of the 17th Annual British Computer Society Conference on Human–Computer Interaction (BCS HCI 2003)*: 87–102. Bath, UK. British Computer Society.

Cockburn, **A.** and **Siresena**, **A.** (2003). Evaluating mobile text entry with the Fastap keypad. *People and Computers XVII (Volume 2): Proceedings of the 17th Annual British Computer Society Conference on Human–Computer Interaction (BCS HCI 2003)*: 77–80. Bath, UK. British Computer Society.

Cockton, **G.** (2004). Value-centred HCI. *Proceedings of the Third Nordic Conference on Human–Computer Interaction*: 149–160. Tampere, Finland. ACM Press.

Combs, **T. T. A.** and **Bederson**, **B. B.** (1999). Does zooming improve image browsing? *Proceedings of Digital Library (DL '99)*: 130–137. New York, USA. ACM Press.

Cooper, **A.** (1999). *The Inmates are Running the Asylum*. Sams Press.

Counts, **S.** and **Fellheimer**, **E.** (2004). Supporting social presence through lightweight photo sharing on and off the desktop. *Proceedings of the SIGCHI Conference on Human Factors in Computing Systems (CHI '04)*: 599–606. Vienna, Austria. ACM Press.

Covey, **S.** (1990). *Seven Habits of Highly Effective People* (1st edn). New York: Free Press.

Crabtree, **A.**, **Benford**, **S.**, **Rodden**, **T.**, **Greenhalgh**, **C.**, **Flintham**, **M.**, **Drozd**, **A.**, **Adams**, **M.**, **Row-Farr**, **J.**, **Tandavanitj**, **N.** and **Steed**, **A.** (2004). Orchestrating a mixed reality game 'on the ground'. *ACM CHI Letters* **6**(1): 391–398.

Csikszentmihalyi, **M.** (1991). *Flow: The Psychology of Optimal Experience*. HarperPerennial.

Cukier, **K. N.** (2005). Let the good times roll. *Intelligent Life* (Summer): 24–25.

Cunningham, **S. J.**, **Jones**, **M.** and **Jones**, **S.** (2004). Organizing digital music for use: an examination of personal music collections. *Proceedings of the 5th International Conference on Music Information Retrieval (ISMIR 2004)*. Barcelona, Spain.

Curzon, **P.**, **Blandford**, **A.**, **Butterworth**, **R.** and **Bhogal**, **R.** (2002). Interaction design issues for car navigation systems. *Proceedings of the 16th British HCI Conference (BCS 2002)*, **2**: 38–41.

Cutting, **D. R.**, **Karger**, **D.**, **Pedersen**, **J. O.** and **Tukey**, **J. W.** (1992). Scatter/Gather: a cluster-based approach to browsing large document collections. *Proceedings of SIGIR'92: the 15th International Conference on Research and Development in Information Retrieval*: 318–329. ACM Press.

de Bruijn, **O.** and **Spence**, **R.** (2000). Rapid serial visual presentation: a space–time trade-off in information presentation. *Proceedings of the Working Conference on Advanced Visual Interfaces*: 189–192.

Derrett, **N.** (2004). Heckel's law: conclusions from the user interface design of a music appliance – the bassoon. *Personal and Ubiquitous Computing* **8**(3–4): 208–212.

Dey, A. K. (2001). Understanding and using context. *Personal and Ubiquitous Computing* **5**(1): 4–7.

Di Pietro, R. and **Mancini, L. V.** (2003). Security and privacy issues of handheld and wearable wireless devices. *Communications of the ACM* **9**: 74–79.

Dillon, A., Richardson, J. and **McKnight, C.** (1990). The effect of display size and text splitting on reading lengthy text from the screen. *Behaviour and Information Technology* **9**(3): 215–227.

Dix, A. (1995). Accelerators and toolbars: learning from the menu. *People and Computers IX (Adjunct): British Computer Society Conference on Human Computer Interaction*: 138–143. British Computer Society.

Dix, A., Finlay, J., Abowd, G. and **Beale, R.** (1998). *Human–Computer Interaction* (2nd edn). Prentice Hall.

Dix, A., Rodden, T., Davies, N., Trevor, J., Friday, A. and **Palfreyman, K.** (2000). Exploiting space and location as a design framework for interactive mobile systems. *ACM Transactions on Computer–Human Interaction* **7**(3): 285–321.

Dourish, P. (2004). What we talk about when we talk about context. *Personal and Ubiquitous Computing* **8**(1): 19–30.

Dray, S. (2001). *Understanding Users' Work in Context: Practical Observation Skills.* Workshop at CHI-South Africa, 10 September 2001.

Dray, S. and **Siegel, D.** (2002). Why do Version 1.0 and not release it? *Interactions* **9**(2): 11–16.

Duchnicky, R. L. and **Kolers, P. A.** (1983). Readability of text scrolled on visual display terminals as a function of window size. *Human Factors* **25**(6): 683–692.

Dunlop, M. and **Davidson, N.** (2000). Visual information seeking on PDAtop devices. *Proceedings of the British Computer Society Conference on Human–Computer Interaction 2000 (Companion)*: 19–20. British Computer Society.

Dykstra-Erickson, E., **MacKay, W. E.** and **Aronwitz, J.** (2001). Perspective: trialogue on design (of). *Interactions* **8**(2): 109–117.

Eagle, N. and **Pentland, A. S.** (2006). Reality mining – sensing complex social systems. *International Journal of Personal and Ubiquitous Computing* **10**(*to appear*).

Eco, U. (1995). *How to Travel with a Salmon and Other Essays.* Harvest Books.

Economist (2004a). Off with the pith helmets. *Economist*, 11 March 2004.

Economist (2004b).Vision, meet reality. *Economist Magazine*, 2 September 2004.

Edwards, A. and **Long, J.** (eds) (1995). *Extraordinary Human–Computer Interaction: Interfaces for Users with Disabilities.* Cambridge University Press.

Erikson, T. and **Simon, H.** (1985). *Protocol Analysis: Verbal Reports as Data*. MIT Press.

Esbjörnsson, M., Juhlin, O. and **Östergren**, M. (2004). Traffic encounters and Hocman: associating motorcycle ethnography with design. *Personal and Ubiquitous Computing* **8**(2): 92–99.

Espinoza, F., Persson, P., Sandin, A., Nyström, H., Cacciatore, E. and **Bylund, M.** (2001). GeoNotes: social and navigational aspects of location-based information systems. *Proceedings of the 3rd International Conference on Ubiquitous Computing*. Atlanta, GA, USA. Springer.

Falk, J. and **Björk, S.** (1999). The BubbleBadge: a wearable public display. *Proceedings of the SIGCHI Conference on Human Factors in Computing Systems (CHI '99), Extended Abstracts*: 318–319. Pittsburgh, PA, USA. ACM Press.

Fallman, D. (2002). Wear, point and tilt: designing support for mobile service and maintenance in industrial settings. *Proceedings of the Conference on Designing Interactive Systems: Processes, Practices, Methods and Techniques (DIS 2002)*: 293–302. London, UK. ACM Press.

Fallman, D. (2003). Design-oriented human–computer interaction. *Proceedings of the SIGCHI Conference on Human Factors in Computing Systems (CHI '03)*: 225–232. Fort Lauderdale, FL, USA. ACM Press.

Frohlich, D. and **Tallyn, E.** (1999). Audiophotography: practice and prospects. *Proceedings of the SIGCHI Conference on Human Factors in Computing Systems (CHI '99), Extended Abstracts*: 296–297. The Hague, The Netherlands. ACM Press.

Frohlich, D., Kuchinsky, A., Pering, C., Don, A. and **Ariss, S.** (2002). Requirements for photoware. *Proceedings of the 2002 ACM Conference on Computer Supported Cooperative Work (CSCW '02)*. New Orleans, LA, USA. ACM Press.

Furnas, G. (1986). Generalized fisheye views. *Proceedings of the Conference on Human Factors in Computing Systems III (CHI '86)*. ACM.

Furnas, G. W. and **Rauch, S. J.** (1998). Considerations for information environments and the NaviQue workspace. *Proceedings of Digital Libraries '98: The Third ACM Conference on Digital Libraries*: 79–88. Pittsburgh, PA, USA. ACM Press.

Gaver, W. (1989). The SonicFinder: an interface that uses auditory icons. *Human–Computer Interaction* **4**(1): 67–94.

Gaver, W., Dunne, T. and **Pacenti, E.** (1999). Cultural probes. *Interactions* **6**(1): 21–29.

Gaver, W., Bowers, J., Boucher, A., Gellerson, H. W., Pennington, S., Schmidt, A., Steed, A., Villars, N. and **Walker, B.** (2004). The drift table: designing for ludic engagement. *Proceedings of the SIGCHI Conference on Human Factors in Computing Systems (CHI '04), Extended Abstracts*: 885–900. Vienna, Austria. ACM Press.

Gaver, W., Beaver, J. and **Benford, S.** (2003). Ambiguity as a resource for design. *Proceedings of the SIGCHI Conference on Human Factors in Computing Systems (CHI '03)*: 233–240. Fort Lauderdale, FL, USA. ACM Press.

Gellerson, H. W., Schmidt, A. and **Beigl, M.** (2002). Multi-sensor context-awareness in mobile devices and smart artifacts. *Mobile Networks and Applications* **7**(5): 341–351.

Glasser, B. G. and **Strauss, A. L.** (1967). *Discovery of Grounded Theory: Strategies for Qualitative Research*. Aldine.

Goldberg, D. and **Richardson, C.** (1993). Touch-typing with a stylus. *Proceedings of the SIGCHI Conference on Human Factors in Computing Systems (CHI '93)*: 80–87. Amsterdam, The Netherlands. ACM Press.

Goldstein, M., Nyberg, M. and **Anneroth, M.** (2003). Providing proper affordances when transferring source metaphors from information appliances to a 3G mobile multipurpose handset. *Personal and Ubiquitous Computing* **7**(6): 372–380.

Gould, J. D., Conti, J. and **Hovanyecz, T.** (1983). Composing letters with a simulated listening typewriter. *Communications of the ACM* **26**(4): 295–308.

Graham, A., Garcia-Molina, H., Paepcke, A. and **Winograd, T.** (2002). Time as the essence for photo browsing through personal digital libraries. *Proceedings of the Joint Conference on Digital Libraries (JCDL '02)*: 326–335. Springer.

Gritner, R. E. and **Eldridge, M.** (2003). Wan2tlk?: everyday text messaging. *Proceedings of the SIGCHI Conference on Human Factors in Computing Systems (CHI '03)*: 441–448. Fort Lauderdale, FL, USA. ACM Press.

Gritner, R. E. and **Palen, L.** (2002). Instant messaging in teen life. *Proceedings of the 2002 ACM Conference on Computer Supported Cooperative Work (CSCW '02)*: 21–29. New Orleans, LA, USA. ACM Press.

Grudin, J. (1990). The computer reaches out: the historical continuity of interface design. *Proceedings of the SIGCHI Conference on Human Factors in Computing Systems: Empowering People (CHI '90)*: 261–268. Seattle, WA, USA. ACM Press.

Grudin, J. (1991). Systematic sources of suboptimal interface design in large product development organisations. *Human–Computer Interaction* **6**(2): 147–196.

Gutwin, C. and **Pinelle, D.** (2003). Designing for loose coupling in mobile groups. *Proceedings of the 2003 International ACM SIGGROUP Conference on Supporting Group Work*: 75–84. Sanibel Island, FL, USA. ACM Press.

Hallnäs, L. and **Redström, J.** (2001). Slow technology – designing for reflection. *Personal and Ubiquitous Computing* **5**(3): 201–212.

Harada, S., Naaman, M., Song, Y., Wang, Q. and **Paepcke, A.** (2004). Lost in memories: interacting with large photo collections on PDAs. *Proceedings of the Fourth ACM/IEEE–CS Joint Conference on Digital Libraries (JCDL 2004)*: 325–333. Springer.

Harper, R. (2003). People versus information: the evolution of mobile technology. *Proceedings of the 5th International Symposium on Human–Computer Interaction with Mobile Devices and Services (Mobile HCI '03)*: 1–14. Udine, Italy. Springer.

Harper, R. and **Sellen, A.** (2001). *The Myth of the Paperless Office*. MIT Press.

Harrison, B. L., Fishkin, K. P., Anuj, G., Mochon, C. and **Want, R.** (1998). Squeeze me, hold me, tilt me! An exploration of manipulative user interfaces. *Proceedings of the SIGCHI Conference on Human Factors in Computer Systems (CHI '98)*: 17–24. Los Angeles, CA, USA. ACM Press.

Hawkins, R. (2002). Ten lessons for ICT and education in the developing world, in *The Global Information Technology Report 2001–2002: Readiness for the Networked World*: Chapter 5. Oxford University Press.

Hazlett, R. (2003). Measurement of user frustration: a biologic approach. *Proceedings of the SIGCHI Conference on Human Factors in Computing Systems*: 734–735. Fort Lauderdale, FL, USA. ACM Press.

Healey, J. and **Picard, R. W.** (1998). StartleCam: a cybernetic wearable camera. *Proceedings of the Second International Symposium on Wearable Computers*. IEEE Computer Society.

Heylar, V. (2000). Usability issues and user perspectives of a 1st generation WAP service. *Proceedings of the Wireless-World Symposium*. Surrey University, UK.

Heylar, V. (2002). Usability of portable devices: the case of WAP, in *Wireless World – Social and Interactional Aspects of the Mobile Age*, **Brown, B., Green, N.** and **Harper, R.** (eds): 195–206. Springer.

Hinckley, K., Pierce, J., Sinclair, M. and **Horvitz, E.** (2000). Sensing techniques for mobile interaction. *Proceedings of the 13th Annual ACM Symposium on User Interface Software and Technology (UIST 2000)*: 91–100. ACM Press.

Hofstede, G. (1997). *Cultures and Organizations: Software of the Mind*. McGraw-Hill.

Holland, S., Morse, D. R. and **Gedenryd, H.** (2002). Direct combination: a new user interaction principle for mobile and ubiquitous HCI. *Proceedings of the 4th International Symposium on Mobile Human–Computer Interaction (Mobile HCI '02), LNCS 2411*: 108–122. Pisa, Italy. Springer.

Horrocks, I. (1999). *Constructing the User Interface with Statecharts*. Addison-Wesley.

Howard, S., Carroll, J., Murphy, J. and **Peck, J.** (2002). Using 'endowed props' in scenario-based design. *Proceedings of the Second Nordic Conference on Human–Computer Interaction (NordChi)*: 1–10. Aarhus, Denmark. ACM Press.

Howell, D. (2001). *Statistical Methods for Psychology*. Wadsworth Press.

Hughes, J., King, V., Rodden, T. and **Andersen, H.** (1994). Moving out from the control room: ethnography in system design. *Proceedings of the 1994 ACM Conference on Computer Supported Cooperative Work*: 429–439. Chapel Hill, NC, USA. ACM Press.

Hughes, J., King, V., Rodden, T. and **Andersen, H.** (1995). The role of ethnography in interactive systems design. *Interactions* **2**(2): 56–65.

Hughes, J. A., O'Brien, J., Rodden, T., Rouncefield, M. and **Blythin, S.** (1997). Designing with ethnography: a presentation framework for design. *Proceedings of the Conference on Designing Interactive Systems: Processes, Practices, Methods and Techniques*: 147–158. Amsterdam, The Netherlands. ACM Press.

Hulkko, S., Mattelmäki, T., Virtanen, K. and **Keinonen, T.** (2004). Mobile probes. *Proceedings of the Third Nordic Conference on Human–Computer Interaction*: 43–51. Tampere, Finland. ACM Press.

Hutchins, E., Hollan, J. and **Norman, D.** (1985). Direct manipulation interfaces. *Human–Computer Interaction* **1**(4): 311–338.

Hutchinson, H., Hansen, H., Roussel, N., Eiderback, B., Mackay, W. E., Westerlund, B., Bederson, B. B., Druin, A., Plaisant, C., Beaudouin-Lafon, M., Conversy, S. and **Evans, H.** (2003). Technology probes: inspiring design for and with families. *Proceedings of the SIGCHI Conference on Human Factors in Computing Systems (CHI '03)*: 17–24. Fort Lauderdale, FL, USA. ACM Press.

Iacucci, G., Kuutti, K. and **Ranta, M.** (2000). On the move with a magic thing: role playing in concept design of mobile services and devices. *Proceedings of the Conference on Designing Interactive Systems: Processes, Practices, Methods and Techniques*: 193–202. New York, NY, USA. ACM Press.

Igarashi, T. and **Hinckley, K.** (2000). Speed-dependent automatic zooming for browsing large documents. *Proceedings of the 13th Annual ACM Symposium on User Interface Software and Technology (UIST 2000)*: 139–148. ACM Press.

Isaacs, E., Walendowski, A. and **Ranganathan, D.** (2002). Mobile instant messaging through Hubbub. *Communications of the ACM* **45**(9): 68–72.

Ishii, H. and **Ullmer, B.** (1997). Tangible bits: toward seamless interfaces between people, bits and atoms. *Proceedings of the SIGCHI Conference on Human Factors in Computing Systems (CHI '97)*: 339–346. Minneapolis, MN, USA. ACM Press.

Isomursu, M., Isomursu, P. and **Still, K.** (2003). Involving young girls in product concept design. *Proceedings of the 2003 Conference on Universal Usability*: 98–105. Vancouver, Canada. ACM Press.

Isomursu, M., Kuutti, K. and **Väinämö, S.** (2004). Experience clip: method for user participation and evaluation of mobile concepts. *Proceedings of the 8th Conference on Participatory Design. Artful Integration: Interweaving Media, Materials and Practices*, **1**: 83–92. Toronto, Canada. ACM Press.

Ive, J. (2004). Design and the environment. *Journal of the Royal Society of Arts* (January): 15.

Jameson, A. (2001). Modelling both the context and the user. *Personal and Ubiquitous Computing* **5**: 29–33.

Jenson, S. (2002). *The Simplicity Shift*. Cambridge University Press.

Jenson, S. (2004). Default thinking: why consumer products fail, in *The Inside Text: Social Perspectives on SMS in the Mobile Age*, **Harper, R.** (ed.). Springer.

John, B. E. and **Kieras, D. E.** (1996). The GOMS family of user interface analysis techniques: a comparison and contrast. *Transactions on Computer–Human Interaction* **3**(4): 320–351.

Johnson, C. (2003). The interaction between safety culture and uncertainty over device behaviour: the limitations and hazards of telemedicine. *Proceedings of the International Systems Safety Conference 2003*: 273–283. Unionville, VA, USA.

Jones, M. and **Marsden, G.** (2004). "Please turn ON your mobile phone" – first impressions of text-messaging in lectures. *Proceedings of the 6th International Symposium on Mobile Human–Computer Interaction (Mobile HCI '04), LNCS 3160*: 436–440. Glasgow, UK. Springer.

Jones, M., Buchanan, G. and **Mohd-Nasir, N.** (1999a). Evaluation of WebTwig: a site outliner for handheld web access. *Proceedings of the International Symposium on Handheld and Ubiquitous Computing., LNCS 1707*: 343–345.

Jones, M., Marsden, G., Mohd-Nasir, N. and **Boone, K.** (1999b). Improving web interaction on small displays. *Proceedings of the 8th World Wide Web Conference*: 1129–1137.

Jones, M., Buchanan, G. and **Thimbleby, H.** (2003a). Improving web search on small screen devices. *Interacting with Computers* **15**(4): 479–495.

Jones, M., Jain, P., Buchanan, G. and **Marsden, G.** (2003b). Using a mobile device to vary the pace of search. *Proceedings of the 5th International Symposium on Human–Computer Interaction with Mobile Devices and Services (Mobile HCI '03)*: 390–394. Udine, Italy. Springer.

Jones, M., Buchanan, G., Cheng, T. -C. and **Jain, P.** (2006). Changing the pace of search: supporting 'background' information seeking. *Journal of the American Society for Information Science and Technology* (accepted for publication).

Jones, S., Jones, M. and **Deo, S.** (2004). Using keyphrases as search result surrogates on small screen devices. *Personal and Ubiquitous Computing* **8**(1): 55–68.

Kallinen, K. (2004). The effects of background music on using a pocket computer in a cafeteria: immersion, emotional responses, and social richness of medium. *Proceedings of the SIGCHI Conference on Human Factors in Computing Systems (CHI '04), Extended Abstracts*: 1227–1230. Vienna, Austria. ACM Press.

Kamba, T., Elson, S., Harpold, T., Stamper, T. and **Sukaviriya, P.** (1996). Using small screen space more efficiently. *Proceedings of the SIGCHI Conference on Human Factors in Computing Systems (CHI '96)*: 383–390. Vancouver, Canada. ACM Press.

Kang, H. and **Shneiderman, B.** (2000). Visualization methods for personal photo collections: browsing and searching in the PhotoFinder. *Proceedings of the IEEE International Conference on Multimedia and Expo (ICME2000)*. New York, NY, USA. IEEE Press.

Kaptelinin, V., Nardi, B. A. and **Macaulay, C.** (1999). The activity checklist: a tool for representing the 'space' of context. *Interactions* **6**(4): 27–39.

Karat, J., Boyes, L., Weisgerber, S. and **Schafer, C.** (1986). Transfer between word-processing systems. *Proceedings of the Conference on Human Factors in Computing Systems III (CHI '86)*: 67–71. ACM Press.

Kaye, J. J. (2004). Making scents: aromatic output for HCI. *Interactions* **11**(1): 48–61.

Kerne, A. (2000). CollageMachine: an interactive agent of Web recombination. *Leonardo* **33**(5): 347–350.

Kjeldskov, J. and **Howard, S.** (2004). Envisioning mobile information services: combining user- and technology-centered design. *Proceedings of the 6th Asia Pacific Conference, APCHI 2004, LNCS 3101*: 180–190. Rotorua, New Zealand. Springer.

Kohtake, N., Rekimoto, J. and **Yuichiro, A.** (2001). Infopoint: a device that provides a uniform user interface to allow appliances to work together over a network. *Personal and Ubiquitous Computing* **5**(4): 265–274.

Korhonen, P. (2000). Usability research in Nokia: evolution, motivation and trust. *Proceedings of the SIGCHI Conference on Human Factors in Computing Systems (CHI '00), Extended Abstracts*: 219–220. The Hague, The Netherlands. ACM Press.

Koskela, T. and **Väänänen-Vainio-Mattila, K.** (2004). Evolution towards smart home environments: empirical evaluation of three user interfaces. *Personal and Ubiquitous Computing* **8**(3–4): 234–240.

Kourouthanasis, P. and **Roussos, G.** (2003). Developing consumer-friendly pervasive retail systems. *IEEE Pervasive Computing* **2**(2): 32–39.

Kurvinen, E. (2003). Only when miss universe snatches me: teasing in MMS messaging. *Proceedings of the 2003 International Conference on Designing Pleasurable Products and Interfaces*: 98–120. Pittsburgh, PA, USA. ACM Press.

Kuutti, K., Iacucci, G. and **Iacucci, C.** (2002). Action to know: improving creativity in the design of mobile services by using performances. *Proceedings of the 4th Conference on Creativity and Cognition*: 95–102. Loughborough, UK. ACM Press.

Landauer, T. (1996). *The Trouble with Computers: Usefulness, Usability and Productivity*. MIT Press.

Landay, J. A. and **Myers, B. A.** (1995). Interactive sketching for the early stages of user interface design. *Proceedings of the SIGCHI Conference on Human Factors in Computing Systems (CHI '95)*: 43–50. Denver, CO, USA. ACM Press.

Lauridsen, O. M. and **Prasad, A. R.** (2002). User needs for services in UMTS. *Wirelesss Personal Communications* **22**: 187–197.

Lee, E. and **MacGregor, J.** (1985). Minimising user search time in menu retrieval systems. *Human Factors* **27**(2): 157–163.

Lee, E., Whalen, T., McEwen, S. and **Lantremouille, S.** (1984). Optimising the design of menu pages for information retrieval. *Ergonomics* **77**: 1051–1069.

Levy, D. (2001). *Scrolling Forward – Making Sense of Documents in the Digital Age*. Arcade.

Levy, D. (2002). The Fastap keypad and pervasive computing. *Proceedings of the First International Conference on Pervasive Computing*: 58–68. Springer.

Liechti, O. and **Ichikawa, T.** (2000). A digital photography framework enabling affective awareness in home communication. *Personal Technologies* **4**(1): 6–24.

Lin, M., Lutters, W. G. and **Kim, T. S.** (2004). Understanding the micronote lifecycle: improving mobile support for informal note taking. *Proceedings of the SIGCHI Conference on Human Factors in Computing Systems (CHI '04)*: 687–694. Vienna, Austria. ACM Press.

Lindholm, C., Keinonen, T. and **Kiljander, H.** (2003). *Mobile Usability – How Nokia Changed the Face of the Mobile Phone*. McGraw-Hill Professional.

Liu, H., Xie, X., Ma, W. and **Zhang, H.** (2003). Automatic browsing of large pictures on mobile devices. *Proceedings of the 11th ACM International Conference on Multimedia*: 148–155. ACM Press

Liu, L. and **Khooshabeh, P.** (2003). Paper or interactive? A study of prototyping techniques for ubiquitous computing environments. *Proceedings of the SIGCHI Conference on Human Factors in Computing Systems (CHI '03)*: 1030–1031. Fort Lauderdale, FL, USA. ACM Press.

Loel, **K.** and **Albers**, **M. J.** (2001). Web design issues when searching for information in a small screen display. *Proceedings of the 19th Annual International Conference on Computer Documentation*: 193–200. Sante Fe, NM, USA. ACM Press.

Loui, **A.** and **Savakis**, **A.** (2003). Automated event clustering and quality screening of consumer pictures for digital albuming. *IEEE Transactions on Multimedia* (September): 390–402.

Luo, **J.**, **Singhal**, **A.** and **Savakis**, **A.** (2003). Efficient mobile imaging using emphasis image selection. *Proceedings of the International Conference on Image Processing* **1**: 13–16. Rochester, NY, USA.

Lyons, **K.**, **Plaisted**, **D.** and **Starner**, **T.** (2004). Expert chording text entry on the Twiddler one-handed keyboard. *Proceedings of the Eighth International Symposium on Wearable Computers (ISWC'04)*: 94–101. Arlington, VA, USA. IEEE.

MacKay, **B.**, **Watters**, **C.** and **Duffy**, **J.** (2004). Web page transformation when switching devices. *Proceedings of the 6th International Symposium on Mobile Human–Computer Interaction (Mobile HCI '04), LNCS 3160*: 228–239. Glasgow, UK. Springer.

Mackay, **W.** (1989). EVA: an experimental video annotator for symbolic analysis of video data. *SIGCHI Bulletin* **21**(1): 68–71.

Mackay, **W. E.** and **Fayard**, **A. -L.** (1997). HCI, natural science and design: a framework for triangulation across disciplines. *Proceedings of the Conference on Designing Interactive Systems: Processes, Practices, Methods and Techniques*: 223–234. Amsterdam, The Netherlands. ACM Press.

MacKenzie, **I. S.** (2002). KSPC (Keystrokes per Character) as a characteristic of text entry techniques. *Proceedings of the 4th International Symposium on Mobile Human–Computer Interaction (Mobile HCI '02), LNCS 2411*: 195–210. Pisa, Italy. Springer.

MacLean, **A.**, **Young**, **R. M.** and **Moran**, **T. P.** (1989). Design rationale: the argument behind the artifact. *Proceedings of the SIGCHI Conference on Human Factors in Computing Systems: Wings for the Mind (CHI '89)*: 247–252. ACM Press.

Mäkelä, **A.**, **Giller**, **A.**, **Tscheligi**, **M.** and **Sefelin**, **R.** (2000). Joking, storytelling, artsharing, expressing affection: a field trial of how children and their social network communicate with digital images in leisure time. *Proceedings of the SIGCHI Conference on Human Factors in Computing Systems (CHI '00)*: 548–555. The Hague, The Netherlands. ACM Press.

Mäntyjärvi, **J.** and **Seppänen**, **T.** (2002). Adapting applications in mobile terminals using fuzzy context information. *Proceedings of the 4th International Symposium on Mobile Human–Computer Interaction (Mobile HCI '02), LNCS 2411*: 95–107. Pisa, Italy. Springer.

Marcus, **A.** (2003).When is a user not a user?: Who are we? What do we do? *Interactions* **10(**5): 28–34.

Marcus, A. and **Chen, E.** (2002). Designing the PDA of the future. *Interactions* **9**(1): 34–44.

Marcus, A. and **Gould, E.** (2000). Crosscurrents. Cultural dimensions and global user-interface design. *Interactions* **7**(4): 32–46.

Marine, L. (2002). Pardon me, but your baby is ugly... *Interactions* **9**(5): 35–39.

Marsden, G. and **Cairns, D. E.** (2004). Improving the usability of the hierarchical file system. *South African Computer Journal* **32**: 69–78.

Marsden, G., **Duquenoy, P.** and **Thimbleby, H.** (1999). Ethics and consumer electronics. *Fourth International Conference on the Social and Ethical Impacts of Information and Communication Technologies (Ethicomp '99)*, **Marturano, A.**, **Rogerson, S.** and **Bynum, T. W.** (eds).

Marsden, G., **Gillary, P.**, **Thimbleby, H.** and **Jones, M.** (2002). The use of algorithms in interface design. *Personal and Ubiquitous Computing* **6**(2): 132–140.

McClarad, A. and **Somers, P.** (2000). Unleashed: Web Tablet integration into the home. *Proceedings of the SIGCHI Conference on Human Factors in Computing Systems (CHI '00):* 1–8. The Hague, The Netherlands. ACM Press.

McGarry, B., **Matthews, B.** and **Brereton, M.** (2000). Reflections on a candidate design of the user-interface for a wireless vital-signs monitor. *Proceedings of the Conference on Designing Augmented Reality Environments (DARE 2000):* 33–40. Elsinore, Denmark. ACM Press.

Milgram, S. (1974). *Obedience to Authority; An Experimental View.* Harper Collins.

Milic-Frayling, N. and **Sommerer, R.** (2002). *SmartView: Enhanced Document Viewer for Mobile Devices.* Microsoft Research (MSR-TR-2002-114).

Millen, D. R. (2000). Rapid ethnography: time deepening strategies for HCI field research. *Proceedings of the Conference on Designing Interactive Systems: Processes, Practices, Methods and Techniques*: 280–286. New York, NY, USA. ACM Press.

Miller, D. P. (1981). The depth/breadth tradeoff in hierarchical computer menus. *Proceedings of the Human Factors Society 25th Annual Meeting*: 296–300.

Miller, G. (1956). The magical number seven, plus or minus two: some limits on our capacity for processing information. *Psychological Review* **63**: 81–97.

Monk, A., **Nardi, B. A.**, **Gilbert, N.**, **Mantei, M.** and **McCarthy, J.** (1993). Mixing oil and water?: Ethnography versus experimental psychology in the study of computer-mediated communication. *Proceedings of the SIGCHI Conference on Human Factors in Computing Systems (CHI '93)*: 3–6. Amsterdam, The Netherlands. ACM Press.

Muller, M. J. (1991). PICTIVE: an exploration on participatory design *Proceedings of the Conference on Human Factors in Computing Systems (CHI '91)*: 225–231. New Orleans, LA, USA. ACM Press.

Muller, M. (2001). A participatory poster of participatory methods. *Proceedings of the SIGCHI Conference on Human Factors in Computing Systems (CHI '01), Extended Abstracts:* 99–100. Seattle, WA, USA. ACM Press.

Munson, J. P. and **Gupta, V. K.** (2002). Location-based notification as a general-purpose service. *Proceedings of the 2nd International Workshop on Mobile Commerce*: 40–44. Atlanta, GA, USA. ACM Press.

Myers, B. (2001). Using hand-held devices and PCs together. *Communications of the ACM* **44**(11): 34–41.

Nam, T. -J. and **Lee, W.** (2003). Integrating hardware and software: augmented reality based prototyping method for digital products. *Proceedings of the SIGCHI Conference on Human Factors in Computing Systems (CHI '03), Extended Abstracts*: 956–957. Fort Lauderdale, FL, USA. ACM Press.

Nardi, B. A. (ed.) (1996). *Context and Consciousness: Activity Theory and Human–Computer Interaction*. MIT Press.

Nardi, B. A. (2000). Interaction and outeraction: instant messaging in action. *Proceedings of the 2000 ACM Conference on Computer Supported Cooperative Work (CSCW 2000)*: 79–88. Philadelphia, PA, USA. ACM Press.

Nardi, B. A. and **O'Day, V. L.** (1999). *Information Ecologies – Using Technology with Heart*. MIT Press.

Nelson, L., Bly, S. and **Sokoler, T.** (2001). Quiet calls: talking silently on mobile phones. *Proceedings of the SIGCHI Conference on Human Factors in Computing Systems (CHI '01)*: 174–181. Seattle, WA, USA. ACM Press.

Nielsen, J. (1993). *Usability Engineering*. Academic Press.

Nielsen, J. (1994). Enhancing the explanatory power of usability heuristics. *Proceedings of the SIGCHI Conference on Human Factors in Computing Systems (CHI '94)*: 152–158. ACM Press.

Nielsen, J. and **Mack, R.** (eds) (1994). *Usability Inspection Methods*. John Wiley & Sons.

Nikkanen, M. (2003). One-handed use as a design driver: enabling efficient multi-channel delivery of mobile applications, in *Mobile and Ubiquitous Information Access*, **Crestani, F., Dunlop, M.** and **Mizzaro, S.** (eds), LNCS 2954: 28–41. Springer.

Nilsson, J., Sokoler, T., Binder, T. and **Wetcke, N.** (2000). Beyond the control room – mobile devices for spatially distributed interaction on industrial process plants. *Proceedings of Handheld and Ubiquitous Computing, Second International Symposium (HUC 2000)*: 25–27. Bristol, UK. Springer.

Norman, D. A. (1988). *The Psychology of Everyday Things*. Basic Books.

Norman, D. A. (1994). *Things That Make Us Smart: Defending Human Attributes in the Age of the Machines*. Addison-Wesley.

Norman, D. A. (1999). *The Invisible Computer: Why Good Products Can Fail, The Personal Computer is So Complex, and Information Appliances are the Solution*. MIT Press.

Norman, D. A. (2004). *Emotional Design: Why We Love (or Hate) Everyday Things*. Basic Books.

Norman, K. L. and **Chin, J. P.** (1988). The effect of tree structure on search in a hierarchical menu selection system. *Behaviour and Information Technology* **7**: 51–65.

Nunez, D. (2002). *A Connectionist Explanation of Presence in Virtual Environments*. MPhil thesis, Department of Computer Science, University of Cape Town, South Africa.

Oviatt, S. (1999). Mutual disambiguation of recognition errors in a multimodal architecture. *Proceedings of the SIGCHI Conference on Human Factors in Computing Systems (CHI '99)*: 576–583. Pittsburgh, PA, USA. ACM Press.

Paap, K. R. (1988). Design of menus. *Handbook of Human–Computer Interaction*: Chapter 10, 205–235.

Palen, L. and **Salzman, M.** (2001). Welcome to the wireless world: problems using and understanding mobile telephony, in *Wireless World: Social and Interactional Aspects of the Mobile Age*, **Brown, B.**, **Green, N.** and **Harper, R.** (eds). Springer.

Palen, L. and **Salzman, M.** (2002). Beyond the handset: designing for wireless communications usability. *Transactions on Computer–Human Interaction* **9**(2): 125–151.

Pascoe, J. (1997). The stick-e note architecture: extending the interface beyond the user. *Proceedings of the 2nd International Conference on Intelligent User Interfaces*: 261–264. Orlando, FL, USA. ACM Press.

Pascoe, J., **Ryan, N.** and **Morse, D.** (2000). Using while moving: HCI issues in fieldwork environments. *ACM Transactions on Computer–Human Interaction* **7**(3): 417–437.

Patel, D., **Marsden, G.**, **Jones, S.** and **Jones, M.** (2004). An evaluation of techniques for browsing photograph collections on small displays. *Proceedings of the 6th International Symposium on Mobile Human–Computer Interaction (Mobile HCI '04), LNCS 3160*: 132–143. Glasgow, UK. Springer.

Pering, C. (2002). Interaction design prototyping: towards meeting the software–hardware challenge. *Interactions* **9**(4): 36–46.

Petersen, M., **Madsen, K.** and **Kjær, A.** (2002). The usability of everyday technology: emerging and fading opportunities *ACM Transactions on Computer–Human Interaction* **9**(2): 74–105.

Picard, R. W. (1997). *Affective Computing*. MIT Press.

Pirhonen, A., **Brewster, S.** and **Holguin, C.** (2002). Gestural and audio metaphors as a means of control for mobile devices. *Proceedings of the SIGCHI Conference on Human Factors in Computing Systems (CHI '02)*: 291–298. Minneapolis, MN, USA. ACM Press.

Plant, S. (2001). *On the mobile – the effects of mobile telephones on social and individual life*. Motorola.

Po, S. (2003). *Mobile Usability Testing and Evaluation*. BIS (Hons) Dissertation, Department of Information Systems, University of Melbourne, Australia.

Poltrack, S. E. and **Grudin, J.** (1994). Organizational obstacles to interface design and development: two participant–observer studies. *ACM Transactions on Computer–Human Interaction* **1**(1): 52–80.

Poupyrev, I., **Maruyyama, S.** and **Rekimoto, J.** (2002). Ambient touch: designing tactile interfaces for handheld devices. *Proceedings of the 15th Annual ACM Symposium on User Interface Software and Technology (UIST 2002)*: 51–60. Paris, France. ACM Press.

Preece, J., **Rogers, Y.** and **Sharp, H.** (2002). *Interaction Design – Beyond Human–Computer Interaction*, John Wiley & Sons.

Pruitt, J. and **Grudin, J.** (2003). Personas: practice and theory. *Proceedings of the 2003 Conference on Designing for User Experience*: 1–15. San Francisco, CA, USA. ACM Press.

Raghunath, M. T. and **Narayanaswami, C.** (2002). User interfaces for applications on a wrist watch. *Personal and Ubiquitous Computing* **6**(1): 17–30.

Reiman, J. (1993). The diary study: a workplace-oriented research tool to guide laboratory efforts. *Proceedings of the SIGCHI Conference on Human Factors in Computing Systems (CHI '93)*: 321–326. Amsterdam, The Netherlands. ACM Press.

Rekimoto, J., **Haruo, O.** and **Ishizawa, T.** (2003). SmartPad: a finger-sensing keypad for mobile interaction. *Proceedings of the SIGCHI Conference on Human Factors in Computing Systems (CHI '03), Extended Abstracts*: 850–851. Fort Lauderdale, FL, USA. ACM Press.

Repo, P., **Hyvönen, K.**, **Pantzar, M.** and **Timonen, P.** (2004). Users inventing ways to enjoy new mobile services – the case of watching mobile videos. *Proceedings of the 37th Hawaii International Conference on System Sciences.*

Resiel, J. F. and **Shneiderman, B.** (1987). Is bigger better? The effects of display size on program reading, in *Social, Ergonomic Aspect of Work with Computers*, **Salvendy, G.** (ed.): 113–122. Elsevier Science Publishers.

Rettig, M. (1994). Prototyping for tiny fingers. *Communications of the ACM* **37**(4): 21–27.

Rodden, K. (2002). *Evaluating similarity-based visualisations as interfaces for image browsing*. University of Cambridge Technical Report, UCAM-CL-TR-543.

Rodden, K., Basalaj, W., Sinclair, D. and **Wood, K. R.** (2001). Does organisation by similarity assist image browsing? *Proceedings of the SIGCHI Conference on Human Factors in Computing Systems (CHI '01)*: 190–197. Seattle, WA, USA. ACM Press.

Rodden, K., Milic-Frayling, N., Sommerer, R. and **Blackwell, A.** (2003). Effective web searching on mobile devices. *People and Computers XVII: Proceedings of the 17th Annual British Computer Society Conference on Human–Computer Interaction (BCS HCI 2003)*: 281–296. Bath, UK. British Computer Society.

Rogers, Y., Taylor, I., Stanton, D., Corke, G., Gabrielli, S., Scaife, M., Harris, E., Phelps, T., Price, S., Smith, H., Muller, H., Randell, C. and **Moss, A.** (2002). Things aren't what they seem to be: innovation through technology inspiration. *Proceedings of the Conference on Designing Interactive Systems: Processes, Practices, Methods and Techniques (DIS 2002)*: 373–378. London, UK. ACM Press.

Roeber, H., Bacus, J. and **Tomasi, C.** (2003). Typing in thin air: the canesta projection keyboard – a new method of interaction with electronic devices. *Proceedings of the SIGCHI Conference on Human Factors in Computing Systems (CHI '03), Extended Abstracts*: 712–713. Fort Lauderdale, FL, USA. ACM Press.

Rosenbaum, S., Cockburn, G., Coyne, K., Muller, M. and **Thyra, R.** (2002). Focus groups in HCI: wealth of information or waste of resources. *Proceedings of the SIGCHI Conference on Human Factors in Computing Systems (CHI '02), Extended Abstracts*: 702–703. Minneapolis, MN, USA. ACM Press.

Roussos, G., Kourouthanasis, P. and **Moussouri, T.** (2003). Designing appliances for mobile commerce and retailtainment. *Personal and Ubiquitous Computing* **7**(3–4): 203–209.

Royce, W. (1970). Managing development of large scale software systems. *Proceedings of the IEEE WESCON*. IEEE.

Sarvas, R., Herrarte, E., Wilhelm, A. and **Davis, M.** (2004). Metadata creation system for mobile images. *Proceedings of the Second International Conference on Mobile Systems, Applications, and Services (MobiSYS '04)*: 36–48. Boston, MA, USA. ACM/USENIX.

Sato, S. and **Salvador, T.** (1999). Playacting and focus troupes: theater techniques for creating quick, intense, immersive and engaging focus groups sessions. *Interactions* **6**(5): 35–41.

Savakis, A., Etz, P. and **Loui, A.** (2000). Evaluation of image appeal in consumer photography. *Proceedings of SPIE Human Vision and Electronic Imaging (3959)*: 111–120.

Sawhney, N. and **Schmandt, C.** (2000). Nomadic radio: speech and audio interaction for contextual messaging in nomadic environments. *ACM Transactions on Computer–Human Interaction* **7**(3): 353–383.

Schach, S. (2002). *Object-Oriented and Classical Software Engineering* (5th edn). McGraw-Hill.

Schilit, B. N., Adams, N. and **Want, R.** (1994). Context-aware computing applications. *Proceedings of the IEEE Workshop on Mobile Computing Systems and Applications*, Santa Cruz, CA, USA. IEEE.

Schilit, B. N., Price, M. N., Golovchinsky, G., Tanaka, K. and **Marshall, C. C.** (1999). As we may read: the reading appliance revolution. *Computer* **32**(1): 65–73.

Schraefel, m. c., Hughes, G. V., Mills, H., Smith, G., Payne, T. R. and **Fey, J.** (2004). Breaking the book: translating the chemistry lab book into a pervasive computing lab environment. *Proceedings of the SIGCHI Conference on Human Factors in Computing Systems (CHI '04)*: 25–32. Vienna, Austria. ACM Press.

Schumann, J., Strothotte, T., Laser S. and **Raab, A.** (1996). Assessing the effect of non-photorealistic rendered images in CAD. *Proceedings of the SIGCHI Conference on Human Factors in Computing Systems (CHI '96)*: 35–41. Vancouver, Canada. ACM Press.

Schusteritsch, R., Rao, S. and **Rodden, K.** (2005). Mobile search with text messages: design and user experience for Google SMS. *Proceedings of the SIGCHI Conference on Human Factors in Computing Systems (CHI '05), Extended Abstracts*: 1777–1780. Portland, OR, USA. ACM Press.

Schwesig, C., Poupyrev, I. and **Mori, E.** (2003). Gummi: user interface for deformable computers. *Proceedings of the SIGCHI Conference on Human Factors in Computing Systems (CHI '03), Extended Abstracts*: 954–955. Fort Lauderdale, FL, USA. ACM Press.

Shneiderman, B. (1987). User interface design and evaluation for an electronic encylopedia, in *Cognitive Engineering in the Design of Human–Computer Interaction and Expert Systems*, **Salvendy, G.** (ed.): 207–223. Elsevier Science Publishers.

Shneiderman, B. (1996). The eyes have it: a task by data type taxonomy for information visualizations. *Proceedings of the IEEE Conference on Visual Languages*: 336–343. IEEE Press.

Shneiderman, B. (1998). *Designing the User Interface: Strategies for Effective Human Computer Interaction*. Addison-Wesley.

Shneiderman, B. (2002). *Leonardo's Laptop – Human Needs and New Computing Technologies*. MIT Press.

Shneiderman, B. (2004). Designing for fun: how can we design user interfaces to be more fun. *Interactions* **11**(5): 48–50.

Siegel, D. (2001). Business: New kid on the block: marketing organizations and interaction design. *Interactions* **8**(2): 19–23.

Silfverberg, M., MacKenzie, I. S. and **Korhonen, P.** (2000). Predicting text entry speed on mobile phones. *Proceedings of the SIGCHI Conference on Human Factors in Computing Systems (CHI '00)*: 9–16. The Hague, The Netherlands. ACM Press.

Smith, S. and **Mosier, J.** (1986). *Guidelines for designing user interface software. Report MTP-10090 ESD-TR-86-278*. The MITRE Corporation, Bedford, MA, USA.

Spence, R., Witkowski, M., Fawcett, C., Craft, B. and **de Bruijn, O.** (2004). Image presentation in space and time: errors, preferences and eye-gaze activity. *Proceedings of the Working Conference on Advanced Visual Interfaces (AVI '04)*: 141–149.

Spinuzzi, C. (2003). Using a handheld PC to collect and analyse observational data. *Proceedings of the 21st Annual International Conference on Documentation*: 73–79. San Francisco, CA, USA. ACM Press.

Spreenberg, P., Salomon, G. and **Joe, P.** (1995). Interaction design at IDEO Product Development. *Proceedings of the SIGCHI Conference on Human Factors in Computing (CHI '95), Conference Companion*: 164–165. Denver, CO, USA. ACM Press.

Starner, T. (2003). The enigmatic display. *IEEE Pervasive Computing* **2**(1): 15–18.

Strachan, S. and **Murray-Smith, R.** (2004). Muscle tremor as an input mechanism. *Proceedings of the 17th Annual ACM Symposium on User Interface Software and Technology (UIST '04)*. Santa Fe, NM, USA. ACM Press.

Suchman, L. (1987). *Plans and Situated Actions*. Cambridge University Press.

Sullivan, K. (1996). The Windows 95 user experience: a case study in usability engineering. *Proceedings of the SIGCHI Conference on Human Factors in Computing Systems (CHI '96)*: 473–480. Vancouver, Canada. ACM Press.

Svanaes, D. and **Seland, G.** (2004). Putting the users center stage: role playing and low-fi prototyping enable end users to design mobile systems. *Proceedings of the SIGCHI Conference on Human Factors in Computing Systems (CHI '04)*: 470–486. Vienna, Austria. ACM Press.

Swierenga, S. J. (1990). Menuing and scrolling as alternative information access techniques for computer systems: interfacing with the user. *Proceedings of the Human Factors Society 34th Annual Meeting*: 356–359.

Taylor, F. W. (1998). *The Principles of Scientific Management*. Dover Publications.

Thimbleby, H. (1990). *User Interface Design*. Addison-Wesley

Thimbleby, H. (1996a). Internet, discourse and interaction potential. *Proceedings of the First Asia Pacific Conference on Human–Computer Interaction*: 3–18. Singapore.

Thimbleby, H. (1996b). Creating user manuals for using in collaborative design. *Proceedings of the SIGCHI Conference on Human Factors in Computing Systems (CHI '96), Conference Companion*: 279–280. Vancouver, Canada. ACM Press.

Thimbleby, H. and **Jones, M.** (2002). Obituary for a fax. *Personal and Ubiquitous Computing* **6**(2): 151–152.

Thomas, P. and **Macredie, R. D.** (2002). Introduction to the new usability. *Transactions on Computer–Human Interaction* **9**(2): 69–73.

Thorndike, E. (1920). A constant error on psychological rating. *Journal of Applied Psychology* **4**: 25–29.

Toyama, K., **Logan, R.**, **Roseway, A.** and **Anandan, P.** (2003). Geographic location tags on digital images. *Proceedings of the 11th ACM International Conference on Multimedia*: 156–166. ACM Press.

Turner, N. (2004). *Augmenting Electronic Programme Guides with Handheld Technology to Better Support Television Planning*. MSc thesis, UCLIC, UCL, London, UK.

UNESCO (2002). *Institute for Statistics, Sub-Saharan Africa Regional Report*. UNESCO, 19 April 2002.

van Rijsbergen, C. J. (1979). *Information Retrieval*. Butterworths.

Vetere, F., **Howard, S.**, **Pedell, S.** and **Balbo, S.** (2003). Walking through mobile use: novel heuristics and their application. *Proceedings of the International Conference of the Australian Computer–Human Interaction Special Interest Group (OzCHI'03)*: 24–32. Brisbane, Australia.

Walton, M. and **Vukovic, V.** (2003). Cultures, literacy and the web: dimensions of information 'scent'. *Interactions* **10**(2): 64–71.

Warren, N., **Jones, M.**, **Jones, S.** and **Bainbridge, D.** (2005). Navigation via continuously adapted music. *Proceedings of the SIGCHI Conference on Human Factors in Computing Systems (CHI '05), Extended Abstracts*. Portland, OR, USA. ACM Press.

Warwick, K. (2002). *I, Cyborg*. Century.

Weberg, L., **Brange, T.** and **Hansson, Å. W.** (2001). A piece of butter on the PDA display. *Proceedings of the SIGCHI Conference on Human Factors in Computing Systems (CHI '01), Extended Abstracts*: 435–436. Seattle, WA, USA. ACM Press.

Weilenmann, A. (2001). Negotiating use: making sense of mobile technology. *Personal and Ubiquitous Computing* **5**(2): 137–145.

Weiser, M. (1993). Some computer science issues in ubiquitous computing. *Communications of the ACM* **36**(7): 75–84.

Weiser, M. and **Brown, J. S.** (1997). The coming age of calm technology, in *Beyond Calculation: The Next Fifty Years of Computing*, **Denning, P.** and **Metcalfe, R.** (eds): 74–85. Springer.

Wigdor, D. and **Balakrishnan, R.** (2003). TiltText: using tilt for text input to mobile phones. *Proceedings of the 16th Annual ACM Symposium on User Interface Software and Technology*: 81–90. Vancouver, Canada. ACM Press.

Winograd, T. (1997). From computing machinery to interaction design, in *Beyond Calculation: The Next Fifty Years of Computing*, **Denning, P.** and **Metcalfe, R.** (eds): 149–162. Springer

Woodruff, A. and **Aoki, P. M.** (2003). How push-to-talk makes talk less pushy. *Proceedings of the 2003 International ACM SIGGROUP Conference on Supporting Group Work*: 170–179. Sanibel Island, FL, USA. ACM Press.

Yee, K. -P. (2003). Peephole displays: pen interaction on spatially aware handheld computers. *Proceedings of the SIGCHI Conference on Human Factors in Computing Systems (CHI '03)*: 1–8. Fort Lauderdale, FL, USA. ACM Press.

Youngs, E. (1998). Evaluating the impact of application, ergonomic and process design on handset success. *Proceedings of User Interface Design for Mobile Terminals*, London, UK.

Zeki, S. (1993). *A Vision of the Brain*. Blackwell.

Zimmerman, J. (2003). Exploring the role of emotion in the interaction design of digital music players. *Proceedings of the 2003 International Conference on Designing Pleasurable Products and Interfaces*: 152–153. Pittsburgh, PA, USA. ACM Press.

Zuberec, S. (2000). The interaction design of Microsoft Windows CE, in *Information Appliances and Beyond: Interaction Design for Consumer Products*, **Bergman, E.** (ed). Morgan Kaufmann.

INTERNET REFERENCES

AmikaNow. *AmikaFreedom for Outlook 98/2000*. http://www.amikanow.com/wireless/kamikafreedom_outlook.asp. Last accessed 12 July 2005.

BBC (2003). *Rickshaws connect India's poor*. http://news.bbc.co.uk/2/hi/technology/3256516.stm. Last accessed 3 February 2005.

Brown, B. and **Weilenmann, A.** (2003). *Design through exploration: using observational methods in ubiquitous technology research*. http://www.dcs.gla.ac.uk/~barry/papers/exploration.pdf. Last accessed 15 January 2005.

Evers, J. (2003). MSN Direct's SPOT service expected by the end of year. *PC World* (5 June), http://www.pcworld.com/news/article/0,aid,111035,00.asp

Exif (1998). *Digital Still Camera Image File Format Standard. Japan Electronic Industry Development Association*. http://www.pima.net/standards/it10/PIMA15740/exif.htm. Last accessed 18 December 2004.

Google. *Google Wireless Services*. http://www.google.com/wireless/. Last accessed 22 February 2005.

International Telecommunication Union (2004). *African Telecommunication Indicators 2004*. http://www.itu.int/ITU-D/ict/publications/africa/2004/. Last accessed 3 February 2005.

Khella, A. and **Bederson, B.** *Pocket PhotoMesa*. http://www.cs.umd.edu/~akhella/pocketmesa.htm. Last accessed 20 December 2004.

Kurakowski, J. (2000). *Questionnaires in usability engineering: a list of frequently asked questions* (3rd edn). http://www.ucc.ie/hfrg/resources/qfaq1.html

Lindholm, C. (2004). *August 2004 – Archives*. http://www.christianlindholm.com/christianlindholm/2004/08/index.html. Last accessed 22 February 2005.

Lindow, M. (2004). *Seeking riches from the poor*. http://www.wired.com/news/business/0,1367,63131,00.html. Last accessed 22 February 2005.

Microsoft (a). *Developing an effective Smartphone user interface*. http://msdn.microsoft.com/library/default.asp?url=/library/en-us/dnsmtphn/html/devSPUI.asp. Last accessed 15 February 2005.

Microsoft (b). *Windows mobile-based PocketPC user interface guidelines – pop-up menus*. http://msdn.microsoft.com/library/default.asp?url=/library/en-us/ui_guide_ppc/html/ppc_popup_menus_ppc_hzth.asp. Last accessed 17 February 2005.

Near Field Communication Forum. *White Paper*. http://www.ecma-international.org/activities/Communications/2004 tg19-001.pdf. Last accessed 11 July 2005.

Nielsen, J. (1997a). *Changes in web usability since 1994*. http://www.useit.com/alertbox/9712a.html. Last accessed 22 February 2005.

Nielsen, J. (1997b). *How users read on the web*. http://www.useit.com/alertbox/9710a.html. Last accessed 22 February 2005.

Nielsen, J. (1997c). *WebTv usability review*. http://www.useit.com/alertbox/9702a.html. Last accessed 22 February 2005.

Nielsen, J. (2000a). *Why you only need to test with 5 users*. http://www.useit.com/alertbox/20000319.html. Last accessed 3 March 2005.

Nielsen, J. (2000b). *WAP field study findings*. http://www.useit.com/alertbox/20001210.html. Last accessed 15 February 2005.

Nielsen, J. (2003). *Do productivity increases generate economic gains?* http://www.useit.com/alertbox/20030317.html. Last accessed 2 February 2005.

Nielsen, J. (2004). *Why mobile phones are annoying*. http://www.useit.com/alertbox/20040412.html

Nokia (a). *Nokia 7600*. http://www.nokia.com/nokia/0,,43867,00.html. Last accessed 2 February 2005.

Nokia (b). *Nokia Research Center – Overview*. http://www.nokia.com/nokia/0,,50249,00.html. Last accessed 15 February 2005.

Opera. *Authoring for small screen rendering – Quick tips*. http://www.opera.com/products/mobile/dev/html/. Last accessed 12 July 2005.

Oxfam (2005). *Mobile phones around the world*. http://www.oxfam.org.uk/coolplanet/kidsweb/bringbring/phoneworld.htm. Last accessed 3 February 2005.

Perlman, G. (1998). *Web-based user interface evaluation with questionnaires*. http://www.acm.org/~perlman/question.html

RCA. *Interaction design*. http://www.rca.ac.uk/pages/research/interaction_design_607.html. Last accessed 17 February 2005.

Sony. *S710a specifications*. http://www.sonyericsson.com/spg.jsp?cc=global&lc=en&ver=4001&template=pp1_1_1&zone=pp&lm=pp1&pid=10179. Last accessed 3 February 2005.

Symbian. *UIQ guidelines – Menus*. http://www.symbian.com/developer/techlib/papers/uiq/uiqstyleguide/Menus.html. Last accessed 17 February 2005.

Tegic. www.tegic.com. Last accessed 3 July 2005.

Vertu. *Vertu – Luxury mobile communications*. www.vertu.com. Last accessed 2 February 2005.

CREDITS

Figure 1.1	MyGROCER showing small screen display attached to shopping cart. Reproduced by permission of Panos Kourouthanassis and George Roussos
Figure 1.2	Fastap keypad. Reproduced by permission of Digit Wireless
Figure 1.3	The Twiddler – active chording for text entry (Lyons *et al.*, 2004). Reproduced by permission of Kent Lyons
Figure 1.4	Peepholes in action – accessing a large personal information space via a small window, Ka-Ping Yee. © 2005 ACM, Inc. Reprinted by permission.
Figure 1.5	The Gummi interface. Reproduced by permission of Sony CSL
Figure 2.1	Sony Ericsson S700. Reproduced by permission of Sony Ericsson
Figure 2.2	Semi-transparent text and widgets as a way of overcoming small screen space while not compromising the principle of visibility (Kamba *et al.*, 1996) © 2005 ACM, Inc. Reprinted by permission.
Figure 2.3	Mobile games portal. Reproduced by the permission of Matthew Fox-Wilson, Ambient Design Ltd
Figure 3.1	Ringtone composition application on a low-resolution, monochrome display. Reproduced by permission of Malcom Barr
Figure 3.2	Hubbub, a mobile Instant Messaging application. Reproduced by permission of Ellen Isaacs
Box 3.5	Shrinking to fit. Extract reprinted by permission of the Microsoft Corporation
Figure 4.2	Examples of mobile prototypes (Nam and Lee, 2003). Reproduced by permission of Tek-Jin Nam
Figure 4.3	Mobile wearable for service technicians (Fallman, 2002). Reproduced by permission of Daniel Fallman
Figure 4.4	Haloes for better map navigation (Baudisch and Rosenholtz, 2003). Reproduced by permission of Patrick Baudisch
Figure 5.1	Home control mobile phone prototype developed through contextual inquiry-style investigations, adapted from Koskela and Väänänen-Vainio-Mattila, 2004
Figure 5.2	Examples of paper-based diary study log sheets (Gritner, R. E. and Eldridge, M. 2003) © 2003 ACM, Inc. Reprinted by permission
Figure 5.3	'Mobile Probes' mobile phone application, adapted from Hulkko *et al.*, 2004
Box 5.11	Extract from Neil Turner's thesis on mobiles and interactive TV: scenarios developed to illustrate design proposals. Text portion reproduced by permission of UCL, London
Figure 6.5	Low-fidelity prototypes of mobile computers and sensors. Reproduced by permission of Jorn Messelter

Figure 6.7	PocketPC device emulator in Microsoft Visual Studio. Screenshot reprinted by permission of the Microsoft Corporation
Figure 6.9	Prototype device. Reproduced by permission of Tek-Jin Nam
Figure 6.10	The cables attached to the mouse wheels allow the PDA to be tracked in two-dimensional space. Reproduced by permission of Ka-Ping Yee
Figure 6.12	The 'sketch' on the right is automatically generated from the volumetric model on the left. Reproduced by permission of Thomas Strothotte
Figure 8.3	Desktop menu branch nodes. Screenshot reprinted by permission of the Microsoft Corporation
Figure 8.4	A section of the 'File' menu from Microsoft Word. Screenshot reprinted by permission of the Microsoft Corporation
Figure 9.5	The Opera mobile browser. Reproduced by permission of Opera software ASA
Figure 9.7	SmartView browsing technique. Screenshot reprinted by permission of the Microsoft Corporation
Figure 9.8	Gateway browser reproduced by permission of Bonnie MacKay
Figure 9.11	Google SMS reproduced by permission of Google
Figure 9.14	Starfield visualisation on a PDA reproduced by permission of M. Dunlop
Figure 10.1	The PhotoFinder system. Reproduced by permission of Ben Shneiderman
Figure 10.2	The process of inferring data from images taken by other people. Reproduced by permission of Risto Sarvas
Figure 10.3	The PocketPC version of PhotoMesa showing all images simultaneously. Reproduced by permission of Ben Bederson
Figure 11.2	CyberTracker iconic interface for the Newton. Reproduced by permission of CyberTracker Software
Table 11.1	Hofstede's dimensions of culture (Marcus and Gould, 2000). © 2005 ACM, Inc. Reprinted by permission
Color plate 1	Thad Starner and the eyeglass output device (Starner, 2003). Reproduced by permission of the Georgia Institute of Technology IBM wristwatch device (Raghunath and Narayanaswami, 2002). Reproduced by permission of IBM Research MediaCup (coffee cup with sensors and communication technologies embedded in base) (Gellerson *et al.*, 2002). Reproduced by permission of Michael Beigl Nokia 770 internet tablet. Reproduced by permission of Nokia
Color plate 2	OK/Cancel. Reproduced by permission of Kevin Cheng Off Panel Productions
Color plate 3	Flowers from dead mobiles. Reproduced by permission of the University of Warwick
Color plate 4	Xerox Parc Tab. Reproduced by permission of Palo Alto Research Centre Inc., a subsidiary of Xerox Corp
Color plate 5	The 'Spinner' music player prototype by Greg Fogel, Sonia Wendorf and Saki Tanaka. Reproduced by permission of John Zimmerman
Color plate 7	Algorithm developed to crop images (Liu *et al.* 2003). © 2005 ACM, Inc. Reprinted by permission

INDEX

1D browsing 261–4
1.5D browsing 264–6
2D browsing 266–9
3G *see* **third-generation**

A

access *see* **information access**
accordion summarization 265, 278
ACDSee 295–6
actions 134
active chording 15
activities 155–6
activities relationship table (ART) 85–7
activity theory 158, 159–60
advertising 127
affordances 46–48
Africa 316–17
alpha versions 188
animated icons 227–28
anonymity 133
anthropology 98, 309–10
Apple 55–7
appliance attitude 11–14, 36
applications 74–7
appropriate technology 318
architecture 5
aromatic output 24–6
ART *see* **activities relationship table**
artifact walkthroughs 140
Asia 316–17
audio recordings 310–11
auditory interfaces 19–20
auto-ethnography 146–7
automatic adaptation 282–3
automatic logging 202
AutoZoom 302–3, 304–6

B

B+Trees 237–41
back-end usability 72–3
background information 283–4
Berners-Lee, Tim 242
beta versions 31, 185–6
between-groups experiments 213
bias 203
binary trees 236–41
biology 96–7
bizware 59–60
BlackBerry 12
blogging 43, 311, 337
blue-skies investigations 125
BlueTooth 149, 280, 309
books 335–6
branch nodes 227, 230
branding 55–8
Brewster, S. 218–9
bridges.org 318–20
browsing
  digital photography 294–300
  information access 249, 255–6, 258–72
Buck test rigs 183–5, 188

C

caller tunes 43
calm technology 308–09
Cameo 12–13
camera phones 46–48, 84
  see also digital photography; multimedia messaging service
Canesta 251
categorizing data 155
category searches 274–5
channels 271
chording 15
Christensen, Clayton 68–9
chronological ordering 291–2, 294
class-inclusion 226, 242
cognitive psychology 96–97
cognitive walkthrough 208
collaboration 139–40
collaboratorium 117
Collapse-to-Zoom 269, 278
collectivism 320–2
communicating ideas 173–4, 191
community benefits 319, 331–3
complementary evaluation 218–19
complex functions 223–46
  alternatives to menus 235–8
  binary trees 237–8, 239–41
  classifications 226–7
  data structures 235, 238
  evaluation 238–41
  hierarchical menus 225–7
  icons 198, 227–33
  linear lists 236
  manuals 233–4
  memory 224–5
  menus 198, 205, 224–45
comprehension 252
computer science 113–15, 119, 237–238
conceptual models 44, 46, 197–8
conferences 336
consent 203–4
consistency 44, 57, 65
constructive interaction 200
content 10, 49
  packaging 271–2
  summarized 259, 265, 278
  see also information access
context
  awareness 217–18
  enquiries 138–40, 145
  evaluation 214–18
  information access 249, 281–2
  menu structure 227
  meta-data 293–4
  prototypes 192
  understanding 135–37, 143–4
contextual walkthrough 208–9
corporate informants 126
costs 319
creative engagement 151–5
cultural probes 151–2
customer experience 5
CyberTracker 325–7
cyborgs 7–8

D

Danfoss 117
debugging 28, 29, 112
DEEP project 327–28
deployment 118–18
Derrett, Nigel 41–2
design principles
  economic impacts 30–1
  emotional impacts 30
  ethical impacts 31–5
  golden rules 44–5
  interactivity 28–35
design space 100–4
developing world
  community benefits 319, 328–33

CyberTracker 325–7
education 327–8
project development 318–20
real access 318–20
societal impacts 320–3
socio-cultural factors 320–4
development 160
dialogs 45
diary studies 141–5
digital photography 289–313
advanced technology 306–7
audio recordings 311
AutoZoom 302–3, 305–6
blogging 311
browsing 294–300
calm technology 308–9
downscaling 300–6
ethnography 290–2
future technologies 312
GestureZoom 304–5, 305–6
meta-data 293–4
rapid serial visual presentation 296–8
screen size 300–1
searching 292–4
social purpose 307–12
speed dependent automatic zooming 298–300, 304–6
timelines 295
treemaps 295–6
users 301–6
video capture 311–12
dimensions of culture 320–4
direct combination 101
direct manipulation 101
direct questioning 99–100
discount methods 145–9
disposable devices 13, 33–5
disruptive innovations 68–9
DoCoMo 64–5
Doodle Pads 18
Dourish, Paul 136
dramatization 153–5
drift tables 153
Dykstra-Erickson, E. 114–15

E

earcons 19, 77
economic impacts
design issues 30–1
developing world 319
texting 61–2
editorial voice 58
education 327–8
elderly people 97
ellipses 227, 230
email 273, 276, 308
emotional impacts 30, 136–8
empowerment 176–8
emulators 179–82
enquiring 138–40
environmental impacts 33–4, 35
ethics
design issues 31–5
interviews 133, 148
prototypes 189
ethnography
digital photography 290–2
interaction design 98, 99–100
methodology 130, 145–9
ethnography-lite 145–6
evaluation 191, 195–220
analysis 241–2
bias 203
classification 196–7
complementary 218–9
complex functions 238–41
conceptual model extraction 197–8
consent 203–4
context 214–18
experimental 209–14

evaluation (*continued*)
heuristic 207–9, 217
hypotheses 210–11
interaction design 94, 106–12
interviews 204–5
non-user methods 207–9
observations 200–2
questionnaires 205–7
Quick and Dirty 197
task selection 212
user selection 211–12
evolutionary prototyping 186
exceptional informants 126, 127
exchanging data 192
expectations 190
experimental bias 203
experimental evaluation 209–14
expert-based reviews 110–12
expressiveness 10

F

Fallman, Daniel 105
Fastap keypads 16–17
feature–persona matrixes 162, 164
feedback 44–6, 48
femininity 320–22
field guides 126
field studies 97–9, 129–30
financial short-termism 28
fish-eye lens visualization 278
flexible organic light emitting diodes (FOLEDs) 251
focus+context 278
focus groups 149–51
FOLEDs *see* **flexible organic light emitting diodes**
formats 249
Frohlich, D. 291–2
front end usability 72–3

G

games 6, 51
GateWay 269–70
gender 99, 320–2
general mobile platforms 183
GeoNotes 140
gestural interfaces 21–6
GestureZoom 303–4, 305–6
goal-led navigation 253–4
goals 134
golden rules of design 44–5
GOMS models 158, 209
Google 275–6, 292
Gould, E. 321–3
graphical user interfaces (GUIs) 71, 116, 244
Greenstone 329–31
grounded theory 158
groupthink 151
GUIs *see* **graphical user interfaces**
Gummi interfaces 21, 22

H

Halo technique 108
Handspring Treo 183–5
haptic interfaces 20–1
hardware
innovation 68–9
integration 178–86
Harper, Richard 10
HCI *see* **human–computer interaction**
Heckel's laws 41–2
Hermes system 87–8
heuristic evaluation 207–9, 217
heuristic reviews 110
hierarchical menus 225–7, 243–4
hierarchical task analysis (HTA) 156–7
high-fidelity prototypes 170–1, 178–86
Hofstede's dimensions of culture 320–4
home control media 138–9

horizontal prototypes 178
HTA *see* **hierarchical task analysis**
Hubbub 75–7
human capacity training 319
human-centered innovations 85–89
human–computer interaction (HCI) 5
Hummingbird technology 149–50
hypotheses 210–11

I

icons
  complex functions 227–33
  conceptual model extraction 187–8
  CyberTracker 325–6
  desktop to mobile 77
identity 55–8
IM *see* **instant messaging**
iMode 9, 42, 62, 64–5
India 318
individualism 320–22
infinite menus 225
InfoDoor 87
InfoPoint 285
informants 126, 127–8
information access 247–88
  automatic adaptation 282–3
  background information 282–4
  browsing 249, 255–6, 258–72
  context 249, 281–2
  developing world 318–20, 324
  digital photography 291–300
  format 249
  guidelines for design 259–61
  information visualization 278–9
  interactivity 249, 252–3
  laid-back search tool 283–5
  mobile information ecologies 52, 280–6
  overviews 259–60
  packaging content 271–2
  peer-to-peer schemes 286
  processing results 284
  schemes for design 261–71
  screen size 250–8
  searching 250, 256–8, 272–9
  simplicity 248–9
  sources 249
  utilizing results 284–5
information ecologies 52, 280–6
information visualization 278–9
innovations 68–9
  adaptation 81–2
  applications 75–8
  desktop-derived 74–81
  disruptive 68–9
  human-centered 85–9
  interface styles 74, 78–81
  real world implications 83–5
  sustaining 68–9
  technology-centered 69–74, 88–89
instant messaging (IM) 75–77
integration165–6, 319
interaction design 93–119
  collaboration 116–7
  definition 95–6
  deployment 117–8
  design space 100–4
  evaluation techniques 94, 106–12
  iterative development 112–13
  multiple viewpoints 113–17
  participation 116
  platform design 102–3
  prototypes 98, 104–10
  understanding users 94, 96–100
interaction prototyping 174–6
interactive television 165–6
interactivity 7–8
  bizware 59–60
  design issues 28–35
  identity 55–7

interactivity (*continued*)
information access 249, 252–4
netware 59
interfaces 14–27
auditory 19–20
Fastap keypads 16–17
gestural 21–6
haptic 20–1
human capabilities 17–27
multimodality 26
Peephole displays 16–17, 18, 23
prototypes 171–2
styles 74, 78–81
International Standards Organization (ISO) 102
internationalization 323–4
interpreting 155
interviews 99, 133, 148, 205–6
intrusion 62, 131–2, 141
investigative methods 1221–68
analysis perspectives 156–60
artifact walkthroughs 140
contextual information 135–40, 143–44
creative engagement 151–55
diary studies 141–5
discount methods 145–9
dramatization 153–5
enquiring 138–40
ethics 133, 148
focus groups 149–51
focusing the study 124–9
identifying people 125–9
log analysis 148–9
magic things 154
observations 130–8, 155–60
online enquiries 148
participant awareness 131–2
personas 160–5
probes 129, 144, 151–3
recruiting subjects 125–9
sampling techniques 125–6
scenarios 160, 163–6
sociologically based 158–60
trends 134–5
understanding people 129–55
iPod 55–8, 156, 283, 295–8
ISO *see* **International Standards Organization**
iterative development 112–13

J

Java 179, 181, 301
Jenson, Scott 110–12
journals 336

K

key presses 205, 209, 235–38, 240–1
key strokes per character (KSPC) 109
keyboards 182
keyphrases 259–60, 265, 274, 276
KLM model 209
Kohonen, Panu 60–1
KSPC *see* **key strokes per character**

L

laid-back search tool 283–5
language 323–4
leaf nodes 227, 230
learning
activity theory 159
evaluation 213
menu structure 225–6
legal frameworks 319–20
Levanto, Elise 134–5
LibTwig 266, 274
liminals 126
linear lists 236
lists 236
local economic factors 319
log analysis 148–9

log sheets 142
long-term orientation 321–2
looping menus 225
low-fidelity prototypes 171–8
low-graphics website versions 262–3

M

MacKensie, Scott 109
macro-economic factors 319
magazines 336
magic things 154
manuals 233–4
many-to-many structures 242–3
mappings 44, 49–51, 57
Marcus, Aaron 40–1, 321–3
market research 126, 211
masculinity 320–2
medical uses 32–3
memory 97, 224–5, 253
memory sticks 285
menus 224–44
  alternatives 235–41
  classifications 226–7
  complex 242–4
  context 227
  data structures 235, 238
  evaluation 197–8, 205, 238–41
  hierarchical 225–7, 243–4
  icons 197–8, 227–33
  learning structure 225–6
  visual language 232–3
meta-data 168, 256, 293–4
mice 182
Millen, David 126
Millennium Bug 40
MMS *see* **multimedia messaging service**
Mobile Digital Library 324, 328–33
mobile probes 144, 152
modalities 18
modeless data entry 18
modes 16
Moore's Law 69–70, 301–2
multi-choice questions 206
multi-tap 15–16, 109
multimedia messaging service (MMS) 6, 61–3, 82, 290, 308
  see also digital photography; video capture
multimodality 26
multiple viewpoints 113–17
music players 137–8, 146–7, 173–6, 190, 281–2
  see also iPod
MyGROCER 14

N

navigation 252–72, 281–2, 324
  see also information access
NaviKey 57
NetFront 263
netware 59
network technologies 280
New Zealand 322, 328–33
Nielsen, Jacob 31, 72, 172, 204, 207–8, 211–12
Nokia 57, 60–1
Nomadic Radio 20, 24
non-auto-scrolling 276
Norman, Donald 11–12, 29, 34, 44, 58, 96, 118
note taking 201
NTT DoCoMo 64–5

O

observations 130–8, 155–60, 199–204
one-handed use 102
one-to-many structures 242–3
online enquiries 148
online manuals 233–4
open-ended questions 206
Opera 263–4
Orange 60

ordered lists 236
organizing data 155
overviews 259–60

P

p2p *see* **peer-to-peer**
packaging content 271–2
page-level schemes 265–6
PalmPilot 9, 12, 23
  desktop to mobile 79
  medical uses 32
  prototypes 171
paperless office 52–3
participant awareness 131–2
participatory design (PD) 116
passive chording 15
PD *see* **participatory design**
PDAs *see* **personal digital assistants**
Peephole displays 16–17, 18, 23, 49
peer-to-peer (p2p) schemes 286
performance issues 182, 191
personal digital assistants (PDAs)
  development 9
  display characteristics 250, 255
  evaluation 201
  observational studies 146
  prototypes 183–4
  searching 256–8
personal organizers 9
personalization 4, 43, 102
personas 160–5
PhotoFinder 293
photography *see* **digital photography**
PhotoMesa 295–6, 297
physical access 318
physical context 214–15
pick-up-and-use devices 13–14
PICTIVE 176
platforms
  design 102–3
  digital photography 306
  prototypes 183–5
PocketPC
  desktop to mobile 78–81
  development 12
  digital photography 295–6
  display characteristics 250
  prototypes 179–80
podcasting 156
political will 320
portability 182
portals 271
Post-It notes 53, 172
power sources 192
power-distance dimension 320–2
PowerBrowser 265–6
predictive text 15–16, 27
privacy 62
probability scores 260
probes 129, 144, 151–3
programmers 113–15, 118
prototypes 169–93
  classification 170–1
  communicating ideas 173, 191
  constraints 191
  cues to users 190
  decision-making 178
  definitions 170
  empowering users 176–8
  evaluation 191
  evolutionary prototyping 186
  expectations 190
  hardware and software integration 178–86
  high-fidelity 170–1, 178–86
  human-centered thinking 85–89
  interaction design 94, 100–6
  interaction prototyping 174–6
  investigative methods 127
  issues 189–91
  low-fidelity 171–8

pitfalls 182
process 187–9
product generation 186–9
revolutionary prototyping 186
self-checking 171–3
psychology 96–7
push-to-talk 78, 81, 98, 143

Q

QOC *see* **Questions-Options-Criteria**
questionnaires 205–7
Questions-Options-Criteria (QOC) 104
Quick and Dirty evaluation 197
QuickSet 26
Quiet Calls prototype 131–2
QWERTY keyboards 78, 273

R

radio frequency identification (RFID) 51
rapid ethnography 145
rapid serial visual presentation (RSVP) 296–8
reading speed 252
real access 318–20
really simple syndication (RSS) 272
recycled handsets 318
reflecting 155
regulatory frameworks 319–20
reliability 206
resources
blogs 337
books 335–6
conferences 336
journals 336
magazines 336
style guides 337–8
websites 337
review-based evaluations 110–12
revolutionary prototyping 186
RFID *see* **radio frequency identification**
ringtones 19, 70–1, 122
Rodden, Kerry 291–3
Rodgers, Yvonne 73–4
RSS *see* **really simple syndication**
RSVP *see* **rapid serial visual presentation**

S

safety 31–3
sampling techniques 125–6
scalar questions 206
scenario prototypes 187–8
scenarios 160, 163–6
Shneiderman, Ben 40, 44–5, 254, 296
screen size 250–8, 300–1
scrolling 252–3, 254, 261, 277, 298–9
SDAZ *see* **speed dependent automatic zooming**
search engines 272, 273
searching
digital photography 291–4
information access 249, 256–8, 272–9
self-checking 171–3
self-reporting 129, 141–5
semantic textual units (STUs) 265
semi-transparent widgets 49–51
short messaging service (SMS)
developing world 327
development 74
information access 275–6
innovations 82
investigative methods 122
usability 61–3
short-term memory 97, 253
short-term orientation 321–2
shortcuts 45
site-level schemes 266
sketching 105, 171–2
skim-reading 259–60
slow technology 43
SmartPad 23

Smartphone 79–81, 103
SmartView 268–70
SMS *see* **short messaging service**
societal impacts 320–3
socio-cultural factors 216–17, 320–22
sociologically based methods 158
software integration 178–86
sources of information 249
South Africa 317–18, 323
spam 83
spatialized audio 20
special needs 26–7
specialist platforms 183–4
specifications 186–7
speech 19–20
speed dependent automatic zooming (SDAZ) 298–302, 304–6
Spinner music player 137
Spinuzzi, Clay 146
Starfield visualization 278–9
Starner, Thad 9
storyboarding *see* **scenarios**
STUs *see* **semantic textual units**
style guides 337–8
Suchman, Lucy 136
summarized content 259, 265, 278
sustaining innovations 68–9
Swiss-Army knife analogy 11–13
Symbian operating system 102–3, 227

T

T9 predictive text 15–16, 27, 109
TAP 81
task analysis perspectives 156–7
techno-fixation 28–9
technology
  acceptance 63–4
  context 216
  innovations 69–74, 87–88
  probes 152
  trust 319
test rigs 183–5, 188
text messaging *see* **short messaging service**
Thimbleby, Harold 29, 118, 237–8
third-generation (3G) devices 12
thrash–discard–revive cycle 147
Tillotson, Jenny 24–6
tilt-based systems 23
timelines 295
TouchEngine 20–1, 23
TouchPlayer 23
transcribing 155
treemaps 296
trends 134–5
triangle icons 227, 230
trust 63–4, 319
turn-taking 62
Twiddler 15, 17

U

UIs *see* **user interfaces**
UML *see* **Unified Modeling Language**
uncertainty avoidance 321–2
undo functions 45
Unified Modeling Language (UML) 160
unistroke entry 109
universal usability 27
upgrade patterns 34–5
usability 5, 27, 40–53
  back-end 72
  complex functions 242–4
  evaluation 107–12
  front-end 72–3
  human-centered innovations 88–9
  information access 252–3, 254
  interaction design 101
  interface styles 78–81
  in itself 44–51
  in life 51–3

short message service 61
technology-centered innovations 88–9
wireless application protocol 72–3
usefulness 41–3
user interfaces (UIs)
desktop to mobile 24, 78–81
interaction design 102–3, 115–16
users
attachment 13
customer experience 5
designers' perceptions 40–1
digital photography 301–6
elderly people 97
ethnography 98, 99–100
evaluation 107–9
gender 99
information access 252–3
interaction design 994, 96–100
manuals 233–4
technology acceptance 63–4
usability 43–53
usefulness 43–5
user experience 54–63
see also evaluation; interactivity

V

validity 206
values 134
Version 1.0 185–6
vertical prototypes 178, 186, 187
Vertu 13
vibration alerts 20–1
video capture 143–4, 153, 200, 311–12
video telephony 70
visibility 44, 48–51
visual anthropology 309–10
visual language 232
Visual Studio 179–80
visualization 278–9
vocabularies 20
voicemail 20

W

WAP *see* **wireless application protocol**
Warwick, Kevin 7–8
Waterfall Model 112
wearable devices 9
website manuals 234
website meta language (WML) 242–3
websites 337
WebTwig 266
Weiser, Marc 53–5
WiFi 216, 280, 328
wireless application protocol (WAP) 9, 70, 72–3, 256–8
within-group experiments 213
within-page navigation 252–3
Wizard of Oz prototypes 175–6
WML *see* **website meta language**
word prediction 109
word-processors 6
working memory 97
writing style 259

X

XLibris 285

Y

zooming 50, 268–70, 3298–306